Fatwa and the Making and Renewal of Islamic Law

In this book, Omer Awass examines the formation, history, and transformation of the Islamic legal discourse and institutions through the lens of a particular legal practice: the issuance of fatwas (legal opinions). Tracing the growth of Islamic law over a vast geographical expanse – from Andalusia to India – and a long temporal span – from the seventh to the twenty-first century, he conceptualizes fatwas as the "atomic units" of Islamic law. Awass argues that they have been a crucial element in the establishment of an Islamic legal tradition. He also provides numerous case studies that touch on environmental, economic, social, political, and religious topics. Written in an accessible style, this volume is the first to offer a comprehensive investigation of fatwas within such a broad spatio-temporal scope. It demonstrates how instrumental fatwas have been to the formation of Islamic legal traditions and institutions, as well as their unique forms of reasoning.

Omer Awass is Associate Professor of Arabic and Islamic Studies at American Islamic College.

Fatwa and the Making and Renewal of Islamic Law

From the Classical Period to the Present

OMER AWASS
American Islamic College

CAMBRIDGE
UNIVERSITY PRESS

CAMBRIDGE
UNIVERSITY PRESS

Shaftesbury Road, Cambridge CB2 8EA, United Kingdom

One Liberty Plaza, 20th Floor, New York, NY 10006, USA

477 Williamstown Road, Port Melbourne, VIC 3207, Australia

314–321, 3rd Floor, Plot 3, Splendor Forum, Jasola District Centre, New Delhi – 110025, India

103 Penang Road, #05–06/07, Visioncrest Commercial, Singapore 238467

Cambridge University Press is part of Cambridge University Press & Assessment, a department of the University of Cambridge.

We share the University's mission to contribute to society through the pursuit of education, learning and research at the highest international levels of excellence.

www.cambridge.org
Information on this title: www.cambridge.org/9781009260879

DOI: 10.1017/9781009260923

First published 2023
First paperback edition 2025

A catalogue record for this publication is available from the British Library

Library of Congress Cataloging-in-Publication data
NAMES: Awass, Omer, 1971– author.
TITLE: Fatwa and the making and renewal of Islamic law : from the classical period to the present / Omer Awass.
DESCRIPTION: New York : Cambridge University Press, 2023. | Includes bibliographical references and index.
IDENTIFIERS: LCCN 2022052227 | ISBN 9781009260909 (hardback) | ISBN 9781009260923 (ebook)
SUBJECTS: LCSH: Fatwas – History. | Islamic law – Interpretation and construction – History. | Islamic law – History.
CLASSIFICATION: LCC KBP491 .A934 2023 | DDC 340.5/922–dc23/eng/20230113
LC record available at https://lccn.loc.gov/2022052227

ISBN 978-1-009-26090-9 Hardback
ISBN 978-1-009-26087-9 Paperback

I dedicate this work to my father, Ahmed Awass, and my mother, Amina Alnini. Neither of whom were learned people, but had a tremendous respect for knowledge. Thus, they always encouraged me to pursue education.

Contents

List of Figures — *page* ix
Acknowledgments — xi

Introduction — 1
Questions Regarding the Authenticity of Early Islamic Legal Material — 4
Outline and Description of the Chapters — 5
Questions on Method and Approach in this Study — 8
Situating this Work within the Literature on Fatwa and Islamic Law — 11

1 Fatwa in the Prophetic and Post-Prophetic Period — 14
Introduction — 14
The Dialogical Style of the Quranic Discourse and the Epistemological Foundations of *Iftāʾ* — 15
The Beginnings of *Iftāʾ* in the Prophetic Practice — 20
Fatwa in the Post-Prophetic Period — 25
Fatwa in the Post-Prophetic Period: Fatwa in the Age of the Early Caliphate — 29
Conclusion — 36

2 Fatwa in the Classical Age — 38
Introduction — 38
Fatwa in the Age of Regional Distinctions — 39
Fatwa in the Age of the *Madhhab* Predecessors — 58
Further Explorations in the Fatwas of the *Madhhab* Predecessors: Usurious Transactions — 65
Fatwa in the Age of the *Madhhab* Predecessors of the Third/Ninth Century: Distribution of Water Resources and Shareholders' Land Rights — 71
Conclusion — 76

3 Fatwa and the Formation of Islamic Legal Discourses, Institutions, and Society — 77
Introduction — 77
The Genesis of Legal Theory, Legal Doctrines, and Institutions in the Late and Post–Abbasid Caliphate Period — 77

Discursive Legal Activity and the Formation of a Muslim Society in Late Antiquity 104
Conclusion 113

4 The Formation of the Islamic Legal Tradition and the Formalization of *Iftāʾ* within the Legal Schools 114
Introduction 114
The Formation of an Islamic Legal Tradition 115
Rules of Fatwa, Classes of Muftīs, and the Authoritative Structure of *Madhhabs* 121
A Note on the Formation of Shīʿī Legal Thought and Institutions 135
A Note on the Formation of the Ibāḍī Legal Thought and Institutions 139
Conclusion 144

5 Fatwa in the Age of the Preponderance of Legal Schools 146
Introduction 146
The Sociohistorical and Political Situation in the Muslim World in the Age of *Madhhab* Preponderance: c. 1100–1850 CE 147
The Systemization and Structuring of Islamic Law: *Fatwas* within the Confines of *Madhhabs* in the Islamic Middle Period 153
Conclusion 196

6 Colonialism, Islamic Law, and the Post-Colonial Fatwa 198
Introduction 198
European Colonization of the Muslim Geographic Periphery in the Nineteenth Century 198
European Hegemony over Muslim Geographic Heartlands in the Nineteenth Century 204
Secular Nationalism and Islamic Reform in the Twentieth-Century Muslim World 209
Modernity and the Change in the Status of Islamic Law in Muslim Societies 212
Fatwas in the Age of Colonialism 218
Fatwa in the Post-Colonial Age 226
Fatwas in the Era of Post-Colonial Muslim Nation-States 227
Fatwas in the Era of Post-Colonial Global Muslim Institutions: The OIC and the IIFA 238
Preliminary Conclusions about Post-Colonial Fatwas 250

Conclusion 253

Glossary 257
Bibliography 263
Index 273

Figures

1 Quranic fatwas *page* 19
2 Prophetic fatwas 23
3 Fatwas in the age of the early caliphate 32
4 Fatwa in the age of regional distinctions 57
5 Fatwa in the age of the *madhhab* predecessors 64
6 Fatwas defining usurious transactions by the *madhhab* predecessors 70
7 Fatwa in the age of the *madhhab* predecessors II: third/ninth century 75
8 Convergence of *ijmāʿ* (consensus) and its forms 83
9 The fragmentation of *raʾy* into specialized forms of legal reasoning 85
10 Illustration of the operation of *qiyās* (analogy) 88
11 The evolution of *qiyās* (textually based analogical reasoning) 89
12 Early process of employing *istiḥsān* (juristic preference) 90
13 Later formulation of the relationship between *istiḥsān* (juristic preference) and *qiyās* (analogical reasoning) 91
14 Al-Juwaynī's (fifth/eleventh) tripartite categorization of jurists 125
15 The structure of iftāʾ within the Ḥanafī *madhhab* according to Qāḍī Khān: (sixth/twelfth): the procedure the *muftī-mujtahid* must follow when issuing fatwas 129
16 Ibn ʿĀbidīn's (thirteenth/nineteenth century) seven levels of *mujtahids* (jurists) in the Ḥanafī school 133
17 Fatwa in the age of preponderance of legal schools 192

18 Fatwa in the age of colonialism: Rashīd Riḍā's fatwas on usury (*ribā*) 224
19 Fatwa in the era of the post-colonial Muslim nation-states I: blood transfusion 231
20 Fatwa in the era of the post-colonial Muslim nation-states II: gender interaction and women's participation in the Muslim public sphere 237
21 Fatwa in the era of the post-colonial Muslim global institutions I: connections between IIFA fatwas and past legal doctrines 245
22 Fatwa in the era of the post-colonial Muslim global institutions II: types of legal rationale manifested in IIFA fatwas 250

Acknowledgments

This book is an augmentation and refinement of my Ph.D. dissertation, which I completed at Temple University in 2014. I would like to express my deepest gratitude to my dissertation advisor Khalid Blankenship who mentored me throughout my graduate studies and continues to support my academic advancement. Without his belief in my potential as a scholar by supporting my pursuit of a Ph.D., I may not have been able to have an academic career. I would like to thank the other members of my dissertation committee, John Raines, Mahmoud Ayoub, and Jayasinhji Jhala, who all provided helpful advice that contributed to the amelioration of this book. John Raines and Mahmoud Ayoub are no longer with us, but I should note that they have played a significant contribution to my general academic maturation and personal growth. John Raines was an academic and activist who ardently pursued various political and social justice causes. In that way, he exemplified the tradition of scholar-activist.

Similarly, Mahmoud Ayoub was not only an academic mentor but also a father and friend to all those whom he taught. Both of these illustrious figures will be missed. I would also like to thank Jayasinhji Jhala for his continued advice and support of my academic career. Without the contribution of all of these scholars, my book would not be what it is today.

Many others have contributed to the development of this book, for which I have acknowledged their specific contributions in various sections of this work. Still, I will simply list their names: Murteza Bedir of Istanbul University, Hamdi Cilinger of Sakarya University in Turkey, Walid Mossad, Adayinka Muhammad Mendes, Ibrahim Khan of the

University of Chicago, and Nadir Begum of Turath Foundation. I would also like to thank Jawad Quraishi of Zaytuna College and Ibrahim Khan of the University of Chicago for specifically assisting with the transliteration of Arabic terms in this book. Lastly, I would like to thank the anonymous reviewers whose insights contributed to valuable revisions of this work. Ultimately, this work is the result of numerous contributions and influences from many scholarly engagements throughout my intellectual formation, all of which I cannot recount here.

Introduction

The aim of this book is to examine the formation and transformation of Islamic legal discourse and the impact of that discourse on Muslim society by analyzing fatwas (religious legal opinions) over the course of Islamic history. Historically speaking, substantive aspects of Islamic law developed out of the material of these fatwas. In the very early stages of Islamic history, there were no formal laws to instruct people in their religious and social concerns, but the manner in which Muslims received guidance with regard to their religious practice was by posting their concerns to early proto-jurists in the form of religio-legal questions, whose responses became known as fatwas. Out of the critical mass of these fatwas, an Islamic legal doctrine took shape and a definitive corpus of Islamic law came into being.

Essentially, my investigation looks at the development and maturation of Islamic law[1] through the lens of a legal practice: the issuance of fatwas. By examining fatwas in different periods of Islamic history from

[1] Lena Salaymeh (2016, 22) eschews a developmental approach to Islamic law that she calls an "origins" approach because she claims that it essentializes Islamic law in that it implies that there is an essentialized subject that is undergoing a linear progression that passes from an earlier stage to a more developed later stage. Moreover, she claims this linear progression is essentializing because it neglects Islamic law's embeddedness in a distinct context (Salaymeh, 23). Her argument is not at all clear to me that taking a developmental approach to Islamic law necessitates essentializing it because one can certainly contextualize that development by showing how the context induced transformations in a certain direction. Nor is it certain that by asserting historical development one is assuming that there is an essentialized subject that is undergoing a linear progression as such a progression need not be conceptualized as an inherent course of history but rather a process that is subject to various historical contingencies.

the beginning until today, I chart the establishment of an Islamic legal tradition and its transformations. More particularly, my analysis draws attention to the way in which fatwas contributed to the formation of Islamic legal reasoning and institutions. Moreover, by analyzing fatwas issued by Muslim jurists from various regions and periods, I identify how fatwas were essential catalysts for historical change, which gives us a better appreciation of the interrelationship between law and society.

Yet even though Islamic legal doctrines and institutions like *madhhab*s (legal schools) partially arose from the discourses and activities associated with the fatwas of early jurists, fatwas in the post-classical period were structured in accordance with the formal rules that governed those discourses and institutions. Hence, there was a reflexive relationship between fatwas and these legal principles, practices, and institutions: Fatwas helped give shape to legal doctrines and legal schools and in turn were later regulated by the constraints of the Islamic legal tradition that they helped construct. This work tries to show how this historical dynamic emerged and what that meant for the transformation of Islamic law in the post-classical period.

This historical foundation provides a basis for a diachronic assessment of the transformations that have taken place in the Islamic legal tradition as a result of the encounter with colonialism. In the latter part of my investigation, I examine how the practice and rationalization of *iftāʾ*, the practice of issuing a fatwa, have changed due to the impact of colonialism on the Muslim world. In this era, the established practices and doctrines of Islamic law were critiqued through the lens of modern Western ideas as well as historical Muslim ideas that were seen to be congruent with "modern" ways of thinking. This spawned colonial-era Muslim movements that sought to reform Islamic law and redefine its relationship with the state and society.

After historically establishing the ideas advocated by reformers, I assess whether those calls for reform have actually affected the practice of Islamic law at the substantive and procedural levels. I do this by subjecting fatwas issued in the colonial and post-colonial period to critical analysis to determine whether the procedures or rationale of fatwas has changed in a fundamental way. The larger themes that I address in my latter analysis are whether the modern trend among some Muslim thinkers and jurists toward contextually oriented legal concepts represents a lasting shift away from the traditional textually oriented legal methodology to produce a new type of discourse that is revolutionizing Islamic law or whether is it a passing phenomenon that will not make a lasting impact on how Islamic law is derived in the future.

Fatwas are the key starting points in addressing these questions because they represent the most elemental dimensions of Islamic law and the new legal developments within it. Thus, they offer vistas on how Muslim religious and legal practice may undergo a change in the future.

In charting the historical development and continuing evolution of Islamic law through the medium of fatwas, I am asserting that fatwas are the atomic components of Islamic legal discourse and practice and, as such, that they tell us a lot about Islamic legal formation. Looking at the development of Islamic legal tradition through the lens of fatwas gives us a sense of how the internal dynamics of the religion of Islam led to this legal formation. In this way, we can chart the origins of the law and the legal tradition from the discursive and social roots of the religion itself.

This investigation seeks not only to map the transformations that have occurred in Islamic legal discourse and tradition through the examination of its elemental components of fatwas but also to allude to the historical impact that this discursive legal practice has had on the history of Islamic civilization. There is a reciprocal relationship between fatwas and social change in Muslim society because fatwas have their origin in the social and religious issues that have arisen in Muslim society since they are legal responses to those issues. Thus, they play the role of indicators of social change as they are a legal representation of that change. On the other hand, since they are legal responses to social changes, they either facilitate those changes by legitimating them or hinder the establishment of those changes by branding them illegitimate.

In addition, fatwas have their origin in civil society because of their dialogical character. This is because they are social exchanges between the public and the *muftī* who responds in legal terms to the public's concerns. Although it is not an exchange between those of equal social status, the process of seeking a fatwa is nonetheless a dialogical activity stemming from the concerns of the Muslim public; thus, this process is spawned by factors in the social environment. We will see later how this peculiar character of *iftā*ʾ (the process of issuing fatwas) is embedded in the discursive sources of Islam that encouraged its dialogical form.

QUESTIONS REGARDING THE AUTHENTICITY OF EARLY ISLAMIC LEGAL MATERIAL

Before outlining the topics addressed in this inquiry, I would like to say a few words about the historical materials used in the first two chapters. Modern Western historical scholarship has problematized many of the historical reports and doubted the authenticity of discourses that were ascribed to authors in the first two hundred years of Islam, claiming that such reports are not authentic reflections of the actual events that took place or that the provenance of these discourses is questionable. This assertion poses a problem for anyone who seeks to make historical claims about the early period of Islam. On the other hand, more recent voices in Western historical criticism have come to question the categorical nature of this assertion that has dominated Western circles of scholarship for much of the twentieth century.

For instance, the work of the German *ḥadīth* critic Harald Motzki titled *The Origins of Islamic Jurisprudence*[2] is an extensive study on certain sections of the *Muṣannaf* of ʿAbd al-Razzāq al-Ṣanʿānī (d. 211 AH), a collection containing opinions about Islamic religious practice from religious figures in the first two centuries of Islam. After analyzing the opinions (fatwas) of religious figures dating from the late first and the early second century of Islam, Motzki argues persuasively that the reported legal opinions found in this work can be safely dated to that period.

Much of the suspicion in Western scholarship about these reports and discourses stems from their preservation in later recorded narrative sources and the lack of documentary (read material) evidence, indicating the authenticity of these reports and discourses. Yet, as some historians assert, information about early Islamic history was recorded in later narrative sources because of the awareness that the materiality of the documents would not be preserved.[3] Lena Salaymeh asserts that "sources that were not written contemporaneously with historical events are not fundamentally ahistorical for several reasons:

1. Contemporaneous sources are not inherently more reliable than later sources;
2. Not all written sources should be categorized as 'later' because the narratives transcribed in them were initially composed orally

[2] See also Motzki's more recent co-authored work *Analysing Muslim Traditions: Studies in Legal, Exegetical and Maghāzī Ḥadīth*, 3, where he critiques some of Schacht's assertions about the inauthenticity of early Islamic traditions.

[3] See Salaymeh (2016, 25), where she attributes this assertion to Chase Robinson.

and transmitted contemporaneously as part of both a narrative-historical and a living legal tradition;

3. Later written sources are based on both oral sources and contemporaneous written texts that are no longer extant ... [that is] contemporaneous written sources that did not survive may be embedded within later written texts;[4]
4. Most of what we know about certain periods of the past come through non-contemporaneous sources, if these are rejected then it becomes impossible to write a history about these periods."[5]

These new developments in Western historical criticism and the critiques of its methodological limitations create room for researchers to make claims about the early Islamic period with some confidence. Yet whether one believes that the historical reports about early Islam, which are used in the initial part of this study, are authentic or not does not take away from what this study seeks to accomplish. What matters most for this investigation is that those who constructed the Islamic legal tradition believed that such reports were accurate and consciously appealed to these representations when forming this tradition. With this in mind, the debate within Western historical scholarship about the historicity of early Islam will not be of concern to this investigation, as my main concern is the construction of a legal tradition regardless of whether the historical information used in that construction was authentic, from the Western point of view, or not.

OUTLINE AND DESCRIPTION OF THE CHAPTERS

Following these preliminary remarks on the historical authenticity of the subject of this investigation, I may now restate the tenor of this study followed by a synopsis of its chapters. *Fatwa and the Making and Remaking of Islamic Law* consists of six chapters and a conclusion. The organization of the chapters is chronological, starting with the early period of Islam moving all the way to the post-colonial Muslim world. Although the work does not focus on any particular period, person, or place throughout, I weave the narrative around the legal practice of *iftāʾ*, whose product is the fatwa – a practice from which Islamic legal norms, methodologies, and institutions emerged. By tracing the path of fatwas in the successive phases of the history of Islamic law, I keep the longue durée of the narrative tightly focused, all the while underlining the range

[4] See also Motzki who similarly argues this point in *The Origins of Islamic Jurisprudence*.
[5] Salaymeh, 32.

of discourses, events, institutions, persons, and places that fashioned the enterprise of Islamic law.

Chapter 1 ("Fatwa in the Prophetic and Post-Prophetic Period") deals with the discursive origins of the fatwa by examining the fatwas during the period of prophecy. My argument here is that *iftāʾ*, the fatwa production process, is fundamentally a dialogical activity that has its discursive roots in the dialogical manner by which both the Quran and the Prophet engaged early Muslim adherents. I then look at some of the fatwas in the post-prophetic period where the early Muslim community faced new sociopolitical challenges and how Muslims resorted to the activity of *iftāʾ* as a socio-legal mechanism for resolving their problems. I show that in their resolutions to these problems, early Muslims employed various approaches of scriptural hermeneutics and legal reasoning that would later become standardized legal precepts in Islamic legal methodology and theory.

Chapter 2 ("Fatwa in the Classical Age") analyzes fatwas from the late first century to the third century of Islam for the sake of discovering the defining features of the fatwa tradition. Here, I show how fatwas became the vehicle actualizing the Quranic ethico-legal norms in the sociohistorical context of Islam. I show how the Islamic legal norms and injunctions that were promulgated by the Quranic discourse and prophetic practice became interpreted, applied, and reinterpreted in various historical and cultural contexts through the process of *iftāʾ*. The forms of legal reasoning and the interpretive devices employed in these fatwas became the basis of an Islamic legal discourse.

Chapter 3 (Fatwa and the Formation of Islamic Legal Discourses, Institutions, and Society) discusses the emergence of distinct Islamic principles and practices in the third/ninth through the fifth/eleventh centuries. I do this by charting the formation of Islamic legal theory and Islamic legal doctrines/schools and show how the substantive and formal roots of these disciplines and institutions partially emerged from the fatwas of previous generations of Muslim jurists. Moreover, I spell out the dialectical relationship that developed between the activity of *iftāʾ* and these new legal formations.

Chapter 4 ("The Formation of the Islamic Legal Tradition and the Formalization of *Iftāʾ* within the Legal Schools") shows how past legal practices played a determinative role in the formation of the Islamic legal tradition. I describe the nature of the relationship of the past to the Islamic legal tradition by looking at the ideas and institutions that came to embody that tradition and how these ideas and practices were shaped by the fatwas of past jurists whose legal pronouncements informed the content of Islamic legal doctrines developed in subsequent centuries. Once this foundation is laid, the remainder of the chapter shows how the establishment and maturation after the fifth/eleventh century of Islamic legal schools, or *madhhab*s, and the legal doctrines that define them led to a structuring of the process of *iftāʾ* where this activity became governed by a set of discursive rules and procedures that contributed to the greater formalization of this legal practice. Muslim jurists within each school now began to lay down rules on how fatwas were to be issued within the confines of the legal doctrines of those schools. In order to understand the form that fatwas take in the post-classical period of Islam, I delineate those discursive rules for fatwa production as found in what is known as *adab al-fatwā* (the protocols of fatwa) literature.

Chapter 5 ("Fatwa in the Age of the Preponderance of the Legal Schools") illustrates more concretely how the discursive rules of fatwa, defined in the previous chapter, were applied in actual fatwas of the period between 1100 and 1850 CE. This was the period when legal schools/doctrines (*madhhab*s) and legal theory (*uṣūl al-fiqh*) were fully established and firmly rooted in Islamic legal practice in ways that they exerted the most influence on the subsequent production of Islamic legal rulings. I accomplished this task by sampling and analyzing fatwas from the period in question. In my selection of fatwas, I choose representative samples of major fatwas in order to show the nature of the activity of *iftāʾ* during this era and how this activity had been transformed since the classical age of fatwa. Moreover, this chapter demonstrates how fatwas helped Muslim society keep pace with social change by modifying the legal corpus that governed it.

Chapter 6 ("Colonialism, Islamic Law, and the Post-Colonial Fatwa") outlines the historical effects that European colonialism had on Muslim society and law in the nineteenth and twentieth centuries. The intellectual challenge posed by Western "modernity" to established Muslim ideas and institutions had a seriously destabilizing outcome. I document the impact of this "modernity" on Muslim thought and society, focusing on the challenges it presented to Islamic legal institutions and how these challenges affected Islamic legal discourse in the colonial period. Building on this historical foundation, I then gauge the impact of modernity on colonial and post-colonial Islamic legal discourse by analyzing fatwas from this period. The purpose of this analysis is to assess how Islamic law and legal institutions have negotiated the challenges of the colonial and post-colonial predicament through the use of traditional legal practices such as fatwa. In addition, the analysis will gauge the extent to which new approaches to legal reasoning represent a substantive transformation in Islamic legal discourse and practice.

Ultimately, the primary question this book seeks to address is how the legal practice of issuing fatwas (*iftāʾ*) played an influential role in the evolution of a distinct legal tradition. Moreover, my investigation sheds light on how this practice was a social instrument that facilitated the formation of an Islamic society that was centered on legal norms and how this practice allowed those legal norms to adapt to sociohistorical changes over time. Thus, fatwas are, in a way, a discursive barometer for measuring change and continuity in Islamic civilization.

Yet beyond discussing the formalities of law, what this work ultimately demonstrates is how a civilization faced with the challenges of history devised its distinctive strategies to cope with those problems. The book shows how Muslims in each historical period asked a different set of questions about the world in which they lived and the kinds of resolutions that they reached. Their queries reflected their concerns of how to live a rational, ethical, and spiritual life in light of the distinctive forms of rationality and values that they espoused, as well as how to regenerate those values despite the vicissitudes of every age.

QUESTIONS ON METHOD AND APPROACH IN THIS STUDY

Before beginning this investigation, I wish to make several clarifications about my approach and theoretical framework. First, I define a fatwa as any statement, oral or written, that establishes the legitimacy or lack thereof of an action, position, or practice and is pronounced by someone who is vested with legal authority, whether the origins of that authority lie in political institutions or simply the religious and social sphere. In defining fatwas in this way, I exclude most juridical decisions (*qaḍāʾ*) from being fatwas because these verdicts did not necessarily establish the legitimacy of human practice, at least in the case of Islamic law. In most cases, juridical decisions merely adjudicated whether those actions were within the bounds of the already established Islamic norms. At the same time, fatwas are different from court decisions because they are not inherently political acts, as they were not always backed by state sanction as in the case of juridical verdicts; hence, they are non-binding by nature.

Moreover, given this definition of a fatwa, I take the statements of early Muslim jurists as fatwas even when we do not always know the social circumstances that brought about their pronouncements. This is because their statements that carried legal implications were not binding during their lifetime in the same way they came to be religiously binding when later generations of legal specialists selected some of those opinions to be especially authoritative and from them formulated legal doctrine (*fiqh*). Even when some of the pronouncements of early jurists made their way into the body of Islamic jurisprudence that came to be known as *fiqh*, at the time that these legal statements were made, they functioned like fatwas in the sense that they were legal responses to religious issues that were of concern to Muslim society and were at the time non-binding. Hence, I use such statements in my work as fatwas. Furthermore, this definition of a fatwa includes short treatises that were written by later legal authorities, treaties that respond to new issues that arose in Muslim society even though we do not have the specific questions that were posed to them that generated their response.

Second, the idea of charting the history of Islamic law though one of its central practices is analogous to creating a discursive map of the enterprise. Mapping generates a portrayal of a subject that focuses on one of its dimensions to the exclusion of all other aspects of its reality. As this is my adopted approach to the study of Islamic law, my attention is not so much focused on the persons, periods, and places that have been integral to the development of the law – and that form the themes of most other studies of Islamic law. Instead, I have chosen to highlight the role of one of its most distinct practices (fatwa-making) that has shaped its trajectory. The benefit of such an analysis is that it allows for the weaving together of diverse persons, periods, places, and principles by considering the common thread of their shared legal practice. This allows us to tie together those seemingly disparate themes and approaches to looking at the law and thus to generate a cohesive picture of our subject.

Third, I utilize Talal Asad's theoretical insight of "discursive tradition"[6] as the overarching framework for understanding the character of the practice of fatwa-making in Islamic history and the enterprise of Islamic law in general. I say that this notion is both a guiding insight and a point for corroboration since Asad's initial proposal and definition of this seminal idea as a way to approach the study of Islam do not give an actual demonstration of how this concept can be applied to real social or historical events. This study demonstrates how Asad's theoretical insight can be applied to the history of Islamic law so that the reader

[6] Asad, 1986, 14.

can appreciate the distinctiveness of this religious enterprise. At the same time, it provides a historical demonstration of one of the ways in which this concept of "discursive tradition" can be more fully articulated to give profound expression to sociohistorical processes.

Beginning with Asad's definition of a discursive tradition as consisting of "discourses that seek to instruct practitioners regarding the correct form and purpose of a given practice that, precisely because it is established, it has a history,"[7] I provide a historical outline, in the first three chapters, of those discourses and evolving discursive practices that come to comprise the Islamic legal tradition. In doing so, I show that this tradition embodies a distinctive modality of how to interact with those fundamental discourses so as to construct a set of legitimate religious practices. I then provide an argument in Chapter 4 as to why the Islamic legal tradition is an exemplary historical illustration of what Asad calls a discursive tradition and how it is distinguished from other discursive traditions.

Fourth, as much as discourses play a fundamental role in defining discursive traditions, they are also shaped by their distinct discursive practices. I alluded to the dialogical character of fatwas as discursive statements that are generated by a dialogical interaction between religious specialists and non-specialists. But such dialogically produced statements also became the medium of legal conversation by which these specialists negotiated their differing legal opinions. From such dialogical engagements that represented a distinct form of discursive practice, foundational discourses were formed and a legal tradition emerged. Thus, the Islamic legal enterprise is not merely a discursive tradition; it must also be understood fundamentally as a dialogically negotiated discursive tradition that arose from this social transactional approach to the law.

Fifth, another aspect of fatwas that is linked to the social processes that inform this dialogically negotiated discursive tradition is their phronetic character. *Phronesis* is an Aristotelian conception denoting a kind of practical reason. As one author describes it: "*phronesis* designates a form of historically informed, prudential judgment which seeks to determine not what is eternally true or valid, but ... 'what is feasible, what is possible, what is correct here and now'."[8] Fatwas reflect this skill by situating universal ethical ideals in a discreet historical moment.[9] So these

[7] Asad, 1986, 14.
[8] Madison, 319.
[9] See Omer Awass' article "Fatwa and the Art of Ethical Embedding" in *Journal of American Academy of Religion (JAAR)* September 2019, vol. 87, no. 3, pp. 765–790.

statements, theoretically speaking, are historically informed discourses and not merely normatively determined judgments. They change as they traverse different times and places. Having this character of historical contingency, they continually reshape the discourses that define this dialogically negotiated discursive legal tradition, thereby maintaining the dynamism of this tradition in various periods and places.

SITUATING THIS WORK WITHIN THE LITERATURE ON FATWA AND ISLAMIC LAW

One thing that stands out when situating this work with existing literature on fatwa and Islamic law is that this is the only book-length treatment in English that charts the history of fatwas from their beginning until today and links that history to the development of the Islamic legal tradition. Although there have been many works on Islamic law, there is a dearth of literature in English on fatwas. What does exist on the topic, for example, are edited volumes that introduce the reader to the genera of the fatwa. But the disparate character of the contributions within such volumes makes it difficult for such works to contain an overarching theme that unifies the various approaches to the study of fatwas.

Other works on fatwas focus on a particular period and/or place and look at how fatwas have been instrumental in the formation of political or social institutions and projects or how fatwas have assisted Muslim societies in responding to contemporary challenges. My work addresses those very same themes but does so over a longer duration and a greater spatial span, showing that those historical processes that are attributed to fatwas, and their corollary practices and institutions, were not merely the result of the contingencies of a particular period or place, but a part of the function of fatwas throughout history. More importantly, considering the long durée also shows us how the practice of fatwas has transformed over time because of the historical changes.

Yet this work is to be situated not only with other works on the fatwa, but because of its broad historical and thematic scope, it also is to be placed in conversation with other general works on Islamic law that are trying to break the existing stereotypes about the misplaced origins and alleged stagnation of Islamic law. This book makes a solid argument for the organic unfolding of Islamic law from the internal discursive and historical dynamics of Muslim civilization itself without denying the influence of other legal heritages on the development of Islamic law. At the same time, it shows how fatwas allowed for the adaptation of the law to changing social and political circumstances. This work never loses sight of this overarching theme even as it delves into the minutia of legal rulings, methods, and practices.

By presenting a logical and historically plausible narrative about the origins and development of Islamic law, it loosens the hold that past academic theories have had on this subject for decades. These theories have rendered that early history as either being shrouded in mystery or a result of some civilizational-wide orchestrated effort to invent an origins story for Islamic law that could legitimate various political and religious agendas. In my estimation, the purveyors of the latter theory have never been able to creditably point to any specific individuals or groups acting in coordination with one another that could plausibly account for this presumption of massive fraud. What such parties may have more convincingly shown is how particular pieces of historical evidence problematize the classical Muslim explanation of the beginning of Islamic law. However, it is beyond the scope of this book to deal with all the claims of these hypercritical historians aside from the arguments I forwarded earlier in this introduction that point to their limitations.[10] Rather what this work merely seeks to achieve in entering that debate, albeit indirectly, is to present a coherent alternative explanation that could render early Islamic law intelligible.

Yet this work also speaks to the Islamic law stagnation debate in Western scholarship, which is said to have taken place in the latter half of the post-classical period (c. 1300) when the formation of Islamic legal schools and legal doctrines had supposedly reached their zenith. I do this by demonstrating how fatwas during this period kept Islamic law current with social changes. What my presentation will show is that Islamic legal institutions were more dynamic than originally perceived even though the pace of civilizational change was more conservative than it was in the formative period since these institutions had reached their developmental maturity. Thus, it adds arguments and evidence to the growing literature in the field that challenges the stagnation thesis of Islamic law.

Yet this work makes important interventions in the study of modern Islamic law. Most works discuss the challenges faced by Islamic law in our times and how colonialism and the post-colonial realities have disrupted the operations of this law within Muslim societies. My work not only furthers this debate but also shows the strategies by which modern

[10] See the section titled "Questions Regarding the Authenticity of Early Islamic Legal Material."

Muslim actors and institutions have been negotiating those challenges to maintain the law's dynamism and relevance in the contemporary period. Some of the unique conclusions reached by this analysis are that despite the continued usage of traditional legal practices like the fatwa in the current situations, what has changed is the strategies of how such practices are employed. The recent production of fatwas is marked by increasing hybridity between modern methods and historical approaches to the law. In making this identification, this work foreshadows the directions that the law will develop in the future.

I

Fatwa in the Prophetic and Post-Prophetic Period

INTRODUCTION

This chapter explores how the Quranic discourse along with the discursive practices of the Prophet Muḥammad contributed to the formulation of formal mechanisms for the instituting of law in the Islamic tradition. More precisely, I analyze how the Quranic and prophetic discursive practices encouraged the practice of *iftāʾ* (the process of generating a fatwa) as a legitimate initiative for generating legal solutions to religious and social problems.

My argument here is that the process of *iftāʾ* is fundamentally a dialogical activity between a seeker (*mustaftī*) who is faced with a religious or social problem and is searching for a resolution to this problem by means of an ethical/legal consultation and a jurist (i.e., *qiyās*) who issues a legal opinion addressing the case that is presented to him. This dialogical nature of the fatwa process has its discursive roots in the dialogical manner by which both the Quran and the Prophet engaged early Muslim adherents. This manner of engagement played a role in facilitating the formal dimensions of *iftāʾ* as the primary mechanism by which Islamic legal opinions would be generated.

The second half of the chapter examines some of the fatwas in the post-prophetic period, where the early Muslim community sought to confront new sociopolitical challenges by resorting to *iftāʾ* as a socio-legal mechanism for problem resolution. As we will see in their resolutions to these problems, they employed various approaches of scriptural hermeneutics and legal reasoning that would later become standardized legal precepts in Islamic legal methodology and theory. More importantly, many of the legal decisions made in this early period set a legal precedent and were adopted in the later formulations of Islamic legal doctrines, hence making this period a crucial one for understanding the development of the institution of fatwa in particular and the Islamic legal tradition in general.

THE DIALOGICAL STYLE OF THE QURANIC DISCOURSE AND THE EPISTEMOLOGICAL FOUNDATIONS OF *IFTĀʾ*

The phenomenon of *iftāʾ* – the practice of making a fatwa – has existed since the very inception of Islam with the revelation of the Quran. This fact is affirmed by the presence of terms in the Quran that indicate that the Prophet Muḥammad was asked questions – for example, *yastaftūnaka* (they seek your opinion/instruction/advice) and *yasʾalūnaka ʿan* (they ask you about) – to which the Quran would respond with legal or theological assertions, depending on the nature of the inquiry.[1]

The manner in which the Quran was revealed facilitated the phenomenon of *iftāʾ*.[2] The Quran was not revealed in one event but was disclosed in portions over many years; this facilitated dialectic interaction between the Quranic discourse and people's religious and social needs. The give and take that arose from people's questions and the subsequent response of the Quranic discourse to these inquiries demonstrate the dialectical aspects of this discourse. This, in turn, created the social dynamic of seeking religious consultation that later became the discursive impetus for the activity of *iftāʾ* in Islam.

Take, for example, the following early Quranic verses that show the dialogical mode of the Quranic discourse responding to the religio-social inquiries or challenges posed by early believers to the Prophet Muḥammad: "And they seek your advice (*yastaftūnaka*), say Allah will give you advice concerning the *kalāla* [those who leave no heir in the direct line]."[3] The internal evidence of Quranic statements such as these – and there are several others that begin with the same or a similar construction – is a clear indication that the Quran, through the medium of the Prophet Muḥammad, engaged in a sort of indirect dialogue with its audience by responding to the inquiries that they posed, as shown by the phrase "they seek your advice" (*yastaftūnaka*).

1 For more on this point, see Hallaq, 1994, 64–65.
2 Riyāḍ, 19.
3 Quran: 4:176. Translation is mine with the exception of the meaning of the term *kalāla*, which is taken from Muhammad Asad's *The Meaning of the Quran*, on verse 4:176.

The nature of fatwa activity presupposes a dialogical mode of interaction between the questioner and the respondent. The Quran served as a catalyst for this dialogical mode because of its interactive mode of revelation. The point here is that the Quranic discourse was not completely monological and that it was responsive to the exigencies of the historical situation. This model of interaction – responding to an inquiry or event – is precisely how the fatwa process operates, showing that it has its methodological foundations in the Quranic discourse itself.

The second respect in which the Quranic discourse catalyzed the activity of fatwa is its explicit recognition that certain Quranic statements were revealed as a response to certain inquiries that were posed to the Prophet Muḥammad, and these statements were introduced by the phrases *yasʾalūnaka* (they ask you) or *yastaftūnaka* (they consult you). The explicit recognition by the Quranic discourse that some of its particular statements were in direct response to certain questions gave legitimacy to people's impulse to inquiry and, hence, the enterprise of pursuing fatwa. This is because this enterprise itself is based on the inquiry posed by a questioner seeking an understanding through the agencies of higher authority. This Quranic discursive practice thus played a foundational role in establishing the practice of fatwa and planting the seeds for a new legal tradition.[4]

It is important to discuss in greater detail the Quranic responses to legal questions posed to the Prophet Muḥammad. This is to illustrate in concrete terms how the Quranic discursive practices became the catalyst for later Islamic legal practices. Although there are many Quranic responses to religio-legal issues, I will restrict my discussion to the verses that begin with the two fatwa-soliciting phrases (*yasʾalūnaka* and *yastaftūnaka*). There are approximately nine verses in the Quran that begin with either of the two *iftāʾ* phrases that are of a legal nature.[5] The questions posed and the responses given are on variant social, economic, and political topics.

[4] Salaymeh (2016: 6) implies in her "contextualist" approach to studying Islamic law that appealing to the internal dynamics within Islam itself to explaining the beginnings of Islamic law constitutes a form of essentialism. Yet identifying, which I do here, the social processes that emerge from people's engagement with scripture is different from saying that such processes are an essential outcome of textual directives. These directives that may give impetus to or facilitate the emergence of certain practices over others were still conditioned by the historical contingencies that play a direct role in shaping those directives' particular social configurations.

[5] There are several more verses dealing with theological topics, some of which I have quoted earlier.

Those issues include the nature of determining times for ritual practice,[6] the legality of fighting during the sacred months,[7] the legality of alcohol and gambling, what to give in charity,[8] the dispensing of the wealth of orphans,[9] sexual conduct during menses,[10] types of lawful food,[11] spoils of war,[12] treatment of women and orphans,[13] and division of inheritance.[14]

The following is a presentation and analysis of one of these verses: "They ask thee (*yasʾalūnaka*) about intoxicants and games of chance. Say: 'In both there is great harm as well as some benefit for man, but their harm is greater than their benefit'."[15] The verse is introduced with the *iftāʾ* phrase *yasʾalūnaka*, indicating that it is a response that was prompted by an inquiry made about the permissibility of intoxicants and gambling, though we are not given the details about who is doing the asking and what prompted that question. In extra-Quranic literature known as *asbāb al-nuzūl* (occasions of revelation), the circumstances of the inquiry that prompted the revelation of this verse are given: "They question thee about strong drink and games of chance..." [2:219]. This was revealed about ʿUmar ibn al-Khaṭṭāb, Muʿādh ibn Jabal, and a group of helpers[16] who went to the Messenger of Allah, Allah bless him and give peace, and said: "'Please give us your verdict about intoxicants and games of chance, for intoxicants suspend people's reasoning faculties, while games of chance waste their money'. As a response, Allah, exalted is He, revealed this verse"[17] (see Figure 1).

This incident shows that it was the initiative of the early Muslim community members whose inquiry precipitated the revelation of those Quranic verses and initiated the establishment of new norms that would transform the practices of this nascent community. The language of the

6 Quran 2:189.
7 Quran 2:217.
8 Quran 2:219.
9 Quran 2:220.
10 Quran 2:222.
11 Quran 5:4.
12 Quran 8:1.
13 Quran 4:127.
14 Quran 4:176.
15 Quran 2:219; translation mine, with assistance from Asad, *The Meaning of the Quran*, 70.
16 The designation of the Muslim natives of Medina (Yathrib) who gave refuge to the Prophet Muḥammad and his Meccan companions when he fled Mecca.
17 al-Wāḥidī, *Asbāb al-nuzūl*, www.altafsir.com/AsbabAlnuzol.aspSoraName=2&āyāh=219&search=yes&img=A accessed January 5, 2012.

verses quoted shows that the practices of drinking alcohol and gambling were not condemned outright nor prohibited, but what is clear is that these practices were seen as doing more harm than good, hence violating the fundamental Islamic legal maxim of maximizing benefit and minimizing harm. Nonetheless, this Quranic verse laid the seeds for the eventual prohibition of these deeply rooted practices, which occurred at a later period through the dictates of other Quranic verses.[18]

Yet what is most interesting about this incident is that it illustrates how members of the nascent Muslim community were internalizing Quranic norms because of their recognition that practices of consumption of alcohol and gambling were inconsistent with those norms, as demonstrated in their reported appeal to the values of reason and conservation in the tradition cited earlier, yet they lacked the authority to implement their point of view on the rest of the community and hence sought a regulation that would reflect that norm as was indicated in their request to the Prophet to give them his "verdict." These advocates did not immediately achieve their objective of decisive legislation prohibiting those practices, but they nonetheless catalyzed the process that led to eventual prohibition. Hence, they were participants in the formation of new practices that were in accordance with the ethos of the new Islamic community.

Another example of Quranic fatwas is the following verses concerning the legal guardian's management of the orphan's wealth:

> And they ask thee (*yas'alūnaka*) about [how to deal with] orphans. Say: "To improve their condition is best." And if you share their life, [remember that] they are your brethren: for God distinguishes between him who spoils things and him who improves. And had God so willed, He would indeed have imposed on you hardships which you would not have been able to bear: [but,] behold, God is almighty, wise![19]

One of the *asbāb al-nuzūl* narrations that set the context for these verses runs as follows:

> Ibn ʿAbbās said: "When Allah, exalted is He, revealed the verse 'And approach not the wealth of the orphan save with that which is better…,' whoever had an orphan's wealth with him proceeded to isolate his food and drink from the orphan's food and drink, and whatever remained of the orphan's food was kept aside until the orphan would use it or it would go bad; and this was a source of anguish for people. They went and mentioned this to the Messenger of Allah, Allah bless him and give him peace, and as a response, Allah, glorified and exalted

[18] See Quran 4:49 and 5:90.
[19] Quran 2:220; translation Asad, 70.

is He, revealed 'And they question thee concerning orphans. Say: To improve their lot is best,' by mixing their food and drink with their food and drink."[20]

This Quranic fatwa for this given situation has a different dynamic than the previously mentioned fatwa. In the previous fatwa on alcohol and gambling, the legislation was wholly initiated by concerns of members of the Muslim community. In this fatwa, according to the narration, the legislation came as a follow-up to and a clarification of a previously legislated practice. In this case, a seemingly unprovoked piece of Quranic legislation requiring that legal guardians show scrupulousness when using the wealth of orphans in their custody seemed ambiguous in terms of its implementation, and this ambiguity created hardship in terms of its practice. This necessitated the practitioners to pursue a fatwa (i.e., for clarification) on how to understand this new practice, whereupon the subsequent portion of the verse (the Quranic fatwa) was revealed as a reply (see Figure 1).

These incidences and their accompanying verses highlight the indirect dialogue taking place between the Lawgiver (God) and members of the first Muslim community and are an indication of the dialogical aspect of the Quranic discourse. This implies that people of the day were taking an active role in determining their religious and social practices by engaging the authoritative discourses with their inquiries. By seeking solutions to the issues that meant the most to them as is represented by the practice of fatwa, ordinary people were (and still are) participating in shaping their religious and social fields. They influence the discourses and the social forces that affect their lives even when they are unable to completely determine them. The dialogical and communicative elements of the Quranic discourse such as the ones displayed in Quranic fatwas facilitated this process.

But more importantly, fatwa as a legal practice derives its basis from the Quranic discursive practice as demonstrated in the examples mentioned earlier. As the authoritative text for Muslims, the Quran's

Case	Ruling/fatwa
Intoxicants and games of chance	Discouraged (later prohibited)
Guardian partaking in food or drink from orphan's wealth	Permitted

FIGURE 1 Quranic fatwas

[20] Al-Wāḥidī, *Asbāb al-nuzūl*, www.altafsir.com/AsbabAlnuzol.asp?SoraName=2&āyāh=220&search=yes&img=A accessed January 7, 2012.

responsive engagement of people's inquiries and concerns provided the epistemological legitimation for the validation of this practice in Muslim life. In other words, fatwa gained its acceptability as a valid form of legal practice and law production because it was something that was enunciated and practiced by the authoritative discourse of Islam (i.e., the Quran). Once validated, *iftāʾ* became one of the foundational practices for the establishment of a whole legal tradition.

THE BEGINNINGS OF *IFTĀʾ* IN THE PROPHETIC PRACTICE

While the Quran was the discursive origin for the legitimation of the usage of fatwa, the prophetic practice was also instrumental in establishing *iftāʾ* as a legal practice in Islam. But how was the art of *iftāʾ* practiced during the career of the Prophet Muḥammad, and what impact did that practice have on institutionalizing fatwa in Muslim legal tradition? What distinguished the prophetic fatwa from the Quranic fatwa, and how were those characteristics instrumental to the development of *iftāʾ* as an Islamic legal institution?

What is distinctive about the prophetic fatwas is the Prophet's occasional use of legal reasoning to justify some of his fatwas, while this feature was on a whole absent from Quranic fatwas. Given that Quranic authority and prophetic authority were seen as epistemologically equivalent from the theological point of view, the Prophet's use of reason in fatwas must have been for pedagogic purposes to show his followers how to arrive at their own legal deductions regarding religious practice.

Let us consider a few illustrations of when the Prophet Muḥammad used reasoning to support his fatwa. First is his fatwa to Maymūna on the legality of benefiting from the skin of a dead sheep. Maymūna mistakenly expanded the range of objects that are legally prohibited by a Quranic verse[21] that prohibits eating the meat of dead sheep that had not been properly slaughtered to include a prohibition of the utilization of its skin for reasons not related to consumption. The Prophet argues that her extension of the prohibition is invalid and that the verse only stipulates the eating of the meat and not the utilization of its skin.[22] In this incident, we see that the Prophet used a sort of hermeneutical reasoning to justify his legal position by showing how the text of the Quran should be understood (see Figure 2).

[21] Quran 6:146.

[22] Muslim, *Ṣaḥīḥ Muslim*, 1:276, *ḥadīth* #100. Beirut: Dar Iḥyāʾ al-Turāth al-ʿArabī, n.d. (cited from Shamela Library software, version 3.61). See also Riyāḍ, 42.

Another example where the use of reasoning in a fatwa is even more pronounced is when the Prophet uses an analogy[23] to justify some of his fatwas: ʿUmar asked about the permissibility of kissing while fasting; the Prophet responded by making an analogy to the performance of the ritual washing of one's mouth as being something allowed during the fast and, hence, on the same grounds argues for the acceptance of the act of kissing while fasting.[24] The point of this analogy is that if swishing water to clean one's mouth without willingly ingesting it does not break one's fast, then neither should kissing one's spouse during the fast as an act of love so long as it does not produce sexual excitement, which is against the spirit of fasting (see Figure 2).

These two examples show how the Prophet Muḥammad contributed to the methodological practices of *iftāʾ* by purposefully displaying legal reasoning when issuing some of his fatwas. There was no need on behalf of the Prophet to enunciate a rationale for his fatwas, as he enjoyed, by Quranic mandate,[25] independent authority to legislate without recourse to an external authority other than the Quran. Nonetheless, in showing his rationale, it should be understood that he was trying to teach his followers the rational basis of Islamic law and the types of rationale that should be employed in its production.[26]

Muslim tradition found in the prophetic practice of *iftāʾ*, especially the types of fatwas where the rationale for his fatwas was enunciated, the methodological seeds that germinated into Islamic legal theory. Take, for

[23] Which is known as *qiyās* in Islamic legal theory and becomes one of the main sources for the production of Islamic law.

[24] See Ibn Ḥanbal, *al-Musnad*, 1:285, *ḥadīth* #138. Beirut: Muʾassast al-Risāla, 2001 (cited from Shamela Library software, version 3.61). See also Riyāḍ, 45.

[25] See Quran 3:32; 3:132; 4:59; 5:92; 8:1; 8:20; 8:46; 24:54; 24:56; 47:33; 58:13; and 64:12 as examples of verses that urge the believers to obey the commands of the Prophet Muḥammad, including in legislative matters. An example of a Qurʾānic statement that indicates the Prophet's authority as being legislative and juridical (binding) in nature and not just religious is the following: "But nay, by thy Sustainer! They do not [really] believe unless they make thee [O Prophet] a judge (*yuḥakkimūka*) in all on which they disagree among themselves, and then find in their hearts no bar to an acceptance of thy decision and give themselves up [to it] in utter self-surrender" (Q. 4:65). This passage is unequivocal in asserting the Prophet's role as judge in all matters, which includes legal issues as implied by the term used to designate this authority: *yuḥakkimūka*. This term and its root *ḥ-k-m* are most often employed when judicial authority is being invoked (see the connotations of the root of the Arabic word *ḥakama* and its various derivations in E. W. Lane's *Arabic-English Lexicon*, 1:616–617).

[26] Al-Sāyis, a contemporary historian of Islamic law, makes a similar assertion in his book *Tarikh al-Fiqh al-Islami*, 42.

example, the two fatwas mentioned earlier where the Prophet in one case based his fatwa on textual hermeneutics and the other on analogy; in the Islamic science of *uṣūl al-fiqh* (Islamic legal theory), textual hermeneutics (e.g., the sections on Quran and *ḥadīth*) and legal analogy (i.e., *qiyās*) comprise more than half of the studies in this discipline.

Muslim scholars have long argued that this science and others have their roots in the Prophet's practice of employing these legal devices in his legal edicts and judgments.[27] The point in this argument is to show how the prophetic practice contributed to the discursive formation of Islamic legal tradition.

On another note, it seemed like the Prophet Muḥammad encouraged *qiyās* (the exercise of using judgment to develop legal rulings) among his followers by affirming the validity of their disparate rulings on various religious matters. For instance, when one of his followers, ʿAmr ibn al-ʿāṣ, became *junub* (referring to the state of greater ritual impurity) and did not have appropriate water to purify himself, he just performed *tayammum* (alternative ritual purification)[28] and performed his prayers and did not repeat them when he eventually found water. This is because at the time of prayer, he had met the requirements to perform the alternative ritual purification (*tayammum*) and hence did not need to repeat the prayer once water was found.[29] Yet, in another setting where his followers found themselves in a similar situation, they did the same. However, when they later found water they performed their prayers again, believing that since the exceptional conditions necessitating the performance of prayer under *tayammum* had been resolved, they were required to perform the prayers anew once water had been found. The Prophet endorsed both opinions/actions as legitimate,[30] seeing that they both had their legitimate recourse to proper reasoning (see Figure 2). This illustrates that variant opinions were accepted so long as the reasoning behind them was valid, thereby encouraging an atmosphere of independent problem-solving that was required when encountering new scenarios that had to be resolved by *iftāʾ* and *ijtihād* (independent legal reasoning).

[27] See Riyāḍ, 44 and al-Sāyis, 41 for examples of Muslim historians of Islamic law who make such assertions.

[28] See Abū Dāwūd, *Sunan Abī Dāwūd*, 1:92, *ḥadīth* #334 and 335. Beirut: Maktabat al-ʿAṣriyya, n.d. (cited from the Shamela Library software, version 3.61).

[29] Abū Zahra, 239.

[30] See *Sunan Abī Dāwūd*, 1:93–94, *ḥadīth* #338 and 339. Beirut: Maktabat al-ʿAṣriyya, n.d. (cited from the Shamela Library software, version 3.61). See also Abū Zahra, 239.

Another example where the Prophet encouraged his followers to practice *ijtihād* was when he gave orders that the army going against the tribe of Banū Qurayẓa should not perform the *ʿaṣr* (afternoon) prayer until they reached there. When the time of *ʿaṣr* seemed to be passing, some within the group understood the command as an injunction to hasten their travel to the destination but not to miss the time to perform the prayer in the process of traveling, and so they prayed on the way. Meanwhile, others interpreted it as a mandatory injunction by the Prophet not to pray *ʿaṣr* except in the territory of the Banū Qurayẓa, and so they did not pray along the way. When they brought the matter to the Prophet, he did not object to either opinion[31] (see Figure 2).

This incident shows that situations or statements could be interpreted differently and still be considered within the range of valid interpretation so long as the language or scenario allowed for it. In addition, the requisites for a fatwa, such as independent legal reasoning, were something cultivated by the Prophet himself. What I am suggesting is that these illustrations of the prophetic practice of *iftāʾ* represent a seminal beginning point for the establishment of the rules that became associated

Case	Ruling/fatwa	Legal reasoning
Usage of skin of a dead sheep (carrion)	Permitted	No analogs to Quranic prohibition for eating carrion; false textual hermeneutics
Permissibility of kissing while fasting	Permitted	Analogous to washing one's mouth while fasting
Repeating prayers with proper ablution after they were performed with alternative ablution (*tayammum*)	Permitted, while not repeating the prayer is also valid	*Ijtihād* (open to various forms of legal reasoning)
The prophetic command to perform *ʿaṣr* prayer at Banū Qurayẓa	Both options for understanding command legitimate	Following literal command or metaphorical interpretation of command

FIGURE 2 Prophetic fatwas

[31] See al-Ṭabarānī's *al-Muʿjam al-kabīr*, v. 19, pg. 79, ḥadīth # 160. Cairo: Maktabat Ibn Taymiyya, second edition, n.d. and al-ḥākim's *al-Mustadrak*, v. 3, pg. 37, ḥadīth # 4333. Beirut: Dār al-Kutub al-ʿIlmiyya, 1990 (both citations from Shamela Library software, version 3.61). See also al-Sāyis, n.d., 40.

with the subsequent practices of *iftāʾ* in particular and Islamic legal theory in general. The Prophet's employing of various methodologies and approaches in generating fatwas, such as the use of textual hermeneutics and analogical reasoning, and his encouragement of others to exercise their own legal reasoning (*ijtihād/raʾy*) to arrive at legal positions became authoritative and foundational norms and practices for the establishment of an Islamic legal tradition.

This is not saying that the entire corpus of prophetic fatwas displayed the same sophistication in the use of legal devices in their pronouncements. In most cases, fatwas do not provide the rationale for their assertion whether they are prophetic or post-prophetic fatwas, but providing the legal rationale in some cases established precedence for how legal reasoning in Islam should be practiced. It is here that the prophetic fatwa can be distinguished from the Quranic fatwas. While the Quranic fatwas have, to use Weber's terminology, an oracular character,[32] in the sense that there is no appeal to rules on how they are arrived at, some of the prophetic fatwas begin to display the rules of their formation as indicated by the examples mentioned earlier, when the Prophet used analogical reasoning to show, for example, that kissing did not negate one's fast.

In asserting that the prophetic practice of fatwa began to establish the legal norms of Islamic legal tradition, I am referring to the formal standards that gave rules for the application of legal decisions. Describing Quranic fatwas as having an oracular character does not mean that they did not establish legal norms. On the contrary, many of the legal norms of Islamic law are a result of the substantive ethical teachings of the Quran. So, although the Quran did not provide much in terms of formal rationality in its fatwas, it certainly did give much in terms of substantive rationality and values for the establishment of Islamic law.

Describing Quranic fatwas as having an oracular character thus refers to the lack of formal rules for their formation, and it is in this formal dimension of law and legal opinions that Weber asserts that legal "norm formation occurs when there is a weakening of the originally purely oracular character of the [legal] decision."[33] It is in this respect that the Prophet's practice of *iftāʾ* catalyzed the development of formal legal norms in his application of rational devices such as analogical reasoning and textual hermeneutics, which became seminal ideas and practices for the formation of Islamic legal theory and tradition.

[32] See Weber, 74.
[33] Weber, 74.

Later, Islamic legal theorists used these prophetic legal practices as legitimating factors in their construction of an Islamic legal theory (*uṣūl al-fiqh*). For instance, classical and medieval Muslim jurists often cited the prophetic traditions mentioned earlier to sanction the exercise of legal reasoning (*ijtihād*)[34] in general and analogical reasoning (*qiyās*)[35] in particular in order to establish new laws that were not directly legislated by the Quran and the prophetic practice. The point here is that Muslim jurists and legal theorists were conscious of the prophetic legal practices when constructing and legitimating the legal methodological tools employed in the derivation of Islamic law, which underlines the importance of these prophetic practices in establishing the Islamic legal discourse.

But what does this discussion of *ijtihād* and *qiyās* have to do with fatwa? Fatwa represents a subcategory of *ijtihād* in that it is a particular activity that is subsumed under the larger category of *ijtihād*. Thus, the licensing of *ijtihād* opened the doors for the practice of *iftāʾ*, both of which were practiced and encouraged by the Prophet himself. Some of the rules for this *ijtihād/iftāʾ*, such as analogical reasoning (*qiyās*), textual hermeneutics (e.g., *dalālāt al-lafẓ*), and the legitimacy of different legal opinions (fatwas), were also established by prophetic practice, which later Islamic legal theorists and jurists saw as the rudimentary legal matter from which to construct the discipline of *uṣūl al-fiqh* (Islamic legal theory). It is obvious by now that these Quranic and prophetic discursive practices provided substantive legal norms, which were the normative material for the formation of an Islamic legal discourse. Yet, these discursive practices also led to the establishment of some of the formal legal mechanisms for the derivation of Islamic law.

FATWA IN THE POST-PROPHETIC PERIOD

There are several ideas to keep in mind before venturing to speak about fatwas in the post-prophetic period. First, the loss of prophetic authority in the issuance of fatwas led to a greater relativity in their legal authoritativeness. During the prophetic period, fatwas issued by the Prophet Muḥammad were considered legal dictates solely based on his prophetic legal authority. Hence, the Prophet's fatwas constituted authoritative

[34] See the following medieval *uṣūl al-fiqh* works that make these points: al-Ghazālī, *al-Mustaṣfā*, 2:392, and al- Rāzī, *al-Maḥṣūl*, 6:20. See also the classical Muslim jurist al-Shāfiʿī's work *al-Risāla*, 299 (translation by Khadduri), where he justifies *ijtihād* by reference to prophetic statements.

[35] See al-Ghazālī, *al-Mustaṣfā*, 2:266–267.

norms that his followers were obligated to practice.[36] Fatwas in subsequent generations lacked that sort of authoritative mandate because those engaging in fatwas lacked the same level of authoritative position that the Prophet had among his followers.[37]

Thus, fatwas issued by learned Muslims after the Prophet's demise were at most considered legal opinions that may or may not have influenced the Muslim community's practices or policies, unless they were adopted and enforced by those in political authority. Nonetheless, despite post-prophetic fatwas not enjoying the same degree of authoritativeness as prophetic fatwas, the combination of prophetic and post-prophetic fatwas provided the legal substance from which Islamic law was derived, as demonstrated later in this investigation.

The second point is the wider social and geographic context in which these fatwas were now issued and the new problems they were designed to address. As the domain of Islam in the post-prophetic period began to expand outside the confines of Arabia, the early Muslims began to encounter new social and political situations that they had not encountered during the prophetic period and that, hence, had not been addressed during his lifetime. These changes in conditions would necessitate new solutions to the challenges that confronted the nascent community, and fatwas were the legal means by which this community dealt with those challenges, as I demonstrate below.[38]

[36] See footnote 25 mentioned earlier for a list of Qur'ānic verses that attest to the Prophet's legal authority. But beyond scriptural evidence, there is historical evidence that supports this contention. The Charter of Medina, for instance, which is accepted as authentic by both traditional Muslim scholarship and Western historians (see Humphreys, 87, for an elaboration of this assertion), contained clauses that gave the Prophet Muḥammad political-legal authority over the city-state polity of Medina. For example, clause 42 of this constitution states: "Whenever among the people of this document there occurs any incident (disturbance) or quarrel from which disaster for them (the people) is to be feared, it should be referred to God and to Muḥammad, the Messenger of God" (source: www.constitution.org/cons/medina/con_medina.htm accessed October 29, 2012). This statement implies that the Prophet's authority entails juridical functions and points to the legally binding nature of his activity. See also the testimony of seventh-century non-Muslim sources (e.g., John bar Penkaye's chronicle) that attest to how early Muslims viewed prophetic dictates as authoritatively binding (see Hoyland, 196–197).

[37] Although it should be noted that for the first two centuries of Islam, there were legal circles, like the Kufan regional school and, eventually, the early ḥanafī school, that viewed statements made by the companions as binding (see Stodolsky, 521). But as the ḥanafī school matured in conversation with other legal circles, the authoritativeness of the companions' statements and practices diminished even in this school. (We shall have more to say about these points later in this investigation.)

[38] An example of the political challenges that resulted from this vast expansion was how to govern the new territories of Persia, the Fertile Crescent, and Egypt. Two basic principles

Third, just as in the prophetic period, post-prophetic fatwas in their early years maintained their character of being impromptu solutions to social or religious problems that arose. *Iftāʾ* as a legal practice was never intended to anticipate legal problems that had not yet arisen, and this attitude was especially the case in the early period of its practice. This is verified by historical reports about the early post-prophetic period that indicate that the Prophet's followers were suspicious of giving fatwas for situations that had yet to arise. One such case was where ʿAmmār ibn Yāsir was sought out by a group for a fatwa on a particular matter. He retorted: "Did this matter occur?" They said no, whereupon he replied: "Let me be until it occurs; if it occurs, then I will undertake the matter for you."[39]

This incident shows that some early Muslims had a disdain for dealing with hypothetical matters and preferred to provide legal judgments on actual issues. This attitude began to change in the following generations of fatwa practitioners, as is shown in the case of ʿAṭāʾ ibn Rabāḥ,[40] who answers what seem to have been hypothetical questions about women converting to Islam and the compensation owed to their non-Muslim husbands.[41] Yet despite this shift in approach to fatwas, fatwas by and large maintained their ad hoc character of being attempted legal solutions for actual religious and social concerns.

Last, the Muslim geographical expansion eventually led to the development of regional schools of law that had their particular approaches to the production of legal decisions. These schools evolved as early as the second generation of Muslims after the death of the Prophet. The appearance of regional legal schools can be explained by several factors that I briefly outline here and expand on later in this investigation. The geographic and social diversity that had developed within the Muslim

were followed during the early period of Islamic conquest: First, the conquering Muslim Arabs were to be prevented from damaging the agricultural society, and second, the new Muslim elite would cooperate with the chiefs and notables of the conquered population. These policies were carried out by separating the conquering Muslim Arabs from the native populations by placing Muslim Arab armies in their own military settlements outside the conquered towns and then working out an arrangement with local elites from the native population that established a governing relationship between the non-Muslim population and their new Muslim suzerains. These Muslim military settlements eventually grew into permanent towns like Basra and Kufa in Iraq, Fustat in Egypt, Qayrawan in North Africa, and Marw in Central Asia (Lapidus, 34, 36).

39 As quoted in Līna al-ḥimsī, *Tārīkh al-fatwā fī al-Islām wa-aḥkāmuhā al-sharʿiyya*, (Damascus: Dār al-Rashīd, 1996), 78. The story was related by al-Dārimī in his *Sunan*, 1:50.

40 Who was among the second generation of Muslims.

41 See Motzki, 110, to reference this fatwa.

community was possibly the first factor that gave impetus for these various regional approaches to law. Another factor had to do with the various learned contemporaries of the Prophet who settled in different regions and influenced subsequent generations of Muslims in these regions with their own interpretations of Islamic teachings in general and Islamic law in particular.[42]

All of the issues and observations about fatwa in the post-prophetic period are best illustrated in the context of examining actual fatwas of this period. So, in the following paragraphs, I will survey fatwas from this period, but it is crucial that I delineate the boundaries of this period. I am calling the first century and a half to two centuries of Islam as the post-prophetic period of fatwas.[43] This age designates the period prior to the evolution of schools of law that established more systematic approaches to law production that I will examine in future chapters. Suffice it to say that the post-prophetic period of *iftāʾ* can also be broken into subperiods all with their own peculiarities and developments in establishing Islamic law and legal practice. In the next subsection, I will examine fatwas in one of these subperiods from those contemporaries of the Prophet Muḥammad who attained legal authority after his demise.

Before starting an analysis of the fatwas from this period, I need to clarify the criteria I used in choosing from the many fatwas that are extant. Similar to the case of the prophetic fatwas, I have chosen fatwas in the post-prophetic period that demonstrate some legal rationale or hermeneutic so as to foreshadow the development of Islamic legal theory in particular and Islamic legal institutions in general. It is important to emphasize that later generations of Muslim legal authorities looked at the practice of their predecessors for insights in establishing a legal tradition.

Yet their predecessors left no theoretical works on legal methodology or law for them to construct this tradition. But it was in the predecessors' actual legal decisions (fatwas) and the rationale employed in them that

42 For example, in Sunnī Muslim tradition, it is recognized that the legal opinions of Ibn Masʿūd (a follower of the Prophet Muḥammad who later settled in Kufa) were the antecedents to the methodological distinctiveness that defined the Iraqi (Kufan) approach to the law.

43 Salaymah (2016: 7) designates this period as "Islamic Late antiquity" as a way of temporally contextualizing Islamic developments within the larger context of the Near East. But as my arguments about the beginnings of Islamic law are focused on the internal dynamics of the Muslim community, I have chosen to use designations that are indicative of that without necessarily diminishing the argument for the importance of viewing the enterprise of Islamic law within a wider spatial and temporal context.

later generations were able to derive legal precepts that eventually served as the material from which a legal tradition was constructed. This is why it was important to select those fatwas that demonstrated types of legal rationale that were the impetus for the development of the Islamic legal tradition in history. This criterion should be kept in mind when thinking about the fatwas that have been subsequently chosen.

FATWA IN THE POST-PROPHETIC PERIOD: FATWA IN THE AGE OF THE EARLY CALIPHATE

This period represents about the first fifty to sixty years after the prophetic period during which many of his contemporary followers continued to live and influence the affairs of everyday Muslim life. This is also the period when the institution of the caliphate was established as a post-prophetic political institution to rule over the quickly expanding Muslim community and empire in lieu of the loss of the Prophet's political leadership. During this period, we witness the Muslim community grappling with new socio-economic and political concerns that were not dealt with in the prophetic period; hence, there was a need for fresh legal decisions to settle the new challenges facing the early Muslim community.

An example of a legal ruling from the age of the caliphate in the domain of political economy was a policy decision on land tax adopted by the Caliph ʿUmar that was treated as a legal opinion (fatwa) and established a political and legal precedent for all policies after him with regard to conquered lands. When the Muslim armies conquered Iraq, they were conflicted on what to do with the area known as the Sawād (fertile area between the Tigris and Euphrates rivers) of Iraq: whether to leave it to be cultivated by the original inhabitants of Iraq and have them pay taxes on its produce or to distribute it among the soldiers who participated in the conquest (a practice known as *qanīma*),[44] as had previously been the practice of the Prophet, based on a Quranic injunction.[45]

The dilemma that ʿUmar faced was that if he distributed it in accordance with the previously established prophetic practice so as to keep with precedence, then a large amount of wealth would have been concentrated in the hands of a few individuals to the detriment of the larger society. This was not the case in the previous distributions by the Prophet Muḥammad, which consisted of small plots of land in desert oasis towns

[44] Abū Zahra, 245. See also al-Tilimsānī, 533–534.

[45] See Quran 8:41.

like Khaybar.[46] Yet if ʿUmar did not distribute the land to the conquering soldiers, then he would be violating the established practice of the Prophet, which was seen as normative by the Muslim community.

ʿUmar, acting on the advice of some of his advisors like Muʿādh ibn Jabal,[47] chose to go against the previously established practice of distributing the land to the conquering soldiers and sought the larger public's interest by leaving usufruct of the land in the hands of the original inhabitants while extracting taxes for the state to be paid out to the troops as stipends.[48] It could be argued that ʿUmar and those who supported his conclusion, in this case, came to this judgment based on *maṣlaḥa* (public interest or the general good), even though this legal decision seemed to have contradicted the established normative/legal practice of the Prophet Muḥammad. Yet the prominent Muslim jurist of the second century of Islam Abū Yūsuf (732–798 CE.) narrates several reports in his book *Kitāb al-Kharāj*[49] that ʿUmar supported his position with the following Quranic verse:

That which Allah giveth as spoil [i.e., *afāʾa*, which is a verbal form of noun *fayʾ*] unto His messenger from the people of the townships, it is for Allah and His messenger and for the near of kin and the orphans and the needy and the wayfarer, that it become not *a commodity [circulating] between the rich among you.* And whatsoever the messenger giveth you, take it. And whatsoever he forbiddeth, abstain (from it). And keep your duty to Allah. Lo! Allah is stern in reprisal.[50]

This verse, which ʿUmar purportedly employed, gives an indication that his decision for the public ownership of conquered lands was something that could be legitimated by a scripturally determined decree and not just a case solely determined by utilitarian considerations of *maṣlaḥa* (public interest/greater good), since it entirely relegates the charge of the spoils (*fayʾ*) to those in governance[51] so as to be utilized for the

[46] Muḥammad Bāqir al-ṣadr, a prominent twentieth-century Shīʿite jurist, argues in his book *Our Economics* (English translation vol. 2. Pt. 2) pgs. 89–99 that the Prophet Muhammad's practice in Khaybar and in other places was to give away the usufruct of the land to the soldiers while keeping the land itself under public ownership. However, the majority of Sunnī Muslim scholars do not agree with this interpretation.

[47] See al-Tilimsānī, 534.

[48] See al-Tilimsānī, 533–534. See also Dennet, 20.

[49] Abū Yūsuf, 23–26. See also al-Sāyis, *Tafsīr āyāt al-aḥkām*, 2:532, and Dennet, 21.

[50] Quran: 59:7. Translation by http://Quranexplorer.com/Quran/ accessed September 17, 2012. Emphasis added.

[51] Muhammad Asad argues that the phrase in this verse "Allah and His messenger" is a metonym for the Islamic cause especially as represented by Islamic governance. See his *Message of the Quran*, 851, n. 8.

greater public interest as indicated by the verse (i.e., the needy, orphans, wayfarers, etc.).[52] Moreover, the verse also gives the moral rationale for the judgment by saying that this *fay*ʾ should not become "a commodity [circulating] between the rich among you," indicating that it should not be a cause for the circulation of wealth among a few. Consequently, not keeping this new-found wealth in the strict domain of those who participated in the conquest served the larger public's interest.[53]

Yet it is very plausible that ʿUmar had the rationale of *maṣlaḥa* primarily in mind when supporting his initial decision and not any particular Quranic injunction because the historical reports say that he only employed the Quranic passage in question several days later when he received opposition to his verdict. Therefore, he sought to bolster the legality of his position and satisfy his opponents who demanded that he uphold the previously established practice of distributing the spoils among the participating soldiers.[54] So one may argue that *maṣlaḥa* was the primary consideration in ʿUmar's fatwa and that the Quranic passage that he employed was for the auxiliary support given the time lag between his initial judgment and his furnishing of Quranic support for his position (see Figure 3).

This legal opinion reveals much about the fatwa-making process and its role in the establishment of the Islamic legal tradition because it illustrates the relationship between Islamic law and society and that the

[52] Yet we mentioned previously that there was another Qurʾānic verse (Q. 8:41) that implied that spoils of war should be largely distributed to the participating soldiers, and this is what the Prophet himself practiced. Thus, there was a conflict between the content of this verse and the prophetic implementation of it and the Qurʾānic verse (Q. 59:7) that ʿUmar employed to bolster his position. Traditionally, Muslim scholars say that the issue is resolved by the different terms used in the two passages to designate the idea of spoils: *ghanīma* and *fay*ʾ. They say that the term *ghanīma*, used in Quran 8:41 that calls for distributing most of the spoils among the participants in the battle, designates the types of spoils taken after armed conflict, while the term *fay*ʾ, used in Quran 59:7 that calls for the withholding of all spoils for public interest, designates the type of spoils that were acquired without armed conflict (see al-Sāyis, *Tafsīr āyāt al-aḥkām*, 2:9 and 2:528). Therefore, both passages are speaking about different subjects, thus reconciling any apparent conflict between them. So ʿUmar's usage of the verse to support his argument was rather inconsistent since the lands of Iraq could not be considered *fay*ʾ per se because they were conquered forcibly and hence had to be considered *ghanīma*. Nevertheless, it was the core principle found in the Qurʾānic verse "that it become not a commodity [circulating] between the rich among you" that Muslim scholars argue is the basis for his argument and not whether the land was *fay*ʾ or *ghanīma*.

[53] See Abū Zahra, *Tārīkh al-madhāhib al-Islāmiyya fi al-siyāsa wa-l-ʿaqāʾid wa-tārīkh al-madhāhib al-fiqhiyya*, for details of the argument.

[54] See Abū Yūsuf, 23–26.

Case	Ruling/fatwa	Legal reasoning	Proto-jurist
Dividing conquered Sawād lands (Iraq) as war booty among Muslim soldiers	Prohibited	Textual hermeneutics and public interest	Caliph ʿUmar I

FIGURE 3 Fatwas in the age of the early caliphate

process of *iftā*ʾ or fatwa production was one of the essential mechanisms mediating this relationship. This reflexivity is manifested in this case as follows: There were Quranic injunctions implemented by prophetic practice that governed how spoils of war were to be distributed based upon certain circumstances that prevailed in Arabia, which then established a normative precedence for how the Islamic polity should deal with spoils. Yet a new situation arose in the conquest of the lands of Iraq where the spoils far exceeded those spoils that were acquired in the Muslim campaigns in Arabia. This then required the old rule to be reworked so that it stayed consistent with the overall aim of the law (public interest or greater good).

So what we see here is a dynamic interplay of legal and social forces where both law and political circumstances affected one another. It is clear that the sociopolitical circumstances in Iraq in the seventh century were different from those of Arabia, necessitating the establishment of new rules to fit the new situation. This was the case in terms of ʿUmar's fatwa, which became a legal precedent for how newly conquered lands (e.g., Iraq, Syria, and Egypt) were to be treated both in his reign and in the reign of those came after him, and it was this decision that later generations of Muslim jurists enshrined in their jurisprudence as the accepted practice by the political authorities (the caliphate). An example of this is the second Muslim century jurist Abū Yūsuf's *Kitāb al-Kharāj,* a legal treatise written for the then Caliph Hārūn al-Rashīd (763–809 C.E.) on how to treat these conquered lands, which was significantly based on the legal positions and practices established during the reign of the Caliph ʿUmar in the early first century of Islam.

Yet if this is the way that sociopolitical circumstances influenced law and subsequent legal tradition, in what ways did this new ruling shape the sociopolitical trajectory of the emerging Muslim society and state? ʿUmar's fatwa had a tremendous impact on the workings of both state and society. On the political level, ʿUmar's policy, adopted in accordance with his fatwa, meant that the Muslim armies would have to be paid in a different manner from which they were paid before, which was directly from the spoils. Since his fatwa and subsequent policy obviated that practice to some degree, there would have to be a new way for soldiers to earn remuneration for their services. So 'Umar, on the advice of his counsels, eventually set up a registry (*dīwān*) where the names of soldiers were recorded and they would receive salaries from the state treasury instead of the spoils of conquest being directly divided among them.[55]

From that point on, the administrative structure of Muslim armies was changed, and this was one ramification that resulted from his fatwa. But paying the soldiers from the public treasury instead of directly from the spoils meant that the state had to adopt a system to generate the revenue that would pay for these expenses. So conquered agricultural lands, such as the Sawād, were taxed instead of confiscated so as to generate revenue for the state. The taxation scheme in the newly conquered land, known as *kharāj*, was often adopted and adapted from the taxation schemes that were already in existence from the previous governing bodies, whether Byzantine or Sassanid.[56]

This opened up new vistas on a socio-economic level, where now the Muslim state could run a treasury where public works were paid for. The irrigation system of the Sawād lands in Iraq had fallen into disrepair during the late Sassanid period. Through the new tax revenue generated from the Sawād tax scheme, the Muslim state was able to repair these irrigation systems and restore the productivity of the land.[57] This had a positive economic impact on the native population that was tilling the land. Moreover, although the cultivators of these lands never gained ownership of them as their ownership of the Sawād lands was transferred from the Sassanid private landlords known as *dhihqān*s to the control of the Muslim state,[58] the policy of not distributing the lands among the Muslim soldiers nonetheless had several consequences: First, it allowed the inheritance of the usufruct of the land to remain with the original cultivators and their heirs, an advantage they did not have in the previous arrangement,[59] and second, it prevented the

55 Hodgson, 1:208; Ra'ana, 111–112. See also Dennet, 29.

56 See Ra'ana, 78, 88, and 90–91 for the various taxation schemes that were adopted in Iraq, Syria, and Egypt.

57 Lapidus, 37–39. See also Dennet, 30.

58 See Ra'ana, 14–15.

59 See Ra'ana, 14–15.

establishment of Muslim-controlled feudal estates that would replace the old feudal estates system that had existed under the Sassanids.[60] This policy probably worked out in the interest of the original peasant cultivators of the land.

My point in this long excursion was to show how this fatwa was both born out of and impacted by the state of affairs at that time, which illustrates the reflexive nature of the process of *iftāʾ* and its relationship to social circumstances. As was the case in the Caliph ʿUmar's fatwa, the new geopolitical scenario that confronted the nascent Muslim state demanded a revision of its previous political practices. But since those political practices were established by scriptural and prophetic authority, those practices became normative. This meant that any newly sanctioned practices would need to attain the same degree of legitimacy to revise the established practices. Fresh legal reasoning was employed that was based on an understanding of the fundamental aims of the scriptural injunctions that trumped any considerations of scriptural literalism with respect to its details.

The newly legitimated political practices that were at first necessitated by the existing circumstances had their corollary effects that transformed the social, economic, and political scene in ways that could not have been initially imagined (e.g., new taxation schemes, the creation of a public treasury, the repair of irrigation systems, revived productivity of land, etc.). These new circumstances, in turn, necessitated their own legal categories that needed to be legitimated by the employment of further legal reasoning. The point is that law is both an effect of certain social dynamics and a cause of some others and vice versa. This is what I mean by the reflexivity of law and society as illustrated by the process of *iftāʾ*.

There is one last thing that ought to be noted about ʿUmar's fatwa on the lands of the Sawād. ʿUmar's argument supporting his legal/policy position was primarily based on the notion of what would be called later in Islamic legal theory *maṣlaḥa mursala* (common good and/or public interest).[61] By initially arguing for the establishment of new political/legal practices with reference to spoils without scriptural evidence but based on considerations of public interest, ʿUmar seemed to be employing this legal technique to support his decision. In doing so, he was revising previous normative practices that had been established by Quranic

[60] See Ra'ana, 14–15.
[61] See Hallaq, 1997, 112–113 for more on this concept.

and prophetic authority. But his subversion of these scripturally based practices was based on his recognition that particular legal or normative rulings in Islam had the aim of serving ultimate ends, such that when these ends were not met by those rulings, then this required that literalism toward the rulings be abandoned in order that the spirit of the law would not be compromised.[62]

ʿUmar's employment of non-scriptural-based reasoning in his fatwas probably set a precedent for some later jurists and theorists, like the founder of the Mālikī legal tradition Mālik ibn Anas, to make *maṣlaḥa* a legal principle by which new Islamic laws can be established.[63] The interesting thing about this principle is that it is based mostly on rational grounds. This is perhaps why not all later Islamic schools of law agreed that this principle could be an independent basis from which particular Islamic rulings may be derived,[64] but there was a general consensus among many prominent Islamic legal theorists, both in the past and today, that the legal principle of *maṣlaḥa* (greater good), in its transubstantiated form of *maqāṣid al-sharīʿa* (the aims of Islamic law), lies ontologically at the very core of Islamic law even when they differ on the epistemological status of *maṣlaḥa* for establishing particular Islamic rulings.[65]

Having surveyed fatwas from the generation of proto-jurists who were both contemporaries of the Prophet Muḥammad and the carriers of his legal legacy to the subsequent generation, it is time to transition to an examination of the *iftāʾ* process in subsequent generations of Muslims after the early caliphate period. We can sum up the period that

[62] This argues against Behnam Sadeghi's (2013: 145) assertion that legal inertia keeps laws effective even when the social contexts and reasons that gave life to the law have changed and may even be borrowed from another tradition without mirroring the values of those traditions. It is clear from ʿUmar's fatwa and the historical circumstances that precipitated it that legal inertia was not at play here and that these circumstances were a factor in legal change. Even though the policy of land taxation that ʿUmar adopted may have originated in a different political setting (Byzantine or Sassanid) with a different legal tradition, the legal reasoning employed in his adoption of the policy shows that it has been re-situated in a new epistemic framework. So, the tenacity of a law may have less to do with legal inertia as Sadeghi states; instead, a law's continuance, despite the change in its justification or context, may simply mean that it has been embedded in a new value system or tradition in which it became integrated and served a new function.

[63] See Hallaq, 1997, 112–113.

[64] See Shafi's argument in his *al-Risāla*, pg. 304–305, against non-scriptural-based legal reasoning.

[65] See Hallaq, 1997, 112–113 for al-Ghazālī's advocacy of *maṣlaḥa* and Hallaq, 1997, 217–219 for Rashīd Riḍā's advocacy of it.

was examined as follows: Islamic legal discourse in this period consisted entirely of the corpus of legal norms and practices that this generation had inherited from the prophetic period with the addition of ad hoc legal decisions (fatwa and *qaḍāʾ*) that this generation produced in response to new circumstances that confronted them.

These legal decisions were in some ways extensions of the Quranic and prophetic legal norms and practices as evidenced in the formulations of their arguments supporting these legal decisions. Yet in their attempt to extend scriptural norms to new situations, they employed various hermeneutical and rational techniques to deduce new legal judgments. But the legal decisions made and legal devices employed by this generation of proto-jurists established legal precedence for future generations of jurists even when they lacked any systematization.

CONCLUSION

What becomes evident from the preceding discussion on fatwas and the process of their production (*iftāʾ*) is that fatwas in this period were impromptu responses to social events. There was no formal paradigm or legal framework that guided how the production of fatwas took place. Instead, situations arose that needed legal solutions, and the solutions (fatwas) that were generated conformed to no particular legal mechanisms other than the preferred legal reasoning of the individual *muftīs* (those pronouncing the fatwas) who issued these opinions. This feature of fatwas has several implications for the understanding of Islamic law and its legal tradition.

The first point, as I show in greater detail in subsequent chapters, is how these fatwas contributed to the formation of emerging Islamic legal doctrines. Given that fatwas are ad hoc responses to arising situations, they tell us that Islamic law is something that grew out of the promptings of everyday events often happening to everyday people.[66] In this respect then, Islamic law is partly an outgrowth of bottom-up social forces given that the very stuff that makes up the law (fatwas) is often provoked by the concerns of ordinary individuals seeking ethical/legal solutions to their everyday problems.

The second point is that out of the legal processes and rationale of these early fatwas, legal discursive practices were constructed by subsequent generations of jurists and proto-jurists who drew on these

[66] For more on this point, see Hallaq, 1994, 61.

antecedents to formulate their own legal methodologies, principles, and doctrines. So the fatwas in this period were crucial in establishing a model from which future legal specialists constructed a legal tradition for Islam. Yet, in the subsequent generations of jurists issuing these fatwas, we will witness an increasing level of formalization and structuring of the legal rationale that legitimates these fatwas. This forms the subject of Chapter 2.

2

Fatwa in the Classical Age

INTRODUCTION

This chapter covers the early history of fatwa and how this institution evolved from the early authoritative discourses and practices of Muslims. More precisely, fatwas from the late first century and second century of Islam will be analyzed so as to discover the defining features of the fatwa tradition and what that may tell us about the development of Islamic law in general.

Moreover, this chapter explores the sociohistorical background of this period, as fatwas are often responses to changes in the sociohistorical environment and therefore these changes tell us a lot about the social processes of fatwa production.

My contention is that fatwas and the process of *iftāʾ* – the practice of fatwa production – are to be understood as a form of the Aristotelian concept of *phronesis*. In regard to *phronesis*, Aristotle asserts the following: "People are in fact prudent (*phronimos*) about something whenever they can calculate well with a view to some serious end in matters which there is no art."[1] Aristotle understood that in matters of practical reasoning (i.e., those concerning human action), there are no hard and fixed rules that can mechanically generate particular decisions as is the case for logic.[2] Moreover, Aristotle relates such practical reasoning to matters associated with application of ethics: "Prudence (*phronesis*) is a true characteristic that is bound up with action, accompanied by reason, and concerned with things

[1] Aristotle, 120.
[2] Madison, 320.

good or bad for a human being."[3] So applying universal ethical norms to a particular situation, for example, requires more than just knowledge of those ethical norms. It also requires the prudence for when, where, and how to apply those norms to the situation that one is faced with.

Iftāʾ is in some essential ways precisely this type of procedure where jurists are attempting to apply general Islamic principles to a particular scenario so as to produce normative guidelines that would inform one's ethico-religious practices. As we will see, fatwa became the means by which the Quranic ethico-legal norms spoken of previously became actualized in the sociohistorical context of Islam. The Islamic legal norms and injunctions promulgated by the Quranic discourse and prophetic practice became interpreted, applied, and re-interpreted in various historical and cultural contexts through the process of *iftāʾ* – by those who had the authority to engage in this process and issue fatwas.

What will also become apparent is that these *muftī*s (those who have the authority to issue fatwas) employed all sorts of legal rationale and hermeneutical devices to reformulate and apply Quranically and prophetically based norms in a way that seemed fitting for the peculiar situations that were faced by the early Muslim community. As will be inferred in the next chapter, the types of legal reasoning and the interpretive devices employed in these early fatwas became the basis of an Islamic legal discourse. This discourse, along with the legal authorities who shaped it, was the genesis of an Islamic legal tradition.

FATWA IN THE AGE OF REGIONAL DISTINCTIONS

By the last quarter of the first century after the advent of Islam, many religious authorities who were contemporaries of the Prophet Muḥammad and carried his religious and legal teachings to the subsequent generation had passed on. Unlike those religious authorities of the first generation who were contemporaries of the Prophet and who continued to reside largely in Arabia proper (particularly the towns of Mecca and Medina) even during the Islamic expansion in the Near East, many of the subsequent generation of religious authorities took up residence in the garrison settlements that were now evolving into proper towns such as Basra and Kufa in Iraq, Marw in Central Asia, and Fustat in Egypt, as well as in other towns in Muslim-governed lands that had already existed prior to the Muslim expansion like Damascus in Syria and Sanaʿa in Yemen.

[3] Aristotle, 120.

The regional diversity of the places where the new religious authority emerged and the changing political circumstances in those areas gave a peculiar coloring to the practice of *iftāʾ* in this period. Therefore, we need to note some of the general characteristics about fatwa during this period so as to understand how the practice of *iftāʾ* developed. The first thing to note is that a distinction developed between the new religious specialists who gave advice on religious matters and the new political leadership. For example, Ibn ʿAbbās, a companion of the Prophet Muḥammad and known for his religious authority, held important political positions during the early caliphate, especially in ʿAlī's caliphal administration, but after the first civil war, he retired from politics and assumed the role of a religious specialist in Mecca.[4] This was in stark contrast to the status of religious specialists in the early Rāshidūn Caliphate period where these figures, who were the close companions of the Prophet Muḥammad, often shared political authority as we have seen earlier in the case of the Caliph ʿUmar.

This gave many of the fatwas during the early post-prophetic period the binding character of *qaḍāʾ* (juridical rulings) because, as has been demonstrated, it was often carried out by those who fused both religious and political leadership like the Caliph ʿUmar. These juridical rulings are what later became known as the *sunna* (established precedence) of those early caliphs. Yet during successive periods, most of the religious leaders become distinct from the political leadership and *iftāʾ* had more of the characteristics of what it finally developed into, which is a legal opinion that has moral and legal authority but does not necessarily have the sanction of the state as it may have had during the time of the early caliphate. This was a result of the two civil wars between opposing camps within the Muslim community, which took place toward the middle and latter part of the first century 35–40/656–661 and 64–73/683–692.

These events brought about the differentiation between the political authorities and most of those who were religiously influential. This was because those who were religiously influential were largely marginalized by the post-Rāshidūn Caliphate political leadership in addition to the fact that the new political leadership was viewed with great suspicion among many early Muslim groups.[5] What further compounded this quandary

[4] For information on Ibn Abbas's distancing from politics, see Vaglieri's article on Ibn Abbas in EI2, v. 1 pgs. 40–41. For the role of Ibn Abbas as a religious specialist, see Hodgson, v. 1, pg. 254.

[5] Indicative of the attitude of many in the early religious establishment toward the Umayyad caliphate, Stodolsky (2012: 512) notes: "As regards the interaction of the Kufan Sunnī scholars with the Umayyads, we observed that another major shortcoming of the

was that political leadership eventually became the hereditary dominion of the Umayyad family.[6] This dynamic is typically illustrated in personalities like the younger contemporary of the Prophet, Ibn ʿAbbās, who was mentioned previously, and later generations of Muslims like Ḥasan al-Baṣrī (d. 728) who became a noted religious figure and abstained from politics in the aftermath of the devastation brought upon the Muslim community by the two civil wars.[7]

Hence, an evolving bifurcation began to take place between religious and political authorities, which precipitated the rise of religious specialists who felt that propagating religious learning and law was the best way to preserve the religious character of the nascent Islamic society from the less religiously authoritative Muslim political leadership. On the whole, many of the members of this new religious authority stayed out of the direct domain of politics and focused their attention on religious learning and law.[8] As we will see, they continued to tackle new legal issues that were continuously arising as a result of the new sociopolitical dynamics created by the Muslim expansions to the Near East and North Africa.

But how did this new group of religious specialists legitimate their legal authority to promulgate law even as they lacked political power? Answering this complex question requires revisiting the discussion on the nature of social transformation affected by the Quranic discourse. The Quranic discourse, with its epistemic and ethical emphasis, brought about novel ways for groups to acquire social legitimation within the nascent Islamic society. Given that the Quran enshrined universal moral values for the Muslim community since these values were derived from scripture and not from custom or tradition, those who were purveyors of this scriptural knowledge and upholders of

discontinuity models of Schacht and Crone and Hinds was to assume despite overwhelming evidence to the contrary that all Muslim scholars followed the precedent of the Umayyads in the first (seventh) century. Schacht, and Crone and Hinds overlooked the influence of the pious opposition, the importance of which Marshall Hodgson stressed long ago. Looking at the lives of four generations of Kufan Sunnī scholars, ʿAlqama, Aswad, and Masrūq in the first, Ibrāhīm, Shaʿbī, and Saʿīd b. Jubayr in the second, Ḥammād and Aʿmash in the third, and Abū Ḥanīfa in the fourth, we observed a common attitude: reverence for companions of the Prophet in general, and the rejection of the Umayyads…."

[6] See Berkey, 84–85 for more details on religious opposition to Umayyad political leadership of that period.

[7] Hodgson, v. 1, pgs. 248–249.

[8] Hodgson, v. 1, 255–256. Yet there were still other camps of religious authorities such as those who went on to form the *Shi'a* and *Khariji* religious groups who took less of a political quietist stance and actively opposed the Muslim regime. See Hodgson, v. 1, 260–263.

its ethical values were given authoritative legitimacy that those in the political corridors, by and large, did not enjoy.

The reason why the new political authorities were increasingly losing their religious and social legitimacy among the larger Muslim public by the beginning of the second century of Islam was because they reverted to previous forms of Arab practice (e.g., favoring kinship ties over religious considerations and Arab political dominance over other ethnic groups in Muslim society) and traditional forms of political legitimation (e.g., hereditary transmission of political power) that in many ways ran against the new religious ethos that the Quranic discourse had planted and was becoming increasingly rooted in segments of the new society in formation.[9] So while the new political elite secured their prominence in Muslim society based on military power and political astuteness along with the claim that they had politically reunited the Muslim community, they lacked both the epistemic and ethical legitimacy that many within the Muslim public sphere increasingly demanded.[10]

This role was now to be filled by a new group of individuals, whom Hodgson calls the "piety-minded."[11] They garnered religious authority within this newly forming Muslim society based on these epistemic and ethical grounds. As the Quranic ethos was becoming increasingly rooted in the evolving Muslim society through the standardization of both doctrine and practice pursued by the piety-minded, Muslims came to expect that the legitimacy of social practices would rest on their reference to scripture (the Quran and prophetic practice) and the practice of the early Muslim community, but not pre-Islamic traditions. Given that these groups of individuals were the carriers and advocates of this scriptural knowledge, they had the epistemic credentials to legitimate their religious authority.[12]

[9] Hodgson, v. 1, 248–252.

[10] It should be noted here that not all individuals in the corridors of political power had lost their religious legitimacy and epistemic authority to influence the early development of Islamic law although over time their authoritative status surely dwindled. For instance, the statements of the pious Umayyad Caliph ʿUmar ibn ʿAbd al-ʿAzīz (r. 99/717–101/720) were seen as religiously authoritative among the Muslim public. Even the statements and practices of his successor, the Umayyad Caliph Yazīd ibn ʿAbd al-Malik (r. 101/720–105/723), at the beginning of the second century of Islam were viewed by the second-century jurist Mālik b. Anas as authoritative (see Hallaq, 2005, 68). Hence, we can say that suspicion of the political authorities was not total, and some early jurists did value their legal opinions.

[11] Hodgson, vol. 1, 250.

[12] See Hallaq, 2005, 66, for the notion of the epistemic quality of religious authority in Islam.

But more importantly, since they were the modelers of Quranic ethical ideals, their religious authority acquired an ethical legitimacy.[13]

In short, the Muslim public regarded them as the defenders, exemplars, and transmitters of the recently established Islamic norms in the face of a relapse to pre-Islamic practices, and in this way, they were seen as the successors of the prophetic tradition, in contrast to the ruling elite. It was from the group of such individuals that a class of legal specialists would emerge by the second century of Islam who in most cases produced and promulgated Islamic legal rulings independently of the state[14] and were more driven by motivations of piety and religious commitment.[15] So, it was in this period that the locus of legal expertise diverged from the political establishment, and from this point on, most of the legal production rested outside the confines of the political authorities.

Having noted the differentiation of political and religious authorities as one of the main developments of legal production during this period, we may now move to another major development. The late first century and early second century witnessed the rise of regional centers of Islamic law (Iraq, Syria, the Hijaz, etc.) with their own approaches to law. Ansari claims, though, that despite each center having its own approach to and doctrines of law, they shared norms from which various questions arose and further elaboration of doctrine occurred. They tended to discuss the same issues, which is an indication that they all had an original source like Quranic norms and prophetic practice.[16]

But why did various approaches to law and differing legal doctrines also develop in these regional centers? If we look at the two main regional centers where most of the eminent legal specialists conducted

[13] See Davutoglu, 123–125, for the nature of sociopolitical legitimation in Islam.

[14] See Ansari, 1966, 88. This of course does not exclude the fact that some of these religious specialists did cooperate with the existing political authorities like the second-century jurist al-Awzāʿī, who cooperated with the Umayyad dynasty in the first half of the second century AH, and the Ḥanafī jurist Abū Yūsuf, who cooperated with the early Abbasid dynasty in the latter half of the second century AH. Yet these represented the exception more than the rule as one can cite counterexamples where religious specialists did their best to distance themselves from the corridors of political power, such as prominent second-century jurists like Abū Ḥanīfa, Sufyān al-Thawrī, Mālik ibn Anas, and al-Shāfiʿī, to name a few from the Sunnī tradition, and Zayd ibn ʿAlī, Muḥammad al Bāqir, and Jaʿfar al-Ṣādiq from the Shīʿite tradition. For more on the cooperation, or lack thereof, of Muslim jurists with the state, see Hallaq, *The Origins and Evolution of Islamic Law*, Chap. 8 ("Law and Politics").

[15] Hallaq, 2005, 63.

[16] Ansari, 1966, 84.

their activities, Kufa (Iraq) and Medina (the Hijaz),[17] we can see that the variant historical and social factors had an effect on the legal edicts that were issued. Ansari says that Kufa, being part of Iraq, which was a part of the Persian cultural orbit prior to the Islamic expansion, had a different intellectual climate than the one that existed in Medina in western Arabia (i.e., the Hijaz). This region was exposed to a greater degree of various religious and philosophical doctrines than Arabia proper.[18]

Moreover, there was a greater degree of ethnic heterogeneity of Arabs from northern and southern regions as well as a more significant number of non-Arab Muslim converts in Kufa than in Medina due to migrations that occurred in the early Islamic period.[19] This made Kufa more of a melting pot of different religious and cultural traditions, which naturally made the place less conservative than other parts of the Muslim world like Medina.

Despite the diversity of legal doctrines that was partially due to geographic considerations, there were signs that distinct legal approaches were in the process of development at the end of the first century and beginning of the second century AH, which formed by the middle of the second century AH into two distinct camps of early Muslim jurists, known as *ahl al-raʾy* and *ahl al-ḥadīth*.[20] Hallaq defines *ahl al-raʾy* as those legalists who favored rational and pragmatic considerations in their jurisprudence and did not restrict their legal production to what was strictly found in the *ḥadīth* traditions (i.e., prophetic sayings),[21] while *ahl al-ḥadīth* were those legalists who preferred the use of *ḥadīth* exclusively, alongside the Quran, to derive jurisprudence with little to no consideration for rational and pragmatic concerns.[22]

[17] Hallaq, 2005, 64–65.

[18] Ansari, 1966, 90.

[19] *EI2*, "Al-Kufa" v. 5, 347.

[20] See al-Sāyis, n.d., 84. Hallaq is of the opinion that this rivalry between the two approaches to law began much later in the middle of the second century AH and only showed the rudimentary beginnings of the rivalry in the beginning of the second century AH (Hallaq, 2005, 75). Yet, one can say that even though the debate between these two schools had not taken shape around the issue of *ḥadīth* in the late first or early second century AH, nevertheless, in this very same period there is a clear rivalry between those who advocated a rational/pragmatic approach (*ahl al-raʾy*) and those who preferred to restrict their religious opinions to previously established norms and practices, or traditionalism (*ahl al-āthār* later evolving into *ahl al-ḥadīth*), as will become evident in the forthcoming discussion.

[21] Hallaq, 2005, 74, asserts that *ahl al-raʾy* "were recognized in terms of their non-reliance on ḥadīth," but this wording is perhaps too strong, as we will find out that this camp did not necessarily shun *ḥadīth* as Hallaq's phrasing implies, but dealt with them differently than the *ahl al-ḥadīth*.

[22] Hallaq, 2005, 74.

One of the factors that contributed to these divergences of methods by early Muslim jurists was their varying social environments. It was in the region of Iraq, particularly the town of Kufa, where advocates of legal pragmatism (*ahl al-raʾy*) were dominant,[23] while it was in the region of the Hijaz, particularly the town of Medina, where advocates of traditionalism more generally were in the ascendency.[24] Social conditions in these two regions differed significantly, and it was probably this difference that contributed to varying approaches to the law.

Iraq's more cosmopolitan environment necessitated that answers to legal problems not be restricted to previously established traditions that had been formed in a different environment; hence, the need to take practical and rational considerations into account when applying Islamic legal norms in the new milieu. On the other hand, the Hijaz, where many traditions (*āthār*) were first transmitted and were in wider circulation, experienced less fluctuation in its simpler mode of life, which mitigated the need to alter the tradition of observing the practice of the previous generation.[25]

These opposing approaches led to some differences in legal opinions and eventually legal doctrines. To illustrate how this opposition played out at the end of the first century of Islam, the following report exemplifies the differences between these two camps of law: A debate took place between the famous Medinan proto-jurist Saʿīd ibn al-Musayyib (d. 94/712) and his younger Medinan contemporary, the proto-jurist Rabīʿa ibn Farrūkh (or Rabīʿat al-Raʾy) (d. 136/753). Rabīʿa asks Saʿīd about the compensation (*ʿaql*) owed to a woman who loses her finger (i.e., due to someone's negligence/recklessness), whereupon Saʿīd answers that it is ten camels. Then Rabīʿa asks about the compensation for two fingers, and Saʿīd answers 20 camels. Rabīʿa then asks the compensation for three fingers; Saʿīd says thirty camels. When Rabīʿa asks him the compensation for four fingers, Saʿīd puzzlingly answers twenty camels.[26]

Rabīʿa, dumbfounded by Saʿīd's response, protests against this judgment by rhetorically asking: "When her injury increased, her compensation becomes less?" That is, it is unreasonable that a greater injury should result in a lesser compensation than a smaller injury. Saʿīd answers this criticism by saying: "Are you an Iraqi?! It is the *sunna* (previously

[23] al-Sāyis, n.d., 85.
[24] al-Sāyis, n.d., 84.
[25] See al-Sāyis, n.d., 84–86, who makes a similar argument.
[26] See Mālik ibn Anas, *al-Muwaṭṭaʾ* (Bewley translation), Section 43.11, pg. 41: "The Blood-Money for Fingers." See also al-Khidri, 93; al-Sāyis, n.d., 87.

established practice)." Saʿīd's reference to Rabīʿa being an Iraqi, although Rabīʿā is a resident of Medina, is a sarcastic comment implying that Rabīʿa is one of those who employ reason/opinion in their juridical judgment in lieu of existing and established practice (*sunna*). Here, Saʿīd is applying the principle established by practice[27] – that a woman's compensation is the same as a man's up to one-third of the indemnity (known as the *diyya*), but after that, she only gets half the indemnity of a man (see Figure 4).

Yet, this conclusion seems illogical from a rational point of view. Nonetheless, the point here is that this dialogue shows that there were early differences in legal approaches in the different regions, as indicated by Saʿīd's objection to Rabīʿa: "Are you an Iraqi?!"; that is, are you one of those who practice *raʾy* (reason/opinion) instead of following established *sunna* (precedence) as was more prevalent in Medina. There are a number of conclusions to be drawn from this incident that shed light on the legal rivalry between rationalists/pragmatists and traditionists in the early Islamic legal formation.

First, despite the preferences toward the use of *raʾy* (discretionary opinion or reason) among the early legal authorities in Iraq and the preference for reliance on *āthār* (reported precedent) or *sunna* (established tradition of predecessors) among legal authorities of the Hijaz, the divide in legal approaches between the two regions was by no means complete. Rabīʿa was a legal authority in Medina, and yet he was considered an advocate of *raʾy* in opposition to the *sunna/āthār* (traditionist) approach that was espoused by most of the legal authorities in Medina. Indeed, he was so much known for his use of *raʾy* that he became known by the epithet Rabīʿat al-Raʾy (Rabīʿa the opinionest).[28]

The same is true for legal authorities in Iraq in that not all of them espoused a rationalist/pragmatist approach, even if that was the dominant school there. The first-century Kufan legal specialist al-Shaʿbī had an aversion to the use of *raʾy* (opinion) in his legal work. In this regard, it has been reported that he once posed the question: If an adult male and a child that was with him were (accidently) killed, would the indemnity be different for the adult because of his maturity or would it be the same as the child's? When people responded that it would be the same, he replied that using analogy (rational consideration in legal cases) is

[27] The later Iraqi school, the main proponents of *raʾy*, claimed that what is meant by the term *sunna* here was not the practice and/or judgment of the Prophet himself but rather that Saʿīd was referring to the practice and/or fatwa of Zayd ibn Thābit, who was one of the learned followers of the Prophet. See al-Khidri, pg. 93.

[28] Al-Khidri, 94.

worthless.[29] The report illustrates how this famous Iraqi legal specialist viewed issues of *ra'y* in legal matters and how his legal approach was closer to that of the Hijazi legal authorities.

The second point that we can conjecture from the Saʿīd's debate with Rabīʿa is that those who advocated *ra'y* at this early stage in the legal debates did not necessarily have a definite legal method worked out that would determine legal cases, at least in the very early period.

Instead, their approach merely consisted of applying the most generally rational or pragmatic consideration to the legal cases that they were confronted with on a case-by-case basis. Rabīʿa did not appeal to any clearly stated principles in objecting to Saʿīd's fatwa other than to appeal to common principles of rationality that would prevent Saʿīd's conclusion from being a logical one. In particular, his argument demonstrates his use of the *a fortiori* (*bi-l-awlā*) argument to expose the absurdity of Saʿīd's position, but he does so in a way that appeals to common sensibility and not to any outlined legal principles.

Yet another fatwa from the late first century AH that is indicative of the approach of *ahl al ra'y* to questions of law is a fatwa by the premiere Kufan (Iraqi) proto-jurist Ibrāhīm al-Nakhaʿī (d. 94/714), a contemporary of the Madinan Saʿīd ibn al-Musayyib, who was just mentioned. Ibrāhīm pronounces a fatwa that if a ring is made of silver and it contains a stone, then it could be bought at any price, whether lower or higher than the cost of the content of silver in it.[30] The contention here is that there is an unequivocal saying (*ḥadīth*) of the Prophet that indicates that transactions involving silver must be traded with an equal measure of silver (its exact exchange value) and that any subtraction or addition to the value of the silver constitutes usury. In his fatwa, Ibrāhīm seems to contravene this economic principle that the Prophet had established, since selling the ring at any price as if it were any commodity whose price is determined by market mechanisms. This would mean that one could buy the ring at a lower cost than the value of the silver in it.

We are not told by the source why Ibrāhīm came to such a decision, but from the scenario presented, we can assume that he was of the opinion that once the stone was conjoined to the silver, the product could no longer be subsumed under the rubric of items considered usurious, which, according to the Prophet's injunctions, could only be exchanged at equal value. Instead, Ibrāhīm must have considered this new product as

[29] Al-Khidri, 94.
[30] Al-Shaybānī, *Kitāb al-Āthār*, v. 2, 733.

a commodity (jewelry) and not strictly silver per se, whose exchange was governed by the prophetically established rule of "like for like." Ibrāhīm's fatwa was then nullifying the specific rules governing the exchange of silver in this case and subjecting this product to the rule of commodity exchanges instead. This fatwa seemed to go against the conservative legal precedent of always exchanging gold and silver in equal measures even when these metals were fashioned into products[31] (see Figure 4).

Yet in another fatwa, Ibrāhīm's legal rationale went against the precedent established by legal authorities in Medina like the Caliph ʿUmar and the wife of the Prophet Muḥammad ʿĀʾisha. This fatwa involved the case of whether it was incumbent to collect *zakāh* (alms tax) on an orphan's wealth. Madinan legal precedent had established that it was incumbent to take *zakāh* on an orphan's wealth.[32] Ibrāhīm, on the other hand, said that it was not incumbent to take *zakāh* on an orphan's wealth until it was incumbent upon him to perform *ṣalāh* (prayer).[33]

In other words, since one can argue that both *ṣalāh* and *zakāh* are fundamental pillars of Islam and it was recognized by all religious authorities that an individual was not held accountable for performance of his *ṣalāh* until he reached the age of maturity/majority, likewise he should not be held accountable for paying his *zakāh* until he reached the same age. Ibrāhīm was making a legal argument by analogy (later termed *qiyās*) to legitimate his position.[34] As we will see later, analogy (*qiyās*) became one of the widely accepted fundamental methodological tools in Islamic legal theory for deriving Islamic law.

At the same time, it can be argued that Ibrāhīm was following the Kufan school's precedent instead of merely going against precedent through the use of his own legal rationale. This is because there is a narration that indicates that the companion of the Prophet Muḥammad Ibn Masʿūd, whose legal decision influenced the legal doctrine of the Iraqi legal school,[35] is said to have given the same fatwa as Ibrāhīm, namely, that *zakāh* was

31 See Mālik ibn Anas, *al-Muwaṭṭaʾ* (Bewley translation), Section 31.16, pgs. 290–293: "Selling Gold and Silver, Minted and Unminted" for reports on how previous legal authorities, including the Prophet Muḥammad, practiced the exchange of these two metals. See also al-Shaybānī, *Kitāb al-Āthār*, v. 2, 733, for how later Iraqi legal authorities like Abū Ḥanīfa disagreed with Ibrāhīm's fatwa and reverted to the wider practice on the exchange of gold and silver.

32 See Mālik ibn Anas, *al-Muwaṭṭaʾ* (Bewley translation), Section 17.6, pgs. 123–124: "The Zakat on the property of Orphans...."

33 Al-Shaybānī, *Kitāb al-Āthaār*, v. 1, 324, #297. See also Ansari, 1966, pg. 105.

34 Ansari, 1966, 105.

35 Al-Sāyis, n.d., 86.

not obligatory on an orphan's wealth.[36] This is why it may be said that Ibrāhīm was opposing the precedent of the Madinan legal authorities and not all authorities since he was certainly in line with the legal precedent of his own regional school. Yet, his use of analogy (*qiyās*) to justify his position, not solely relying on the legal precedent set by his predecessors, illustrates nicely how those proto-jurists who became known as *ahl al-raʾy* (advocates of reason/opinion)[37] were willing to use rational means to justify their legal positions and were less dependent on observing tradition, as was the case for the *āthārists* (traditionists) (see Figure 4).

These two fatwas by Kufan proto-jurist Ibrāhīm al-Nakhaʿī and the previous fatwa/debate by the Madinan Saʿīd ibn al-Musayyib illustrate the contentions in legal approach that existed between the various regional centers in the Muslim world at the end of the first century AH, especially the methodological differences that existed between rationalists/pragmatists and traditionists, which led to variations in legal doctrines in these different regions. This rivalry between the regional legal school in Iraq, which came to represent the legal approach of *raʾy* (discretionary opinion), and the regional school in Hijaz, which came to represent the legal approach of *āthār* (traditions), continued well into the second century AH and further advanced the sophistication of Islamic legal theory.

Yet it must not be overstated in this representation of these opposing camps that they were polar opposites of one another where *ahl al-raʾy* were thoroughgoing rationalists who did not take into account prophetic traditions (*ḥadīth*) or the legal precedence of their predecessors as represented by the term *āthār*. At the same time, neither should *ahl al-āthār/ḥadīth* be viewed categorically as those who completely shunned reason or considerations of pragmatism in their legal deductions or who were blindly committed to tradition. In both schools, it was not a matter of either *raʾy* or *āthār/ḥadīth*, but rather it was a matter of the degree to which either one of these approaches was relied upon that gave the schools their distinctions.[38]

36 Al-Shaybānī, *Kitāb al-Āthār*, v. 1, 325, #298.

37 El Shamsy (2013:25) aptly describes the methodology underlying the *raʾy* approach: "the process of *raʾy* begins with an assumption that both debates share; this is progressively extended by one of the debaters through *raʾy* questions in order to show either that his own opinions are consistent or that his opponent's opinions are inconsistent with their common assumption." This approach can be seen in my analysis of Ibrāhīm's fatwa where he starts with the accepted position that prayers are not incumbent upon a minor and then analogically argues that it would be fundamentally consistent that another important practice in Islam, such as almsgiving, be treated likewise.

38 Ansari, 1966, 113.

For example, there was a debate that took place toward the middle of the second century AH between Abū Ḥanīfa (d. 150/767), the premier jurist representing the Iraqi school and *ahl al-raʾy* during his time, and al-Awzāʿī (d. 157/773), the premier jurist in Syria at that time and a representative of the traditionist camp that eventually morphed into *ahl al-ḥadīth* (advocates of *ḥadīth*, where *ḥadīth* is a subset of *āthār*). The legal issue of debate was about the correct manner in which the ritual prayer (*ṣalāh*) is to be performed. Al-Awzāʿī asks Abū Ḥanīfa why the practitioners of the Iraqi school of law do not raise their hands in the *ṣalāh* during the transitions into and out of prostrations. Abū Ḥanīfa responds that there exists no authentic report (*ḥadīth*) that the Prophet Muḥammad had practiced this.[39]

Al-Awzāʿī responds by narrating a *ḥadīth* with a chain of narration containing Madinan authorities that indicated that the Prophet did indeed engage in this practice. Thereupon, Abū Ḥanīfa responds with a *ḥadīth* of his own narrated by Kufan authorities that the Prophet did not engage in that practice. A debate ensues between the two jurists about the greater authoritativeness of the opposing reports based on the authority of those who transmitted them. Abū Ḥanīfa at this juncture argues for the greater authoritativeness of his *ḥadīth* on the assumption that the transmitters of his report had a greater understanding of the law than al-Awzāʿī's transmitters[40] (see Figure 4).

This is but one illustration that the proponents of *raʾy* relied on *ḥadīth* to justify their positions. Yet when they did rely on scriptural sources or the legal precedent of those before them for their judgments or their fatwas, they seemed more circumspect about the source and usage of *ḥadīth* and tended to rely on those normative sources and precedents that were prevalent in their region,[41] even when the diffusion of *ḥadīth* in their region was less than in other regions like the Hijaz.

As this case illustrates, for the proponent of *raʾy*, it was not a question of whether *āthār/ḥadīth* was an authoritative source of the law but rather when and how to use *ḥadīth* that distinguished the proponents of *raʾy* from the proponents of *ḥadīth*.[42] For Abū Ḥanīfa, the authoritativeness of the *ḥadīth* that was to influence religious practice was to be based on the narration of those who understood the aims of the law. Here is where the proponents of *raʾy* were more guarded and critical in utilizing *ḥadīth/āthār*

[39] Al-Khidri, 94; al-Sāyis, n.d., 87–88.
[40] Al-Khidri, 94–95; asl-Sāyis, n.d., 87–88.
[41] Al-Sāyis, n.d., 86.
[42] Abū Zahra, 260.

than their counterparts and were not reluctant to employ their rational faculties and practical sensibilities when they felt the need to.[43]

Yet Abū Ḥanīfa's response to al-Awzāʿī's argument is perhaps more emblematic of the Ḥanafī's attitude toward this growing proliferation and authoritativeness of *ḥadīth* in general and not simply a matter of preference for regional practice. The *raʾyist* approach, especially that of the Ḥanafīs, to *ḥadīth* was methodologically different from that of the traditionist-influenced jurist like al-Awzāʿī because the Ḥanafīs did not allow for the contents of *ḥadīth* with a singular chain of narration (*āḥād*) to modify the implications of practice that arise from the Quran or widely known *ḥadīth* (*mashhūr*) because these *ḥadīths*, with a singular chain of transmission (*āḥād*), could not be treated as affording the same epistemological certainty as the Quran or popularly established practices.[44] This principle that an *āḥād ḥadīth*, which the Ḥanafīs called *shādhdh*, could not modify an established practice is more clearly enunciated by the response of Abū Yūsuf (Abū Ḥanīfa's protégé) in rebutting al-Awzāʿī's position on whether a cavalryman who brings two horses to battle should receive two shares of the booty. Supporting the Ḥanafī position that such a cavalryman receives one share, Abū Yūsuf says:

It has not reached us from the messenger of Allah, may peace and blessings be upon him, nor from one of his Companions that any of them allotted a share for two horses except for one *ḥadīth*, and the single report according to us is anomalous (*shādhdh*); we do not follow it. As for al-Awzāʿī's statement that the imams governed this way and that the people of knowledge held this position, this is like the doctrine of the people of the Hijaz. This is not accepted and [is] transmitted from ignorant people! Who is the imam who governed this way and the scholar who held this position so that we can look to see whether he merits transmission [of knowledge] from him and whether he is trustworthy concerning knowledge? How is it that shares are distributed for two horses but not for three; from where is this? How is it that a share is allotted for a horse which is tied in its place of

[43] Sadeghi (129) questions whether the prophetic practice formed part of the Ḥanafī canon since Abū Ḥanīfa and al-Shaybānī quote prophetic statements and then give rulings that are contrary to them. Yet this assessment of the Ḥanafīs' approach to *ḥadīth* and law in general is not accurate because they stipulate that the *ḥadīth* must be widely circulating (*mashhūr*) before it can be binding in modifying established practice (see Sodolosky, 522). In other words, if a *ḥadīth* is transmitted with a single chain of narration (*āḥād*), it is not authoritative enough in their methodology to change an established ruling. Moreover, the Ḥanafīs may disagree on methodological grounds whether a *ḥadīth* with a particular implication (*khāṣṣ*), for example, can modify a Qurʾānic statement that has a universal implication (*ʿāmm*) because in their legal methodology, statements that have universal implication (*ʿāmm*) are definitive (see Sodolosky 2012: 520).

[44] Stodolsky, 242.

rest and which is not fought upon, while he [the cavalryman] fought only upon the other [horse]? Think about what we mention and what al-Awzāʿī said, and consider its consequences.[45]

However, there is one more fatwa case study that I will add here that highlights not only the methodical differences between regions but also the historical trend toward the commitment toward distinct lines of legal authority. This trend toward personal authority formation is crucial to understanding the subsequent development of legal schools. Moreover, it looks at fatwas emerging from another region within the Iraqi orbit that played an influential role in the early debates on Islamic law: Baṣra. This case study analyzes the fatwas of Jabir ibn Zayd (d. 93/711) and his disciple Abū 'Ubaydah Muslim ibn Abī Karīmah (d. 145/762) regarding the correct duration for a claimant to possess an abandoned property.

The first-/seventh-century Baṣran proto-jurist and the precursor to the Ibāḍī school of law Jabir ibn Zayd was asked by a man from al-Baṣra stating: What do you say about a man who had a house in al-Baṣra that became ruined, but he became so preoccupied with travel and other concerns that he was not able to tend to it? When he returned another man had occupied it, and for twenty-five to thirty years, he acquired it (*ḥazāhā*), fixed it, and resided in it [with the knowledge of the original owner]. Then the original owner was prevented from take-up a case to evict the occupier. Jabir responded that he would not legitimate the original owner's case to retrieve the home that was resided in for that duration while the owner was present when the squatter acquired, occupied, and fixed it, and all the while the owner did not attempt to change that [situation] or object to it. Thus, Jaber concludes the owner has no legal right to reclaim property through a court case nor has the moral legitimacy to do so.[46]

Jabir ibn Zayd's fatwa appears to be based on a legal norm that was established in a statement (*ḥadīth*) attributed to the Prophet narrated by Jaber himself although he does not cite it directly in this case. This *ḥadīth* comes through a Baṣran chain of transmission and is found in an Ibāḍī

[45] As cited in Stodolsky, 274. El Shamsy (2013: 27) asserts that the *ra'y* approach of the ḥanafīs favored widely accepted (*mashhūr*) reports containing maxim-like rules that could be extended to a broad array of similar cases. As a result, reports dealing with individual cases were often rejected whenever they conflicted with the implications of the general rule. Yet as the above quotation from Abū Yūsuf reveals, reports were rejected particularly because of their singular (*āḥād*) chain of transmission, not merely because they went against an established general rule. Such singular (*āḥād*) reports were not seen as having the sufficient epistemological primacy to modify these general rules.

[46] Abū Ghānim, vol. 3, 149.

collection of *ḥadīth* (*Musnad al-Rabī'*): "whoever acquires (*ḥazā*) a land and resides on it for *ten* years, while the [potential] litigant (*al-khaṣm*) is present and s/he does not change or deny [that acquisition], it [the land] is for the one who acquired and resided on it and the litigant has no right to it."[47] Yet there is another statement attributed to the Prophet found in another Ibāḍī collection of legal opinions (*al-Mudawwanna al-Kubrā*) that is transmitted by Medinan narrators that says: "Whoever acquires (Haza) a thing for *ten* or *twenty* years or more, it is his."[48] So, there are conflicting narrations about the proper duration that establishes the right of acquisition of abandoned or unclaimed property.

Considering Jaber's legal case and other legal norms arising from the prophetic statements, Abū 'Ubaydah (d. 145/762) gave his fatwa that anyone who acquired an abandoned home or property for twenty years without any objection from others, the property is his/hers. If someone later objects while s/he was all long witness to this acquisition and brings proof of ownership, s/he has no right to possession of that property.[49] How does Abū 'Ubaydah conclude that twenty years is the duration for establishing the right of possession of abandoned/unclaimed property, while in the case brought to Jabir ibn Zayd the duration was twenty-five or thirty years? Al-Rabī 'ibn al-Ḥabīb (d. 170/786) (a disciple of Abū 'Ubaydah) explains that Jabr ibn Zayd was merely responding to the scenario spelled out to him and that the duration stipulated in that case was not a minimum requirement for determining a right of possession, but rather that it had merely met the minimum standard of years.[50] So, Abū 'Ubaydah's stipulation of twenty years was not a departure from Jabr ibn Zayd's judgment but rather an affirmation of it. Seemingly, the reason Abū 'Ubaydah arrived at such a conclusion was that one of the mentioned prophetic statements gives twenty years as one of two possibilities for establishing this minimum duration.

But why does Abū 'Ubaydah affirm twenty years rather than ten years as the minimum duration for establishing the right of possession? Despite the existence of a report from the Prophet that unambiguously states that ten years is the duration, a report that narrated Jaber himself with a Baṣran (Iraqi) chain of transmitters, Abū 'Ubaydah states that Jaber ibn Zayd preferred the twenty-year duration out of precaution

47 Al-Rabī', 135. Emphasis added.
48 Abū Ghānim, vol. 3, 147. Emphasis added.
49 Abū Ghānim, vol. 3, 149.
50 Abū Ghānim, vol. 3, 150–151.

(*iḥtiyāṭ*).[51] It is not explicitly stated in the sources, but one would presume that the reason Jaber sided on the side of caution by choosing the longer duration despite the shorter duration that was stipulated in his own narrated prophetic report was because of the ambiguity in the reporting of the prophet's statements on this issue.

The prophetic statements reported from a Medinan line of transmitters that were documented in later Ibāḍī sources of law listed that duration as either being ten or twenty years. Having awareness of the existence of these conflicting reports presumably guided Jaber's opinion to take precautions and choose the longer duration even if this duration conflicted with the reported statement of the Prophet that he narrated.

So, it seems that Jaber ibn Zayd's use of precaution (*iḥtiyāṭ*) in his legal opinions established juridical precedence that subsequently influenced Abū 'Ubaydah's fatwas on this issue. Moreover, we are told by these sources that Abū 'Ubaydah used to also practice precaution (*iḥtiyāṭ*) in his other legal opinions regarding stipulations of duration in matters of religious practice if there was doubt about the proper duration.[52] Thus, it seems that precaution (*iḥtiyāṭ*) became a preferred legal approach when deciding matters among this circle of jurists, who would eventually be viewed as the predecessors of the Ibāḍī school of law.

Yet others within this circle of (proto-Ibāḍī) jurists dissented from Abū 'Ubaydah and Jabir's opinion about the legitimate duration to establish the right of possession of abandoned property (*iḥāza*). 'Abd Allah ibn 'Abd al-Azīz (a second-/eighth-century disciple of Abū 'Ubaydah) advocated for the adoption of the ten-year duration limit. His rationale for this is that both the jurists of Iraq, particularly Kufa (read advocates of *ray*/reason), and the jurists of Medina (read advocates of *athar-ḥadīth*/precedence) have a consensus that the duration for establishing the right of possession is ten years based on a shared report from the Prophet transmitted by their respective authorities saying: "whoever acquires (*ḥazā*) possession of property or resides in it (*ammarahū*) for ten years, it

[51] Abū Ghānim, vol. 3, 151. I am grateful for the assistance of Dr. Khalfān al-Mundhirī of Sultan Qaboos University, Muscat, Oman, and Dr. Muṣṭafā ibn Ṣalāḥ Bājū of Algiers, Algeria, editor of Abū Ghānim's *al-Mudawwanna al-Kubra* that is used in this section. Both of whom through personal oral and written communications provided valuable information regarding the concept of "*iḥtiyāṭ*" as employed in Ibāḍī *fiqh* and information regarding some of the narrators in the chains of transmission used in this section. Nevertheless, I take full responsibility for the claims made and the arguments advanced in this section.

[52] Abū Ghānim, vol. 3, 152.

is for him/her."[53] This *ḥadīth* does not have the same ambiguity regarding the duration as the other mentioned prophetic report narrated by Medinan authorities found in the Ibāḍī sources.

Abū 'Ubaydah seems to have been aware of such a prophetic report since after all he was one of the transmitters of the first-mentioned report narrated by Baṣran authorities that affirmed the same thing. Yet he dismissed their relevance stating that he was unsure regarding the intent and interpretation of this report.[54] Abū 'Ubaydah seems to have placed greater reliance on the understanding of his master Jabir ibn Zayd on the correct manner of practice of this prophetic norm than he does with the understanding of the implications of the prophetic statements that were forwarded by other groups of jurists. This interpretation of Abū 'Ubaydah's juristic approach is supported by one of his statements indicating that the mere knowledge of prophetic traditions does not qualify one to understand their juristic implications: "Every man of traditions (*ṣāḥib ḥadīth*) who has no *Imam* [guide/leader] in jurisprudence is gone astray. If God had not favored us with Jabir ibn Zayd, we too would have gone astray."[55] So, Abū 'Ubaydah's fatwa leans more toward the greater authoritativeness of a particular lineage of jurists (read Jaber ibn Zayd) rather than the majoritarian position of the Medinan and Iraqi practice.

On the other hand, his disciple 'Abd Allah ibn 'Abd al-Azīz seems more inclined to the majoritarian view given that he believed that their practice was based on a well-founded report from the prophet. Also, his statement indicates that his dissent from the position of his adopted Baṣran lineage of jurists was his juristic assumption that independent reasoning should not supersede authentic reports about prophetic practice even such reports originated from individuals or groups outside of his espoused circle of jurists: "What the Prophet said is the truth, and prophetic practice (*sunna*) is more obligatory to be followed if it is an authentic practice of the prophet. As for independent reasoning (*qiyās*),[56]

[53] Abū Ghānim, vol. 3, 151.

[54] Abū Ghānim, vol. 3, 152.

[55] As cited in Ennami, 84.

[56] It has to be said here that Ibn Aziz's use of the term *qiyās* in this statement, usually meaning analogy, is to be interpreted more broadly to mean independent reasoning since there seems to be no use of analogy per se in the legal reasoning of Jaber's or Abū 'Ubaydah's fatwas. What we had instead is a departure from some interpretation of prophetic precedent based on the concept of precaution; hence my rendering of the term *qiyās* here as independent reasoning. My interpretation of the term *qiyās* is supported by Ṭāriq Al-Shaybānī's claim that early Ibāḍī authorities would use the terms *ra'y*, *qiyās*, and *ijtihād* interchangeably to mean forms of independent reasoning (see Ṭāriq Al-Shaybānī, pgs. 19–20).

although it may be established (*taqaddumuhū*) it should not supersede the prophetic practice since its authority is even more established."[57]

Ibn 'Abd al-Azīz characterizes the positions of his predecessors that aired on the side of precaution when it came to protecting the rights of the original owners of the property as being a form of independent reasoning that ignores the strong textual evidence to the contrary. On the other hand, his contemporaries within this Baṣran circle of jurists like al-Rabīʿ disagreed with his departure and stuck to the position that was established by the precedence of this particular Baṣran line of jurists dismissing the majoritarian position on this issue that was advocated by Ibn Abdul Aziz. Thus, because of the judgment of Jaber ibn Zayd on this issue, its further clarification and delineation by Abū 'Ubaydah, and its confirmation by al-Rabīʿ, it became the adopted legal position in the early Ibāḍī school law;[58] a school that took shape around the legal opinions of this line of Baṣran authorities.

The immediate takeaway from this discussion is that Jabr ibn Zayd, a Baṣran (Iraqi) jurist, was seemingly in line with his Iraqi milieu as an advocate of *ra'y* given his less conservative tendencies to go against the precedent (*athar/ḥadīth*), even those precedents – like the *ḥadīth* mentioned earlier – which he narrated. This interpretation of Jaber's legal approach is not merely deduced from this scenario, but there are other situations where he acted likewise as reported in non-Ibāḍī sources. For instance, Jaber in one opinion goes against the established prophetic norm of prohibiting bribery by stating that there was nothing more beneficial to people than bribery during the days of an unjust government official.[59] Here, he seems to be adapting the prophetic norm against bribery to the particular political necessities that people faced at the time. Furthermore, he also went against the fatwa of his teacher Ibn Abbas, allowing a person to have sisters as concubines.[60] Thus, this tendency toward departing from precedent and affirming his own legal opinion is well attested.

Jaber's disciple Abū 'Ubaydah, on the other hand, is the one who displays more conservative tendencies by sticking to the precedent (*athar*) and the legal approaches (e.g., precaution) of his juristic master in his fatwas as demonstrated by his dismissal of other legal authorities' interpretations

57 Abū Ghānim, vol. 3, 152.
58 Abū Ghānim, vol. 3, 151–152.
59 See *Al-Muṣannaf* by 'Abd al-Razzāq al-Ṣana'anī for the *ḥadīth* on bribery and Jaber's reaction regarding bribery cited earlier. Accessed online at https://shamela.ws/book/84/3830 April 15, 2022.
60 Motzki, 2002, 190.

Case	Ruling/fatwa	Legal reasoning	Proto-jurist	Region
Compensation (ʿ*aql*) owed to a woman who loses her fingers	1. Half the compensation as a man when all four fingers lost, but full compensation with less than four 2. Full compensation of man	1. Established practice (*sunna*) and legal precedence 2. Logical argument	1. Saʿīd ibn al- Musayyib 2. Rabīʿat al-Raʾy	1. Medina 2. Medina
Buying silver ring with stone	Can be bought at price lower or higher than the silver content in it	Silver ring no longer considered usurious item because of the stone	Ibrāhīm al-Nakhaʿī	Kufa
Alms tax (*zakāh*) on orphan's wealth	Not incumbent	Analogy (*qiyās*) to the incumbency of prayer for the orphan	Ibrāhīm al-Nakhaʿī	Kufa
Raising hands in the prayer (*ṣalāh*) while transitioning between different postures	1. Incumbent 2. Not incumbent	1. *Ḥadīth* from Madinan authorities establishing the practice 2. *Ḥadīth* from Kufan authorities establishing opposite practice	1. al-Awzāʿī 2. Abū Ḥanīfa	1. Damascus 2. Kufa
Duration for right to possess abandoned property	1. Ten Years 2. Twenty Years	1. *Ḥadīth* and practice of Kufan and Madinan authorities 2. Precaution (*iḥtiyāṭ*) and precedence of Baṣran authorities	1. Majority of Muslim jurists from Iraq and Medina 2. Jaber ibn Zayd and Abū ʿUbaydah	1. Iraq and Medina 2. Baṣra

FIGURE 4 Fatwa in the age of regional distinctions

of legal norms in favor of Jaber's. It is this emerging conservative attitude among late second-century jurists of viewing the legal approaches and opinions of some earlier jurists as authoritative in distinction to other earlier jurists is what lays the seeds for the formation of schools of law known as *madhhabs*. I will demonstrate later in Chapter 4 that this distinct genealogical line of Baṣran legal authorities highlighted in this fatwa (Jaber Ibn Zayd – Abū 'Ubaydah – al-Rabīʿ) becomes the authoritative juristic basis for the formation of an Ibāḍī *madhhab*. It is this sort of authority formation that will be explored further in the next section.

Yet what this case and the earlier case of the debate between Abū Ḥanīfa and Al-Awzāʿī also show is that the law in the age of regional distinctions did not merely indicate distinct methodologies of approaching the law but also that each region had its distinct line of authorities whose fatwas formed the precedents for how the legal norms were to be interpreted and applied. So, a legal norm as embodied by a statement from the Prophet, for example, was not sufficient enough to establish or modify regional practices. Rather it was whether such a statement was accepted by the regional authorities, and how they interpreted it was what established the legal precedence in any one region.

What these last two fatwa case studies show is that despite the objections of the advocates of *ra'y* to the attempts by traditionists to modify well-established regional practices through the use of *athar/ḥadīth*, the movement toward traditionism throughout the second century, as represented by those who were proponents of the practices of the earlier predecessors, continued to gain momentum. This movement developed a narrower focus than in the past. Its new legal doctrinal focus was to insist that there was only one type of practice/precedent that was to be seen as ultimately authoritative in the formulation of Islamic law and that was the practice of the Prophet himself, as represented, particularly, in *ḥadīth* discourse. So those who advocated *āthār* or traditionism in contrast to *ra'y* at the end of the first century became known as *ahl al-ḥadīth* in the second, and they continued to oppose the use of *ra'y* in matters related to the formulation of the religious law.

FATWA IN THE AGE OF THE *MADHHAB* PREDECESSORS

The contentious legal issues that arose in the latter part of the first century and early part of the second century, such as doctrinal and methodological differences, continued to influence the legal debate during the latter part of the second century AH. Yet there were important legal developments in this century that gave the fatwas made by legal authorities a more permanent place in Islamic legal doctrines than previous fatwas had ever had before. Legal pronouncements and approaches to the law made by these second-century jurists became the axis around which later jurists constructed Islamic legal schools, known as *madhāhib* (sing. *madhhab*), in the following three centuries. Moreover, it was from these jurists that newly forming legal schools took their names. It is the fatwas of these jurists that we examine in this section to determine how these legal opinions influenced the evolution of legal ideas in Islam.

Our analysis focuses on the fatwas of three leading jurists of the second/eighth century after whom three of the several Sunnī schools of Islamic law are named:[61] Abū Ḥanīfa (d. 150/767), after whom the Ḥanafī school of law is named; Mālik ibn Anas (d. 179/795), after whom the Mālikī school of law is named; and Muḥammad ibn Idrīs al-Shāfiʿī (d. 204/819), after whom the Shāfiʿī school of law is named.

In addition, we examine the rulings of two other leading jurists of the second/eighth century whose legal opinions were just as crucial to the formation of the Ḥanafī school as the opinions of Abū Ḥanīfa himself: Abū Yūsuf (d. 182/798) and Muḥammad ibn al-Ḥasan al-Shaybānī (d. 189/804), the protégés of Abū Ḥanīfa. It may even be argued that al-Shaybānī is more important to the formation of the Ḥanafī school of law than Abū Ḥanīfa since he was one of the earliest collectors of the legal opinions of the Iraqi school of jurists, from which the Ḥanafī school of law emerged, as well as a jurist in his own right who issued fatwas along the lines consistent with the Iraqi legal tradition.

Let us begin by looking at some of the fatwas of Abū Ḥanīfa. One position where Abū Ḥanīfa goes against the opinions of the majority of other jurists of his time concerns the stipulation requiring a female to have a male guardian (known as a *walī*) to procure a marriage and validate the marriage contract. Abū Ḥanīfa's position is that this stipulation is not mandatory,[62] and his rationale is that if it is agreed upon that a woman has complete guardianship over her wealth, then she also ought to have complete guardianship over her right to marriage.[63] This fatwa is interesting in that it appears to make an analogical argument (*qiyās*) that draws on the legitimacy of another recognized legal rule and ignores the

[61] The actual discussion of the formation of Islamic legal schools that took place in the third/ninth through fifth/eleventh centuries will be reserved for the upcoming chapters.

[62] Al-Sarakhsī, *al-Mabsūṭ* (Beirut: Dāar al-Maʿrifa), 5:10 (cited from the Shamela Library software, version 3.61).

[63] Abū Zahra, 276.

scriptural text (*ḥadīth*) that makes the presence of a guardian a precondition for the validity of the marriage contract[64] (see Figure 5).

This fatwa has several interesting features. One of these is that Abū Ḥanīfa draws upon established economic practice (a woman's complete guardianship over her wealth) to legitimize practices in the social sphere (granting women complete guardianship in marriage). This example of Abū Ḥanīfa's fatwas, and similarly those of Ibrāhīm al-Nakhaʿī before him, demonstrates that utilization of analogical reasoning in juristic decisions was rife among those jurists who belonged to the Iraqi school. In fact, it is within their circles that the term for legal analogical reasoning, *qiyās*, as a specific form of the more general applications of reasoning (*raʾy*) was coined. Ahmad Hasan asserts that the early Iraqis used this term to mean a more systematic reasoning about the law and drawing legal parallels between legal cases than the more general application of legal opinion signified by the term *raʾy*.[65] At the same time, the Iraqi circle of jurists did not employ the term *qiyās* during this period in the exact same way as the very structured legal reasoning that was defined by later Shāfiʿī legal theorists.[66]

Yet as much as Abū Ḥanīfa and his protégés Abū Yūsuf and al-Shaybānī employed *qiyas* to justify their legal opinions, they often employed other forms of legal reasoning to validate their fatwas that ran counter to *qiyās*; this is because they felt that for certain cases analogical reasoning produced undesirable legal outcomes. Among the early counter-*qiyās* legal instruments they used was *istiḥsān*, where the jurist makes a judgment based on his juristic preference consciously going against what the *qiyās* (analogical argument) would require. This Iraqi school was (in)famous for employing such a legal device in some of its rulings, much to the irritation of those *ḥadīth* advocates who felt that this form of legal deduction was based on sheer caprice.

It is not clear what criteria legitimated the employment of *istiḥsān* by these Iraqi jurists, but Ahmad Hasan seems to think that public interest was the motive for its use.[67] An example of *istiḥsān* is the case of Abū Ḥanīfa disapproving of the practice of *ishʿār* (making an incision in the flesh of the sacrificial animal) on the hajj pilgrimage because he viewed

[64] Al-Tirmidhī, 2007, 461, *ḥadīth* #, 1103.

[65] Hasan, 140–141. Although, as we have pointed out in footnote 102, a *raʾy* argument did display a general structure from which *qiyās* arguments emerged.

[66] Hasan, 144. I will have more to say about the development of *qiyās* in the following chapter.

[67] See Ahmad Hasan, *The Early Development of Islamic Jurisprudence*, 146.

it as a cruel disfiguration of the animal. This was his judgment despite *ḥadīth* that approved of the practice of *ishʿār*. The fifth-/eleventh-century Ḥanafī jurist al-Sarakhsī (d. 493/1090) explains that Abū Ḥanīfa was opposed to *ishʿār* because this custom was extreme and caused the animal harm. Therefore, despite the evidence of *ḥadīth* saying otherwise, Abū Ḥanīfa made the counterjudgment of banning it on the basis of *istiḥsān* (juristic preference)[68] (see Figure 5).

Among other forms of legal reasoning that were employed by second/eighth-century jurists was Mālik's alleged use of legal reasoning without a direct scriptural warrant, like public interest (*maṣlaḥa*), to validate his fatwas. A fatwa by Mālik that perhaps illustrates his usage of the principle of public interest is his position on eating carrion out of necessity when there is edible food that is not owned by the person in question. It is prohibited to eat carrion meat in Islamic law as a result of a specific injunction stated in the Quran,[69] but necessity would suspend this injunction. But what should be done in the case where there is edible food that does not belong to the individual who is in need? Mālik states that if this person believes that eating the foods (fruits, crops, and sheep) that belong to others would get him prosecuted as a thief, then he should eat the carrion, but if he thinks that the owners would recognize the dire situation and not prosecute him, then he should eat from the edible food.[70]

The Quranic injunctions do provide an annulment of the prohibition against eating carrion when necessity calls for it by an absence of edible food,[71] yet the scenario in this fatwa is different in that edible food is present, yet it is not owned by the starving person. For this case, the scriptural injunctions (Quran or *ḥadīth*) and Mālik's own Medinan legal tradition are silent, hence forcing jurists like Mālik to produce a ruling that is consistent with the overall moral and legal norms prescribed by scripture. So, in light of the absence of an authoritative ruling in this case, it seems that Mālik resorted to a form of legal reasoning known as *istiṣlāḥ*[72] (i.e., seeking the public interest [or *maṣlaḥa*] based on presumed universal legal norms). This is where he engages in a sort of legal calculus as to what constitutes correct action (see Figure 5).

We should clarify at this point the similarity that exists between the legal principle of *istiḥsān* that Abū Ḥanīfa allegedly employed in his fatwa

[68] Hasan, 146–147.
[69] Qurʾān, 2:173 and 16:115.
[70] Mālik ibn Anas, 1982, Section 25.7, pg. 227.
[71] Quran, 2:173. Also Quran 16:115.
[72] See Hallaq, 2005, 208, for a precise definition of this term.

against branding sacrificial animals and the principle of *istiṣlāḥ* that Mālik allegedly used to justify his fatwa on the legality of eating carrion. Their point of similarity is that they are both forms of legal reasoning that are employed to validate legal opinions independently of any scripturally mandated injunction, legal derivation through *qiyās* (analogical reasoning), or forms of legal precedent or consensus. Yet where *istiḥsān* and *istiṣlāḥ* diverge is with respect to how they deal with direct scriptural evidence or scripturally derived evidence that has a bearing on the case at hand.

In the case of *istiṣlāḥ* (seeking public interest or the common good), there is a complete absence of direct scriptural injunctions or scripturally derived rulings that have a bearing on the case, hence forcing the jurist to resort to this form of independent reasoning to solve his case, as we have seen in Mālik's fatwa on eating carrion. On the other hand, in the case of *istiḥsān* (juristic preference), there exists scriptural evidence or scripturally derived evidence through *qiyās* that has a bearing on the case in question, yet the jurist acts independently to annul the legal implication of that evidence presumably to avoid what he sees as an undesirable outcome. Such was the case in Abū ḥanīfa's fatwa on the branding of sacrificial animals.

If Abū Ḥanīfa and Mālik were more liberal in their use of extra-scriptural legal methods like *istiḥsān* and *istiṣlāḥ* in making legal derivations, al-Shāfiʿī, the younger contemporary of these two jurists, was much less inclined to employ extra-scriptural legal methods other than strict *qiyās* for social situations that were not explicitly addressed in scriptural sources. This is because he advocated restricting jurisprudence to matters found in the scriptural sources alone (Quran and prophetic practice) or to those legal opinions that enjoyed unanimous consensus (*ijmāʿ*). Those situations on which these legal sources were silent should be dealt with by the strict use of legal analogy carried out on the basis of scripturally established norms.[73]

An illustration of al-Shāfiʿī's use of *qiyās* can be found in his fatwa establishing the financial liability of children toward their father if the parents are unable to support themselves. In presenting his case, he initiates his argument in reverse by citing the scriptural passages in the Quran and prophetic *ḥadīth* that support the idea that the father is obligated to

[73] See al-Shāfiʿī's treatise entitled *al-Risāla* (trans. Khadduri, 1987), which was partly written to counter other methodological trends like *istiḥsān* in support of *qiyās*. See, for example, *al-Risāla*, 306 where he restricts jurisprudence to those sources just mentioned.

support his children in their youth.[74] He then proceeds to argue by analogical deduction that the father is entitled to the same right against his children if he has no means to support himself. This is because his circumstance now falls within the rubric of the legal principle that was operative in the scripturally mandated obligation of the father to support his children: direct lineage coupled with the incapacity to support oneself. Once these very same conditions apply to the father – that he shares the same lineage and is financially incapacitated – then he is entitled to the same rights from his children as the obligation he once had toward them.[75]

What is interesting about this fatwa and the analogical reasoning that al-Shāfiʿī displays in it is his identification of legal principles that are operative in scriptural injunctions. It is those legal principles that are anchors for legal injunctions pronounced by the scriptural sources even when these legal principles are not necessarily explicitly mentioned in the scriptural sources. It is by this token that scriptural injunctions can be analogically extended to different cases if these cases share the same operative legal principle of the original case. He recognized that in order for analogical legal reasoning to be valid, it has to meet a certain condition, namely, that both the original case and the novel case share an essential attribute – what he called the *maʿnā* –[76] for the legal judgment of one to be carried over to the other (see Figure 5).

In this way, al-Shāfiʿī further methodologically grounded *qiyās* as a legitimate legal tool by which to derive law. Although *qiyās*, as a term and a device, was employed and developed by the Iraqi regional school best represented in the second century AH by Abū Ḥanīfa and his protégés, it was refined and elevated by al-Shāfiʿī as the premiere methodological tool by which new laws might be derived for situations that had no precedents. As such, al-Shāfiʿī, even in his opposition to the overall approach of the Iraqi regional school, with its notoriety of being home to *ahl al-raʾy* (the advocates of opinion), accepted certain methods of their legal reasoning that he saw as being in consonance with the scriptural sources.

At the same time, his rejection of other non-scriptural sources of law, like the employment of *istiḥsān* (juristic preference), and his restriction of the legitimate means of deriving new jurisprudence to legal devices such as *qiyās* show how the arguments of *ahl al-ḥadīth*, as a faction opposed to any non-scripturally based legal opinions, were gaining traction among

[74] Al-Shāfiʿī, 1987, 309–310.
[75] Al-Shāfiʿī, 1987, 310.
[76] Al-Shāfiʿī, 1987, 309.

Case	Ruling/fatwa	Legal reasoning	Jurist	Region
The presence of a male guardian (*walī*) for females for the validity of marriages	Not incumbent	Analogy (*qiyās*) to accepted ruling that females have complete guardianship over their wealth	Abū Ḥanīfa	Kufa
Ishʿār (branding a sacrificial animal)	Not approved	*Istiḥsān* (juristic preference) contrary to *ḥadīth* allowing it	Abū Ḥanīfa	Kufa
Eating carrion (not *ḥalāl*) or eating someone else's crops (theft) when in dire need	1. Eat carrion if presumed that the owner of crops will prosecute 2. Eat crop if the owner will not prosecute	1. *Maṣlaḥa* 2. *Maṣlaḥa*	Mālik ibn Anas	Medina
Financial liability of children toward father if he is unable to support himself	Incumbent	Analogy *qiyās*) to scripturally mandated liability of father to support children	al-Shāfiʿī	Medina and Egypt

FIGURE 5 Fatwa in the age of the *madhhab* predecessors

jurists in the late second century. Although *qiyās* was not accepted as a legitimate source for deriving law by *ahl al-ḥadīth*, who restricted legal reasoning to the direct derivation of law from scriptural injunctions, al-Shāfiʿī recognized the main argument of *ahl al-ḥadīth* because *qiyās* itself was a form of scripturally based reasoning and was not as remote from scripture as *istiḥsān* and *istiṣlāḥ* were.

FURTHER EXPLORATIONS IN THE FATWAS OF THE *MADHHAB* PREDECESSORS: USURIOUS TRANSACTIONS

The previous section individually examined the fatwas of the *madhhab* predecessors in terms of how each jurist approached the process of law-making and the distinct types of legal reasoning he utilized and ultimately contributed to the Islamic legal tradition. We now examine the legal opinions of Abū Ḥanīfa, Mālik, and al-Shāfiʿī not so much in terms of addressing disparate and particular religious or social happenings but in terms of how each one of these jurists employs fatwas to expand the legal reach of scriptural norms. For this analysis, I cross-examine their juristic opinions (fatwas) on a common theme, namely, the types of exchange that constitute usurious (*ribāwī*) transactions. By looking at their legal pronouncements on one topic, we can gain a broader perspective on the types of legal reasoning and hermeneutical strategies each uses to justify his opinions. It will become apparent form this analysis that although each jurist recognizes the same source of authoritative norm – namely, a report from the Prophet Muḥammad – they each nevertheless interpreted and rationalized the scripturally derived norms differently.

To start with, their legal rulings on this issue are stated with reference to the prophetic report that stipulates that six types of goods (wheat, barley, dates, salt, gold, and silver), when exchanged for the same type, must be in equal quantities and must be exchanged on the spot or else the transaction is considered usurious.[77] Thus, there are two ways in which transactions in these goods can be considered usurious: first, if any one of these goods is exchanged for the same type in unequal measure, and second, if any one of these goods is exchanged for its same type in different time periods, that is, if there is a delay in the delivery/exchange of the one item for the other.

[77] Al-Shaybānī, *Kitāb al-Āthār*, 2:736. See also Māalik ibn Anas, 1982, 31.17, pg. 292 (although this report does not mention salt) and al-Shāfiʿī, *Kitāb al-Umm*, 4:32, for a similar prophetic report.

As will become clear, each of the fatwas of these three jurists expanded the scope of usurious transactions to include other types of goods not specifically mentioned in the prophetic tradition about usurious exchanges. Each of their fatwas was an attempt to interpret the legal norm that the Prophet had established, and based on their understanding of its aims, they tried to extend or limit the reach of this norm. In examining the actual content of their fatwas, I will only consider those fatwas that address one of the two types of usurious transactions – namely, those regarding an unequal exchange of the same type of item – while disregarding scenarios invoking the other condition of whether they are exchanged on the spot or not.

Let us begin our comparative analysis with a look at several fatwas of Abū Ḥanīfa on what constitutes usurious transactions. For example, he is of the opinion that the exchange of two loaves of bread for one is a legitimate exchange and non-usurious.[78] On the surface, this is completely in line with the literal reading of the prophetic tradition in that bread is not one of the goods that are addressed in that *ḥadīth* and hence is not directly subject to the prohibition of being exchanged in unequal quantities. On the other hand, when rendering his opinion about the unequal exchange of iron or copper, Abū Ḥanīfa is of the opinion that these types of items, when exchanged within the same category, must be exchanged on an equal basis or else the transaction is considered usurious,[79] and this is despite the fact that neither iron nor copper was included in the prophetic prohibition on usurious exchanges.

The question arises, why would the unequal exchange in bread be considered differently than the unequal exchange of iron or copper in the fatwas of Abū Ḥanīfa? The answer lies in the rationale he gives in both fatwas. In the case of bread, he says that this category of goods is not sold by measurement of weight or volume,[80] while his rationale for his opinion in the case of iron and copper is that they are sold by weight measure.[81] Hence, Abū Ḥanīfa's legal position expands the prophetic prohibition on usury to include all products/items that are sold by measure of volume or weight. For Abū Ḥanīfa, all types of goods whose exchange takes place by means of volume or weight measure must be exchanged in equal measure or else the transaction is usurious.[82] So the six items that were stipulated

[78] Al-Shaybānī, *al-Ḥujja ʿalā ahl al-Madīna*, 2:619.
[79] Al-Shaybānī, *al-Ḥujja ʿalā Ahl al-Madīna*, 2:659.
[80] Al-Shaybānī, *al-Ḥujja ʿalā Ahl al-Madīna*, 2:619.
[81] Al-Shaybānī, *al-Ḥujja ʿalā Ahl al-Madīna*, 2:659.
[82] Khin, 496; Wheeler, 21.

in the *ḥadīth* were seen by Abū Ḥanīfa as just specific examples of a more general category of things that are exchanged by measure of volume or weight. So, exchange in terms of volume and/or weight represents the attribute that is the common ground for all the six goods mentioned in the *ḥadīth* and is the basis for extending the verdict on those items to other items not specifically mentioned in the prophetic tradition.[83]

Mālik, on the other hand, has a different set of criteria by which he extends the prophetic prohibition of usurious exchanges and what he considers the fundamental cause for considering things usurious or not. For instance, he says in one fatwa that foods of the same type are not to be exchanged except in equal measure.[84] Yet on another occasion, he gives the fatwa that certain kinds of fruits like watermelon and cucumbers can be exchanged in unequal measure since they are not food that can be dried and stored; in other words, they are perishable.[85] In another fatwa, Mālik says that it is legitimate to exchange metals – other than gold or silver, which are overtly stipulated in the mentioned prophetic tradition – of the same type like copper or iron in unequal measure.[86]

So, what can we deduce from these cases about how Mālik has understood the principle stemming from the normative statements of the Prophet Muḥammad that determine usurious transactions? Like those of Abū Ḥanīfa, Mālik's fatwas indicate that the principle of usurious transactions is not to be limited to the six goods mentioned by the *ḥadīth* because he, too, expands the range of usurious transactions. Yet judging from his fatwas, the criterion which he seems to believe is that the operative principle behind usurious transactions is different from that of Abū Ḥanīfa. We can see this by the fact that he allows things that are measured by volume or weight (e.g., copper and iron) to be exchanged in unequal measure contrary to Abū Ḥanīfa's position.

But on the other hand, he stipulates that foods are not to be exchanged in unequal measure unless they cannot be dried and stored (i.e., they are perishable). So for Mālik, the legal attribute underlying the prophetic prohibition on what constitutes usurious exchanges seems to be that category of goods that consists of non-perishable foods. On the other hand, gold and silver are included in the prohibition on the principle that they are metals used as instruments of universal valuation.[87] In other words,

[83] Khin, 496.
[84] Mālik ibn Anas, 1982, Section 31.22, pg. 295.
[85] Mālik ibn Anas, 1982, Section 33.15, pg. 290.
[86] Mālik ibn Anas, 1982, Section 43.21, pg. 300.
[87] Khin, 498.

Mālik saw those four food items mentioned by the Prophet as specific examples of a more general category of foods that were non-perishable, hence deriving the principle that non-perishable foods of the same category should be exchanged in equal measure or else the transaction would be considered usurious.[88]

Mālik's fatwa on usurious transactions are narrower in scope than that of Abū Ḥanīfa's since Mālik stipulates that in order for the transaction to be usurious, it must be an unequal exchange of only non-perishable food items, exempting gold and silver from this condition. Abū Ḥanīfa's view, by contrast, identifies the basis for the ruling as an unequal exchange of any good that is measured by volume or weight, excluding only those things that are not subject to this condition, such as things that are exchanged by counting. So, for Abū Ḥanīfa, the type of item exchanged (whether it be a food or a non-food item) is immaterial to the determination of usurious transactions. For him, it is only the manner in which an item or good is exchanged (i.e., by volume or by weight) that is legally considered for determinations of usury.

Moreover, Mālik also bifurcates the legal principles (or attributes) that he thinks lie behind the prophetic statement governing usurious transactions by asserting a separate standard for gold and silver because they are means by which the value of things is determined and another standard for foods because those foods that were mentioned are non-perishable. Abū Ḥanīfa, on the other hand, asserts a singular principle that he thinks governs usurious transactions – namely, all things exchanged by measure of volume or weight – hence not paying heed to the substantive differences between goods but rather looking at the formal characteristics that tie various goods together.

In lieu of these legal opinions, al-Shāfiʿī adds his own perspective as to what exchanges constitute usurious transactions. He is of the opinion that all things that are eaten or drunk (foods and/or medicines),[89] along with gold and silver, must be exchanged in equal quantities when exchanging them for goods of the same kind or else the transaction would be considered usurious.[90] Whatever is eaten or drunk, regardless of its perishability (a decisive factor for Mālik), is subject to the rules governing usury.[91] Moreover, whether or not the exchanged goods in question are measured by volume and/or weight – the main consideration underlying

[88] Khin, 498–499.
[89] Al-Shāfiʿī, 2004 4:34.
[90] Al-Shāfiʿī, 2004 4:37.
[91] Al-Shāfiʿī, 2004 4:33.

Abū Ḥanīfa's position – is of no consequence so long as they are eaten or drunk.[92] If they are not eaten or drunk and are other than gold and silver, then they are not subject to the principle of usurious exchanges in the eyes of al-Shāfiʿī.[93]

Al-Shāfiʿī's rationale for interpreting the prophetic injunction on usurious transactions in this way has several levels of explanation. In terms of his stipulations on the equal exchange of gold and silver, this is just a literal reading of the prophetic injunction; in the case of these two metals, he believes, like Mālik, that no analogies to other goods/item should be made to gold and silver because they are substances by which all other products are assigned values.[94] On the other hand, the restriction of the principle of usurious transactions on the other four food items that are explicitly mentioned in the prophetic injunction is expanded by al-Shāfiʿī to include all those products that are edible (food, drink, medicine, etc.). His justification for expanding the circle of items subject to the principle of usurious transactions to include all items that are eaten or drunk is his belief that the four food items cited by the Prophet are just examples of things that are widely consumed for people's benefit, and if any product contains the same core attribute of edibility as those items that are explicitly mentioned in the ḥadīth, then it should be treated by analogy in a legally similar way[95] (see Figure 6 for a summary of all these legal positions).

What is interesting about the fatwas of Abū Ḥanīfa, Mālik, and al-Shāfiʿī on what constitutes usurious transactions is that each of their positions is anchored in the same scriptural prescription (in this case a prophetic tradition), from where each jurist then moves beyond the specific scripturally mandated injunctions to a more universal rule that could be applicable to situations that extend beyond the immediate circumstances that might have given rise to those scriptural prescriptions. In doing this, each jurist tried to find a unifying legal principle, deduced from the scriptural particulars, from which to draw in other cases under its legal rubric. This extension of authoritative legal norms to new cases became one of the hallmarks of the fatwa process in particular and Islamic law in general.

92 This is implied from his discussion on selling foods/drinks in countable quantities as opposed to measure them by weight or volume. See al-Shāfiʿī, 2004 4:33.

93 Al-Shāfiʿī, 2004 4:37.

94 Al-Shāfiʿī, 2004 4:32.

95 To see the full extent of his argument on this issue, see al-Shāfiʿī, 2004 4:33–34. See also Khin, 499.

Scriptural norm	Ruling/fatwa	Legal principle	Jurist
Unequal exchange or bartering of wheat, barely, dates, salt, gold, and silver constitutes usury	– Exchange of two items of bread for one is not usurious – Unequal exchange of metals (copper or iron) is usurious	Unequal exchange of things measured by volume and weight constitutes a usurious transaction. Unequal exchange of items that are sold by counting does not constitute a usurious transaction	Abū Ḥanīfa
	– Unequal exchange of some foods is usurious (e.g., bread), while the unequal exchange of others (e.g., watermelon) is not usurious – Unequal exchange of metals (except gold and silver) is not usurious	Unequal exchange of non-perishable foods is usurious, but the unequal exchange of perishable foods is not usurious. Unequal exchange of non-food items (other than gold and silver) is not usurious	Mālik ibn Anas
	– Unequal exchange of foods, drinks, and medicines is usurious – Unequal exchange of metals (aside from gold and silver) is not usurious	– Unequal exchange of all edible goods is usurious – Unequal exchange of non-edible goods (besides gold and silver) is not usurious	al-Shāfiʿī

FIGURE 6 Fatwas defining usurious transactions by the *madhhab* predecessors

This extended demonstration of the overlapping fatwas by the *madhhab* predecessors reveals several characteristics about the formation of Islamic law and its forms of legal reasoning. First, all these jurists, whether they were considered inheritors of the advocates of *raʾy* like Abū Ḥanīfa or advocates of tradition (*āthār/ḥadīth*) like Mālik and al-Shāfiʿī, held the prophetic practice as represented in *ḥadīth* as a source of authoritative legal norms. Moreover, advocating traditionalism in the law did not necessarily mean literal observance of the scriptural sources, as can be seen from al-Shāfiʿī's extension of the legal reach of the aforementioned *ḥadīth* on usury, for example. Last, despite their agreement about the sources of legal norms (in this case, the prophetic *ḥadīth*), jurists did not necessarily interpret such sources uniformly, which led to a diversity in legal opinions. Yet, the plurality of these opinions was nevertheless realized with reference to a common set of discursive strategies that attempted to reveal the legal intent of the norms embedded in the scriptural evidence; this is indicated by the fact that all three jurists abstracted beyond the particularities of the text so as to discover the core legal precept that defined usurious transactions. All this shows that these jurists were contributing to the formation of a common legal tradition with its own distinctive qualities that will be elaborated in the forthcoming chapters.

FATWA IN THE AGE OF THE *MADHHAB* PREDECESSORS OF THE THIRD/NINTH CENTURY: DISTRIBUTION OF WATER RESOURCES AND SHAREHOLDERS' LAND RIGHTS

Historical and Legal Background to the Fatwas

Yaḥyā ibn al-Ḥusayn (d. 298/911), aka al-Hādī ilā al-Ḥaqq, was a jurist in the latter part of the third/ninth–tenth century who came from Medina, established himself as a ruler in the northern highlands of Yemen and established the emerging Zaydī Shīʿī branch of Islam there.

Yaḥyā ibn Hussein (al-Hādī) was a learned grandnephew of Zayd and, thus, according to juristic stipulations of Zaydī Islam, a qualified legal authority in this emerging legal school. In addition, al-Hādī was influenced by the views of his grandfather al-Qāsim ibn Ibrāhīm al-Rassī, whose legal opinions in the earlier part of the third/ninth century were foundational to the establishment of an early Zaydī legal doctrine espoused by Zayd's followers in Iraq and the Caspian Sea region.[96]

[96] Madelung, 478.

Yet, al-Hādī's legal opinions in the latter part of the third/ninth century were just as crucial to the formation of a Zaydī legal doctrine and school because it was his interpretation of Zaydī Islam that he established in Yemen is what survived Zaydīsm to this day. Therefore, his ideas influenced the course of the remaining branch of the Zaydī madhab throughout history.

Hence, I consider him a madhab predecessor of the Zaydī legal school, although he thrived two generations later from the earliest shapers of Zaydī legal doctrine like his grandfather. His legal opinions are primarily found in two of his works on law: *Kitāb al-Aḥkām* and *Kitāb al-Muntakhab*.

Geographic Context of the Fatwa

Northern Yemen, the area where al-Hādī ruled, was a region with a longstanding agricultural tradition dating back to two millennia before al-Hādī's rule. Even though Yemen did not have rivers from which to irrigate its agriculture similar to its regional river valley civilizations like those of the Nile, Tigris, and Euphrates, historically, it managed its rainwater resources to irrigate its farms.[97] In this environment, issues regarding agricultural and water management have been prevalent, thereby contextualizing one of al-Hādī's fatwas that I will analyze here on the rights to the distribution of water resources.

Methodological Basis to Al-Hādī's Fatwas

The two short fatwas chosen for analysis here come from *Kitāb al Muntakhab*, which is a collection of some of al-Hādī's legal opinions that were solicited by his disciple Muḥammad ibn Sulaymān al-Kūfī, who later collated these opinions into this work. Before al-Hādī answers al-Kūfī's legal questions, he admonishes al-Kūfī on the proper methodological basis by which to accept his views: Do not take these opinions based on observance of authority (*taqlīd*) but rather on legal proofs (*hujjah*).[98] This methodological precept foreshadows a defining characteristic of the Zaydī legal school, which maintains that for a jurist to be qualified to issue legal opinions, they must possess all of the tools

[97] Macktintosh-Smith, 24.
[98] Al-Kūfī, 21.

for independent legal reasoning (*ijtihād*) and not base their opinions on precedent.

Al-Kūfī further interrogates al-Hādī's proposition as to what legal sources constitute the proper grounds for this legal reasoning. Al-Hādī replies that are three sources of the law: the Quran, consensually established prophetic practice (*ijmāʿ ʿan al-rasūl*), and intellect/reason (*ʿaql*).[99] From this response, there are several pertinent points to notice as to what it implies regarding the evolving trends in Islamic legal reasoning during the third/ninth century. First, al-Hādī affirms the authority of the *sunna* but only that which has been established by consensus (*ijmāʿ*) or a collective agreement. By holding this position, he is reflecting the earlier antithesis of the second-century Iraqi school – a school from which al-Hādī's legal opinions genealogically evolve from – to *aḥad ḥadīths* that were narrated with but a few lines of transmission (see the Awzaʿī-Abū Ḥanīfa debate expounded earlier).

Second, the affirmation of intellect/reason as a basis of the law is a tacit acceptance of the implicit position of the advocates of *ra'y* that reason and not mere revelation formulate law.

Furthermore, it is an indication that the early iteration of the Zaydī school had not accepted the limitation on the role of reason in the formulation of the law to *qiyās* (analogy) that later advocates of ḥadīth like al-Shāfiʿī acknowledged. As we will later find out, subsequently, Zaydism limits the role of reason in lawmaking to *qiyās* (analogy). Nevertheless, 'aql (intellect/reason) becomes the precursor to the establishment of *qiyās* as a legal principle in the Zaydī legal school.

Analysis of Fatwa on Distribution of Water Resources

Al-Kūfī asks al-Hādī how should a stream (*sayl*) be divided up between farm fields (*ḍayāʿ*). Al-Hādī responds by saying that if water is plenty, those who are engaging in crop farming (*ṣāḥib al-zāriʿ*) can hold the stream water until the water reaches one's shoelaces (*al-sharakayn*). In contrast, those involved in palm cultivation should keep the water until it comes to the ankles (*al Kaʿbayn*); then, they should send the water downstream for the other fields to do likewise until all the fields are irrigated.[100] Thus far, al-Hādī does not offer explicit normative support for his legal opinion. Yet, implicitly one can surmise that his answer is based

[99] Al-Kūfī, 21.
[100] Al-Kūfī, 362.

on his knowledge of what was a reasonable amount of water that the agricultural sciences of his day and region determined was necessary for a successful yield for each of these crops. One would not expect that there would be a normative basis for such a rational determination, yet al-Hādī's opinion normalizes that determination based on his political and legal authority.

Al-Kūfī then asks, if the water from the stream is not enough to reach the end of the fields, how should the water be distributed? Al-Hādī responds by saying that the upstream fields should receive less water than the amount initially stipulated (and presumably, the same would be the case for the fields downstream). He based this decision on a similar decision taken by the Prophet regarding the Stream of Mahrūr that would run through Medina when the people downstream complained about the people upstream diverting its waters when its water was scarce.[101] In this case, al-Hādī uses the *sunna* to legitimate his legal opinion affirming his previously stated legal methodology that prophetic practice is the only type of legal precedent that is independently normative to establish law.

Al-Hādī's Fatwa on the Plot Distribution of Shareholders of a Field

Al-Kūfī asks, are people who have shared ownership of a field obliged to give contagious plots to the small shareholders when they decide to split up the area on the presumption that dispersing their plot shares would have negative consequences for the small shareholders? Al-Hādī responds that the larger plot shareowners would be obliged to give contagious plots to the more minor plot shareholders if the dispersion of their properties would lead to their inability to sell or farm on them, thereby bringing them harm. Al-Hādī based his decision on the prophetic report that states: "Do no harm, and neither harm should be done on to you" (*lā ḍarara wa lā ḍirār*).[102] The significance of this prophetic statement is that it became an axiomatic legal principle within the Islamic legal tradition for guiding the determination of cases such as the one al-Hādī was confronted with. Moreover, this statement demonstrated universal legal principles that underlie the practice of Islamic legal reasoning (Figure 7).

[101] Al-Kūfī, 362.
[102] Al-Kūfī, 362.

Case	Ruling/fatwa	Legal reasoning	Jurist	Region
How should stream water be divided between upstream and downstream fields?	-Crop fields should take in water up to the height of shoelaces -Palm fields should take in water up to the height of the ankles	Reasonably determined necessity and agricultural custom (*'urf*)	Yaḥyā ibn al-Ḥusayn al-Hādī	Yemen
How should stream water be divided between upstream and downstream fields when the stream is insufficient to reach downstream?	Upstream fields should receive less than what is usually stipulated	*Sunna*: the prophet's precedent in Medina with Mahrur Stream	Yaḥyā ibn al-Ḥusayn al-Hādī	Yemen
If shareholders divide their plot between themselves, can the small shareholders demand from the large shareholders that their shares be divided/made contagious?	Yes, if dividing the small shares non-contagiously brings harm to small shareholders	*Sunna*: prophetic report/principle states: "Do no harm…."	Yaḥyā ibn al-Ḥusayn al-Hādī	Yemen

Figure 7 Fatwa in the age of the *madhhab* predecessors II: third/ninth century

CONCLUSION

The legal activity of the religious specialists of the late first, second, and third centuries of Islam generated much difference among them on how they should go about this legal enterprise, and out of that tension, a legal discourse began to emerge dialectically. However, there was a common thread running through their differences and debates, namely, that the past was normative. It did not matter whether one was a jurist who advocated *ra'y* (opinion/reason) or one who advocated *āthār/ḥadīth* (tradition/prophetic tradition) or whether one was an Iraqi-based jurist or a Hijazi-based jurist; the past, in one way or another, served as a source of standards for the promulgation of legal opinions.[103]

Of course, various parties had different views on how and what aspects of the past were to serve as normative standards for the contemporary situation, yet all were unanimous in agreeing that the revelatory period of Islam, as represented in the scriptural discourses of the Quran and prophetic traditions (*ḥadīth*), was to play a paramount role in informing a jurist's legal outlook and, to a good extent, substantively regulate his legal decisions. Where they differed in this respect was on how to interpret and apply the norms found in these past discourses to their own conditions.

This is where these jurists and proto-jurists applied their *phronetic* wisdom, or *phronesis*, to use Aristotelian terminology, to understand and apply the normative principles found in these historical and authoritative discourses and traditions to their peculiar circumstances. What emerged out of these exercises of practical reasoning is not just a mass of legal doctrines but also a repertoire of legal techniques and hermeneutical methods that would shape the future of Islamic legal discourse. Moreover, these early jurists, perhaps by virtue of existing themselves in what later generations viewed as the normative past, became the authoritative references from which a legal tradition would emerge in the subsequent period. We explore these issues in greater detail in Chapter 3.

[103] See Edward Chase, "Law and Theology," in *A Companion to Law and Legal Theory* (Blackwell Publishing, 1999), for his elaboration on Harold Berman's notion of historical jurisprudence for more on the idea that the past is a source of norms.

3

Fatwa and the Formation of Islamic Legal Discourses, Institutions, and Society

INTRODUCTION

The previous chapters mapped the practice of *iftāʾ* in the first three centuries of Islam, giving a detailed analysis of the forms of legal reasoning that were being cultivated by this legal activity. The current chapter examines how those modes of rationality and socio-legal practices gave rise to distinct forms of legal discourses and institutions. Over the next two centuries, Muslim jurists would amend and synthesize the legal approaches and principles of their predecessors, paving the way for the formation of an Islamic legal system. The central role of fatwas in this process will be highlighted. But before undertaking this exposition, we first present some historical considerations and legal developments necessary for giving context to the discussion.

THE GENESIS OF LEGAL THEORY, LEGAL DOCTRINES, AND INSTITUTIONS IN THE LATE AND POST–ABBASID CALIPHATE PERIOD

The fourth/tenth and fifth/eleventh centuries ushered in new political realities that had a profound impact on Muslim society. The effective disintegration of the Abbasid Caliphate by the fourth/tenth century brought about a political fragmentation that had not been witnessed before in Muslim society where Muslims no longer found themselves ruled by a unified caliphate but by smaller parochial states. This fragmentation allowed for new dynamics to come into play, and the Muslim scholarly elite found themselves in some ways to be a unifying force for Muslim society through the dissemination of their religious teachings.[1]

Despite the political fragmentation of the caliphate, Muslims could travel anywhere where it formally ruled, and no matter who the ruler was, they could expect to be governed by a similar set of ethico-legal norms that came to be known as the Sharīʿa. Of course, Sharīʿa law was cultivated by Muslim scholars in general and Muslim jurists in particular. This unifying role that these ethico-legal norms played in Muslim society increased the prestige of those who had cultivated those norms, the *ʿulamāʾ* (lit. "those who possess knowledge," or scholars), as they became to be known. This further lent legitimacy to their project of elucidating the legal tradition that now played an even more central role in Muslim society.[2]

Concomitantly, during the fourth/tenth and fifth/eleventh centuries, a more precisely defined Islamic legal discourse began to emerge and take shape, building on the legal discourses of the previous centuries. Out of the debates and legal decisions of early jurists and the legal reasoning they employed in their decisions, later jurists began to construct more systematic legal doctrines and methodologies out of which an Islamic legal tradition came to be formed. In the next several sections of this chapter, we examine the formation of the Islamic legal tradition as represented in the genesis of legal schools (*madhhab*s), the establishment of legal doctrines, the development of an Islamic legal theory (*uṣūl al-fiqh*), and how fatwas played an integral role in the realization of these legal institutions.

Before embarking on such an analysis, it is important first to contextualize the discussion by outlining the historical legal developments of the period in question. In his book *The Evolution of Islamic Law*, Wael Hallaq describes the post-Shāfiʿī era of classical Islamic legal discourse as the period of "Great Synthesis" partly between the two major trends in Islamic law: the advocates of *raʾy* (rationalist/pragmatist) and the advocates of *ḥadīth* (prophetic tradition).

Among the historical factors that contributed to the process of synthesis between the two approaches of legal jurisprudence are the following:

First, by the end of the second/eighth century, there was an increase in the mobility of Muslim scholars, which enabled them to travel to the

1 For more on these points, see Hallaq, 2005, 183–184; Hodgson, 1974, 1:349–350; Lapidus, 1973, 40; and Zaman, 1997, 5–7.

2 For more on this point, see Lapidus, 1973, 37–40.

various regions of the Muslim world in pursuit of Islamic knowledge.[3] This greater mobility, Hallaq argues, increasingly exposed Muslim scholars to the religious and legal practices of different regions (what Hallaq calls the living sunnaic practices).[4] This greater exposure to different ideas and methods created an atmosphere of consolidation and synthesis. This trend is probably best represented by the second-/eighth-century jurist al-Shāfiʿī with whose fatwas we dealt in the previous chapter. Al-Shāfiʿī was born in Palestine and at a very young age went to study in the cities of Mecca and Medina. He would later go on to study in Yemen and Iraq, eventually settling in Egypt where he developed a following for his jurisprudence.[5] Thus, al-Shāfiʿī illustrates this growing cosmopolitanism among Muslim scholars as he traversed most of the major centers of Islamic learning of his time. This cosmopolitanism was a necessary ingredient that spawned the sort of synthesis of legal ideas in which al-Shāfiʿī himself would play a large role.

Second, the growing proliferation of *ḥadīth* provided a unified rubric to consolidate all the variant legal practices in different regions under the banner that law should be primarily derived from sacred text and less from independent rational or pragmatic judgments that vary from one region to another.[6] This is why later jurists like Muḥammad al-Shujāʿ al-Thaljī (d. 267/880), a prominent Iraqi Ḥanafī jurist,[7] tried increasingly to align the forming Ḥanafī legal doctrine with the normative implications found in the continually proliferating *ḥadīth* literature even though Abū Ḥanīfa's circle were traditionally considered *ahl al-raʾy*.[8]

Third, some traditionists (*ahl al-ḥadīth*), including certain later Ḥanbalīs[9] and other traditionalists like the Mālikīs, accepted some elements of the

[3] This increased mobility of Muslim scholars during this period is documented in the works of later Muslim writers such as the fifth-/eleventh-century Muslim scholar al-Khaṭīb al-Baghdādī's (d. 463/1071) *al-Riḥla fī ṭalab al-ḥadīth* (Traveling for the pursuit of *ḥadīth*), which documents the travels that many scholars undertook in pursuit of prophetic traditions.

[4] Hallaq, 2005, 120.

[5] For more on the life of al-Shāfiʿī, see Abū Zahra, 422–437; al-Khidari, 156–158; and al-Sāyis, n.d., 117–119.

[6] Hallaq couches his argument in terms of the growing authority of *ḥadīth* in Islamic discourse (see Hallaq, 2005, 122). Alternatively, one may argue that it was the proliferation of *ḥadīth* rather than the growth of its authority that facilitated this process.

[7] Hallaq, 2005, 215.

[8] Hallaq, 2005, 126–127.

[9] Followers of Aḥmad ibn Ḥanbal, one of the leading figures in the *ḥadīth* (traditionist) movement in the third/ninth century, were ambivalent about *qiyās* (analogy) as a means of determining practice and preferred to restrict himself to what was in the corpus of *ḥadīth*, even when some *ḥadīth* were judged weak in terms of authenticity. See Abū Zahra, 514–515, and Vickor, 101–102.

rationalist legal methodology of the advocates of *raʾy*, such as the use of *qiyās* (analogy) and even the use of non-textually based methods like *istiḥsān* (juristic preference).[10] This may mark the beginning of the shift in the traditionalist camp's ambivalent attitude toward non-textually (that is, non-*ḥadīth*) based inquiries into the law or non-regionally based legal practices. Their adopting rationalist tools like *qiyās* and *istiḥsān* meant that they were accommodating the mainstream project toward synthesis instead of exclusion.

Toward the end of the last chapter, we identified the sort of discursive transformations that eventually occurred in many of the legal hermeneutical concepts and the legal rationales that were developed in the first three centuries of Islam. There, we pointed out how a number of legal concepts and methods from the early period ultimately underwent a process of dialectic development by which many of these earlier concepts became differentiated and synthesized into newer legal concepts in the process of trying to resolve the scripturalist and extra-scripturalist approaches to the law. We now revisit those legal changes with the explicit purpose of showing how those conceptual transformations eventually led to the synthesizing of an Islamic legal theory.

Before discussing the theoretical and historical processes that led to the formative development of Islamic legal theory as a distinct discourse between the third/ninth and fifth/eleventh centuries, it should be noted that theorization about the law was already taking place at the end of the second/eighth and the beginning of third/ninth centuries, with al-Shāfiʿī playing a particularly important/prominent role in this process. In his treatise *al-Risāla*, al-Shāfiʿī defines the legitimate sources of Islamic law (Quran, *ḥadīth*, *ijmāʿ*, *qiyās*, *istiḥsān*, etc.) and charts a course on the proper means for how this law is to be derived from its sources and how it is to be reconciled when the sources seem to lead to conflicting legal ends.[11]

It was for the first time that a Muslim jurist was writing about the law theoretically, in the sense that al-Shāfiʿī's objective in this work was not to resolve actual legal cases but to define a methodology of how to approach legal issues. *Al-Risāla* represents the first conscious discursive effort to theorize Islamic law[12] and thus stands as a watershed in the

[10] Hallaq, 2005, 127.

[11] See al-Shāfiʿī, *al-Risāla*, trans. Majid Khadduri (London: Islamic Texts Society, 1987).

[12] This is different from saying that *al-Risāla* represents the first work on *uṣūl al-fiqh*. What is being asserted here is that al-Shāfiʿī's efforts in this work represent rudimentary

history of that law. What must be said here is that al-Shāfiʿī's *Risāla* does not expound the full-fledged Islamic legal theory (*uṣūl al-fiqh*) in the same way that was developed by later theorists, but it certainly handles in broad strokes most of the major themes that comprised the more fully developed theory of the later periods and the relations of those themes to Islamic legislation, including, for example, *ijtihād* (legal reasoning) and *naskh* (abrogation).

All these themes constituted the core issues of the more completely evolved Islamic legal theory, as we discuss later in this chapter. Moreover, al-Shāfiʿī's systematic, albeit basic, treatment of these issues abstracted from the actual process of *iftāʾ* allows us to describe his efforts as an embryonic stage of the formation of Islamic legal theory. This is why one may speak of the development of Islamic law in terms of a pre- and post-Shāfiʿī era because his period represents an era where explicit theorization of the law begins to take place, hence representing a turning point in Islamic law.

Moreover, it is worthy to note that al-Shāfiʿī's theorizing about the law was born out of the great legal debates between the various second/eighth-century jurists and the legal methodologies they employed as well as the overarching approaches to the law that were represented by the different factions such as the *ahl al-raʾy* and the *ahl al-ḥadīth*. When examining his *Risāla*, one can recognize that al-Shāfiʿī was trying to reconcile these opposing camps by synthesizing what he felt were the best legal methodologies and approaches to the law in each of these opposing factions.

For example, as much as he espoused *ḥadīth* as an exclusive substantial source of Islamic law along with Quran – to the pleasure of the *ḥadīth* faction – he accepted at the same time key elements of the *raʾy* faction, such as *qiyās*, as legitimate methodological procedures that would tie human rationality to the revelatory truth. In this way, we can see that the embryonic stages of consolidation and synthesis of the law had begun taking place by the end of the second/eighth and the beginning of the third/ninth centuries. We shall have more to say about these points in the following section.

steps toward the development of an *uṣūl al-fiqh* discourse. Modern Western scholarship disagrees on whether al-Shāfiʿī should be considered the founder of *uṣūl al-fiqh*. See Hallaq, "Was al-Shāfiʿī the Master Architect of Islamic Jurisprudence?" [bibliographical info.], and Joseph Lowry, "Does Shāfiʿī Have a Theory of 'Four Sources' of Law?" [bibliographical info.].

The Transformation of Key Islamic Legal Concepts and the Creation of Islamic Legal Theory

One of the early legal concepts that was used by Muslim jurists is the concept of *ijmāʿ* (consensus). In the pre-Shāfiʿī era, *ijmāʿ* was understood as being the agreement of a particular region of the Muslim world (such as Kufa or Medina) on a question of religious/legal practice. This was often expressed in the early legal literature in statements such as "the opinion on which the people of Kufa agree" or, in the case of Medina, "the matter on which we agree."[13] Later, *ijmāʿ* was redefined as the consensus of the whole Muslim community as represented by its *mujtahids* (jurists).[14] Moreover, any matter resolved through *ijmāʿ* was now seen as providing certain (*qāṭiʿ*) knowledge about the authoritativeness of the legal judgment in question and not just speculative (*ẓannī*) knowledge[15] (see Figure 8).

It is worth noting here that *ijmāʿ* (consensus), operationally speaking, came to be comprised of essentially two types: what could be called *ijmāʿ* of interpretation and what could be called *ijmāʿ* of innovation. *Ijmāʿ* of interpretation essentially meant scholars and jurists of the Muslim community had reached an agreement in interpreting the implications of scriptural texts, which in turn gave rise to unanimity on certain religious beliefs and practices. So, *ijmāʿ* of interpretation had its fundamental basis in scriptural texts (Quran and *ḥadīth*) in that these scriptural sources were the starting point from which a legal consensus of this type was reached. In other words, this type of *ijmāʿ* was not an agreement reached on a legal issue not addressed by the scriptural sources, but rather it was an agreement about how to understand what the scriptural sources were telling Muslims about how to perform their religious practices (see Figure 8).

A very basic example of *ijmāʿ* of interpretation is the consensus of Muslim scholars across the board about the absolute necessity of the religious practice of the five pillars of Islam (testimony of faith, prayer, charity tax, fasting, and pilgrimage) by all Muslims despite their sectarian

[13] Hallaq, 2005, 110.

[14] See al-Shāfiʿī's argument for *ijmāʿ* as representing the legal consensus of the entire Muslim community in *al-Risāla*, 287. After al-Shāfiʿī, the consensus of the Muslim community became interpreted as the consensus of the community of Muslim jurists.

[15] See the assertion of the third-/ninth-century theologian and jurist Ibrāhīm b. ʿUlayya (d. 218/834) in his debate with al-Shāfiʿī, which must have taken place no later the first decade of the third/ninth century as al-Shāfiʿī died during that period, where he unequivocally states the definitive certainty of *ijmāʿ*: "Consensus is proof that supersedes anything, because it excludes the possibility of error" (El Shamsy, 59). See also Hallaq, 2005, 138.

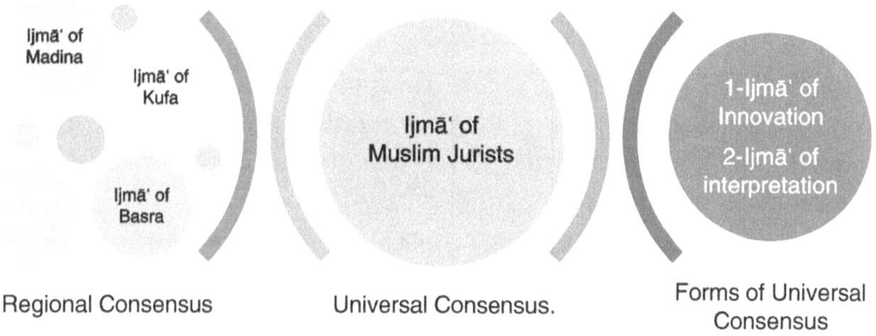

FIGURE 8 Convergence of *ijmāʿ* (consensus) and its forms

views.[16] All these practices are born out of actual scriptural injunctions[17] and not out of any independent opinion of jurists about what constitutes the fundamentals of Islam; their unanimous consensus that these practices are fundamental constitutes an agreement of interpretation of how to understand the implications of those scriptural injunctions. This *ijmāʿ* of interpretation makes up the vast majority of cases of consensus that have been reached by jurists in the history of Muslim jurisprudence.

On the other hand, there is the *ijmāʿ* of innovation, where scholars and jurists reach a consensus about a religious belief or religio-legal practice concerning matters not directly addressed by the scriptural sources. In this type of *ijmāʿ*, the religio-legal matter that is presented to the jurists is completely novel in that it has no explicit scriptural mention and yet jurists are able to reach unanimity about the sanction or lack thereof for such a belief or practice in the religion.

This type of consensus, which did not have a direct scriptural basis – although it is said to have indirect roots in scriptural injunctions – occurred with much less frequency in the history of Islamic jurisprudence than the *ijmāʿ* of interpretation.[18] Yet most cases of this type of *ijmāʿ*

[16] Of course, there were some groups that were deemed fringe by the major Muslim sects, like perhaps the Ismāʿīlīs, that did not affirm the necessity of acting upon all of these pillars.

[17] See, for example, the prophetic tradition (*ḥadīth*) found in the collection of al-Bukhārī, 1:11, *ḥadīth* #8. Dār Ṭawq al-Najāh, 1422 AH: "Islam is founded on five things: declaring that there is no god but God and that Muḥammad is His messenger, establishing prayers, giving alms, pilgrimage (*ḥajj*), and fasting Ramaḍān." *Ḥadīth* cited from Shamela Library software (version. 3.61). Translation is mine.

[18] As an example of this type consensus, Ibn Ḥazm, in his work *Marātib al-Ijmāʿ* (Levels of consensus) in the chapter on "al-Sabq wa-l-ramy" (chapter on racing and archery), says that there is no disagreement among jurists on the permissibility of giving prizes for horse racing. Retrieved from the Shamela Library program (version 3.61), January 6, 2015).

were more confined to a unanimous agreement among jurists ascribing to a certain school of jurisprudence or *madhhab* rather than a consensus reached by all the jurists of Islam. This point is evident from the fact that each school has issues for which jurists of that school converge upon one and the same opinion, while jurists from other schools hold a different opinion on the same issues.

The second major concept critical for the development of the synthesis in Islamic legal discourse that took place in the third/ninth and fourth/tenth centuries is the transformation of the legal concept of *qiyās* (analogy). In the pre-Shāfiʿī period, arguments from qiyās were undifferentiated and those types of arguments were subsumed under the all-inclusive category of *raʾy* (legal opinion) or *ijtihād* (legal effort/reasoning). These categories included all juridical conclusions that were not directly stated by authoritative texts and/or were not established religio-legal practices of particular regions but rather were based on personal reasoning instead (see Figure 9).[19] We can see that *qiyās* was employed in the first century of Islam in the form of the *a fortiori* argument seen in the following legal judgments: Wine is prohibited to drink; therefore, although less offensive, it is also prohibited to sell.[20]

In the middle of second/eighth century, the Iraqi school (read Abū Ḥanīfa and his protégés) began to use the term qiyās to mean a more systematic reasoning about the law and drawing legal parallels between legal cases,[21] as we saw in the case of Abū Ḥanīfa's legal reasoning in his fatwas examined in the previous chapter. The manner of usage of qiyās in this period shows that it was increasingly becoming differentiated from the more general application of legal opinion signified by the term *raʾy*.[22] Still, at this stage, Iraqi jurists did not mean by the term qiyās the very structured operation that the term would eventually connote when later defined by post-Shāfiʿī legal theorists.[23]

One example of this rudimentary understanding of qiyās comes from the Iraqi jurist al-Shaybānī, one of the protégés of Abū Ḥanīfa. The Medinan school critiqued Abū Ḥanīfa's legal position that laughter not only invalidates ritual prayer (*ṣalāh*) but also invalidates the state of ritual purification (*wuḍūʾ*) that is a precondition for prayer. Al-Shaybānī

[19] Hallaq, 2005, 114–115.

[20] Hallaq, 2005, 115–116.

[21] Ansari, 165, and Hasan, 1970, 140. See also El Shamsy, 22–28 for the evolution of *raʾy* reasoning within the early Iraqi school.

[22] Ansari, 269–270, and Hasan, 1970, 140–141.

[23] Hasan, 1970, 144.

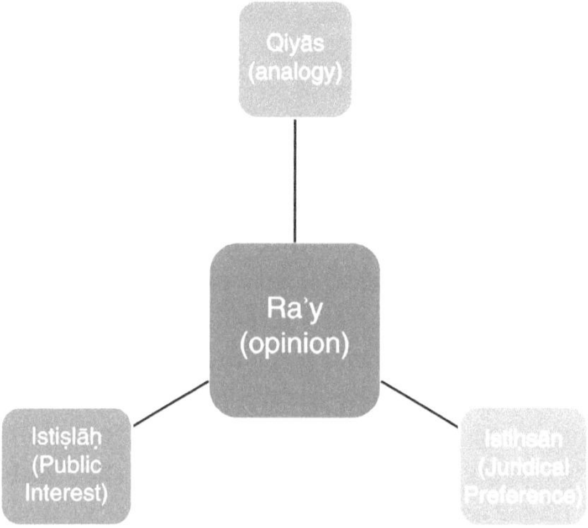

FIGURE 9 The fragmentation of *ra'y* into specialized forms of legal reasoning

seems to agree with the Medinan position, against his own school, that laughter does not invalidate ritual purification by saying that even if there were no *athar* (authoritative precedent) on this issue that would decisively decide the case, qiyās (read reason) would necessitate that one adopt the Medinan position.[24] We can see from this usage that qiyās was still a far cry from the very formal operation it would become in later legal theory.

By the time of al-Shāfiʿī toward the end of the second/eighth century, as qiyās was becoming more distinguished from other forms of *ra'y/ ijtihād*, it gained greater acceptability from some members of the traditionist camp. For those who were more committed to the sustained implementation of *ḥadīth* like al-Shāfiʿī, qiyās became an acceptable form of *ra'y/ijtihād*,[25] as opposed to other forms of legal arguments considered in the category of *ra'y* (e.g., *istiḥsān*) that were rejected by this group[26] (see Figure 11).

[24] Hasan, 1970, 143. The case is but one example that speaks against El Shamsy's seemingly totalizing interpretation of the character of all Islamic legal practice prior to al-al-Shāfiʿī as being communal and/or regional in scope (El Shamsy, 85 and 177). Indeed, this case and many others show that scholars from different regions were willing to forgo their regional and communal practice if presented with sufficient evidence to the contrary. For more on this assertion, see Stodolsky, 283–284.

[25] See al-Shāfiʿī, *al-Risāla*, "Qiyās," 289–290.

[26] See al-Shāfiʿī, *al-Risāla*, "Istiḥsān," 305, where he rejects *istiḥsān*. See also Hallaq, 2005, 117.

Al-Shāfiʿī's conception of *ijtihād* was that it was limited to qiyās, as he states unequivocally in his famous treatise *al-Risāla*.[27] This delimiting of *ijtihād* was an obvious move to narrow the scope of *raʾy* (reason/opinion), specifically as practiced in the form of *istiṣlāḥ* (public interest or common good) and *istiḥsān* (juristic preference) as forms of legal reasoning that did not directly rely on scriptural evidence. This emphasis on textuality was the new paradigm on which al-Shāfiʿī wanted the law to solely rely,[28] and qiyās was one of the primary means of extending the scope of this textuality, its relevance, and its jurisdiction to new socio-legal issues.

Al-Shāfiʿī provides a justification for this stance on *ijtihād* in *al-Risāla* where he says that one cannot pursue *ijtihād* (independent reasoning) without seeking the proper means (*dalāʾil*, or indications/proofs) by which that reasoning can take place and that *qiyās* is exactly that form of proper reasoning.[29] This is because al-Shāfiʿī believed that one cannot rationalize without some established principle (reasoning does not take place in a vacuum; it has established premises) and, based on those original principles, one extends a judgment to something else that shares characteristics (or what he called *maʿnā*) with the original principle (premise/case).[30]

Put more figuratively, al-Shāfiʿī likens the behavior of the jurist in his legal reasoning to that of a buyer/seller in the market, saying that just as the purchaser needs to assess at least two things (lit. qualities: *maʿnayayn*) before making a purchase from the market – namely, the intrinsic worth of the product and the value of similar products on the market – before determining its value, so too does the jurist need to assess the case presented to him and seek its likeness in other cases that have been already established before determining his judgment on it.[31] So it seems that for al-Shāfiʿī, all reasoning (*ijtihād*) has its basis in analogical reasoning (qiyās), where there is something that is already established [in this legal scenario: either scripture or an original legal case based on scripture] and what applies to that established case by analogy (qiyās) is extended to other cases that share an essential characteristic (*maʿnā*) with it (see Figure 11).

27 See al-Shāfiʿī, *al-Risāla*, 288, where al-Shāfiʿī unequivocally states this point. See Abū Zahra, 455, where he quotes a passage from al-Shāfiʿī's *Risāla* stating this point; see also Hallaq, 1999, 23.

28 This claim is the fundamental point that El Shamsy extensively argues for in his work *Canonization of Islamic Law* (2013).

29 Al-Shāfiʿī, *al-Risāla*, 505.

30 Abū Zahrah 457.

31 See al-Shāfiʿī, *al-Risāla*, 506–507, where he makes such an argument. See also Abū Zahra, 457.

In the post-Shāfiʿī period, with the exception of the ultra-traditionists like the Ẓāhirīs and some Shīʿī schools like the Ithnā ʿAshariyya (Twelver Shīʿī), we see greater acceptance of qiyās as a valid way to derive Islamic law at least among Sunnī traditionists. But its greater acceptance as a valid means of employing rationality in the derivation of law becomes limited only to two cases: when there is a new case about which the revealed texts are silent or when there is a new case on which no *ijmāʿ* (consensus) has been reached by the scholars.[32]

Yet even after the acceptance of qiyās by most camps of the debate in the early period, the concept still underwent an evolution. For example, al-Shāfiʿī established that the operation of qiyās was based on a rationale, which he called *maʿnā* (characteristic/attribute/quality), shared between the scenario that had a textually established legal injunction and the new situation that was not directly addressed by scripture. But during the transformation of legal discourse after al-Shāfiʿī, this rationale was no longer dubbed *maʿnā* and was later denoted by the term *ʿilla* (legal cause), which was a more clearly defined concept than its predecessor and played a more explicit role in legitimating the operations of qiyās. For example, al-Shāfiʿī never defined precisely what he meant by the term *maʿnā*, which he claimed was the shared characteristic between the two cases that legitimated the analogy (qiyās) between them.

On the other hand, in post-Shāfiʿī legal theory, the *ʿilla* was defined as that essential characteristic of the original case that was the effective cause that substantiated a particular ruling. The existence of this characteristic in new cases becomes the reason for the extension of that ruling in original case to those new cases that share that characteristic (*ʿilla*).[33] Moreover, the operations of qiyās become more technically defined in this post-Shāfiʿī period, as later legal theorists insisted that qiyās must contain four essential elements in order to be qiyās proper (see Figure 10):

1) A new legal case not addressed by the scriptures (Quran and *ḥadīth*) or *ijmāʿ* (consensus).
2) An old legal case that was resolved by recourse to the norms of scripture or *ijmāʿ* (consensus).
3) The legal cause (*ʿilla*) shared by both cases, which ties them together conceptually.

32 Hallaq, 2005, 141.

33 Illustrations of this formulation of *ʿilla* will be given in the subsequent pages once the operations of the newly formulated concept of *qiyās* have been defined.

4) The inference by which the ruling of the old case is now applied to the new case based on the legal attribute (*ʿilla*) shared by the two cases (Figure 10).[34]

In this way, *qiyās* became the premier analytic procedure that helped mediate the tension between human rationality and revelation/tradition that had existed between the more rationally inclined *ahl al-raʾy* and the more scripturally inclined *ahl al-ḥadīth*. *Qiyās* delineated the proper role rationality would play in respect to the established scripture/tradition in the socio-legal sense: by interpreting and extending the relevance of scripture to new situations. This device bridged the dichotomy between reason and revelation (Figure 11).

However, unlike al-Shāfiʿī, who felt that qiyās was the only legitimate source of law after scripture (Quran and *ḥadīth*) and consensus (*ijmāʿ*), some jurists, while accepting qiyās, felt nevertheless that limiting jurisprudential deductions to those reached by the procedure of qiyās severely constrained legal possibilities. Hence, they advocated the inclusion of other legal procedures that would rectify in their opinion undesirable legal conclusions reached by qiyās and would expand the scope of the production of legal judgments. Among the two main legal tools that this latter group of jurists advocated were the legal concepts of *istiḥsān* (juristic preference) and *istiṣlāḥ* (arguments of public interest or the common good).

Counter to al-Shāfiʿī's reproach of *istiḥsān*, ḥanafī jurists in the fourth and fifth centuries AH responded that *istiḥsān* as used by

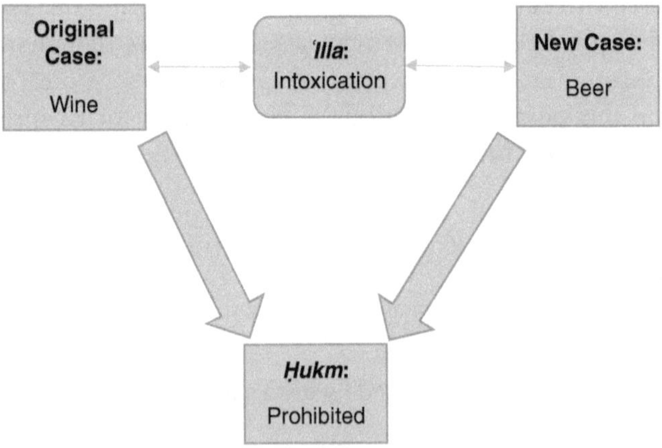

FIGURE 10 Illustration of the operation of *qiyās* (analogy)

34 Hallaq, 2005, 141.

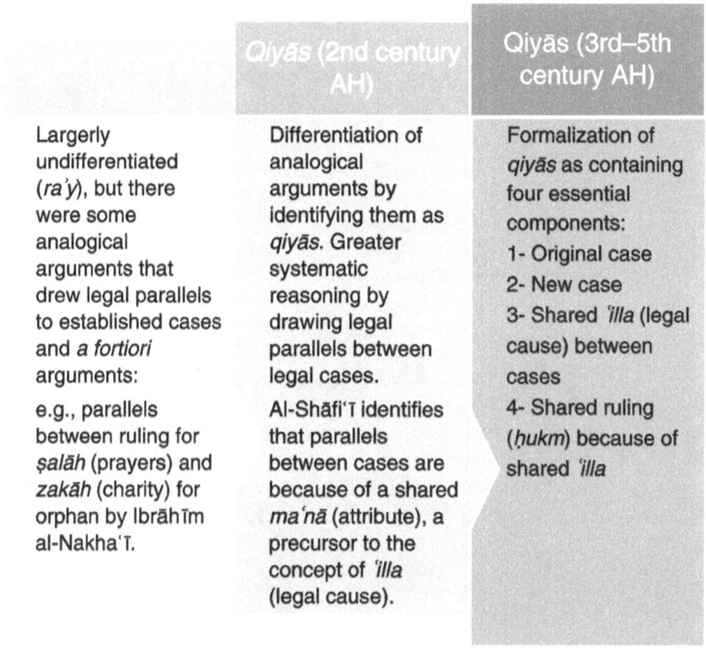
Qiyās (2nd century AH)
Qiyās (3rd–5th century AH)
Largerly undifferentiated (ra'y), but there were some analogical arguments that drew legal parallels to established cases and a fortiori arguments:
e.g., parallels between ruling for ṣalāh (prayers) and zakāh (charity) for orphan by Ibrāhīm al-Nakha'ī.
Differentiation of analogical arguments by identifying them as qiyās. Greater systematic reasoning by drawing legal parallels between legal cases.
Al-Shāfi'ī identifies that parallels between cases are because of a shared ma'nā (attribute), a precursor to the concept of 'illa (legal cause).
Formalization of qiyās as containing four essential components:
1- Original case
2- New case
3- Shared 'illa (legal cause) between cases
4- Shared ruling (ḥukm) because of shared 'illa

FIGURE 11 The evolution of *qiyās* (textually based analogical reasoning)

second-/eighth-century jurists of the Iraqi school was not a form of arbitrary judgment based on the whimsical preferences of particular jurists,[35] as al-Shāfiʿī had alleged. Rather, it was a legal mechanism for replacing a less desirable ruling that was based on *qiyās*[36] for another ruling that seems better even when it lacked explicit textual (scriptural) evidence or formal reasoning.[37] According to the advocates of *istiḥsān*, on some occasions *qiyās* produced undesirable results, hence necessitating that jurists make adjustments in their rulings so as to mitigate these undesired consequences when strictly adhering to *qiyās* (see Figure 12).

But to alleviate the critique of arbitrariness that al-Shāfiʿī and others claimed about *istiḥsān*, these later Ḥanafīs argued that *istiḥsān* did not arbitrarily obviate the consequences of *qiyās*, but particularized (*takhṣīṣ*) its scope. As we mentioned earlier, at the very heart of analogical reasoning of *qiyās* was the legal cause (ʿ*illa*) that was shared by both the original ruling derived from textual indicators and the new case that needed a

[35] Zysow, 400.
[36] Zysow, 399.
[37] Zysow, 399–400.

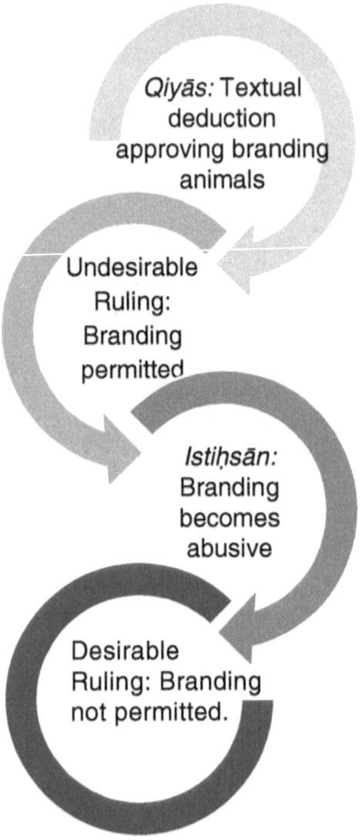

FIGURE 12 Early process of employing *istiḥsān* (juristic preference)

ruling (*ḥukm*). The ruling (*ḥukm*) of the original case was analogically extended to the new case based on their shared legal cause (*ʿilla*) as well as all other cases that shared this attribute.

An example where ḥanafīs felt that *istiḥsān* should modify a ruling reached by *qiyās* was in the case of predatory animals and predatory birds. Scriptural evidence established that the flesh of predatory animals is ritually impure; therefore, its consumption is prohibited. By analogy, then, Muslim jurists prohibited the consumption of predatory birds because they share the same legal cause, or *ʿilla*, of being predatory beasts and thus are ritually impure to consume. Also, food left behind by a predatory bird should by analogy be considered ritually impure and prohibited for consumption, since that was the case for a carcass left behind by a predatory animal. But according to juristic preference (*istiḥsān*), the food left behind by predatory birds is lawful to consume[38] (see Figure 13).

The reason given for this was that when predatory animals eat, their impurity is transmitted to the food through the saliva in their mouths.

[38] Hallaq, 1997, 109.

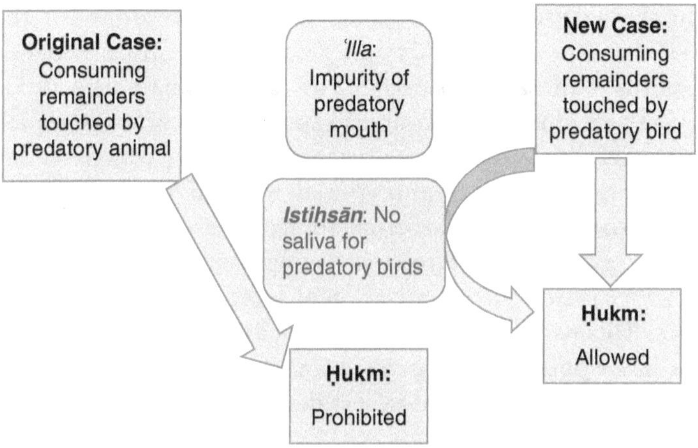

FIGURE 13 Later formulation of the relationship between *istiḥsān* (juristic preference) and *qiyās* (analogical reasoning)

Predatory birds, on the other hand, eat by means of their beaks, which are made of bone that remains dry while they eat; hence, no bird saliva is transmitted to the prey. Therefore, jurists modified the legal conclusions that would have been reached by *qiyās* (the prohibition of consumption of food that had been touched by predatory birds) to reach another conclusion that was reasoned through *istiḥsān* (the lawfulness of eating food touched/eaten by a predatory bird).[39]

So, what the proponents of *istiḥsān* claimed was that it did not obviate all the implications of the *qiyās* in question, but it merely particularized the scope of its legal cause (*ʿilla*) so that its consequences (the ruling, or *ḥukm*) would apply in certain situations and not in others due to some impediment (*mānīʿ*) that prevented consequences of that legal cause from being transposed to the case in question.[40] This operation was dubbed as *takhṣīṣ al-ʿilla* (particularizing the legal cause), and Ḥanafīs saw that this rationale is what lay at the core of the operations of *istiḥsān*.[41] Hallaq summarizes the operation of *takhṣīṣ al-ʿilla* in the following manner:

> Limitation occurs when the reasoner argues that the ratio of a case X and the rule generated by X is Y, but due to an impediment (*mānīʿ*) existing in the case, X is restricted in its scope; the resultant being the rule that is not Y but Z.[42]

[39] Hallaq, 1997, 109–110.
[40] Zysow, 403. See also Hallaq, 1997, 109.
[41] Zysow, 404.
[42] Hallaq, 1997, 110.

It was in this way that later Ḥanafīs were able to argue for the legitimacy of the notion of *istiḥsān* as a reasonable legal hermeneutical device and not an arbitrary practice as al-Shāfiʿī had alleged. Of course, they had to argue why recourse to such a legal tool was needed to rectify negative legal conclusions reached by *qiyās*, which by this period was emerging as the quintessential form of legal reasoning among many jurists and legal theorists. So, *istiḥsān* was reformulated not as the arbitrary negation of *qiyās* as its opponents had portrayed it but rather as a measured particularization of some of the legal implications of *qiyās*. This particularization was seen as a necessary intervention because if the operations of *qiyās* were left unmodified in certain circumstances, then that may lead to less desirable legal consequences in some cases.

Istiṣlāḥ (arguments of public interest or common good), on the other hand, was less controversial than *istiḥsān* among the early jurists and legal theorists largely because it was not defined as counter-*qiyās* in the same way that *istiḥsān* had been, hence leaving less of a debate about its legitimacy among the *qiyās*-favoring jurists and theorists. Nevertheless, the legal concept of *istiṣlāḥ* (arguments of public interest) also needed some legitimation since it too seemed like a form of non-scriptural legal reasoning, which was coming under increasing scrutiny by later generations of jurists, especially those jurists who wanted to maintain scriptural/textual hegemony over the law (i.e., those who inclined toward this orientation were the advocates of *ḥadīth*).

The point here is that the advocates of the legal principle of *istiṣlāḥ* (sometimes referred to as *maṣlaḥa mursala*) propose that new legal rulings can be generated by reference to this principle without explicitly relating the law to some established scripturally based injunction.[43] The basis of the newly proposed ruling would be an appeal to general legal principles that are rationally deduced and are purported to be the aims of the law (*maqāṣid al-sharīʿa*).[44] The idea here is that the whole enterprise of Islamic law is based on a set of legal principles that are inferred from the details of scripturally based legal rulings, and it is these general legal principles that the law is said to be serving.

Even when most jurists and legal theorists agreed that the purpose in the promulgation of Islamic laws was to achieve some utility or public good, many of them still were not completely comfortable with the idea

43 See Hallaq, 1997, 112, and Zysow, 394–395.

44 See Hallaq, 1997, 112.

that legal injunctions could be legislated entirely from general legal principles without some direct or indirect reference to the text/scripture. This was especially the case given the growing domination of the textualist paradigm on the outlook of Muslim jurists.[45]

Nevertheless, *istiṣlāḥ* did not suffer from the same stigma from which *istiḥsān* suffered in that it was not explicitly defined as a counterbalancing mechanism to *qiyās* and hence did not seem directly to oppose legal conclusions reached through *qiyās*. This helped *istiṣlāḥ* achieve greater acceptability among later Muslim jurists and theorists than did *istiḥsān*, but because of the lack of formal structure in this type of argumentation and the open-ended juristic possibilities that could be reached by its implementation, it never won explicit universal recognition by all schools of Islamic legal thought as an independent legal methodology to establish laws.

Ultimately, it would be only *qiyās* (analogical reasoning) and *ijmāʿ* (consensus) that gained universal acceptability among the surviving Sunnī schools of law and some Shīʿī sects like the Zaydī school as extra-scriptural means/sources of deducing law.[46] Other forms of legal reasoning like *istiḥsān* and *istiṣlāḥ* never reached the same level of acceptability as *qiyās* and *ijmāʿ*, but were nevertheless legitimated by some juristic schools like the Ḥanafī and Mālikī schools and legal theorists and not by others. Islamic legal theory, or what was termed *uṣūl al fiqh* (lit. the sources of law), came to be comprised of some universally accepted elements and other methodologies that were disputed among different camps of law.

In the end, Islamic legal theory was comprised of a blend of scriptural and extra-scriptural sources and methodologies for deriving Islamic law. On a scriptural level, all schools of law, whether Sunnī, Shīʿī, or other, accepted that the Quran and prophetic practice (*sunna*) represented the undisputed substantive sources of Islamic law. On the extra-scriptural level, all surviving Sunnī schools of law also accepted *ijmāʿ* (juristic consensus) and *qiyās* (analogical reasoning) as being legitimate methodologies or sources from which Islamic legal injunctions might be produced. This rendered all other forms of legal reasoning that were developed in the second/eighth and third/ninth centuries partial and secondary in the refined formulation of Islamic legal theory (*uṣūl al-fiqh*) that matured by the fifth/eleventh century.

[45] See Hallaq, 1997, 112.
[46] Abū Zahra, 663.

Yet this whole excursion into the conceptual development of these legal principles was to show the very dialectic manner in which Islamic legal theory was formulated. This legal theory was devised out of the rudimentary legal concepts that began to circulate in the legal discussions of the second/eighth and third/ninth centuries and that were further differentiated and developed over the next several centuries with other legal concepts. But even more important than recognizing the differentiation process that took place in the evolution of Islamic legal theory is the recognition of the discursive origins of the formation of Islamic legal theory.

Islamic legal theory partially has its discursive origins in the process of *iftāʾ* and its by-product, the fatwa. Despite being influenced by other factors, Islamic legal theory in some ways grew organically out of the practice of fatwas of the previous centuries. In the first three centuries of Islam, the modes of legal reasoning employed in fatwas and other juristic discourses displayed embryonic legal concepts, and stemming from those discussions, a legal theory began to emerge. It was the methodologies that those early jurists employed that came to dominate the discussion of the proper means by which Islamic law could be pronounced. So, it was from the discursive activity of fatwa that elements of a legal theory were extracted and articulated.

Hence, we conclude from this that theoretical speculation about the law was an afterthought of actual legal practice as quintessentially represented by the practice of *iftāʾ* (the art of making fatwa). In other words, Islamic law was not formed as a product of explicitly articulated legal principles; rather it was the legal practices that ultimately determined the course of the law. This fact highlights the critical role that fatwas and *iftāʾ* played in the formation of Islamic law and how the very roots of this legal formation lie in this legal practice.

The Construction of Islamic Legal Doctrines and Schools

As much as the second/eighth and third/ninth centiuries legal activity played an integral role in the eventual establishment of a more sophisticated legal hermeneutics in the subsequent centuries, it also played an integral role in supplying many of the authoritative legal figures that would act as the starting point for the construction of Islamic legal schools, known as *madhāhib* (sing. *madhhab*). What do we mean by an Islamic legal school, or *madhhab*? A "school," in the intellectual sense, represents "persons who hold a common doctrine or accept the same teachings or follow the same method."[47] Hallaq defines the juristic *madhhab* of Islam as "a group of jurists and legists who are strictly loyal to a distinct, integral, and most importantly, collective legal doctrine attributed to an eponym, as master-jurists, so to speak, after whom the school is known to acquire particular, distinctive characteristics."[48]

In other words, persons belonging to a *madhhab* were those who followed a common legal doctrine that had its roots in the legal activity of a person or group of independent jurists. These master-jurists after whom the legal schools were named were often those jurists who had offered legal opinions in the second century like Abū Ḥanīfa, Mālik, and al-Shāfiʿī in the Sunnī legal tradition and Jaʿfar al-ṣādiq and Zayd ibn ʿAlī among Shīʿīs. There were schools that were formed around the figures of third-/ninth- and fourth-/tenth-century jurists like Dāwūd al-Ẓāhirī and Ibn Jarīr al-Ṭabarī; yet all of those legal schools did not survive for reasons that are probably too complex and not well understood to get into here.

What is clear is that schools that were formed around the figures of second-century jurists did have a lasting impact on the way the jurisprudence and the legal tradition of Islam developed, and this would have an impact on the way fatwas were issued from then on as will be shown.

Western academics dispute whether the eponyms of these schools can indeed be considered true founders of the schools of law as Muslim tradition asserts,[49] but this debate is immaterial to the argument being made here. What is important is that the schools of law in their final development became the fundamental institutions that determined the course of Islamic jurisprudence for the next millennium.

Nevertheless, one may assert that the authority that has been ascribed to these master-jurists may not have been totally capricious and may have been a result of the distinctive methodological awareness that they displayed in their legal activity and that was recognized by later jurists. This methodological distinctiveness served as the fundamental pillar from which the schools of jurisprudence were later constructed. This was shown in the previous chapter where the fatwas/rulings of second-century jurists and their legal debates employed distinctive legal methodologies and forms of legal reasoning to legitimate their fatwas.

47 See Hallaq, "From Regional to Personal Schools of Law? A Reevaluation," 2001, 5, where he quotes this dictionary definition of an intellectual school. See also Makdisi, 1981, 1, who defines a school in a similar manner.

48 Hallaq, 2005, 152.

49 See Hallaq, 2005, 158–161; Hallaq, 2003, 62; also Melchert's *The Formation of Sunnī Schools of Law* for an elaboration on this point.

The process of authority construction and the formation of legal schools in one particular case will be examined to see how a legal school arose from the embryonic discourses of earlier reputed master-jurists. To illustrate how these schools came into being, an outline of the construction process of the Ḥanafī *madhhab* from the third/ninth to the fifth/eleventh century will be taken up here.

In the third/ninth century, the Ḥanafī jurist Muḥammad ibn Shujāʿ al-Thaljī was instrumental in grounding legal opinions of the second-century predecessors of the Ḥanafī school (Abū Ḥanīfa, Abū Yūsuf, and Muḥammad al-Shaybānī) more centrally within the discourse of *sunna/ḥadīth* (prophetic practice)[50] as a way of legitimating these opinions within the increasingly synthesized *raʾy-ḥadīth* legal paradigm that was taking hold after al-Shāfiʿī. This is because not all legal opinions in the second century were necessarily rationalized or legitimated through the explicit use of scriptural sources such as the Quran and the prophetic traditions. In many cases, it was just assumed that the jurists were indeed grounding their legal opinions within the scriptural sources and/or legal precedent (*athar*). With the growing ideological push toward explicit grounding of opinion in *ḥadīth*, these assumptions were no longer acceptable. This situation brought about a growing inclination among legal specialists who leaned toward certain master-jurists to explicitly ground the legal opinions and practices of these master jurists within the discourse of *ḥadīth*.

This movement toward grounding legal opinions within the universalizing discourse of *sunna/ḥadīth* was greatly facilitated by the appearance of exclusive compilations of prophetic traditions (*ḥadīth*) in the third/ninth century (e.g., the collections of al-Bukhārī and Muslim). The existence of these compilations allowed for the legal opinions that were prevalent in certain regions (Kufa and Medina, for example) to now be grounded in the recently proliferating discourse of *ḥadīth* instead of their own local legal precedent, which had access to certain prophetic practices and not others.[51]

But at the same time, the proliferation of the prophetic *sunna* in the form of *ḥadīth*, in contradistinction to other forms of traditions and precedence, itself was reflexively caused by the growing ideological prestige

[50] Hallaq, 2005, 126–127. It should be noted that al-Shaybānī's works already show a greater concern than those of his predecessors with ḥadīth as proof texts, as in his *Kitâb al-Ḥujjah 'alâ ahl al-Madînah*, as well as his version of *al-Muwaṭṭa'*. I am thankful to Dr. Khalid Blankinship for this astute observation.

[51] See Hallaq 108–109 for a similar argument.

of *ḥadīth* among second-century jurists such as al-Shāfiʿī as the ultimate source of law after the Quran. This was seen to be the case even when *ḥadīth* did not possess an absolutely certain pedigree like those with a singular chain of transmission (*āḥād*); a criterion – which we demonstrated in the previous chapter – that early Ḥanafī and Māliki jurists insisted upon before modifying their regionally established legal practice and precedent. Because of people like al-Shāfiʿī, *ḥadīth* was now becoming the sole substantive source of Islamic legislation aside from the Quran. The growing appeal of the position of advocates of *ḥadīth* (*ahl al-ḥadīth*) was possibly due to the fact that prophetic *sunna* was something that was universally accepted among all legal authorities in the different regions of the then Muslim world, in contrast to other forms of *sunan* (practices/precedence) that might have been authoritative in one place and not another (e.g., Mālik's notion of *ʿamal ahl al-Madînah* or "the practice of the people of Medina").

Hence, the prophetic *sunna* as discursively embodied in *ḥadīth* was seen as an attractive epistemological starting point from where the variant legal practices and doctrines that were prevalent in various places could converge to create a universal legal doctrine that would unify Muslim religious practice. In other words, the ideological push toward *ḥadīth* fed the growing movement of *ḥadīth* compilations, which in turn fed the growing movement toward *ḥadīth* conformity.[52]

But the idea behind this push toward coalescing legal opinions within the discourse of *ḥadīth* was not to necessarily completely reformulate the juristic opinions of the second-/eighth-century jurists to fit the letter of the *sunna/ḥadīth*, but to show how the diversity of legal opinions was consistent with this prophetic practice or *sunna*[53] as represented in *ḥadīth* and that the divergence found in these legal opinions as pronounced by these second-/eighth-century master jurists stemmed from a different understanding and application of the *sunna/ḥadīth* to the various legal scenarios. Hence, the various legal factions could legitimately claim to have a consensus on what constituted the basis of the law (*uṣūl al-fiqh*) and at the same time have divergent views about its implications.[54]

Let us now examine how this legal reformulation played out in the construction of the Ḥanafī school of law. If the push toward grounding and consolidating legal opinions of master jurists within the discourse

[52] See Hallaq, 2005, 76, who concurs with the final point.

[53] Wheeler, 72.

[54] Wheeler, 74–75.

of *ḥadīth* was accelerating in the third/ninth century by jurists who had Ḥanafī leanings like al-Thaljī, this process was continued by figures like al-Ṭaḥāwī in the fourth/tenth century. Wheeler states: "According to al-Ṭaḥāwī the conflict of opinions is due either to authorities extracting different principles from different texts (read *ḥadīth*) or differently applying the same principle to new circumstances."[55]

Al-Ṭaḥāwī's works *Sharḥ Maʿānī al-āthār* and *Ikhtilāf al-Fuqahāʾ* tried to do just that by illustrating how second-/eighth-century jurists like Abū Ḥanīfa, Mālik, and al-Shāfiʿī interpreted and applied *ḥadīth* differently to arrive at their divergent legal conclusions. In addition, al-Ṭaḥāwī usually attempted to persuade the reader of the soundness of the position of the Ḥanafī jurists so as to show the legitimacy of their legal reasoning and interpretive scheme of the *sunna* and thereby the legal authoritativeness of Abū Ḥanīfa and his protégés as founders of a legal school.[56] In the same vein, the fourth-/tenth-century Quranic commentator with Ḥanafī leanings al-Jaṣṣāṣ carried out a similar program to al-Ṭaḥāwī's, by demonstrating in his work *Aḥkām al-Quran* how the legal opinions of the second-/eighth-century Ḥanafī jurists were consistent with the intent of the legal injunctions of the Quran.[57]

If third-/ninth- and fourth-/tenth-century jurists like al-Thaljī and al-Ṭaḥāwī focused their attention on showing how the legal opinions of Abū Ḥanīfa and his protégés Abū Yūsuf and al-Shaybānī were both grounded in and consistent with *ḥadīth*, fifth-/eleventh-century Ḥanafī-inclined legal theorists like al-Dabūsī (d. 430/1039) and al-Sarakhsī (d. 483/1090) had a different focus. They instead attempted to show how, on epistemological and methodological grounds, second-/eighth-century Ḥanafī jurists could diverge in their legal opinions from their counterparts like Mālik and al-Shāfiʿī despite sharing the same substantive and authoritative basis of the law (Quran, *sunna*/*ḥadīth*, *ijmāʿ*, and *qiyās*).

[55] Wheeler, 101. With parenthesis indicating additions by the author.

[56] See Wheeler, 100–109, for illustrations. This interpretation of al-Ṭaḥāwī's project draws a different conclusion from El Shamsy, who claims that later Ḥanafīs like al-Ṭaḥāwī were influenced by al-Shāfiʿī who began to uphold the authoritativeness of (disembedded) *ḥadīth* and bring the Ḥanafī school in line with that approach to the law. To support his view, El Shamsy claims that al-Ṭaḥāwī even uses the same argument (Quranic verse) that al-Shāfiʿī uses to argue for the authoritativeness of the sunna as a way of indicating that al-Ṭaḥāwī was influenced by al-Shāfiʿī (El Shamsy 2013: 206). But an alternative interpretation is that all such arguments merely became a part of the common stock of ideas that were used by the advocates of *ḥadīth* tradition, which al-Shāfiʿī and others (like al-Ṭaḥāwī) borrowed to bolster the support of this growing movement.

[57] See Wheeler, 109–112 for details.

In this way, these legal theorists were giving theoretical and methodological legitimation for the authoritativeness of Ḥanafī legal opinion and, by extension, legitimating the distinctiveness of this school of law.

For instance, al-Dabūsī states that the three foundational figures of the Ḥanafī *madhhab* – Abū Ḥanīfa, Abū Yūsuf, and al-Shaybānī – methodologically held that a *ḥadīth* of the Prophet with a single chain of transmission (*khabar aḥad*) was to be preferred to an injunction reached through *qiyās* to a more established scriptural source like the Quran, while Mālik held that *qiyās* to a more established scriptural source that has been transmitted recurrently (*mutawātir*) has greater authority than a prophetic *ḥadīth* with a single chain of transmission.[58]

This argument revolves around the epistemological principle that a prophetic report with a single chain of transmission only leads to speculative/indefinitive (*ẓannī*) knowledge, while a report that is transmitted recurrently (*mutawātir*) leads to definitive (*qāṭiʿ*) knowledge. So the central focus of the debate is whether to accept the legal implications of *ḥadīth* whose epistemological basis is less certain over the legal implications derived indirectly through analogy to a textual source (e.g., Quran or *ḥadīth* with a recurrent chain of transmission) that has a sounder epistemological basis. Although the *sunna/ḥadīth* is on a whole of greater authority in determining law than *qiyās*, nevertheless, not all *ḥadīth* were considered of equal epistemological value in determining law. Moreover, what this shows is that, among some of the jurists, an analogy to a better established scriptural source can be given greater authority than some *ḥadīth*.[59]

Al-Dabūsī illustrates how this methodological difference between the Ḥanafīs and Mālik leads to variant conclusions in the law even when they are in agreement with regard to the authoritative sources of the law: "Our companions (Abū Ḥanīfa and his protégés) say that semen is a

[58] Wheeler, 134.

[59] This is different from El Shamsy's assertion that the early Ḥanafīs only accepted a *ḥadīth* if it was embedded in regional community practice and that it was later Ḥanafīs like al-Ṭaḥāwī who incorporated disembedded *ḥadīth* into the Ḥanafī school, thus bringing about a convergence between the rationalist and traditional movements (El Shamsy 2013: 207). For the early Ḥanafīs at least, it was more a question of the epistemological authoritativeness of a disembedded *ḥadīth*, as I have shown earlier and as is argued here by al-Dabūsī, rather than whether a *ḥadīth* was embedded in communal tradition that determined whether a *ḥadīth* would influence religious practice. El Shamsy's assertation about embeddedness of *ḥadīth* in communal tradition is correct about Mālik's legal orientation, but he seems to overgeneralize this orientation to the Ḥanafīs, thereby giving greater prominence to al-Shāfiʿī's accomplishments.

physical impurity which must be purified by rubbing the [affected] cloth when it [the semen] is dry. We take this from a report (*ḥadīth*). According to Mālik, it is not purified except by washing with water, like [is the case with] urine."[60] As Wheeler points out: "The differences between Ḥanafīs and Mālik, in this case, are explained in terms of disagreement over the evaluation of the relative authority of the different sources."[61] In other words, Mālikīs discount the *āḥād ḥadīth* on semen in favor of a *qiyās* to the ruling on urine, which has been established in a text with higher epistemic authority than the reported *ḥadīth*.

What this shows is that even when there was a broad agreement on the general outlines of a legal theory (*uṣūl al-fiqh*) among the Sunnī legal factions[62] that gave a hierarchy to the authoritative sources of the law (Quran, *sunna/ḥadīth*, *ijmāʿ*, and *qiyās*), later jurists and theorists believed that some of the legal differences that existed among second/eighth-century jurists like Abū Ḥanīfa, Mālik, and al-Shāfiʿī came down to the legal approach and manner of application of these foundational sources of law rather than being genuine differences on what constituted the sources of the law.

These divergent approaches and methodologies that later legal theorists deduced from the earlier legal opinions ended up acting as the foundational principles of the different legal schools. So, as much as *uṣūl al-fiqh* was formulated to show the foundations of Islamic law in general, the methodological variations of how to approach those sources of the law are what constituted the foundations of the Islamic legal schools (*uṣūl al-madhhab*).[63] The core principles of these methodological foundations were seen as having been instituted by the second-/eighth-century jurists who became the madhhab predecessors of the legal schools.

The point here is that these second-/eighth-century jurists showed some methodological clarity and innovativeness in deriving Islamic law from the various scriptural and extra-scriptural sources, which gave them an aura of legal authoritativeness in subsequent generations that previous "proto-jurists" had never acquired despite their tremendous contributions to cultivating the law. Examples of their innovativeness were their appeals to legal concepts such as *qiyās*, *istiḥsān*, *istiṣlāḥ*, *ijmāʿ*, *ʿamal*,

[60] As quoted in Wheeler, 135. Materials in parenthesis are my additions to the text/translation.
[61] Wheeler, 135.
[62] Large portions of this legal theory were also accepted among some Shīʿite groups like the Zaydī school.
[63] More will be said about this later in this work.

etc., which were explicitly defined by them even when such concepts had been established and employed in earlier periods. The fact that these second-century and early third-century jurists were beginning to name their methodological devices for deriving the law was an indication of their efforts to theorize the law.[64] So, the way in which they theorized and applied these legal principles gave each of them a distinctiveness that was perhaps less clear in their predecessor's jurisprudence, which earned them the distinction of being seen as the founders of legal approaches that culminated in the founding of legal schools.

If Islamic legal theory (*uṣūl al-fiqh*) was the source of unity of Islamic law for jurists, the foundational principles/practices of the schools (*uṣūl al-madhhab*) were definitely a source of distinction and legitimation of the divergent legal procedures and judgments. Rationalizing these differences allowed for diversity within the law that could accommodate manifold situations without constricting legal possibilities. Chapter 4 will explore in greater detail these legal approaches and methodological considerations that defined the different legal schools.

As a final note, it should be asserted here that in the same way that Islamic legal theory (*uṣūl al-fiqh*) was derived from the actual jurisprudential practices of earlier Muslim jurists, the foundational legal principles/practices (*uṣūl al-madhhab*, lit. foundation of the school) and legal doctrines that came to comprise and define the legal schools were also products of the same jurisprudential practices, for which fatwas represented the discursive traces. The preservation of these fatwas allowed later generations of jurists and legal theorists to abstract these general legal principles even when earlier jurists did not always explicitly articulate them in their own jurisprudential rationalizations. Yet, these legal rationalizations and discursive practices remained embedded in their legal conclusions (fatwas).

So, fatwas were crucial to the formation of Islamic law and its institutions. But even if fatwas played a fundamental role in the formation of these disciplines and institutions, once these institutions came into being, they altered the course of fatwas ever after. Because of the formation of the legal institutions such as legal theory and legal schools, the process of *iftāʾ* (fatwa-making) took on a slightly different character in that its ad hoc character in the previous period became much more structured once this legal tradition became fully formed and operative in the later period. This will also be examined in greater detail in the following chapter.

[64] See Alparslan, pg. 91, who argues that naming of activities and concepts is an important stage in the development of a discipline.

Fatwa as the Substantive Basis of Islamic Legal Doctrines

In the last two sections, the development of Islamic legal theory (i.e., *uṣūl al-fiqh*) and Islamic legal schools (*madhāhib*) was charted, showing how fatwa played an integral role in those two formations. In this section, a mapping of the process of formation of Islamic legal doctrines will be undertaken, showing how previous fatwas/rulings were the raw materials from which these doctrines were formulated.

It is apparent by now that Islamic law was not simply an outgrowth of official legal institutions like the activity of judges and courts, but primarily the growth of independent activities of Muslim jurists (*faqīhs* or *muftīs*) who tried to address people's day-to-day problems in terms of the ethical precepts of Islam. So unlike Western case law, legal judgments of the courts do not comprise the substantive portion of Islamic law. Islamic law was not produced by government-sanctioned activity conducted by representatives of the state such as judges and legal pronouncements of courts. Rather, jurisprudential production in Muslim history on a whole lay outside the confines of the state.[65]

Instead, independent jurists elaborated Islamic law by providing their legal rulings (fatwas) on various social and religious matters. After amassing a critical mass of fatwas, the jurists were able to synthesize these fatwas into a legal doctrine that would regulate Muslim religious practice, ranging from ritual practice to the economy.[66] Historically speaking, the classic Islamic legal corpus as represented in legal compendiums (*fiqh*) did not just spring up at once early in this history of Islam, as we have no legal text dating back to the first or early second century of Islam as we do in the case of fatwas dating back to these periods.[67] Furthermore, logically speaking, it is presumed that the corpus of Islamic legal doctrines, or *fiqh*, must have been constituted from primordial legal matter that served as its substantive source.

[65] Hallaq, 1994, 56–57.

[66] Hallaq, 1994, 55.

[67] One can argue that the legal works from the second century of Islam such as Mālik's *al-Muwaṭṭa'*, al-Shaybānī's *Kitāb al-Āthār*, and al-Shāfi'ī's *Kitāb al-Umm* are essentially books of fatwa. Even if they were historically not designated as books of fatwa, they are in fact just that since they contain the legal rulings of these jurists and the jurists of previous generations, which has been loosely defined as fatwa in the introduction of this work. The content of these works is certainly closer to resembling fatwas than *fiqh* in both their substance and structure since they represented independent legal rulings of those jurists of those times that had not attained primacy and bindingness, like *fiqh*, until later periods. Hence, these rulings started off like fatwas and later were integrated into *fiqh* by means of a process that will be demonstrated in this section.

The legal compendiums that later came into being were a result of the increasing sophistication of Islamic civilization and the need for more standardized sources of information that could answer peoples' religious/legal questions.

Fatwas are the logical and historic link to the development of Islamic legal doctrines that came in the form of *fiqh* compendiums. This is because when a critical mass of fatwas was reached and those fatwas became legally authoritative among Muslim jurists, they must have felt a need to synthesize these disparate fatwas into coherent legal texts for didactic purposes of teaching and disseminating the law. This indicates that the very substance of Islamic law partly arose from the activity of producing fatwas, which indicates a relationship of dependence of standardized law on this type of jurisprudential activity (*iftā'*).

Yet the argument for a relationship between fatwa and the growth of Islamic legal doctrine is not solely based on logic; there is historical evidence that Muslim jurists incorporated fatwas in their authorship of Islamic law compendiums. Here is some of the evidence:

1. The famous Ḥanafī jurist al-Nasafī stated that he included fatwas in his legal manual Kanz al-daqā'iq.[68]
2. The Mālikī jurist al-Ḥaṭṭāb included hundreds of fatwas of Ibn Rushd al-Jadd[69] and al-Burzulī in his commentary on the foundational Mālikī text al-Mukhtaṣar of Khalīl ibn Isḥāq.[70]
3. The Shāfiʿī jurist al-Nawawī is also reported to have included fatwas in his commentary on al-Muhadhdhab.[71]

Not all aspects of fatwas were fit for inclusion in the legal corpus of Islamic law (*fiqh* compendiums) because of the didactic and reference-like quality of these legal manuals. So an assimilation process was established where fatwas would be formatted to accommodate the structure of these legal texts. There were two ways by which fatwas were synthesized into an Islamic legal corpus: *tajrīd* and *talkhīṣ*. This two-fold process is as follows:

1. Tajrīd (abstracting): stripping the fatwa of elements that were not necessary for the works of legal doctrine. This might include the reasoning that a muftī (jurist consult) would have given to support the fatwa or the names of the parties mentioned in the fatwa.

[68] Hallaq, 1994, 40.
[69] The grandfather of the Muslim philosopher and jurist Ibn Rushd.
[70] Hallaq, 1994, 41.
[71] Hallaq, 1994, 41.

These were extraneous details not appropriate to include in legal compendia that represented the various legal doctrines.[72]

2. Talkhīṣ (abridgment): summarizing important elements of the fatwa such as documents that were included in the fatwa and are integral to understanding its context.[73]

But not all fatwas of jurists finally ended up in the legal compendiums that codified the doctrines of the legal schools; so which fatwas were included in this legal literature? Generally speaking, there were several criteria that helped jurists decide that certain fatwas should be universally accepted and included in the *fiqh* compendia. The medieval Muslim jurist al-Awazajandī listed some of these criteria:

1. Relevance: whether the fatwas were relevant to the society for which the jurist authoring the *fiqh* compendium was writing.[74]
2. Need: if it was determined that the issue handled by the fatwa needed to be known by ordinary people for their religious practice.[75]
3. Frequency: This point is a product of the other two criteria, but the way in which jurists can determine whether certain fatwas were needed and relevant to the context was by the frequency with which the fatwas were issued on a particular matter.[76]

Through such legal processes of inclusion, conversion, and synthesis of the fatwas of early master-jurists and subsequent major jurists, later Muslim jurists established legal doctrines that guided and informed the religious practice of the Muslim community. These legal doctrines took the pedagogic form of legal compendia that standardized the major doctrines of the legal schools. So, fatwas were one of the sources that formed the substantive basis of Islamic law by providing the basic legal material from which Islamic legal doctrines were formulated.

DISCURSIVE LEGAL ACTIVITY AND THE FORMATION OF A MUSLIM SOCIETY IN LATE ANTIQUITY

It can be argued that legal activity and practices in the forgoing chapters were not only fundamental to the formation of legal doctrines and institutions but were also a critical process to the formation of Islamic society

[72] Hallaq, 1994, 44–45.
[73] Hallaq, 1994, 45.
[74] Hallaq, 1994, 49.
[75] Hallaq, 1994, 49.
[76] Hallaq, 1994, 49.

itself. From the very inception of the Islamic community in Medina, a legal charter was established to govern the relationship between the various groups constituting that ethnically and religiously diverse community. So, from the very beginning, the Islamic vision drew a connection between law and society that was mediated by the agency of the state. Over the course of time, the Muslim state began to lose its legitimacy among some groups in the nascent Muslim community as a result of civil wars and usurpation of power by agents who were less inclined to pursue that Islamic vision, which led to a crisis among those groups of Muslims who were committed to that original vision.

As the hope for establishing religiously sanctioned government faded among those committed to an Islamic vision, it became clear to some that alternative methods had to be resorted to in order to salvage what remained of that vision and reconstitute the unity of the Muslim community in spite of the political division and the sociological challenge of cultural heterogeneity that were brought in by early and rapid expansion of the Muslim state.[77] For this group, the elaboration of legal norms was the means by which unity and purpose of the Muslim community could be maintained. By legitimating and advocating certain socio-religious norms and practices that would be commonly adhered to, they were forging a religio-legal basis for social cohesion.

But what precisely was the vision that they had sought in light of the seemingly insurmountable political challenges and the sectarian and social disunity that had become endemic in the community? The hallmark of this vision is epitomized in the Quranic phrase "People of the Book." This notion is used in the Quran as an epithet for Jews and Christians to show that which they have in common with Muslims, which was the possession of a revealed scripture that was the authoritative basis of the community. Moreover, this descriptor encapsulated an ideal for the foundation of these communities, which were largely based on knowledge and discursive learning as opposed to ethnic solidarity or political motivations.

[77] El Shamsy (2013: 4–5) supports this assertion by claiming that the impetus for what he calls the "canonization" of Islamic law was a crises of identity and authority experienced by the Muslim community that was rooted in the rapid spread of Islam that led to the "influx and rising prominence of new Muslim converts from diverse backgrounds ... and the dissolution of the tribal solidarity and ethnic homogeneity that had sustained the initial wave of expansion." My argument though does not center on the notion of "canonization" of texts as much as it centers on tradition formation, which instructs its practitioners on the appropriate discursive practices for interacting with such texts.

The fact that people were distinguished by reference to books meant that their communities were modeled on a framework of textual authority. This new conceptual framework played a large role in guiding the actions of those pietistic groups who sought to engender an alternative model of civilizational (ummatic) purpose and unity in the midst of political illegitimacy, religious sectarianism, and the prevailing cultural heterogeneity. In essence, what these groups attempted to do was to reconstitute the social milieu in Muslim-controlled lands in light of the new sources of knowledge and values as represented by the textual[78] authority of the Quran and in later times more definitively by the prophetic practice.[79]

In trying to establish a community based on a model of textual authority, what I have called here "the People of the Book" model, these pietistic groups were projecting the text (the Quran) onto the social world. This projection took the peculiar form of law as the primary embodiment of the values propounded by the text as the sort of social mechanism that could forge a basis for this new society in contradistinction to the order that was being imposed by the political establishment or the existing social realities. Moreover, by linking community to textuality, this model affirmed that the primary mode of rationality displayed by this society was what could be described as hermeneutical in character – a type of rationality that is bounded by an established body of knowledge where the main function of this (scriptural) rationality is to interpret this knowledge in such a way that links it to peoples' social world. Thus, it was a type of reasoning that was not solely based on pure reason or social convention.

[78] It should be understood that when textuality is invoked here, I simply mean a set of ideas or discursive statements that are ascribed to a definitive author(s). As is known, the Quran, for example, was not primarily transmitted in the form of a text in its early history; instead, it could be described initially as an oral document. Yet despite this oral form of transmission, the Quran describes itself as a book, hence expanding the definition of book (text) to fit the definition that I outlined earlier.

[79] El Shamsy (2013: 5) fundamentally concurs with this idea of a community centered around textual authority when he asserts that by seeking a new foundation for religious authority other than the established communal practice, canonization offered a way forward from regional, legal, and communal impasses by vesting authority in a fixed category of textual sources that could be the subject of analysis by religious experts. Yet it is my contention as I am arguing here that this canonization, El Shamsy's designated term for the evolving relationship of the early Muslim community with a set of texts, precedes the late second-century legal debates and arguably can be traced back to the inception of Islam itself. This assertion is the case if one has a fluid notion of textuality that includes a set of orally preserved and transmitted discourses that functioned as texts such as the early Quran and *ḥadīth* (see previous footnote for more on this notion of textuality).

The importance of hermeneutics in its mediating role of interpreting the implications of this textual authority gave rise to another form of authority that would have this mediating task: hermeneutical authority as represented by the early religious specialists and proto-jurists. Their precise function was to act as custodians of these textual authoritative sources by preserving and explicating the religious ramifications of these texts. As far as law was concerned, two hermeneutical approaches/parties developed early on representing this hermeneutical authority: the advocates of *raʾy* and the advocates of *athar* (being a material embodiment of traditionalism), with each approach being concentrated in certain regional centers.

The advocates of *raʾy* were the more reason and context-centered group of proto-jurists who were less conservative in their approach to the law. They approached legal issues using pragmatic and rational grounds when no explicit injunctions were found in the Quran or an "established"[80] prophetic practice or when injunctions deduced from these textual sources seemed to run counter to the broader aims of the norms advocated by those textually authoritative sources. This is not to say that they did not rely on the precedents of their regional religio-legal practice (e.g., Iraq), and in this sense, they too were traditionalist, but their legal practice was seemingly more heavily swayed toward rational and contextual considerations than that of other early groups.[81] One can say that the general interpretative approach of this party was inclined toward an intentionalist theory hermeneutics[82] where they sought to discover and implement whenever possible the intent behind the textual legal injunctions rather than stick to the formal letter of the text. Hence, this approach represented a heterogeneous approach to the formation of the legal corpus given that rationality is a culturally influenced faculty and hence varied from one region to another in this nascent Muslim society.

On the other hand, the advocates of *athar* were the more tradition-centered party that approached legal issues from the point of view of precedents set by previously established religious authorities, like the

[80] With the term "established," I am alluding to the Ḥanafī rejection of modifying what they considered established legal practice based on *ḥadīth*s that were supported by singular chains of transmission (*āḥād*), which I have discussed earlier.

[81] To highlight this rationalist streak, El Shamsy points (2013: 27) out that the *raʾy* approach of the Ḥanafīs favored widely accepted (*mashhūr*) prophetic reports that contained maxim-like rules that can be extended to a broad array of other similar cases.

[82] For more on the intentionalist theory hermeneutics, see Steven Mailloux's "Interpretation" pg. 123 in *Critical Terms for Literary Study*, ed. Lentricchia and McLaughlin. University of Chicago. Chicago: 1990.

practice of the Prophet, the early caliphs and the Companions of the Prophet, and those who came shortly after them. Their general interpretive approach inclined toward a formalist theory hermeneutics[83] where a more literal understanding of the textual sources and precedential practices were favored over the functionalist approaches of their adversaries. This approach was more conservative given that there was a specific and given body of knowledge to draw from in the formation of the legal corpus.[84]

The tensions between the two parties created by their varying approaches eventually created a marked transformation in the Islamic legal discourse. It was perhaps understood that the position of advocates of *raʾy* (pragmatists/rationalists) would not bring about the uniformity sought by the pietistic groups[85] within the diverse cultural milieu of the early Muslim state because of the naturally heterogeneous production of legal opinions that was inherent to the *raʾy* approach. The perceived advantage of the "*atharist*" (traditionalist) approach was that it would produce a more uniform code of law that would foster cultural unity among the heterogeneous ethnic and sectarian groups within Muslim society. In due time, the debate began to turn in the traditionalists' favor, and the notion of *raʾy* came under increasing attack by its opponents.

By the early beginning of the third/ninth century, the advocacy for tradition was increasingly moving away from the idea of regional legal precedents and morphing into a particular form of traditionalism marked by a more universally accepted precedent of *ḥadīth* and whose advocates became known as *ahl al-ḥadīth*. This movement distinguished itself by advocating for the sole legal authoritativeness of the practice of the Prophet to the exclusion of any other tradition. Although this movement increasingly gained ground on the advocates of *raʾy*, this did not mean that the *raʾy* approach was being completely abandoned. Some within this new reconstituted traditionalist camp saw some elements of the rationalist approach as being beneficial to the project of creating the new legal discourse that was to act as the foundation of the nascent Muslim community.

83 For more on the formalist theory hermeneutics, see Steven Mailloux's "Interpretation" pg. 123 in *Critical Terms for Literary Study*, ed. Lentricchia and McLaughlin. University of Chicago. Chicago: 1990.

84 This more conservative approach is highlighted in Mālik's critique of the *raʾy* approach where he claimed that it made legal opinions unstable because they were always susceptible to change when a better *raʾy* argument was furnished for another opinion. See El Shamsy 2013: 28.

85 Those groups who had a shared Islamic commitment for shaping early Muslim society, which included members from both the advocates of *raʾy* and the advocates of *athar*.

For instance, al-Shāfiʿī, as a self-proclaimed traditionalist albeit with rationalist tendencies, argued for the validity of *qiyās* (analogical reasoning) – which was employed by the advocates of *raʾy* and, as I have demonstrated earlier, particularly by the jurist Abū Ḥanīfa and his followers – as a valid legal method for generating laws for situations that were not directly legislated by the Quranic text or the prophetic practice as textually represented by *ḥadīth* reports. In making his argument for the legitimacy of *qiyās*, al-Shāfiʿī used the traditionalist approach by appealing to the Quranic text for its legitimation;[86] nonetheless, this does not take away from the fact that *qiyās* was one of the main legal devices used by the advocates of *raʾy*, and in arguing for its validity, he was accepting some of the rationalist methods into his own traditionalist approach. Yet, there were other legal methods employed by the advocates of *raʾy* that al-Shāfiʿī criticized as being capricious such as *istiḥsān* (juristic preference).

My point here is that the *raʾy* (rationalist) approach just did not disappear as a result of the criticism by the advocates of *ḥadīth* (traditionalists). Instead, it underwent a transformation by becoming more differentiated (*qiyās*, *istiḥsān*, etc.), whereby some elements of it became absorbed into the new synthesizing universal legal discourse as seen in the case of al-Shāfiʿī. It is my contention that even other elements of the *raʾy* approach, which were seemingly rejected by the traditionalist camp, were actually reconstituted and adopted by them. Take, for example, the element of *istiḥsān* that al-Shāfiʿī criticized in his work *al-Risala*[87] as being capricious adjudication that does not explicitly link legal opinion to authoritative text. One can say that it was explicitly rejected outright by the traditionalists; on the other hand, one can argue that the concept of *istiḥsān* underwent a metamorphosis that made it more acceptable to the traditionalist camp and that is in its reconstitution as *ijma'* (juridical consensus).

More precisely, *istiḥsān*, a legal device that did not require direct scriptural reasoning to legitimate its legal conclusions, was readapted by the traditionalists to become *ijmāʿ* (consensus) by recognizing the legitimacy of that process of juristic preferences when carried out collectively by a group of jurists and not just the individual jurist. So *ijmāʿ*, the consensus

[86] See al-Shāfiʿī, *al-Risala* (1987: 295), where he argues for the legitimacy of practicing *ijtihād* (legal reasoning, which he equates with *qiyās*) based on the implications of Quranic verses.

[87] See al-Shāfiʿī, *al-Risala* (1987: 304), for more on this point.

of a group on a legal opinion without explicitly linking that opinion to any authoritative text, can be seen in some ways as the universalization of *istiḥsān* by making that seemingly intuitive and individual procedure a collective one. Thereby, *ijmāʿ* transformed *istiḥsān* into a socio-rational process that grants it a greater degree of legitimacy with those who had opposed *istiḥsān* due in large part to its new communicative form that allowed for the input of a culturally and regionally diverse group of jurists.

As can be seen from this interpretation, the fragmentation of the method of *raʾy* and the reorientation of its constituent elements allowed for a transformation of the legal discourse creating the conditions for a legal synthesis that would foster the civilizational unity sought by pietistic groups. But the transformations of the discourse did not only occur in the *raʾy* approach. Similar transformations occurred in the advocates of the *ḥadīth* approach as well.

I mentioned earlier that advocates of a regional traditionalism like Mālik and al-Awzāʿī and their followers were increasingly coming under the sway of the advocates of *ḥadīth*. The denotation of the earlier term *athar*, a signification for traditionalism, referred to a group that advocated the past communally established precedent and practice (*sunna*) of the learned members of the Muslim community as a source of legitimation for Islamic jurisprudence. But the notion of *sunna* became more differentiated; one particular practice emerged as the primary form of *sunna* that trumped all other types, which served as a precedent in the formation of Islamic law among the advocates of tradition, namely, the *sunna* of the Prophet Muhammad. Thus, the *sunna* of the Prophet became increasingly differentiated from other *sunan* (sing. *sunna*).[88] Furthermore, this *sunna*, which had earlier been propagated as stories, reports, and the living practice of particular regions, increasingly began to take the distinct discursive form of *ḥadīth*: individual reports about the prophet Muhammad that were accompanied by a chain of transmission that purportedly traced the genealogy of the report back to him.

This differentiation process in the concept of *sunna* was probably an important historical step in facilitating the cultural galvanization sought by the pietistic groups for two reasons: One, the *sunna* of the Prophet was universally accepted among all the different groups, whether from the advocates of *raʾy* or *ḥadīth*, merely because of the special place that he held

[88] See Hallaq, 2005, pg. 69 for more on this point.

in Islam even though they interpreted the content of this *sunna* differently, while the other *sunan* did not have such universal appeal among all groups. Second, the casting of the *sunna*, or practice, of the Prophet Muḥammad into the atomized discursive format of *ḥadīth* (singular statements) further helped in the universalization and diffusion of this prophetic *sunna* because the presentation of the *sunna* in this format – in the form of a discursive text rather than a living tradition – made it more easily transferable from one region to the next in the then known Muslim world.

To elaborate further on this last point, the *isnād* (chain of transmission) of the *ḥadīth* provided a mechanism for de-centering the prophetic *sunna* from regional specificity of a lived tradition by creating networks of *ḥadīth* reporters that spanned across space so that information (*ḥadīth* in this case) was made more accessible across regions. In other words, *ḥadīth*, as "atoms of information," were able to traverse regional limitations through an *isnād*. The *sunna* of the Prophet in this atomized form (*ḥadīth*) was easier to transfer than whole regional traditions (e.g., the "practice of the people of Medina") across locals. So not only was the differentiation of the *sunna* of the Prophet a part of this social trend toward universalization of norms of religious practice, but its framing into discursive statements of *ḥadīth* also helped to facilitate the diffusion of that *sunna*.

The increasing differentiation of the notion of *sunna* into the specific *sunna* of the Prophet – as the practice that stands apart from other living practices (*sunan*) – as an authoritative source of Islamic law led to other transformations in the legal discourse. One such transformation is the consolidation of the concept of *ijmāʿ* as a legal mechanism for interpreting and legislating law. I have already mentioned how *ijmāʿ* from one angle can be viewed as a universalization of the notion of *istiḥsān* through collectivization of juristic opinions or preferences. This collectivization of opinion was seen as legitimate within traditionalist quarters because inherent to their notion of the *sunna* of the previous generations was the notion of the legitimacy of the collectivity and the consensual nature of established practice. Given this background, *ijmāʿ* can be seen as a new form by which old legal devices that had been previously espoused by both rationalists and traditionalists as legitimate sources of law could be reconstituted in a new legal form that was mutually accepted by the different sides.

All in all, this discursive process of epistemological fragmentation and reconstitution of previous legal concepts and methods was an attempt to create a legally uniform discourse that would be a social basis for the religious unification of the various ethnic and denominational groups that were found in early Muslim society. The conceptual basis for this legal consolidation is one which attempted to posit a specific relationship between community and text by which both the community and the text are reflexively defined and bound through the hermeneutical authority of the emerging group of religious specialists.

Some authors posit the transition of the Islamic legal enterprise from a communal-centered tradition to a canon-centered individualism inaugurated by al-Shāfiʿī.[89] What this chapter shows is that major transformations in the developing legal tradition were not caused by the conscious efforts of one individual but were the result of a collective and dialogical process between a community of jurists. Moreover, the hypothesis that the pre-Shāfiʿī state of legal affairs was merely communally embedded discourses and practices oversimplifies the situation. The fact is that the authority of scriptural sources (the canon) was more or less present during the earlier period of regionally centered legal traditions although there were differences on how to interpret and operationalize those sources. What we showed here is that in the post-Shāfiʿī period, we see a growing consensus between the variant legal circles on the fundamental set of interpretive tools by which to deal with such texts.

The relationship between the community and its sacred texts will be explored further in the next chapter in the discussion of the formation of an Islamic legal tradition. But one other dimension that emerges from the historical processes discussed in this section that I would like to highlight here is the dialogical character of these conceptual transformations and epistemic group realignments, for which the practice of fatwa-making played a critical role. All of these ideational dialectics and consensus-building measures were largely part of dialogically negotiated engagement between various parties who on a whole shared equal epistemic and political status and had a broad but common vision as to how Islamic society should come into being. This communicative scholarly engagement had its roots in the fatwa-making process itself where the dialogical manner of the production of fatwas served as an archetype for how various factions transacted with one another. Furthermore, the fatwas that were issued from this procedure were the carriers of embedded legal concepts that were the matter from which the legal tradition was negotiated. More will be about this in the subsequent chapter.

[89] See El Shamsy (2013:6) who is the proponent of this argument.

CONCLUSION

The first five centuries of Islam were the foundational period in which Islamic legal ideas and institutions evolved and when many of their defining characteristics were conceived and refined. This is why this formative period came to occupy a special place in the collective memory of participants of this developing legal tradition, and the legal ideas and experiences emerging from this period became memorialized by the discourses (e.g., legal theory and doctrines) and associations (e.g., legal schools) that were established by later generations. There is no doubt that the idealization of this period in the history of Islam in general and the history of Islamic law in particular is a result of the construction of later generations who looked at their past with a growing sense of grandeur because of the achievements of their predecessors, whether those achievements were real or imaginary. Yet it was those achievements that later generations did not forget and felt an urgent need to emulate that ultimately brought about the growth of an Islamic tradition, which will be explored in more detail in the next chapter.

As a final note, this presentation of the development of the Islamic legal system is somewhat self-contained in that it has tried to show how it emerged from some early Muslim juristic discourses and practices. In reality, though, what has been mentioned here are not the only elements that went into building this legal system, and neither was this system insulated from the outside influence of other cultures and legal traditions.[90] Islamic law and civilization as a whole is an original synthesis of ideas, experiences, and practices from within the religion itself and those elements that at the onset were outside of it but were later assimilated within the particular rationality of its tradition. This is what made all those elements Islamic, whether they originated with Muslims themselves or were borrowed from other cultures and heritages. But what I have demonstrated is that even if not all aspects of the tradition come from within the religion itself, at least the fundamental pillars of this tradition come from its primary scriptural sources and the Muslim community's experience and engagement with those foundational texts. This idea will be explored further in Chapter 4

[90] See Lena Salaymeh, *The Beginnings of Islamic Law: Late Antique Islamicate Legal Tradition*, which argues for the influence of Jewish and other Near Eastern legal traditions on Islamic law.

4

The Formation of the Islamic Legal Tradition and the Formalization of *Iftāʾ* within the Legal Schools

INTRODUCTION

In Chapter 3, the formations of Islamic legal theory and Islamic legal doctrines/schools were charted, showing how the activity of fatwa was integral to these legal formations. It also indicated how all the contending legal groups and approaches had one common theme that gave unity to their desperate messages, which was the authoritativeness of the past in terms of formulating present religio-legal practice. This attitude would serve as a starting point for the formation of an Islamic legal tradition that had its own distinctiveness based on its historical experience. If the past is a fundamental starting point of any tradition, the past played a very determinative role in Islamic tradition in general and in the Islamic legal tradition in particular. One of the objectives of this chapter is to define the precise nature of the relationship of the past to the Islamic legal tradition by looking at the ideas and institutions that came to embody that tradition and how they came about.

The analysis of the Islamic legal tradition will be done in light of Talal Asad's notion of Islam as a discursive tradition, and this notion will be developed and its implications explored specifically with reference to the evolution of Islamic law. Asad describes the Islamic discursive tradition as "simply a tradition of Muslim discourse that addresses itself to conceptions of past and future, with reference to a particular Islamic practice in the present."[1] This seminal idea of how to conceptualize the general enterprise of Islam will be developed within the framework of the history

[1] Asad, 1986, 14.

of Islamic legal practice. The second part of this chapter will chart how the establishment of Islamic legal schools (*madhhab*s) in turn influenced the process of fatwa pronouncements. Even as *iftāʾ* was an integral element in the establishment of these legal practices and institutions, once these legal institutions were configured, they, in turn, regulated the process of fatwa formation by governing the manner in which these fatwas would be produced as well as constraining the range of legal possibilities of fatwas.

Fatwas after the fifth/eleventh century became increasingly restricted by the established legal schools (*madhāhib*), in that the fatwas issued after the fifth/eleventh century had to be consistent with the legal doctrines that were the discursive embodiment of those schools. Muslim jurists within each school now began to lay down rules regarding how fatwas were to be issued within the confines of the legal schools and the rules of their own schools in particular. The literature that attempted to define these rules became known as *adab al-fatwa* (the etiquette of fatwa), which started to come into being in the late fifth/eleventh century around the time when the development of the institution of legal schools (*madhāhib*) reached a stage of greater maturity. These works attempt to define the qualifications and categories of muftīs who could issue fatwas, what legal doctrinal rules they must observe in issuing their fatwas, and the procedures that muftīs must observe in pronouncing their fatwas. Our aim in detailing these typologies is to define the discursive rules set by jurists and legal theorists of this period regarding how fatwas were to be issued and who had the right to issue them. This discussion will contextualize the argument in the next chapter that aims to determine how muftīs of the post-classical period maneuvered in and around these discursive rules when producing their fatwas.

THE FORMATION OF AN ISLAMIC LEGAL TRADITION

Experiences and events of the past were integral to the formation of Islamic law as those experiences and events were transmitted to subsequent generations. Later generations viewed those past experiences as having an aura of authority that normatively shaped their contemporary practices. In this way, Islamic law can be viewed as a legal tradition. But what is tradition and what makes the Islamic legal enterprise a legal tradition? More importantly, what sort of legal tradition is the Islamic legal tradition? Tradition is not merely a transmission of ideas from the past, but a belief in their present value.[2] In this sense, tradition is distinct from habituated custom in the fact that it consists in some ways of conscious recognizing and choosing.

Krygier notes three fundamental characteristics of any tradition. First, its *pastness*: the belief of the participants in that tradition that it originated at some point in the past. Second, its *authoritative presence*: Although it originated in the past, it has significance for the lives and activities of those who presently participate in it. Third, *transmission*: Traditions are not merely discontinuous projections of the past on the present; there is continuity in their conveyance from one generation to the next whether this transmission was deliberate or not.[3] So a necessary consequence of this third characteristic is that traditions are fundamentally social[4] because they are born in and sustained through the constant interactions of groups.

This investigation of the history of Islamic legal discourse shows that it can be construed as a tradition as delineated by Krygier. First, the substance of these discourses and practices indeed originated in the past, starting with the fact that their normative basis is found in textual sources from the past, such as Quran and *ḥadīth,* as well as the formulation and formalization of the law coming from authoritatively recognized jurists of the past. Second, those legal discourses that were formulated in the past were viewed as authoritative by subsequent generations as evidenced by the formation of Islamic legal schools, legal theory, and legal doctrines that were initiated by jurists from previous centuries. Last, the opinions of past legal authorities were continually passed down and transmitted to later generations either orally, as was primarily the case with first-century legal authorities, or through writing, as was predominately the case for jurists starting in the latter half of the second century onward.

But more importantly, if Islamic law represents a legal tradition, what sort of tradition is it? In a seminal article written more than three decades ago, Talal Asad stated that Islam, more broadly, should be viewed as a discursive tradition.[5] Asad gives a distinct definition of this type of tradition as consisting of "discourses that seek to instruct practitioners regarding the correct form and purpose of a given practice that, precisely

[2] See Max Radin's "Tradition." The Encyclopedia of the Social Sciences, 1934, vol. 15, pg. 62.

[3] Krygier, 240.

[4] Krygier, 240.

[5] Asad, 1986, 14.

because it is established, it has a history."[6] So, what is unique about Asad's understanding of a discursive tradition is that it centralizes discourse as a mediating principle between past and present. For Asad, traditions are comprised of discourses that link the past, present, and future through the medium of continuously transmitted pedagogic instructions on the purpose and correct form of practices.[7]

For Asad, Islam is a discursive tradition precisely because it is related to certain foundational texts such as the Quran and *ḥadīth* (prophetic traditions).[8] It is this concept of discursive tradition that will be employed here in describing the Islamic legal tradition. If the entire enterprise of Islam can be described as a discursive tradition, then its legal tradition, which is a subset of it, may be described as a discursive legal tradition as well. This is because the Quran and *ḥadīth* are as much the starting points of the legal tradition of Islam as they are the foundations of the Islamic tradition writ large.

This is because the dialogical manner of Quranic declarations facilitated the epistemological and historical establishment of legal practices like *iftāʾ* by which many ethico-legal norms were transmitted. *Iftāʾ* was both encouraged and employed in the Quranic discourse, thereby inaugurating a practice that would be the quintessential method of promulgating Muslim law and extending the reach of those Quranic norms. In addition, the Quran's dialogical approach, especially with regard to seeking fatwas (see, for example, Qur'an: 2:189; 2:217; 2:219; 2:220; 2:222; 4:127; 4:176; 5:4; 8:1),[9] facilitated the practice of its ethico-legal norms, as the practitioners of the Qur'an's injunctions were in some ways active participants in the formation of those norms through their inquisitiveness. At the same time, the gradual way those norms were introduced (over a period of twenty-three years) enabled the transformation of both individuals and community, thus fostering the evolution of Muslim legal subjects and society.

The prophetic practice (*sunna*) played a supportive role in the process of forming this discursive legal tradition. The Prophet Muḥammad was the legal authority who enforced Quranic legal norms in the nascent Muslim community, and his practice became the framework for how

[6] Asad, 1986, 14.

[7] Asad, 1986, 14–15; see also Mahmood, 114–115, for an interpretation of how to understand Asad's notion of tradition.

[8] Asad, 1986, 14.

[9] See Chapter 1 where some of these verses have been analyzed with respect to their grounding of the practice of fatwa.

these norms would be understood and implemented. Moreover, the legal rationale and interpretive tools that he employed to extend the scope of these Quranic norms paved the way for later generations to understand how to derive the law from both the Quranic norms and his example. Later, the prophetic practice would be discursively embodied in what would be known as collections of *ḥadīth*. The corpus of *ḥadīth* would be a secondary source from which legal norms and injunctions would be derived in the Islamic legal tradition as established by Islamic legal theory (*uṣūl al-fiqh*).

So, the basis of the Islamic legal discursive tradition was the textual authority that was exerted by Quran and *ḥadīth* as the core discourses that defined this tradition. At the same time, it is because of this textual authority of the Quran and *ḥadīth* that the Islamic legal tradition can be described as a discursive tradition because they were the reference points for the legitimation of statements or practices within that legal tradition. Thus, this Islamic discursive tradition is, as Saba Mahmood has pointed out, "a mode of discursive engagement of sacred text,"[10] and its legal tradition is the quintessential example of this mode of discursive engagement.

But just as these foundational texts stand at the core of the discursive tradition of Islam in general, and the discursive Islamic legal tradition in particular, they are not the only discourses that comprise this tradition. Charles Hirschkind asserts that Asad's notion of Islamic discursive tradition ought to be understood as a "historically evolving set of discourses, embodied in the practices and institutions of Islamic societies...."[11] Historically speaking, distinct legal discourses that were based on these foundational sacred texts did evolve, giving rise to a discursive legal tradition. To use Ovamir Anjum's words in describing the Islamic discursive tradition, this legal subtradition likewise "would be characterized by its own rationality and styles of reasoning" in that its theoretical considerations and premises emanate "from the content and form of the foundational discourses (the content and context of scripture, the historical experience of Islam in its formative years, etc.)."[12]

[10] Mahmood, 115.
[11] As quoted in Ovamir Anjum, "Islam as a Discursive Tradition: Talal Asad and His Interlocutors," 662, in Comparative Studies of South Asia, Africa and the Middle East, vol. 27, no. 3, 2007
[12] Anjum, 662.

The method of these legal discourses were hermeneutical in character, largely disposed to explicating the legal implication of the foundational sacred texts of Quran and *ḥadīth*. The textual authority of the Quran and *ḥadīth*, in terms of providing the substantial and normative basis of the law, would eventually necessitate the growth of hermeneutical discourses that would interpret those texts. This would eventually give rise to specialists whose epistemic function was to hermeneutically mediate between the larger public and these foundational sacred texts, thereby giving rise to authoritative discourses that would supplement the content and implications of the foundational and authoritative discourses of scripture.[13]

Yet these supplementary hermeneutical discourses, especially those related to law, arose from dialogical interactions between these specialists and the discursive vehicle that was the facilitator for these (legal) exchanges, which was the fatwa. As statements representing the legal implications of the sacred text were themselves the product of dialogical engagements between specialists and non-specialists, fatwas were also about how specialists communicated and negotiated their various opinions with one another. From this communicative practice that was discursively represented by unitary statements emerged more established and elaborate secondary discourses. This is because embedded within these statements were the legal concepts and methodologies that were cultivated by this dialectic process, which enabled these emerging discourses to exercise their hermeneutical function. Moreover, fatwas' phronetic character of matching norms to the particular historical context always situated the universal norms found in these discourses to contemporary realities, thereby keeping the discursive legal tradition dynamic.

These hermeneutical legal discourses developed these rational and interpretive tools (e.g., *qiyās*/analogy, *istiṣlāḥ*/public interest, and other hermeneutical devices) that were often embedded within fatwas, for which these evolving devices would both clarify the intent of scriptural norms and extend their reach to new legal domains. Furthermore, it was in defining a set of distinctive discursive methods of how people could interact with these sacred texts and their secondary discourses that made the Islamic legal tradition a unique discursive tradition.

From these legal discourses, a body of authoritative legal doctrines (*fiqh*) and legal theory (*uṣūl al-fiqh*) arose that would become the bedrock

[13] This statement can be said of any of the subtraditions within the larger Islamic discursive tradition not just its legal tradition.

of the Islamic legal tradition. Moreover, out of the legal opinions and methods of this class of authoritative legal specialists, the institution of Islamic legal schools (*madhāhib*) came into being. These doctrines, theories, and institutions would give shape to a peculiar legal tradition that was in some ways unique to the Islamic legal tradition[14] that evolved as a result of the distinctive historical experiences of Muslim peoples. But more importantly, these discursive formations and their resulting practices would become the determinative matrix that would shape all future Islamic legal discourses in general and the fatwa tradition in particular.

Saba Mahmood asserts Talal Asad's notion of Islam being a discursive tradition because its "pedagogical practices articulate a conceptual relationship with the past, through an engagement with a set of foundational texts (the Quran and the ḥadīth), commentaries thereon, and the conduct of exemplary figures."[15] Moreover, she interprets Asad's concept of Islamic discursive tradition as representing a particular modality of Foucault's notion of a discursive formation where "reflection upon the past is a constitutive condition for the understanding and reformulation of the present and the future. Islamic discursive practices link practitioners across the temporal modalities of past, present and future through a pedagogy of practical, scholarly, and embodied forms of knowledge and virtues deemed central to the tradition."[16]

This conception of tradition is an apt description of the Islamic legal tradition because it was formed from a series of past discourses and discursive practices that were always related to existing realities. The Qur'an and *ḥadīth* legitimated legal principles and practices (e.g., Quranic dialogical fatwa engagement, prophetic use of *qiyās*, as well as substantive legal norms from which legal doctrines were formulated), which were employed by later jurists to legitimate their own jurisprudential views and practices. These foundational discourses gave impetus to those legal principles and practices that were elaborated and expanded upon by jurists who constructed a system of rules (legal rationales and hermeneutical tools such as the science of *uṣūl al-fiqh* or the formulations of legal doctrines based on the rules of the legal schools, or *madhāhib*) that would regulate the legal understanding and implications of those texts as to how they should inform the religious practices of the Muslim community.

[14] See Hallaq, 2004, 164–165, on this point.
[15] Mahmood, 115.
[16] Mahmood, 115.

Secondary discourses like fatwas and discursive practices like *qiyās* and *istiḥsān* from the earlier generation of jurists and theorists mediated between these foundational sacred texts and the community and hence established the hermeneutical authority of those early jurists whose ideas and views shaped the future course and practice of Islamic law. This hermeneutical authority was later institutionalized in the form of Islamic legal schools and doctrines (*madhāhib*) and Islamic legal theory (*uṣūl al-fiqh*), whereby future generations would formulate the law and establish religious practices in reference to these past legal authorities and their institutionalized legal discourses. This authoritativeness of past legal discourses and the personalities associated with them became the constitutive condition for the understanding of Islamic law and how it should be formulated in the present and future. This point will be explored in greater detail in the next section.

In closing, it is important to stress not only the discursive elements of the Islamic legal tradition but also the dialogical dimensions of its formation. I have outlined how the practice of fatwa shaped the legal discourses and institutions that came to be the defining markers of this legal tradition. I have indicated the social transactive character of fatwa processes but only alluded to how it influenced the way this tradition came to be. The practices associated with fatwa production spawned the social conditions that made this Islamic legal tradition not only discursive but also a dialogically negotiated tradition. The dialogical interactions of jurists were meditated through the fatwas they were issuing, and through this communicative activity, a legal tradition was eventually negotiated that then determined which discourses and practices were to be seen as authoritative. This dialogical dimension is an equally distinctive quality of this tradition, and this is why I call the enterprise of Islamic law a "dialogically negotiated" discursive tradition.

RULES OF FATWA, CLASSES OF MUFTĪS, AND THE AUTHORITATIVE STRUCTURE OF *MADHHABS*

Up until the fifth/eleventh century, Muslim legal theorists affirmed that any jurists who sought to give fatwas must be at the level of *mujtahid*, by which they meant a jurist who had the legal capacity to derive his legal opinions directly from the sources of the law and hence had the same level of juristic competence as those who were considered founders of the legal schools. Later, this level of *ijtihād* (legal competence) would be designated as *mujtahid muṭlaq* (an absolutely independent jurist) to distinguish this level of jurisprudential status from newer categories of *muftīs* that were being introduced as the Sunnī Islamic legal schools (*madhhabs*) were becoming ever more differentiated in their structure by the end of the fifth/eleventh century.

This movement toward greater differentiation of categories of *muftīs* and levels they occupy within the hierarchy of Islamic legal schools began to restrict how fatwas were to be issued to what was consistent with the established legal doctrines. The beginning process of this classification of *muftīs* and their fatwas can actually be traced to the late fifth-/eleventh-century Shāfiʿī jurist and legal theorist Abū al-Maʿālī al-Juwaynī (d. 478/1085), who discusses this matter in his work titled *Ghiyāth al-umam*.

In respect to classes of *muftīs*, al-Juwaynī delineates what explicitly appears to be a three-tiered scheme. At the top of the scheme is the class of *muftī* who is designated as a *mujtahid*. The *mujtahid* is the *muftī* who has encompassed all the legal capacities to make *ijtihād* (in this context, it means independent legal reasoning to make assertions about the law without reference to established legal doctrines).[17] Al-Juwaynī says that to achieve this legal capacity, the *mujtahid* must have the following six attributes: first, competence in the Arabic language because the sources of the law stem from Arabic literary sources (Quran, *ḥadīth*, and previous legal judgments) and thus necessitate that one be highly proficient in Arabic as it is the means to comprehending the Islamic law;[18] second, knowledge of verses in the Quran that deal with legal injunctions as well as knowing those that are abrogated and whether those verses have universal or particular implications;[19] third, to have knowledge of the *sunna* (prophetic practice) because most legal injunctions come from this corpus; moreover, the *mujtahid* should know how to navigate through this literature by possessing knowledge of the various sciences of *ḥadīth* as well as distinguishing between those aspects of the *sunna* that have legal implications from those that do not.[20] Fourth, the *mujtahid* must have knowledge of legal doctrines of past *mujtahids* so as not to promulgate fatwas that go against an established *ijmāʿ*, or the consensus of previous jurists.[21] Fifth, he must possess a comprehensive understanding of the means of

[17] Al-Juwaynī, 285.
[18] Al-Juwaynī, 286.
[19] Al-Juwaynī, 286.
[20] Al-Juwaynī, 286–287.
[21] Al-Juwaynī, 287.

qiyās (legal reasoning) and the level of authoritativeness of legal proofs.[22] Lastly, the *mujtahid* must be pious in order for his fatwas to have currency,[23] although this is not an absolute condition for the legitimacy of his *ijtihād* with reference to himself even though others should not accept his fatwa unless he is pious.[24]

Al-Juwaynī goes on to say that this category of *mujtahid-muftī* need not follow the previously established doctrines of the *madhhabs* but should issue fatwas in accordance with his own legal reasoning that may be followed by others even when there are established legal doctrines.[25] Al-Juwaynī asserts that this type of *mujtahid* probably no longer exists in his age (see Figure 14 for a summary of the different levels of *mujtahids* in al-Juwaynī's system).[26] Therefore, he goes on to spell out the description of the second class of *muftīs*, who are, more or less, followers of already established legal doctrines as represented by the *madhāhib* (sing. *madhhab*). Their main function is to transmit those doctrines through their fatwas to the layman.[27] So this type of *muftī* is not autonomous in his fatwas since he does not have the capacity for independent legal judgment directly from the sources of the law (Quran, *ḥadīth*, *qiyās*, etc.),[28] even though he does have the capacity to reach legal conclusions that are consistent with the *madhhab* that he professes (see Figure 14).

Furthermore, this type of *muftī* is usually faced with two types of situations: one where he is asked about the legal status of a state of affairs that has been addressed by the established doctrines and one where he is asked about a circumstance that has not been explicitly addressed by the previous doctrine.[29] As for the first case, he must transmit the teachings of the *madhhab* with regard to the case at hand.[30] As for the second case, when he is faced with a situation that has not been previously addressed in the legal doctrine of the *madhhab*, al-Juwaynī affirms that this class of *muftī*, who is not autonomous from the legal doctrines of the school, is of two kinds. The first kind is one who is capable of transmitting the explicit legal doctrines of the school and extending the legal implications of those doctrines to similar scenarios. In addition, this kind of *muftī* is able to sort

22 Al-Juwaynī, 287.
23 Al-Juwaynī, 288.
24 Al-Juwaynī, 291.
25 Al Al-Juwaynī, 298.
26 Al-Juwaynī, 300.
27 Al-Juwaynī, 300–301.
28 Al-Juwaynī, 300–301.
29 Al-Juwaynī, 301.
30 Al-Juwaynī, 301.

out and select (*taḥrīr wa-taqrīr*) the legal positions that properly represent the school from those other positions that are seen as inferior. But he does not have the legal capacity to decide legal cases that are not explicitly determined by the legal doctrine (*ghayr manṣūṣ*) based on cases that are explicitly decided by the doctrine (*manṣūṣ*).[31] This is because he lacks the full means of legal reasoning (*masālik al-aqyisa*) and the capacity to deduce legal implications (from the established doctrines).[32] However, al-Juwaynī is quick to assert that this level of *muftī* may deal with some legal cases that are not explicitly dealt with by the doctrine of the *madhhab* if such cases are unambiguously implicit in the stated doctrine (*fī maʿnā al-manṣūṣ*).[33] On the other hand, there is a level of *muftī* within a *madhhab*, whom he calls the independent jurist within the *madhhab* of an absolute jurist (*al-faqīh al-mustaqill bi-madhhab imāmihi*), who comprehends the legal rationale and methodology (*aqyisa wa-ṭuruq*) underlying the doctrines of his *madhhab* and hence is able to decide legal cases that are not explicitly stated in the doctrine based on those that are stated.[34]

In summary, it seems that al-Juwaynī's presentation of the classification of *muftī*s is somewhat ambiguous, but I can discern two main types: one who is a *mujtahid* (an absolutely independent jurist) who does not follow an established doctrine and is capable of independently forming his own legal opinions. Examples of this type are the purported founders of the legal schools in the second/eighth and third/ninth centuries. Moreover, it is completely legitimate for laypersons to follow such a *muftī-mujtahid*, if one actually exists, at the expense of following an established doctrine of a legal school of a past *muftī-mujtahid* (for example, one of the *madhhab* predecessors of the four Sunnī *madhhab*s).

The second type of *muftī* is one who is not completely independent of the established doctrines of the legal schools and issues fatwas that must be consistent with the doctrines of the particular *madhhab* to which he subscribes. Under this second type of *muftī*, there are two subtypes: One is the *muftī* who is capable of dealing with legal cases that are not explicitly dealt with in the legal doctrine of the *madhhab* by inferring their solutions from cases that have been determined in the doctrine, while the other subtype of *muftī* is only able to issue legal opinions that transmit the explicitly stated doctrines of the school and cannot render legal decisions for new cases.

[31] Al-Juwaynī, 303.
[32] Al-Juwaynī, 306.
[33] Al-Juwaynī, 303–304.
[34] Al-Juwaynī, 306.

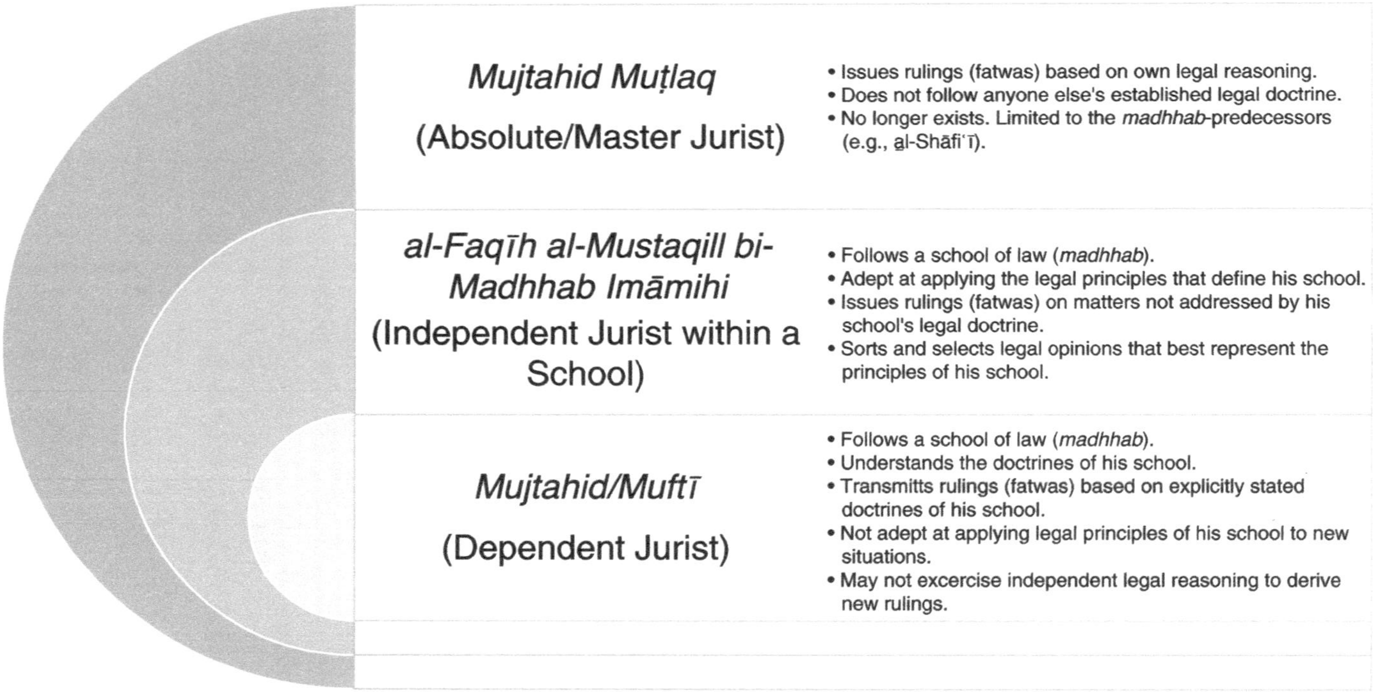

FIGURE 14 Al-Juwaynī's (fifth/eleventh) tripartite categorization of jurists

If al-Juwaynī's exposition represented the early stages of formalization of ranks within legal schools, later expositions of this matter became more sophisticated in their stratifications of *muftī*s as well as detailing the legal competence needed to make fatwas within the boundaries of a *madhhab*. Take, for instance, the sixth/twelfth-century independent Ḥanafī jurist (*mujtahid*) Qāḍī Khān (d. 592/1195) who prefaces his fatwa collection, known as *Fatāwa Qāḍī Khān*, describing what a *muftī* (*rasm al-muftī*) is within the bounds of his Ḥanafī school. This represents an earlier attempt by a member of the Ḥanafī school to circumscribe the activity of fatwa and the classifications of *muftī* within his *madhhab*.

He says the *muftī* of his era that belongs to his *madhhab*/school (*aṣḥābinā*, lit. "our companions") is one who, when asked about a legal matter that had been addressed before and whose solution is found in the authoritative doctrines of the Ḥanafī school (*ẓāhir al-riwāya*), should issue a fatwa in accordance with those established legal opinions, provided that the authorities of the school had reached a consensus (consensus in the opinions of the master jurists of the school: Abū Ḥanīfa, Abū Yūsuf, and al-Shaybānī). Such a *muftī* must not resort to his own view even if he is an experienced *mujtahid* (absolute jurist).[35] Qāḍī Khān justifies this position by claiming that the correct legal opinion most probably lies with the authorities of the *madhhab*/school (*aṣḥābanā*), and the *muftī*'s legal reasoning (*ijtihād*) probably does not match theirs.[36]

Moreover, this *muftī* should not be concerned with other jurists who disagree with the founders' authoritative positions nor should he be satisfied with his own legal proof (*ḥujja*) for his position because they (the master jurists of the school: Abū Ḥanīfa, Abū Yūsuf, and al-Shaybānī), more than anyone else, understood the legal evidence (*'adilla*) and were most capable of distinguishing between the types of legal evidence that were sound from those that were unsound.[37] What Qāḍī Khān is speaking of here is the type of *muftī* that reached the level of *mujtahid* (an independent jurist) within the Ḥanafī school, but not absolutely independent to go against the purported founders and absolute *mujtahid*s of his legal school. This category is similar to the second category of al-Juwaynī's classification of *muftī*s (see Figure 13). On the other hand, if there is a difference

[35] Qāḍī Khān, v. 1, 2. *Fatāwa Qāḍī Khān* as printed on the margins of *al-Fatāwa al-Hindiyya* by Shaikh Nizam.

[36] Qāḍī Khān, v. 1, 2. *Fatāwa Qāḍī Khān* as printed on the margins of *al-Fatāwa al-Hindiyya* by Shaikh Nizam.

[37] Qāḍī Khān, v. 1, 2–3. *Fatāwa Qāḍī Khān* as printed on the margins of *al-Fatāwa al-Hindiyya* by Shaikh Nizam.

of opinion among these early authorities of the *madhhab* (Abū Ḥanīfa, Abū Yūsuf, and al-Shaybānī), then he should see where Abū Ḥanīfa agreed with one of his two associates (either Abū Yūsuf or al-Shaybānī), then take that legal position because the greater preponderance of legal proofs lies with the two of them.[38] Now, if Abū Ḥanīfa's opinion goes against the opinions of his two associates in matters regarding human transactions (*mu'āmalāt*), then the *muftī* should take the legal opinions of Abū Ḥanīfa's two associates (Abū Yūsuf and al-Shaybānī) in those matters because there is consensus among later jurists in the Ḥanafī *madhhab* on this position.[39] As for other legal areas where there is a dispute between Abū Ḥanīfa and his associates, the *muftī* who is at the level of independent legal reasoning (*mujtahid*) within the confines of the Ḥanafī school should take the position to which his own reasoning has led him[40] (see Figure 15).

Qāḍī Khān then goes on to describe the qualifications of the *muftī* that is described as a *mujtahid* (independent jurist) within the Ḥanafī school. There seems to be a difference in opinion by the later authorities in the *madhhab* as to what constitutes a *mujtahid* (independent jurist) within the school. Some said that if he is a person who exercises *ijtihād* (legal reasoning) on ten issues and gets eight of them right, then he is a *mujtahid*. Other authorities said that he must have memorized the *al-Mabsūṭ*, al-Shaybānī's work that first laid out the legal doctrine of the Ḥanafī school, in addition to memorizing some of the principles of *uṣūl al-fiqh* (legal theory) like *naskh* (abrogation); in addition, he must be familiar with the customs of people.[41] Qāḍī Khān never quite decides on which of the two criteria mentioned would be the decisive one in determining who is a *mujtahid* within the Ḥanafī *madhhab*.

But if the legal solution to an issue that arises is not found in the past authoritative doctrines (*ẓāhir al-riwāya*), then this *muftī-mujtahid* should resort to the legal principles of the *madhhab* to resolve the issue. But if there is a legal opinion that is not found in the authoritative doctrines (*ẓāhir al-riwāya*), yet the later (independent) jurists within the *madhhab* are unanimous about their legal position on the issue, then the *muftī* should take their position. But if the later jurists disagreed on a position,

[38] Qāḍī Khān, v. 1, 3. *Fatāwa Qāḍī Khān* as printed on the margins of *al-Fatāwa al-Hindiyya* by Shaikh Nizam.

[39] Qāḍī Khān, v. 1, 3. *Fatāwa Qāḍī Khān* as printed on the margins of *al-Fatāwa al-Hindiyya* by Shaikh Nizam.

[40] Qāḍī Khān, v. 1, 3. *Fatāwa Qāḍī Khān* as printed on the margins of *al-Fatāwa al-Hindiyya* by Shaikh Nizam.

[41] Qāḍī Khān, v. 1, 3. *Fatāwa Qāḍī Khān* as printed on the margins of *al-Fatāwa al-Hindiyya* by Shaikh Nizam.

then the current *muftī* should exert his own legal reasoning and take the position that seems correct to his own reasoning[42] (see Figure 15).

Finally, Qāḍī Khān delineates the rules governing the second level of *ijtihād/iftā'* within the bounds of the Ḥanafī school, which is the domain of the *muftī* who is considered a *muqallid* (a dependent or relative jurist). He does not specify the criteria that define this type of *muftī* as he does for the *muftī* who is a *mujtahid* other than to say that he does not meet the criteria for being a *muftī-mujtahid*. He says this category of *muftī* should take the answer from whoever he believes is the most knowledgeable person [a *mujtahid* or independent jurist] in the law and attribute the opinion to him. If the most knowledgeable person is in another region, then the *muftī* should write to him for a response[43] (see Figure 15).

Qāḍī Khān's presentation of the categories of *muftī*s does not explicitly mention the category of *mujtahid muṭlaq* (absolute/autonomous/master jurist), but it is very clear that there is such a category of *mujtahid*s for him. This category of *mujtahid*s is represented by what I am calling the early *madhhab* predecessors of the Ḥanafī school, Abū Ḥanīfa, Abū Yūsuf, and al-Shaybānī, who are, as he has implied, beyond reproach in terms of their capacity for legal reasoning. One reaches the conclusion from the tenor of his discussion that such *mujtahid*s no longer exist and are only a part of the past, although he is not explicit about it as al-Juwaynī is. Furthermore, Qāḍī Khān's presentation of the categories of *muftī*s does not seem directly to address the *mujtahid* who is independent in his legal reasoning but is not independent enough in his *ijtihād* to reach the capacity of *mujtahid muṭlaq* (absolute jurist) and to found his own legal doctrine.

Despite the general character of Qāḍī Khān's presentation of the types of *muftī*s, he nevertheless makes a significant advance in delineating the discursive rules for legitimate engagement of fatwas within the confines of his particular *madhhab* for the types that he does describe. For example, unlike al-Juwaynī's presentation, which talks more generally about the levels of required legal capacities and competencies for a *muftī* to make fatwas, Qāḍī Khān unequivocally tries to spell out in more detail what that would mean particularly in the Ḥanafī *madhhab*. This is especially pronounced where he specifies what exactly represents authoritative doctrines in this school (*ẓāhir al-riwāya*) and where later *muftī*s were

[42] Qāḍī Khān, v. 1, 3. *Fatāwa Qāḍī Khān* as printed on the margins of *al-Fatāwa al-Hindiyya* by Shaikh Nizam.

[43] Qāḍī Khān, v. 1, 3. *Fatāwa Qāḍī Khān* as printed on the margins of *al-Fatāwa al-Hindiyya* by Shaikh Nizam.

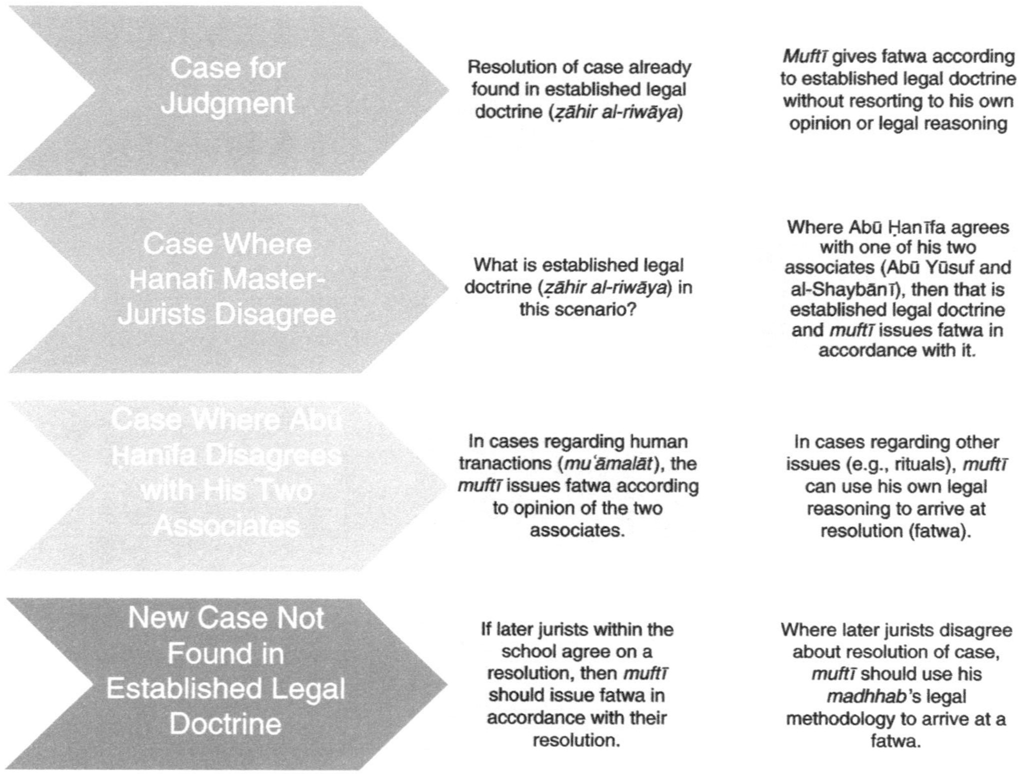

Case for Judgment
Resolution of case already found in established legal doctrine (ẓāhir al-riwāya)
Muftī gives fatwa according to established legal doctrine without resorting to his own opinion or legal reasoning
Case Where Ḥanafī Master-Jurists Disagree
What is established legal doctrine (ẓāhir al-riwāya) in this scenario?
Where Abū Ḥanīfa agrees with one of his two associates (Abū Yūsuf and al-Shaybānī), then that is established legal doctrine and muftī issues fatwa in accordance with it.
Case Where Abū Ḥanīfa Disagrees with His Two Associates
In cases regarding human tranactions (mu'āmalāt), the muftī issues fatwa according to opinion of the two associates.
In cases regarding other issues (e.g., rituals), muftī can use his own legal reasoning to arrive at resolution (fatwa).
New Case Not Found in Established Legal Doctrine
If later jurists within the school agree on a resolution, then muftī should issue fatwa in accordance with their resolution.
Where later jurists disagree about resolution of case, muftī should use his madhhab's legal methodology to arrive at a fatwa.

FIGURE 15 The structure of iftāʾ within the Ḥanafī *madhhab* according to Qāḍī Khān (sixth/twelfth): the procedure the *muftī-mujtahid* must follow when issuing fatwas

situated with respect to those doctrines. Moreover, he tries to describe the criteria for a *muftī-mujtahid* in the Ḥanafī school in exact terms (e.g., having memorized the *Mabṣuṭ* or getting eight out of ten legal issues right) so that we know exactly how these *muftī*s are circumscribed by the boundaries of the school to which they belong.

What we may surmise thus far from this whole discussion about the discursive rules of fatwas and the ranking of *muftī*s that was being formulated by Muslim jurists between the fifth/eleventh and sixth/twelfth centuries is that fatwas were no longer free exercises in legal reasoning in which a jurist was expected to look directly at the textual sources of the law (Quran and *ḥadīth*) as well as other legal precepts and contextual evidence so as to seek the legal norms from which he could formulate responses to deal with ever new cases with which he was confronted. Instead, fatwas became ever more confined to transmitting or extending the legal implication of already existing legal doctrines and/or legal methodologies defined by classical Muslim jurists and legal theorists. This conservative approach to *iftā*ʾ would become the uncontested manner, with few exceptions, in which fatwas would be issued during the period of *madhhab* preponderance (c. 1100–1900), which will be illustrated in the next chapter through an analysis of fatwas from this period. But to deepen our understanding of the development of the discursive rules for fatwas and the structuring of *madhhab*s, an examination of *adab al-fatwa* literature from later periods of the age of the preponderance of *madhhab*s will be explored here so as to show how this structuring of fatwas continued to evolve after the initial period.

For this task, I have chosen a work that represents the culmination of *madhhab*-centered legal thinking: the ideas of the famous thirteenth-/nineteenth-century Ḥanafī jurist Ibn ʿĀbidīn (d. 1252/1836). He represents the last generation of traditional Muslim jurists who formulated Islamic law within the confines of *madhhab*s prior to the call for modern reforms that were to shake the foundations of Islamic law in the latter part of the nineteenth century.[44] So in a way, his thoughts represent the pinnacle of the systemization of Islamic law before the modern challenge. More particularly, an examination will be undertaken of his treatise

[44] There was an internal Muslim reform movement in the eighteenth century by Muslim scholars, some of whom also challenged the confines of the *madhhab*. This movement may have contributed to the changes in Muslim institutions that began to be noticed in the late nineteenth century and early twentieth century, but this work will not discuss that eighteenth-century reform movement as its historical impact on Muslim society remains somewhat understudied. For more on this movement, see the works of Aḥmad Dallal.

ʿUqūd rasm al-muftī where he describes how fatwa in the Ḥanafī *madhhab* is regulated. This description reveals the structure of the Ḥanafī *madhhab* as a whole and how fatwas fit into that overall structure.

First, Ibn ʿĀbidīn starts his treatise with a rule that any *muftī* should follow: He must give a fatwa in accordance with the legally preponderant position (*rājiḥ*) of his *madhhab*. Ibn ʿĀbidīn claims that there is an *ijmāʿ* (consensus) among Muslim jurists about this position.

Moreover, he states that it is not permitted for a *muftī* to issue fatwas based on weak legal opinions (*marjūḥ*) within his *madhhab*.[45] From these initial statements, the reader gets a sense of how fatwas became confined to the doctrines and legal methodologies that had been established by the legal schools.

He then goes on to outline a hierarchy for jurists who occupy different authoritative levels within the Ḥanafī *madhhab*. This structure that Ibn ʿĀbidīn lays out consists of seven levels (*ṭabaqāt*).[46] The first, which stands at the very top of this classification, is the level of the absolute independent jurists of Islamic law (what he calls *al-mujtahidīn fī al-sharʿ*), which consists of the *madhhab* predecessors of the four Sunnī legal schools[47] (Abū Ḥanīfa, Mālik, al-Shāfiʿī, and Ibn Ḥanbal). These were the second-/eighth- and third-/ninth-century jurists some of whose legal opinions were examined in previous chapters. His claim is that this class of jurists established original legal principles and extracted doctrine from the sources of the law without imitating other jurists in their legal principles or their doctrines[48] (see Figure 16).

The second level of jurists/*muftī*s within the Ḥanafī school consists of those who, he claims, are independent jurists but within the limits of the Ḥanafī *madhhab* (*mujtahidūn fī al-madhhab*). Examples of such figures in the Ḥanafī school are Abū Ḥanīfa's two protégés Abū Yūsuf and Muḥammad al-Shaybānī. Ibn ʿĀbidīn claims that what makes them

[45] Ibn ʿĀbidīn, 2000, 5.

[46] It should be pointed out that Ibn ʿĀbidīn's typology of *muftī*s within the Ḥanafī *madhhab* is not original. In fact, this typology was already outlined three centuries earlier by the Ottoman Shaykh al-Islām Aḥmad Ibn Kamāl Pashazadeh (d. 940/1533). See Hallaq's exposition of Ibn Kamāl's typology in *Authority, Continuity, and Change in Islamic Law*, 14–17. Nevertheless, Ibn ʿĀbidīn's treatise represents one of the last efforts to expound the character of fatwa within the confines of a *madhhab* before the advocacy of modern reforms for Islamic law and institutions; hence, it gives a good indication for the endpoint of the evolution of this traditional institution prior to the modern challenge. Moreover, there will be other aspects of this treatise that will highlight the operations of fatwa within a *madhhab* that make this treatise a good reference for our discussion.

[47] Ibn ʿĀbidīn, 2000, 6.

[48] Ibn ʿĀbidīn, 2000, 6.

independent jurists within the *madhhab* was their ability to deduce rulings in accordance with the legal principles (*qawāʿid*) established by their mentor, Abū Ḥanīfa. Thus, even when they extract different legal rulings than he, they nevertheless confine these deductions in accordance with the legal principles that Abū Ḥanīfa established[49] (see Figure 16).

At the next (third) level are the subsequent generations of Ḥanafī jurists from the third/ninth to the fifth/eleventh century (e.g., al-Ṭaḥāwī, al-Jarrāḥ, al-Bazdawī, al-Sarakhsī, etc.), who are what he calls the independent jurists in particular legal cases (*mujtahidūn fī al-masāʾil*). These are cases where there is no established legal doctrine (*la riwāyah*, lit. no narration) from the *madhhab* predecessors or the master jurists (Abū Ḥanīfa and his protégés). Ibn ʿĀbidīn tells us that this level of *muftī* may not go against the fatwas of the founders of the *madhhab*, but he may select from those opinions that seem most in keeping with the principles of the *madhhab* and promote those as the official position of the school.[50] He may also establish new legal rulings (fatwas) on new cases based on the legal principles established by the founders[51] (see Figure 16).

Ibn ʿĀbidīn sees these first three levels of jurists to one extent or another as *mujtahids* (independent legal reasoners). On the other hand, jurists at levels four through seven are no longer viewed as independent jurists (*mujtahidūn*), or those who can make *ijtihād* (deducing new rulings through independent legal reasoning). Instead, these levels of *muftī*s are in the realm of what is known as *taqlīd*,[52] which may be defined as the opposite of *ijtihād* in the sense that those who make *taqlīd* do not arrive at legal rulings independently, but depend on and follow those rulings that have been established in the legal doctrine of the *madhhab*. So from this level onward is what we may call the level of dependent or limited *muftī*s, as their legal activities are restricted to legal principles and rulings established by the previous three levels.

Level four *muftī*s consist of those jurists whose task is to engage in the activity of what is designated as *takhrīj* (extrapolation) and are known as *mukharrijūn*. Their capacity to make *takhrīj* of rulings is a result of their competence in legal principles (of the *madhhab*), and hence they are tasked to "resolve juridical ambiguities and tilt the scale in favor of

[49] Ibn ʿĀbidīn, 2000, 6.
[50] Ibn ʿĀbidīn, 2000, 7.
[51] Ibn ʿĀbidīn, 2000, 7.
[52] Ibn ʿĀbidīn, 2000, 7.

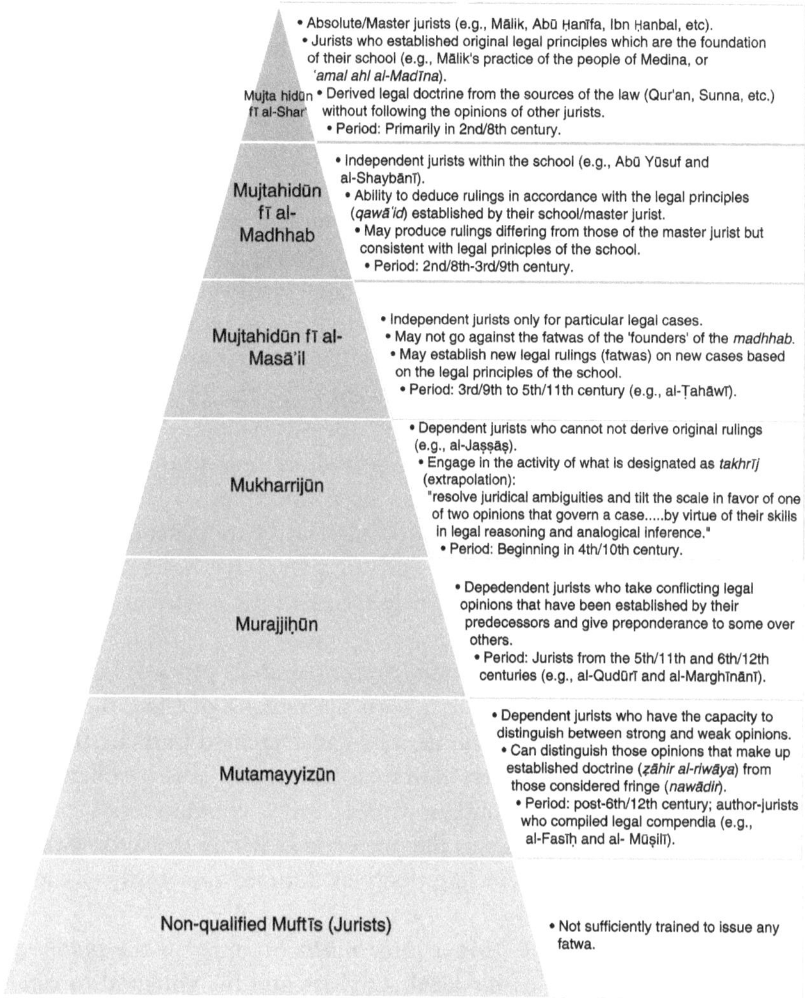

FIGURE 16 Ibn ʿĀbidīn's (thirteenth/nineteenth century) seven levels of *mujtahids* (jurists) in the Ḥanafī school

one of two opinions that govern a case ... by virtue of their skills in legal reasoning and analogical inference."[53] An example of a Ḥanafī jurist in this category is al-Rāzī (al-Jaṣṣāṣ).[54] The fifth level consists of those jurists who are considered *murajjiḥun* (those who give preponderance

[53] Hallaq, 2004, 16. See also Ibn ʿĀbidīn, 2000, 7.

[54] Ibn ʿAbidīn, 2000, 7. See editor's footnote #2 that identifies the name al-Rāzī with the fourth-century Ḥanafī jurist al-Jaṣṣāṣ.

to one opinion over another). Examples of jurists that fit this category are those Ḥanafī jurists from the fifth/eleventh and sixth/twelfth centuries like al-Qudūrī and al-Marghīnānī, whose task is to take conflicting legal opinions that have been established by their predecessors and give preponderance to some over others using the established standards of the *madhhab*[55] (see Figure 16).

The sixth level consists of those dependent *muftī*s who have the capacity to distinguish (*mutamayyizūn*) strong from weak opinions, as well as those opinions that make up established doctrine (*ẓāhir al-riwāya*) from those that are considered fringe (*nawādir*). Examples of this type are those post-sixth-/twelfth-century author-jurists who compiled legal compendia of the doctrines of the Ḥanafī school like al-Fasīḥ (d. 680/1281) and al-Mūṣilī (d. 683/1284) – the authors of *al-Kanz* and *al-Mukhtār*, respectively – whose task in these legal compendia is to present the established legal doctrines of the school and keep out of their works those legal opinions that are considered weak.[56] Those belonging to the seventh and final level are not real jurists or *muftī*s at all; rather, they are poorly trained jurists who are incapable of issuing sound fatwas.[57]

Following are some observations on Ibn ʿĀbidīn's proposed configuration. The first observation is that with the passing of time, the Ḥanafī *madhhab* and the *madhhab*s in general had increased in their structural complexity since the early period of their formation. This is evidenced by the fact that Ibn ʿĀbidīn's configuration of *muftī*s contains twice as many levels or categories of jurists as the one expounded by the sixth-/twelfth-century Ḥanafī jurist Qāḍī Khān that was outlined previously (six levels versus three).

Second, the lower the level a jurist/*muftī* occupies in the *madhhab*, the lesser is the extent of his legal activities and his potential to establish legal opinions, or fatwas. Moreover, the increasing stratification of *muftī*s/jurists was in some ways a function of time. The farther in time jurists seemed to be from the *madhhab* predecessors, the lower the status they occupied in the juristic typology. All these observations point to the notion that the scope of fatwa became much more confined and structured the more the institution of *madhhab*s became established and differentiated in Islamic history.

55 Ibn ʿĀbidīn, 2000, 7.
56 Ibn ʿĀbidīn, 2000, 7.
57 Ibn ʿĀbidīn, 2000, 7.

In conclusion, it is hoped that the foregoing discussion has created a better understanding of how Islamic legal schools (*madhhab*s) operated in shaping Islamic law and the role they played in formalizing the process of fatwa-making. In short, one can say that a *madhhab* consists of several layers of precedential legal opinions that are canonized in certain texts. Some of those texts (*kutub al-furūʿ*) structure those legal opinions in such a way that the greatest priority is given to the legal opinions of the earliest master jurists, followed by the opinions of subsequent generations of jurists who claimed to follow the legal methods of the founding masters when introducing new aspects to the legal doctrine of the school. Another way to view a *madhhab* is to see it as a legal field where a set of interdependent relationships exist between a constellation of legal opinions/texts and people/scholars, all of which are stratified in a hierarchical matrix. This matrix aimed to preserve, generate, and disseminate Islamic law in a systematic fashion, ensuring its continuity over space and time.[58]

A NOTE ON THE FORMATION OF SHĪʿĪ LEGAL THOUGHT AND INSTITUTIONS

So far in my investigation, very little has been said about the development of law and legal institutions within Shīʿī Islam. This is because the development of a distinctive Shīʿī legal theory and of Shīʿī institutions did not occur until centuries after their Sunnī counterparts. This is despite the fact that they had undergone in some respects a process of legal evolution similar to that of Sunnī law, but at later periods.[59] This lag is partly due to the distinctiveness of Shīʿī Islam, which followed the teachings of charismatically inspired leaders (Imams) from the descendants of the Prophet Muḥammad, seeing them as a continuation of the his religious legacy and hence leaving little need for this community to develop a law when they had direct religious guidance from such religiously authoritative leaders.

There are two main legal schools (*madhhab*s) in *Shīʿī* Islam: Zaydī and Twelver Shīʿī (aka Imāmī or Jaʿfarī), which developed independently of one another because of their variant historical trajectories in the

[58] George Makdisi described *madhhab*s as a professional legal guild (see Stewart, 28), but such a description is not the best way to conceive of this organization because it lacked any formal membership or administrative staff that guilds would be expected to have. Instead, a *madhhab* is what Max Weber would call a voluntary association because it claimed authority over voluntary members and had rationally established rules (Weber, 1978, v. 1, 52).

[59] Stewart, 14–15; Vikor, 126–128.

formative period.[60] Moreover, as Knut Vikor notes, they do not have "a common original Shīʿī legal theory," and they each independently emerge out of a "common source of Muslim legal thought."[61] Despite their different paths of historical development, they share a common ground in the theological sphere, in that they both believe that the religious teachings of the descendants of the Prophet carry greater authority than those of other Muslims.

Zaydi Islam had its roots in a second-century political movement that drew its inspiration from the aborted revolution of the great-grandson of the Prophet Zayd ibn ʿAlī (d. 122/740) against the late Umayyad dynasty. The adherents of the Zaydī school claim that their legal lineage goes back to the teachings of Zayd ibn ʿAlī. Yet, Zayd and his early followers espoused legal opinions that were not too distinct from the Kufan/Iraqi (read advocates of *ra'y*) mainstream.[62] But by the early part of the third/ninth century though, this politically repressed movement began to develop a distinct legal doctrine centered on the charismatic authority of Zayd and the routinized legal authority of Zayd's decedents and his immediate relatives who supported Zayd's political cause.[63]

Among the personalities who developed Zaydi legal doctrine in the early third/ninth century were Zayd's grandson Aḥmad ibn ʿIsa ibn Zayd (d. 247/861) and al-Qāsim ibn Ibrāhīm al-Rassī (d. 240/860), which served as a basis for practice for Zaydī communities in Iraq and the Caspian Sea region.[64] Yet the Zaydī legal school did not flourish until a Zaydī state was established in the northern highlands of Yemen by al-Rassī's grandson Yaḥyā ibn al-Ḥusayn (al-Hādī) (d. 298/911). Al-Hādī legal teachings and judgments, as documented in two works, *Kitāb al-Aḥkām* and *Kitāb al-Muntakhab*, became the basis of the Zaydī *madhhab*'s legal doctrines in Yemen. In Yemen, this sect continues to survive despite its disappearance in other regions of the Muslim world.[65]

According to Zaydī political theology, the Zaydī community was to be led by a descendent of the Prophet Muḥammad, although from no particular hereditary line. This leader's religious authority is not as absolute

[60] Vikor, 122.

[61] Vikor, 122. Stewart also affirms that the emergence of Twelver Shīʿī legal ideas and institutions took place within the wider legal developments occurring in Sunnī jurisprudence (Stewart, 14–15).

[62] Heidar, 192.

[63] Heidar, 192, and Madelung, 478.

[64] Madelung, 478

[65] Haykal, 6. See also Madelung, 479, and Vikor, 122.

as in the case of Twelver Shīʿism; however, this leader (Imam) had to be a *mujtahid* (absolute independent jurist).[66] This stipulation probably led to less stratification of jurists within the Zaydī *madhhab* than in the Sunnī schools, given that Zaydīs would have access to such a *mujtahid* in every generation that would lead not only the community but also who shape their law. In Chapter 2, where I analyzed al-Hādī's fatwas, the early Zaydī school accepted the Quran, *sunna* (prophetic practice), and *ʿaql* (intellect/reason) as the legitimate sources for lawmaking. However, later, they narrowed the scope of *ʿaql* to *qiyās* (legal analogy). The legally distinguishing attribute of the Zaydī *madhhab* is that its adherents opposed the validity of *ijmāʿ* (consensus of Muslim jurists) as a jurisprudential means of establishing law.[67] Yet, in terms of legal doctrine, the Zaydī *madhhab* is closer to the four Sunnī schools than the Twelver Shīʿa are.

The Twelver Shīʿī (Imāmī) *madhhab*, on the other hand, settled on the legal authority of Shīʿī scholars who were seen as deputies of the religious authorities (Imams), who were from a particular hereditary line of the Prophet Muḥammad's decedents, when the last of these religious authorities disappeared in the third/ninth century. During the post-Imamate period of Shīʿī Islam, there were two paths that Shīʿīs followed in terms of religious legal practice: One was to attach themselves to an existing Sunnī school of law;[68] the other was to form their own distinct school of law (*madhhab*), which received a major push after the formation of the Safavid state in Iran in the tenth/sixteenth century that adopted Twelver Shīʿism as state ideology.[69] Yet it can be argued that the legal works of the fifth-/eleventh-century Shīʿī jurist al-Shaykh al-Mufīd (d. 413/1022) already represent a concerted effort toward the development of a distinct doctrine of Twelver Shīʿī law.[70]

During the initial formation of the Twelver Shīʿī *madhhab*, the stratification of *muftīs*/*mujtahids* was not as apparent as in the case of the Sunnī schools around the same period. This is evidenced by the lack of such classifications of *muftīs* in Shīʿī legal works. For example, in his work on

[66] Haykal, 6–7.
[67] Vikor, 123–124.
[68] Stewart, 62.
[69] Vikor, 127–128. In this brief discussion of the development of Twelver Shīʿī jurisprudence, I am ignoring the eleventh/ seventeenth-century anti-*madhhab* Akhbārī movement because ultimately the pro-*madhhab* movement of the Uṣūlīs becomes the preponderant position within the Twelver Shīʿī community. For more on this debate, see Stewart pgs. 175–208.
[70] Stewart, 128.

Twelver Shīʿī (Imāmī) legal theory entitled *Mabādiʾ al-wuṣūl*, al-ʿAllāma al-Ḥillī lists the qualities of the person who has the right to make *ijtihād*. The qualities of such a *mujtahid* are similar to those described of the *mujtahid mustaqill* (absolutely independent jurists) within the Sunnī schools.[71] There is nothing in his work about the sort of hierarchical stratifications of *muftī*s who can issue fatwas at different levels of authority, which was already a trend within the Sunnī *madhhab*s of that period. In al-Ḥillī's presentation of *ijtihād*, there is only the *mujtahid-muftī*, on the one hand, and the non-*mujtahid* layman or learned man,[72] on the other, both of whom ought to follow a *mujtahid-muftī*. Even as late as the tenth/sixteenth century, the adherents of Twelver Shīʿī *madhhab* may not have developed a stratified matrix of *muftī*s/*mujtahid*s in their school, as is shown in the absence of such discussions in their *adab al-fatwā* discourse. For example, in his work *Munyat al-murīd*, the famous Twelver Shīʿī scholar of the tenth/sixteenth century, Zayn al-Dīn ibn Muḥammad ibn ʿAlī (d. 966/1558–1559), known as al-Shahīd al-Thānī, discusses the qualities of the *muftī* who has the right to make *ijtihād* (legal innovation through issuing of fatwas). Once again in this discussion, the *muftī* is described as an absolute *mujtahid*, and there seem to be no secondary or tertiary levels of *ijtihād* as there were in the *adab al-fatwā* literature among Sunnī scholars centuries earlier.[73] This gives some indication that a stratification of the Twelver Shīʿī *madhhab* analogous to that of the Sunnī legal schools did not occur until later.

Once a distinct Twelver Shīʿī legal school emerged sometime after the tenth/sixteenth century, its adherents too developed a hierarchy and structure for their legal institution by the middle of the nineteenth century that are somewhat different from the Sunnī schools. The tripartite system of *muftī*s/*mujtahid*s went as follows: *mullā*, *ḥujjat al-Islām*, and *āyatullāh*. At the lowest level were the *mullā*s, who were not legitimized to make *ijtihād* or issue fatwas at all, as they were simply to act as religious guides to laymen in the community.[74] In the middle comes the *ḥujjat al-Islām*, who can infer legal opinions when the *āyatullāh*s have not taken a legal position on the issue.[75]At a higher level of *ijtihād* are the *āyatullāh*s, from

[71] al-Ḥillī, 240.

[72] Someone presumably learned in law but not qualified to make independent judgments about the law.

[73] See Zayn al-Dīn ibn Muḥammad ibn ʿAlī's (al-Shahīd al-Thānī) discussion in *Munyat al-murīd* about *adab al-fatwā* pgs. 275–305.

[74] Vikor, 134.

[75] Vikor, 135.

whom arises the highest level of religio-legal authority in the Twelver Shī'ī school: the *marja*'s. The *marja*'s are in a sense absolute independent *mujtahid*s whom all lower authorities must follow. The *marja*'s achieve their special rank through the recognition of other *āyatullāh*s.[76]

In terms of legal theory, where Twelver Shī'ī law is distinguished from its Sunnī counterpart is in its refutation of the validity of *qiyās* (legal analogy) as a legitimate legal device for deducing law. This is despite the fact that it affirms *qiyās*'s corollary, *ta'diyat al-ḥukm* (transitiveness of the rule),[77] which allows the ruling of one case to be transferred to another because of their similarities. On the other hand, it does not oppose *ijmā'* (consensus) as a legitimate means of arriving at a legal injunction, but narrows its scope to jurists whose consensus is legitimate to the Twelver Shī'ī fold.[78]

This concludes our brief presentation of the development of law and legal institutions in Shī'ī Islam. More will be said about Shī'ī legal thought when we address some of the fatwas from Shī'ī legal schools in the following chapter, yet the main point of this brief discussion is to show the points of convergence and divergence between Sunnī and Shī'ī *madhhabs*. Moreover, it is to be inferred that Shī'ī legal schools developed in conversation with the legal discourses that were influenced by earlier Sunnī legal thought, and hence, they did not have a completely independent path of evolution even when there are clear marks of distinction between Sunnī and Shī'ī legal schools.

A NOTE ON THE FORMATION OF THE IBĀḌĪ LEGAL THOUGHT AND INSTITUTIONS

The Emergence of the Ibāḍī *Madhhab* until the Second/Eighth Century

The early foundations of the Ibāḍī *madhhab* emerge from the legal activity and opinions of early Baṣran authorities like Jaber ibn Zayd (d. 93/711) and Abū 'Ubaydah Muslim ibn Abī Karīmah (145/762); proto-jurists whose opinions I examined in Chapter 2. The fatwas of Jaber played a crucial role in the formulation of both early Sunnī and Ibāḍī legal doctrines. His early influence on proto-Sunnī law is attested to by the preservation of many of his legal opinions in early Sunnī sources

[76] Vikor, 135.
[77] Stewart, 107–108; Vikor, 130–131.
[78] Stewart, 160; Vikor, 134.

of law.[79] Yet it was within Ibāḍīsm that Jaber's legal opinions had the greatest influence. This is because the early shapers of the Ibāḍī legal tradition, like Abū 'Ubaydah and al-Rabī' (d. 170/786), decided to make Jaber's opinions and approach to Islamic law the focal point of their legal discussions in distinction to other proto-jurists who thrived in the Baṣran and more broadly in the Iraqi (read *ray'ist*) regional milieu. This is because Jaber, despite his universal appeal among different theological and political groups in early Islam, was seen by members of Ibāḍī circles as someone sympathetic if not supportive of their theological views and political program.[80] Hence, they decided to centralize his legal views as the departure point from which to construct their distinct approach to the law.

As was alluded to earlier, Jaber's legal approach was in line with the Iraqi legal environment where proto-jurists from this region were predominately advocates of *ra'y*. As I have shown when analyzing his fatwa on the right to possession of unclaimed properties (AKA *iḥ āza*), Jaber diverged from the prominent legal precedence on the issue that was even supported by a prophetic tradition in which he was a principal transmitter. The cause of his divergence as is reported in Ibāḍī sources was his legal consideration of precaution (*iḥtiyāṭ*) or persevering property rights. This exercise of precaution by Jaber seemingly led his disciple Abū 'Ubaydah to make this consideration a predilection in his legal approach.[81] Yet despite Jaber's legal contributions, it is arguable whether Jaber can be considered the madhhab predecessor of the Ibāḍī school of law. This is so because he was not so doctrinally or methodologically distinguished from his Iraqi *ra'yist* contemporaries like Ibrāhīm al-Nakhaʿī and others to say that his legal ideas represented a separate school. In addition, his broad appeal, where he had disciples from outside those who were sympathetic to the Ibāḍī political movement and who transmitted and integrated his opinions in proto-Sunnī legal discussions, makes it difficult to argue that his contributions were what solely precipitated the formation of the Ibāḍī *madhhab*.[82]

The early development of a distinct Ibāḍī legal school lies in the attitudes to the law taken up by Jaber's second-century disciples like Abū

[79] See, for example, *Al-Muṣannaf* of 'Abd al-Razzāq al-Ṣana'anī where over twenty legal opinions are recorded for Jaber ibn Zayd that I have been able to trace.

[80] Wilkinson, 187–188; 194–195.

[81] See Abū Ghānim, vol. 3, 152.

[82] This is not to say that Jaber's legal opinions were not crucial to the formation of Ibāḍī legal doctrine, but his approach to the law was not the decisive factor in the formation of the Ibāḍī madhhab.

'Ubaydah, al-Rabī', and others who consciously took steps to distinguish a historical basis to the law that they would view as authoritative. Given the distinct political theology and political activities of this particular circle of Jaber's disciples that pitted them against the reigning Umayyad political authorities, they opted to separate from the larger Muslim political body and establish a legal doctrine that could govern the members of this distinct community. Such a legal doctrine drew its distinctions not so much with having divergent views from the majoritarian legal opinions but from being constructed from this circle of jurists' specific engagement with the legal opinions of Jaber ibn Zayd, whom they now deemed as the sole legal authority from all other legal predecessors for whom they would center their legal conversations.[83]

This attitude was demonstrated earlier in my analysis of Abū 'Ubaydah's fatwa, which uses Jaber's legal opinion and principles as the starting precedent to argue his position. Al-Rabī' then confirms this as the established position among this circle of jurists and thus undermining 'Abd Allāh ibn 'Abd al-Azīz's efforts to modify this position by appealing to the precedent of the majority of jurists outside of this particular Baṣran circle. This is how these legal arguments led to the establishment of an authoritative legal doctrine, leading to an establishment of an earlier version of an Ibāḍī *madhhab*.

Yet it was not merely this practice that brought about the early formation of this school but the conceptualization of that distinguishing practice as introduced by Abū 'Ubaydah of the "[True] Bearers of Knowledge" (*ḥamalat al-'ilm*).[84] This concept becomes the basis of legitimation for establishing authoritative lines of jurists whose opinions come to define the early Ibāḍī *madhhab*: Jaber–Abū 'Ubaydah–al-Rabī' or Jaber–Dhammam–al-Rabī'.[85] Al-Rabī' cements the establishment of these authoritative lines by authorizing the legal opinions of his predecessors in a series of written works (*Athar al-Rabī'*, *Musnad al-Rabī'*, etc.) that are attributed to him.[86] Although this emerging Ibāḍī legal doctrine is not drastically different from the legal positions of the wider circle of early Muslim jurists,[87] it is distinguished by the specific lines of authority that legitimate that doctrine. This specific set of authorities is what defines

[83] Ennami, 84.
[84] For more on this concept, see Al-'Aghbarī 68–70 and Ennami 101–105.
[85] Ennami, 110; Francesca, 213; and Al-Kharusi, 14–15.
[86] Ennami, 110; Francesca, 213; and Al-Kharusi, Chap. 1.
[87] Al-Kharusi, 162.

a school, and it is what defined the early formation of the Ibāḍī *madhhab* that took shape by the end of the second and early third century.

Later Development of the Ibāḍī *Madhhab*: Third to Sixth Centuries

In the third century, Ibāḍīsm experienced a political resurgence with the establishment of the Ibāḍī Rustumī dynasty in North Africa (modern-day Algeria) that was independent of the Sunnī Abbasid Caliphate centered in Baghdad. There were also Ibāḍī domains that came into existence in southern Arabia (Oman/Yemen) around the same time. This allowed for some of the members of the new vanguard of Ibāḍīsm (*ḥamalat al-ʿilm*) to migrate from their regional center in Basra, Iraq, to these regions so as to embed Ibāḍīsm into the sociopolitical fabric of those regions through the implementation of Ibāḍī law at the level of governance.[88] All the while, the Ibāḍī legal discourse remained in conversation with the legal developments occurring within the larger Islamic legal tradition that was taking place in the third and fourth centuries.[89] The legal synthesis that took place between the advocates of *ray'* and the advocates of *ḥadīth* and the proliferation of *ḥadīth* throughout Muslim lands during the third and fourth centuries was re-aliening the legal commitments of the various groups (see Chapter 3). The Ibāḍīs were no exception to this trend, and by the fourth century, Ibāḍī jurists and legal theorists began steering the Ibāḍī *madhhab* along with these new developments.

The proliferation of *ḥadīth* further facilitated within the Ibāḍī madhhab, which always acknowledged the prophetic practice as a source of law,[90] the integration of more *ḥadīth* into their legal analysis from Sunnī sources beyond what prophetic statements were already embedded in the Ibāḍī *athar* tradition. This impact of this diffusion was already having an impact on Ibāḍī law beginning in the fourth century when major Omani Ibāḍī jurists like Abū Saʿīd al-Kudamī (fourth/tenth century) issued legal opinions guided by *ḥadīth* that went against the precedent within the madhhab.[91]

[88] See Al-ʾAghbarī, 66–67, and Muʿammar, 500, for the propagation of Ibāḍīsm by the "Bearers of Knowledge" into North Africa leading to the establishment of Rustumī dynasty. See Wilkinson 215–219 for the propagation of Ibāḍīsm into Oman and Yemen.

[89] Al-ʾAghbarī, 89–91.

[90] See Ennami 112–113 for statements from Jaber ibn Zayd and Abū ʿUbaydah supporting this assertion.

[91] Al-Kharusi, 13.

Nevertheless, one should not overstate the impact of this integration of non-Ibāḍī-sourced *ḥadīth* on the overall trajectory of the *madhhab* because this newfound ḥadīth was always viewed through the prism of established Ibāḍī practice. Hence, such *ḥadīth* literature may have enhanced the legitimacy of Ibāḍī practice, and in some cases, it modified it, but *ḥadīth* was never the sole determiner of it. The prophetic practice as embodied in *ḥadīth* was authoritative but only understood by the guided Ibāḍī hermeneutical authority of the "*ḥamalat al-'ilm*" (Bearers of Knowledge). Therefore, the absorption of Sunnī-sourced *ḥadīth* led to some convergence between Sunnīs and Ibāḍīs but never quite made the Ibāḍī madhhab lose its distinct identity and character.[92] If that were not the case, the Ibāḍī *madhhab* would not have currently maintained differences in legally guided ritual and social practice such as wiping on the leather sock in ablution or the legitimacy of the marriage of fornicators, which went against some explicit injunctions of *ḥadīth* found in Sunnī sources.[93]

The convergence between Ibāḍīsm and the wider Islamic legal tradition occurred not only with the absorption of Sunnī-sourced *ḥadīth* but also with the Ibāḍī acceptance in the fourth and the fifth centuries of the maturing Islamic legal theory (*usul al-fiqh*) that was being cultivated by non-Ibāḍī jurists. So, the aforementioned al-Kudamī and his contemporary 'Abd Allah ibn Baraka (fourth/tenth century) began to speak of the foundations of Ibāḍī law as being based on four sources – mirroring the systemization of their Sunnī and in some instances their Shii counterparts – Quran, *sunna* (prophetic practice), *ijmā' l'ittifaq* (consensus/agreement), and 'aql/ *ra'y* (intellect/opinion).[94] Al-'Awātibī (fifth/eleventh century) and Abū Ya'coub al-Warajalanī (d. 570/1174) continued this systemization of Ibāḍī law under these theoretical categories, which continued to draw the Ibāḍī legal discourse closer to the mainstream legal tradition. Eventually, Ibāḍī law accepted the same four sources of law as categorized in Sunnī legal theory: Quran, *sunna*, *ijmā'*, and *qiyas*.[95] However,

[92] Wilkinson overstates the impact of the integration of Sunnī-sourced *ḥadīth* into Ibāḍīsm saying that it led a process of Sunnīzation of Ibāḍīsm, which he called "normalization." As I have pointed out, Ibāḍī convergence with non-Ibāḍī practices and traditions was a part and parcel of the movement of consolidation and synthesis that was occurring within the wider Islamic legal tradition. Yet, every madhhab retained its own particularities and character even with the movement toward such convergence.

[93] See Ennami pgs. 139–149 for a lengthy discussion of the differences between Ibāḍī and Sunnī rulings.

[94] T. al-Shaybānī, 20.

[95] See T. al-Shaybānī, 19–32.

Ibāḍī *athar* (precedent) continued to influence how such categories would be interpreted and implemented and is what maintained the distinctness of the Ibāḍī *madhhab* despite the trend toward convergence.[96]

Yet the increasing systemization of Ibāḍī law and its convergence with Sunnī law never led to the stratification of their *madhhab* in the same way that Sunnī *madhhabs* have undergone. So, similar to Twelver Shīʿī and the Zaydī *madhhabs*, *ijtihād* continued to be unrestrictedly practiced by anyone who was qualified to issue legal opinions.[97] Yet, in Ibāḍīsm, even if one were to attain the level of the absolute *mujtahid* (*mujtahid muṭlaq*), one is still expected to remain an adherent to the Ibāḍī *madhhab* along the broad contours of the precepts and early precedence that defined that school even though they may differ with their *madhhab* predecessors on particular aspects of the doctrine. An example that is cited in the Ibāḍī *madhhab* of those who attained that status of absolute jurists but remained as Ibāḍī adherents is the before-mentioned Abū Saʿīd al-Kudamī (fourth/tenth century) and Nur al-Dīn al-Salīmī (d. 1914) in modern times.[98]

CONCLUSION

The Islamic legal tradition was a result of slow discursive and dialectic processes that gave this tradition its particular qualities. This tradition was discursive in the sense that it emerged from a set of foundational discourses and subdiscourses that were a starting point for its legal doctrines and practices. Yet it was the dialectic and dialogic engagement of those foundational discourses by the participants and specialists of this tradition that produced a legal structure that gave this tradition the form by which it shaped the legal activity in subsequent generations.

An example of the distinct forms of this tradition was the classification of *muftī*s and the systemization of fatwas that came into being with the maturation of the legal schools. Islamic legal schools did not have formal ecclesiastic bodies that supervised the activity of *iftāʾ* in accordance with the rules that were spelled out in the *adab al-fatwā* literature. The categorization of *muftī*s and levels of *iftāʾ* merely meant that there were a set of mutually recognized rules among jurists that would govern how fatwas were to be issued and who was entitled to do so. In other words, there

96 Wilkinson, 414, 419.
97 Muʿammar, 62–63.
98 Al-Kindī, 128.

were no formalized or elected groups of *muftī*s in each *madhhab* who would administer the activity of fatwa and ensure that such rules were observed. Instead, their shared recognition of different levels of epistemic authority was a result of a consensus among these later jurists.

However, the model of a stratified hierarchy of *madhhab*-affiliated jurists that was taking shape in Sunnīsm never gained the same traction in non-Sunnī schools of law except in late post-classical Twelver Shīʿī (c. 1850), albeit in a less differentiated way. Thus, the understanding of *madhhabs* in these minority schools took on a different hue than it did in the majoritarian schools. *Madhhabs* in this understanding merely meant the existence of a distinct legal doctrine that was established by past authorities whose legal ideas continued to be the focal point of the legal discussions of subsequent adherents who further developed and modified that doctrine. Not central to this non-Sunnī understanding of a *madhhab* is the idea that there is a descending hierarchy of authorities that is correlative to the temporal distance of subsequent authorities from the *madhhab* predecessor(s).

In the following chapter, we examine actual fatwas from the post-classical period, showing how these constraints were observed and how *muftī*s had to navigate through and around them to issue their fatwas. These *madhhab* constraints by no means closed off innovation in Islamic law, but they did circumscribe the aspects of the law that could receive new attention. These ranks and rules in a sense produced continuity in the law that was perhaps necessary for the law to develop further. But, as we will notice in the next chapter, change was inevitable, and this required *muftī*s to keep up with these changes through new fatwas that were in congruence with established legal rulings and the discursive rules that governed their fatwas.

5

Fatwa in the Age of the Preponderance of Legal Schools

INTRODUCTION

The last chapter demonstrated how Islamic legal schools became the paradigm through which Islamic law was articulated. This was illustrated by the development of discursive rules that regulated the manner by which fatwas were to be issued and the rank of those *muftī*s who would be issuing them. In this chapter, I intend to illustrate more concretely how those rules were applied in actual fatwas of this period, by sampling and analyzing fatwas from the post-classical period (c. 1100 to 1850 CE), as this was the period when legal schools/doctrines (*madhhab*s) and legal theory (*uṣūl al-fiqh*) were fully established and firmly rooted in Islamic legal practice so that they exerted the most influence on Islamic legal production. More broadly though, this period in the lands of Islam represents a unity from the perspective of the maturity, continuity, and influence of Muslim religious institutions on Muslim society, such as Muslim theological schools, Sufi *ṭarīqa*s (mystical orders), and *futuwwa* organizations (social and guild fraternities).

In this selection of fatwas, representative samples of major fatwas will be chosen so as to show the nature of the activity of *iftāʾ* during this era and how this activity had been transformed since the classical age of fatwa. The criteria for such selections will be revealed in later sections of this chapter. Yet it is not the only goal of this chapter to show the discursive activity of *iftāʾ* during this period. This chapter aims indirectly to demonstrate how fatwas helped Muslim society keep pace with social change by modifying the legal corpus that governed it. This demonstration makes clear that the impetus for fatwas stems from sociohistorical circumstances, yet at the same time these fatwas influence the human practices that shape social reality. It is this dialectic between law and society that this chapter will attempt to bring to light. In order to achieve this objective, a sketch of the sociopolitical circumstances of this period will be outlined so as to historically contextualize the fatwas of this period.

THE SOCIOHISTORICAL AND POLITICAL SITUATION IN THE MUSLIM WORLD IN THE AGE OF *MADHHAB* PREPONDERANCE: C. 1100–1850 CE

From the point of view of political and social developments, the period of *madhhab* preponderance may be more conveniently divided into two phases: 1100–1500 and 1500–1850 CE. Most generally speaking, the phase between 1100 and 1500 CE, especially in its first half (1100–1300), witnessed greater political fragmentation of the geographic heartlands of Muslim society centered in the Near East and Central Asia than what had existed in the earlier post-caliphate period (c. 950–1100 CE). The region came under the control of smaller independent dynasties like the Ayyubids, Seljuks, and Ghaznavids who controlled most of the Muslim geographic heartland after the initial demise of the caliphate.[1]

Moreover, the period between 1100 and 1300 CE was also known for the specter of foreign threats such as the Crusades and the Mongol invasions in the heartlands of Islam and the Reconquista in Spain that brought large swaths of Muslim lands under foreign control.[2] Nevertheless, the political fragmentation of previous Muslim states in the Muslim heartlands (Seljuks and Fatimids) spurred alternative political movements that brought about the formation of new dynastic states like the Zengid and Ayyubid that gained ascendancy in Syria and Egypt during the twelfth century and slowly restored the lands lost to the Crusaders. These dynasties supported Sunnī Muslim orthodoxy and tended to patronize the *ʿulamāʾ* and Muslim religious institutions like mosques and *madrasas*.[3] During the twelfth and thirteenth centuries, *ʿulamāʾ* from all over the Muslim world flocked to the centers of the Zengid–Ayyubid state and then the Mamluk state (1250–1517 CE) that was centered in Cairo.[4] This was in part due to the financial support of scholars by these dynasties,

[1] Hodgson, v. 2, 263; Lapidus, 201; Wink, v. 2, 9.
[2] Hodgson, v. 2, 263; Sonn, 79–85; Wink, v. 2, 11–12.
[3] Hodgson, v. 2, 266; Lapidus, 291; Sonn, 87–88.
[4] Lapidus, 291.

but one must also consider the factor that many of these scholars were more likely driven out of their homelands in Iran, Iraq, and Central Asia as a result of the Mongol invasions of those areas during the thirteenth century as well from Spain and Palestine as result of the Reconquista and the Crusades, respectively. Gilbert shows that nearly half the resident *ʿulamāʾ* of twelfth- and thirteenth -century Damascus were immigrants.[5] For example, Ibn Taymiyya, a scholar whose fatwas will be considered later in the chapter, was one such immigrant scholar to Damascus from Harran, which is in present-day Turkey, where his parents fled because of the Mongol invasions.

As a result of this state patronage, this period witnessed a shift in the relationship between the *ʿulamāʾ* and the Muslim political elite. In the age of caliphate, the *ʿulamāʾ* maintained an overall economic and political independence from the governing elite. Toward the end of the fifth/eleventh century, the relationship between the Muslim scholarly elite drew closer to the Muslim political elite because of their patronage. This increasing trend toward state support for scholarship took greater hold under the Seljuk dynasty of Iran, Iraq, and Syria in the late fifth/eleventh century with the establishment of the Nizamiyya colleges, and this patronage continued throughout the period of the twelfth to fifteenth century under the Ayyubid and Mamluk states of Syria and Egypt and the Ilkhanid and Timurid dynasties of Iran and Iraq.[6] Moreover, in the same period, there was a greater number of *ʿulamāʾ* who were employed in state service.[7] This closer cooperation between the *ʿulamāʾ* and the rulers and the patronage of the *ʿulamāʾ* by the political elite signified a greater loss of economic and political independence for the *ʿulamāʾ* during this period, which increased the tendency of making them instruments of the Muslim state and increasing the legitimacy of those in power.[8] The trend of the religious establishment drawing closer to the circles of the political elite became even stronger in later periods, especially under the Ottoman dynasty.[9]

During this period, Islamic law, as embodied in the legal doctrines of the *madhhab*s, maintained a central position and was made always relevant to changing conditions through the fatwas practiced by jurists, who

[5] Gilbert, 112–113.
[6] Arjomand, 269–276.
[7] See Gilbert, 126, who documents this fact for the Ayyubid state.
[8] See Arjomand, 279–283, and Gilbert, 132–133, for more on this point.
[9] Lapidus, 207.

were respected by Muslims throughout the lands of Islam.[10] Yet the pace of change in Islamic law that was facilitated by fatwas in the pre-modern period was evolutionary and organic in that there were no major breaks in the way the law was conceived or practiced. There were only piecemeal and particular modifications of the law when circumstances necessitated those changes.[11] *Madhhab*s influenced this conservative pace of change in the Islamic legal system through their established legal doctrines that now confined the scope of fatwas in terms of new legal production to those matters that were not directly addressed by those doctrines (as I will demonstrate in the next section of this chapter).

To comprehend how fatwas were integral to the cultivation and maintenance of Islamic law, one need only look at the practice of Muslim judges (*qāḍī*s) in their court proceedings.

Fatwas, which reflected the authoritative doctrines of the *madhhab*s, were often requested by judges from *muftī*s in hard cases, and these fatwas "normatively constituted the basis of the *qāḍī*'s ruling."[12] As Hallaq notes, this phenomenon explains why court decisions in themselves were not deemed authoritative or binding precedents in Islamic law as was the case in common law legal systems. This also explains why the decisions of Muslim courts were never kept and published as was the case for common law courts.[13]

Hence, Islamic law, on a whole, was not a product of state machinery and was largely cultivated by *muftī*s who were agents of civil society, that is, "separate and self-conscious networks or institutions independent of the state or in opposition to the state"[14] – and not agents of the state.[15] So, the development of Islamic law had relative independence from the state and was somewhat impervious to the changes of dynasties and political rule.[16] Although Islamic law was relatively autonomous from the state, the state-sponsored courts and *qāḍī*s (judges) who were enforcing these rules were not. While the muftī largely derived his authority from the

[10] Hodgson, v. 2, 351–352.
[11] Hallaq, 2009, 183.
[12] Hallaq, 2009, 177–178. See also Burak, 29–30, who shows how fatwas operated in the Mamluk dynasty's judicial apparatuses serving as the normative basis of judicial rulings.
[13] Hallaq, 2009, 178.
[14] Vikor, 185–186.
[15] Vikor, 188.
[16] Vikor, 187. Burak argues that a branch of the Ḥanafī *madhhab* that was connected to the Ottoman state was affected doctrinally by the machinations of the state (see Burak, 18), but in my later analysis of a fatwa by the Ottoman chief muftī, I will demonstrate how Burak's claim is an overstatement.

public based on his epistemic standing even if he served in the capacity of a state official, the *qāḍī*, on the other hand, acquired his primary authority from the state. So, Sharīʿa courts were an apparatus of the state but were based on laws that were "outside the state's domain."[17] So while the *qāḍī* was a state official, muftīs, on the whole, were members of civil society so long as they were able to play their role as explicators of the law apart from state apparatuses such as the courts.[18] This relationship would change in the future as some later Muslim ruling dynasties like the Ottomans incorporated the office of muftī into the state machinery.

If the first phase of the age of *madhhab* preponderance represents the height of political fragmentation, the latter period, from c. 1500 to 1800 CE, represents a period of greater political integration and consolidation around three major empires that arose in the Muslim world: the Ottomans in Anatolia, Southeastern Europe, and the Middle East and North Africa; the Safavids in Persia; and the Mughals in India. During this period, there was even greater rapprochement and integration between government institutions and the *ʿulamāʾ* and religious institutions.[19] During the previous period, the *ʿulamāʾ* had lost some degree of their autonomy and became somewhat subordinated to the military regimes that came into ascendancy in the Muslim world, but in this age of great Muslim empires, they lost even more of their autonomy as many of the religious institutions and cultural forms were brought into closer relation to these imperial institutions.[20]

In the Ottoman Empire, "the *ʿulamāʾ* came under state control, but in doing so they brought the Sharīʿa into the center of state life."[21] The sultan achieved greater authority over those social domains that were under the influence of the Sharīʿa, but at the same time, the Sharīʿa and *ʿulamāʾ* were more recognized in the operations of the government.[22] The *ʿulamāʾ* came to have great power and prestige in the Ottoman state. Training and testing were required to acquire their official ranks as *qāḍī*s (judges) and muftīs,[23] and they were well organized and had a considerable degree

[17] Vikor, 187.
[18] Vikor, 187–188; Tucker (1998, 21) asserts that this was also the case of non-state appointed muftīs during Ottoman times.
[19] Burak's work (2016) demonstrates this point amply in the case of the Ottoman Empire. See also Hodgson, v. 3, 5.
[20] See Burak, 10–11, and Hodgson, v. 3, 105.
[21] Hodgson, v. 3, 105.
[22] For more details on this point, see Burak, 39–43. See also Hodgson, v. 3, 106, and Lapidus, 217.
[23] Burak, 133.

of impunity to the extent that the chief muftī (*shaykh al-Islam*) was given the authority to issue a deposition to the sultan if he was deemed unfit.[24]

Yet, there were imperial policies and administrative ordinances known as *qānūn*, which were legislated by the ruler and were not the product of the jurists' discourses, but were nevertheless Sharīʿa legitimated by the *ʿulamāʾ* through various Sharīʿa principles such as *ʿurf* (custom) and/or *al-siyāsa al-sharʿiyya* (ethical diplomacy). The purpose of these imperial *qānūn* ordinances was to address those aspects of public order that had not been addressed by Sharīʿa law directly because they were specific to the particular political framework of whatever imperial court was issuing them. These policies and ordinances were certified by the appointed *ʿulamāʾ* as long as they were not inconsistent with the Sharīʿa.[25]

On the other hand, the Safavid dynasty of Persia was an exception to the trend of close collaboration between the religious establishment and imperial court. The Safavid dynasty was driven by religious zeal to propagate Twelver Shīʿī Islam (Imāmī or Jaʿfarī Shīʿīs) among its majority Sunnī subjects and thus invited and patronized many foreign Twelver Shīʿī *ʿulamāʾ* to Persia so as to achieve its ideological goals,[26] and many foreign Shīʿī scholars were invited to Persia.[27] The Safavids nevertheless "continued to operate on the earlier model of maintaining a degree of separation between the military/political sovereign and the Sharīʿa establishment."[28]

Part of the reason why there was a more tenuous relationship between the Twelver Shīʿī religious establishment and the imperial court in the Safavid state was that Twelver Shīʿī *ʿulamāʾ* were not accustomed to cooperating with the political establishment, since there were not many

24 Hodgson, v. 3, 108. The deposition of no fewer than ten Ottoman sultans was finalized and legitimated by the fatwas of the chief muftīs of the empire dating back as early as Sultan Osman II in 1622 CE and as late as the last Ottoman Sultan Mehmet VI in 1922 CE (I am grateful to the Ottoman historian Mehmet Ipsirli, Professor Emeritus of History at Istanbul University, for providing me this information through personal communication).

25 For more on *qānūn*, see Hallaq, 2009, 200, and Hodgson, v. 3, 109. Burak argues how the sultan's edicts (*qānūn*) went as far as to influence the substantive doctrines and institutional structures of Islamic (Ḥanafī) law (see pg. 10 and pg. 213), yet my later analysis of the fatwa by an official Ottoman chief muftī will show that this assertion is somewhat misplaced.

26 For more on this point, see Newman's article on religious trends in the Safavid dynasty under the entry "Safawids" in EI2, v. 8, pgs. 777–780.

27 S. H. Nasr, pg. 162, and Hourani pg. 187 in Dabashi, S. H. Nasr, and W. Nasr's *Expectations of the Millennium: Shi'ism in History*.

28 Hallaq, 2009, 202.

instances in the history of Islam where an independent state[29] emerged that openly professed the ideology of Twelver Shi'ism.[30] Twelver Shīʿīs were a minority group, and most ruling dynasties in the Muslim world up until that time had been Sunnī. Hence, the Twelver Shīʿī religious establishment developed a suspicion of political powers, and this attitude was hard to overcome even when the new Safavid state actively promoted Twelver Shīʿī doctrine.[31]

Yet, most reservations that the Twelver Shīʿī religious establishment had about the Safavid state were eventually overcome as subsequent Safavid rulers in Persia moved away from the millenarian tendencies of the early regime toward accepting a more orthodox form of Twelver Shīʿism.[32] With continued Safavid patronage of Shīʿī *ʿulamāʾ* and the building of Shīʿī institutions like religious schools and mosques, many Twelver Shīʿī *ʿulamāʾ* by the early seventeenth century came to support the Safavid dynasty's legitimacy and drew closer to the imperial court by accepting official state religious posts.[33] One such position was that of the *ṣadr*, an appointed religious state official who was to act as a liaison between the political court and the religious establishment.[34]

The third major Muslim dynasty in this period was the Mughals in India. Unlike the Ottoman and Safavid dynasties, whose rulers had fairly uniform policies toward Islam and Islamic institutions, in Mughal India, this varied significantly according to the ruling emperor. For example, toward the earlier stages of the empire during the reign of Emperor Akbar (r. 1556–1605), traditional Muslim *ʿulamāʾ*, for example, were more alienated from the courtly circle as a result of Akbar's religiously syncretic positions,[35] while during later stages of the empire, in the reign of Emperor Aurangzeb (r. 1658–1707), Islam and the traditional *ʿulamāʾ* establishment

29 The Buyid dynasty in fifth/eleventh-century Iraq and Persia is but one of the few examples of a ruling elite that had a Twelver Shīʿī orientation and supported Shīʿī causes yet remained symbolically under the suzerainty of the Sunnī caliphate.

30 See R. M. Savory's article on the dynastic, political, and military history of the Safavids in EI2, v. 8, pg. 765.

31 I will show that the tenth/sixteenth-century fatwa of the Twelver Shīʿī jurist al-Karakī that I will analyze later in this chapter is an attempt to get Shīʿī scholars to overcome their negative attitude toward political power, especially in regard to the Safavid dynasty.

32 See Arjomand, 184–185 in Dabashi, S. H. Nasr, and W. Nasr's *Expectations of the Millennium: Shi'ism in History*.

33 For more details, see Newman's article on the Religious Trends in the Safavid Dynasty under the entry "Safawids" in EI2, v. 8, pgs. 778–779

34 Hodgson, v. 3, 53; Lapidus, 242.

35 Lapidus, 372; Sonn 100–101, 105.

were given greater authority in the state. For example, one of the major contributions to Sharīʿa law in India was his commissioning of a Ḥanafī legal compendium known as *Fatwa-i ʻAlamgiri* (also known as Al-Fatāwa Al-Hindīyya), which was commissioned by Emperor Aurangzeb himself.[36]

All in all, the Islamic religious establishment and the Muslim state became ever closer in the age of *madhhab* preponderance (c.1100–1900 CE), and the distance that had previously existed between them in the formative period was bridged. The legal and political impact of this new cooperation between the religious establishment and the state will be better assessed in the next section when we look at fatwas that were issued during this period by muftīs some of whom were under the patronage of these various Muslims states.

THE SYSTEMIZATION AND STRUCTURING OF ISLAMIC LAW: *FATWAS* WITHIN THE CONFINES OF *MADHHABS* IN THE ISLAMIC MIDDLE PERIOD

The remainder of this chapter will illustrate how fatwas were issued in the post-formative period of Islamic law, which approximately spans from the sixth/twelfth century all the way to the tenth/sixteenth century, under rules and restrictions of the legal schools (*madhhab*s) that were preponderant in this age. In selecting the fatwas that would illustrate this point, I used the following criteria to determine which of the many thousands of fatwas best suited the objectives of this investigation: First, the selected fatwa had to be issued by a famous jurist/muftī of a particular legal school (*madhhab*). This would better ensure that the fatwa was in some ways looked at as having greater authority and thus put into practice, given the stature of the jurist in question. Second, the rationale used in the fatwa should in some way reflect the need to navigate through the discursive rules of the *madhhab*, established legal theory *(uṣūl al-fiqh)*, and/or a dominant legal precedent to which the muftī issuing the fatwa adhered. Third, the selected fatwa should in some way have promoted a change in the religio-legal practices or precedent, thereby illustrating the continually evolving character of Islamic law. Fourth, the fatwa chosen should be of sufficient length to demonstrate the types of legal rationale that were developed in that particular period. Fifth, the fatwa should have been precipitated by a change in social or historical circumstances and conditions. Hence, this analysis will not deal with fatwas that are

[36] Guenther, 212.

concerned with ritual or strictly religious matters, as those types of practices tend to show more continuity over time than they do change. Lastly, these fatwas should be concerned with sociohistorical issues of universal significance or scope and not be confined to the concerns of individuals or particular groups.

The last two criteria ensure that this discussion of fatwas is taken out of the strict realm of purely legal discussion into the realm of social reality, which fatwas influenced and were influenced by. It should be noted that not all the fatwas selected for this investigation met all the criteria mentioned earlier, as it was a difficult task to sift through thousands of fatwas and find ones that would simultaneously meet all the criteria that were set. Nevertheless, if a particular fatwa met most of the criteria and was particularly illustrative of some of the criteria in some salient way, then it was selected as an example of fatwas from this period.

The fatwas chosen were issued by muftīs from varied geographic locations around the Muslim world during this period, which will also demonstrate patterns of uniformity and diversity of the practice of *iftāʾ* in different cultural and regional settings. In addition, the fatwas chosen for this analysis represent a broad spectrum of fields dealing with social, economic, and political issues as well as fatwas that emerge from muftīs who represent various ideological and sectarian trends. So the idea is to be as inclusive as practically possible in the fatwa selection for this investigation so as to get an accurate representation of the fatwa activity of this period.

Ibn Rushd al-Jadd's Fatwa on Pardoning or Punishing for Murder: c. Sixth/Twelfth Century

The Andalusian Mālikī jurist Ibn Rushd al-Jadd (d. 520/1126)[37] issued a fatwa in a criminal case of murder that took place in Cordoba in the year 516/1122.[38] The case involves a father who was murdered by an intoxicated person where the deceased was survived by three minor

[37] To be distinguished from his famous philosopher-jurist grandson, who is also called Ibn Rushd (d. 1198).

[38] This particular fatwa of Ibn Rushd al-Jadd is found in the collections of Ibn Rushd's fatwas, and Hallaq has translated an unabridged version of this fatwa in his book *Authority, Continuity and Change in Islamic Law*. Hallaq's translation and some of his commentary will be utilized in this analysis. Nevertheless, this analysis will have a greater reliance on the original Arabic version of the fatwa that is found in Ibn Rushd's collection of fatwas because the circumstances surrounding the fatwa are presented there with more detail. See Ibn Rushd, v. 2, fatwa # 385, pg. 1196. See also Hallaq, 2004, pgs. 195-200 for translation of this fatwa.

children,[39] who became the focus of the debate in the fatwa. Moreover, the agnates in this case are the victim's brother and the brother's adult children, who demanded the execution of the murderer.[40] The fatwa adjudicates whether the agnates of a murdered victim have the right to call for the immediate execution of the murderer or whether the minority children of the murdered victim have the right to pardon the murderer once they reach the age of majority.

Ibn Rushd's stance is that minority children should be allowed to attain the age of majority and be given the choice to pardon or punish the perpetrator, thus circumscribing the right of the agnates to exact immediate punishment.[41] It should be noted that the position that Ibn Rushd takes is counter to the established position of the doctrine of the Mālikī *madhhab*, which gives the agnates the authority to exact immediate punishment.[42] So here Ibn Rushd's fatwa goes against the established doctrine, which impels him to give a full argument to justify his point of view.

In his fatwa, Ibn Rushd decides to correct what he believes is a widespread misperception that no muftī should go against the established doctrine of his adopted school. Ibn Rushd responds to this assertion by claiming instead that no muftī should follow or issue legal opinions according to an existing doctrine unless he knows that it is sound.[43] This clears the way for him to argue his case against the established legal ruling of the school. What he asserts in this fatwa necessitates that the muftī knows more than just the doctrine itself, including the legal rationale establishing its soundness.

After establishing his right to disagree with the established Mālikī doctrine, Ibn Rushd attempts to give justification for his legal position by quoting the relevant proof texts that support his position. On this point, he quotes relevant passages of the Quran (2:178; 17:33) and several *ḥadīth*s that establish the right of the heir of the victim to seek punishment or pardon the killer.[44] Ibn Rushd is aware that the discursive legal tradition is grounded in the sacred text of the Quran and *ḥadīth* and hence the importance of offering an interpretation of these sources that would legitimate his point of view and avoid the point of view of Mālikī

39 Ibn Rushd, v. 2, fatwa # 385, pg. 1197. See also Hallaq, 2004, 206.
40 Ibn Rushd, v. 2, fatwa # 385, pg. 1197. See also Hallaq, 2004, 200.
41 Ibn Rushd, v. 2, fatwa # 385, pg. 1198. See also Hallaq, 2004, 195.
42 Ibn Rushd, v. 2, fatwa # 385, pg. 1197. See also Hallaq, 2004, 195.
43 Ibn Rushd, v. 2, fatwa # 385, pg. 1197. See also Hallaq, 2004, 195–196.
44 Ibn Rushd, v. 2, fatwa # 385, pgs. 1198–1200. See also Hallaq, 2004, 196–197.

tradition, which he believes is inconsistent with the implications of those sacred texts as well as with the Mālikī *madhhab*'s own legal principles for arriving at valid rulings.

Ibn Rushd claims that some jurists who interpret the stated Quranic passages assert that it is not the right of the agnates to pursue punishment before the minor children come of age because it would negate the children's right to pardon and receive the blood money. He also claims that this last stated opinion is analogous to the legal rights of minor children in non-penal cases that are not transferred to the closest relatives such as cases of preemption, where the child is allowed to attain the age of majority and claim his/her rights. Ibn Rushd tries to situate these opinions among jurists of his own school and jurists of other schools like al-Shāfiʿī,[45] knowing that in order to advance his argument he needs to show that there is a precedent for his position.

Once he shows that some of the preceding jurists held his view, thereby giving his opinion greater legitimacy, Ibn Rushd then begins to undermine the legal basis of the established position of the Mālikī school. The Mālikī school relegates the right of punishment to the agnates if the victim's heirs are minors, and the adherents of this school established this legal position through the legal hermeneutics of *istiḥsān* (juristic preference), obviating the conclusion based on *qiyās* (juristic inference or analogy), which preserves the minor children's right to attain age so that they may determine whether they want to pardon or punish.[46]

The point that Ibn Rushd makes here is that legal rulings that are established by the legal rationale of *qiyās* (juristic inference) are stronger than those opinions established by other forms of legal rationale because *qiyās* is one of the four unanimously accepted means of establishing law in Islamic legal theory, while *istiḥsān* is not.[47] Ibn Rushd claims that the justification for those who base their judgment on *istiḥsān* is their belief in the greater value of punishment over that of pardoning. Ibn Rushd states that this is because the punishment is seen as a deterrence from committing a crime, and those who argue for the greater value of punishment find support for their view in the Quranic verse which encourages

[45] Ibn Rushd, v. 2, fatwa # 385, pg. 1199. See also Hallaq, 2004, 197.

[46] Ibn Rushd, v. 2, fatwa # 385, pg. 1201. See also Hallaq, 2004, 198.

[47] It should be recalled from the previous discussion that the legal ruling that is established through the hermeneutics of *istiḥsān* is, by definition, one that annuls an opposite legal ruling that has been established through *qiyās* for some overarching reason necessitating such invalidation. Hence, for those who advocate *istiḥsān*, it is only used in rare occasions where the conclusions reached by *qiyās* have created odd situations that jurists believe run counter to the spirit of the law.

punishment by stating: "There is life in retaliation...."[48] Ibn Rushd disagrees with this point of view and claims that the value of pardoning overrides that of punishment and finds support in another set of Quranic passages (3:133–134; 42:20; 42:43) that speak of the merits of pardoning wrongdoers.[49] He also quotes a *ḥadīth* of the Prophet that indicates that he encouraged the heirs of victims to pardon murderers.[50] Therefore, he concludes that since pardoning is recommended, the minor children should be allowed to attain the age of majority so as to be given the opportunity to practice the greater of the two rights of pardoning.[51]

In the latter part of the argument for his position, Ibn Rushd handles those elements of legal theory (*qiyās* and *istiḥsān*) that are relevant to the case at hand and tries to show that the theoretical basis of his opponents' position (*istiḥsān*) is weak given that their rationale for this basis (the greater value of punishment that would necessitate a speedy verdict) is not supported by his hermeneutics of Quranic values that give greater weight to clemency. Moreover, Ibn Rushd argues that rulings based on *qiyās* have the preponderant position in the legal principles of the Mālikī *madhhab;* hence, this ruling based on *istiḥsān* is in violation of those principles[52] (see Figure 15).

As was shown in the previous chapters, fatwas prior to the establishment of the *madhhab*s' legal doctrines were a matter of debate between jurists and the legal positions they espoused. Once some of these personal legal positions evolved into doctrines of the legal schools, the debate about legal opinions (fatwas) was no longer strictly a matter of one independent jurist advancing the legal rationale for his position against the opinion of another. The matter now became much more complex and restricted, as Ibn Rushd's fatwa shows, where jurists now had to deal with established legal doctrines to which they adhered and had to situate their own legal opinions within the crafted opinions of preceding jurists in their legal school.

Hence, Ibn Rushd's fatwa shows us that the character of the fatwa process (*iftāʾ*) had changed during the period when legal doctrines were becoming established and accepted. Now the debates about legal opinions were anchored in the doctrines of the legal schools, and these debates

48 Quran: 2:179.
49 Ibn Rushd, v. 2, fatwa # 385, pg. 1201. See also Hallaq, 2004, 198.
50 Ibn Rushd, v. 2, fatwa # 385, pg. 1202. See also Hallaq, 2004, 199.
51 Ibn Rushd, v. 2, fatwa # 385, pgs. 1201–1202. See also Hallaq, 2004, 199.
52 See Hallaq's interpretation of Ibn Rushd's argument in Hallaq, 2004, 200–201.

were largely restricted to the dependent jurists who were affiliated with a *madhhab*. The purpose of these intra-doctrinal debates was to work out the proper legal doctrines and opinions in accordance with the legal principles and precedent of each school, and they were less concerned about the legal doctrines and opinions of opposing schools.

But how did the political authorities and the Mālikī school receive Ibn Rushd's fatwa? The authorities seem not to have paid heed to Ibn Rushd's fatwa and executed the murderer on the request of the agnates, keeping with the legal position found in Mālikī doctrine.[53] Moreover, later Mālikī jurists viewed Ibn Rushd's contrarian fatwa with mixed reactions. Some felt that he was within his rights as a high-ranking scholar in the Mālikī *madhhab* to issue such a fatwa that opposed the official position of the school but nevertheless considered his opinion to be weak; hence, the fatwa was never incorporated subsequently into the legal doctrine of the Mālikī school, as evidenced by the absence of his ruling in the legal compendia that represent the established legal doctrines of the school.[54]

Regardless of the failure of this fatwa to influence the verdict in the case or ultimately change Mālikī legal doctrine, this fatwa is an important indicator of how fatwas in the age of the preponderance of legal schools had to be rationalized within the limits of the school if they were to be accepted at all. Although Ibn Rushd was probably considered a *mujtahid* (independent jurist) within the Mālikī school who had the proper authoritative rank to issue such a fatwa that opposed the previously established precedence of the Mālikī school, not all fatwas that were issued by such high-ranking jurists were necessarily accepted subsequently as authoritative positions of the *madhhab*. These fatwas had to be scrutinized by later high-ranking jurists (*murajjiḥ*s) who had the authority to select or reject such legal opinions that would be incorporated into the official ruling of the school.

Ibn Taymiyya's Fatwas on Mongol Incursions into Syria (c. 1300)

In this section, two fatwas will be analyzed simultaneously that deal with the same topic and are issued by the Ḥanbalī[55] jurist and theologian

[53] See Hallaq, 2004, 200, for this information.

[54] For more on this point, see Hallaq, 2004, pgs. 202–204.

[55] In reference to Aḥmad Ibn Ḥanbal (d. 241 AH/ 855 CE), the madhhab predeccessor of the Ḥanbalī school of law, which is the fourth and final Sunnī *madhhab* after the Ḥanafī, Mālikī, and Shāfiʿī schools.

Taqī al-Dīn Aḥmad Ibn Taymiyya (d. 728/1328), who was a resident of Damascus during the reign of the Mamluks. Although he was an adherent of the Ḥanbalī school of law, he was less inclined than his contemporaries to show complete deference to the rulings that had been established in his own school of law.[56] He was critical of the legal doctrine of *taqlīd* (strict observance of a particular school of law) that had become established by his time.[57] This did not mean that he rejected the authority of the rulings of the *madhhab*s, but he more than anyone did not feel that a qualified *mujtahid* (jurist) ought to be confined to the previous rulings reached through consensus by the schools of law. Ultimately, it was the textual authority of the Quran and sunna that held supremacy, which either affirmed or rejected the rulings reached by the early master *mujtahid*s of the *madhhab* and the consensus reached after them.[58] Nevertheless, he was solidly within the Ḥanbalī tradition, as most of his views abide by the rulings of that school of law.[59]

However, what is most important here is to spell out the political context in which these fatwas of Ibn Taymiyya were composed. The fatwas of concern here are those which he issued regarding the three invasions of the Tatars, or Mongols, into Syria that took place in the years 699/1299–703/1303 under the Ilkhanid Tatar ruler of Iran, Ghazan (r. 694/1295–704/1304).[60] The subject of these fatwas was whether it was legitimate for the Muslims in the region of Syria to take up arms to resist the Tatars, given that the Tatar leadership had become Muslim. The fact that the invaders were Muslims created confusion in the ranks of the Muslim populace of the region probably because they were not sure whether the events signified an inter-dynastic rivalry between the Tatars and Mamluks, which the Muslim populace had witnessed many times in the history of Islam (with the usual response by the populace being to remain aloof), or whether this was a genuine foreign invasion that required the resistance of all Muslims. This much can be surmised from the questions that were posed to Ibn Taymiyya, asking him to clarify matters for them.

[56] See Ibn Taymiyya's fatwa invaliding the repudiation of marriage when a husband divorces his wife three times in one sitting in *Fatāwa Ibn Taymiyya al-Kubra*, v. 3, pg. 224.
[57] See Laoust, 954, for more on this point. Also, Hodgson, v. 2, 471.
[58] Laoust, 954.
[59] Hodgson, v. 2, 471.
[60] Bonney, 113. See also Laoust, 951.

Before undertaking a detailed analysis of Ibn Taymiyya's response to the questions, I offer here some general observations about the structure of Ibn Taymiyya's fatwas. His arguments in these fatwas employ three types of authoritative evidence to prove his point of view: first, the textual authority of Quran and *ḥadīth*; second, the hermeneutical authority of the early jurists (Abū Ḥanīfa and his protégés, Mālik, al-Shāfiʿī, and Aḥmad Ibn Ḥanbal and his protégés), who in Islamic tradition are said to be the originators of the Sunnī legal schools. Third, Ibn Taymiyya invokes the historical precedents of early Muslims and their responses to similar predicaments. So, these types of evidence represent the three levels of authority that Ibn Taymiyya recognizes in these fatwas as the proper grounds by which to outline his response.

With these preliminary observations about Ibn Taymiyya's fatwas on the Tatars, we can now turn to their actual content. Ultimately, what Ibn Taymiyya tries to prove in his fatwas is that the Tatars cannot be considered legally Muslims even though they declared the profession of faith (*shahada*), so it was necessary to resist them as foreign invaders who would bring great harm to Islam and Muslims if they were not stopped. His main argument in his fatwas to prove this point is to illustrate the Tatars' utter disregard for the Sharīʿa (the normative ideals of Islamic law) by citing numerous examples of their contravention of it, including their complete contempt for the sanctity of Muslims in the transgressions they committed against Muslim lives, properties, and sacred places.[61] In addition to the monstrosities they perpetrated against Muslims, Ibn Taymiyya argues that their total neglect for performing fundamental Islamic practices such as prayer (*ṣalāh*) and charity (*zakāh*) and their equating the religion of Islam with other religions call their faith into question.[62] Moreover, he adds that the motives behind the Tatars' aggression are to fight not for the sake of Islam but for the sake of Mongol glory and supremacy along with their scrupulous observance of their codified Mongol traditions (the Yasa) and not the Sharīʿa of Islam.[63]

After making these preliminary remarks, he starts his argument by showing how the Quran does give license for Muslims to fight those groups of Muslims who make professions of faith yet try to circumvent fundamental practices of Islam. In this regard, in the second fatwa, he

[61] See, for example, Ibn Taymiyya's *Majmuʿ Fatāwa Ibn Taymiyya*, v. 28, pgs. 275–276, where he says this in his first fatwa, and pg. 283, where he states this in the second fatwa.
[62] Ibn Taymiyya, *Majmu Fatāwa Ibn Taymiyya*, v. 28, pgs. 283–284.
[63] Ibn Taymiyya, *Majmu Fatāwa Ibn Taymiyya*, v. 28, pgs. 283–284.

quotes Quranic passages to prove his point. One such passage is Quran 2:277–279, which instructs those Muslim groups engaging in the practice of usury to desist from doing so or else risk being fought against by the Prophet Muḥammad.

But for Ibn Taymiyya, it does not suffice to quote Quranic passages that aid his point of view. He takes his argument to another level by quoting *ḥadīth*s of the Prophet Muḥammad that in his view foretold the coming of deviant Muslims groups like the Khawārij and their destructive effects on the Muslim community. These *ḥadīth*s give license for Muslims to militarily oppose those groups. Moreover, he shows that when such groups like the Khawārij and those factions of Muslims who reneged on paying the alms tax (*zakāh*) after the death of the Prophet Muḥammad arose during the time of the early caliphate, the Muslims justifiably took up arms against them because they had transgressed against the Sharīʿa, or rulings of Islam.[64]

These episodes provide the historical precedents to legitimize Ibn Taymiyya's view about the Tatars.

After detailing the response of the early Muslim caliphate to renegades against its authority and/or against the Sharīʿa, Ibn Taymiyya proceeds to discuss the stances that the early master jurists of the *madhhab*s took with regard to these rebellions against the early caliphate and the legal legitimacy of each group fighting in these conflicts. He says that Abū Ḥanīfa and his protégés, al-Shāfiʿī, and some of the protégés of Aḥmad Ibn Ḥanbal claim that all groups opposing the Muslim caliphate during the first civil wars are to be considered renegades (*bughāh*) whether it was the camp of al-ṣiffīn, al-Jamal, or others.[65] After a long digression about the legal stances of these jurists on how to deal with renegades, he proceeds to assert that Mālik, the advocates of *ḥadīth*, and the majority of subsequent jurists of the *madhhab*s distinguish the rebellions of the Khawārij and the tribes involved in the wars of apostasy from the rebels in the case of the battles of al-Jamal and al-Ṣiffīn. He claims that the latter groups may be seen as renegades against the political authority, while the case of the Khawārij and the camps involved in the wars of apostasy were renegades against the very religion of Islam and its Sharīʿa.[66]

Recalling the historical and legal precedents along with the normative principles of the sacred texts is central to Ibn Taymiyya's argument,

[64] Ibn Taymiyya, *Majmu Fatāwa Ibn Taymiyya*, v. 28, pgs. 279–280.
[65] Ibn Taymiyya, *Majmu Fatāwa Ibn Taymiyya*, v. 28, pg. 280.
[66] Ibn Taymiyya, *Majmu Fatāwa Ibn Taymiyya*, v. 28, pgs. 280–281.

because he recognizes that the Muslims view the early history of Islam as normative, and so much of that history determines how Muslims over time have interpreted the norms that are found in their sacred texts. But looking at the structure of Ibn Taymiyya's argument in his fatwas, one sees that as a Ḥanbalī jurist-consult, he appealed far less to the authoritative hierarchy of his own *madhhab*, or any other *madhhab* for that matter, than other jurists of his time. Even though he did not confine his argument to the authoritative juridical structure of his school of law or any other school, he is careful to include the juridical stances of all four master jurists of the schools about the events and the camps in the early Muslim civil wars so as to extrapolate from that what their position would be in the case of the Tatars.[67] The point here is that Ibn Taymiyya knows that the authority of the *madhhab*s cannot be ignored even when he chooses not to confine himself to their stances when arguing his point of view, because he is well aware of the power that *madhhab*s were exerting on the legal discourse of his period (see Figure 15).

It is hard for us to measure the political impact of Ibn Taymiyya's two fatwas against the Tatar invasions into Syria during the period 699/1299–703/1303, the period in which these fatwas were issued. What can be said, though, is that the Mamluk authorities of this period did urge Ibn Taymiyya to exhort the Muslims of Syria to engage in jihad against both the Mongols and the remaining crusading states in the area.[68]

When looking back at Ibn Taymiyya's two fatwas concerning the Tatars, one recognizes that his legal discourse represents a kind of integrative jurisprudence where politics, morality, and history coalesce to cope with realities of the present without necessarily disregarding the legal precedents that had been established before him nor confining himself to the conclusions that were reached in those precedents. It was this sort of flexibility that allowed Islamic legal discourse to continue to evolve even when this discourse took on a particular stamp during the age of *madhhab*s. Fatwas like those of Ibn Taymiyya were legal practices that were crucial to that process of adaptation.

[67] See, for example, in the second fatwa where Ibn Taymiyya accepts Aḥmad Ibn Ḥanbal's legal position, that captured property of the Khawārij is to be considered war booty, from which Ibn Taymiyya infers that the Khawārij were to be viewed as non-Muslims and likewise the Tatars by analogy. See Ibn Taymiyya, *Majmu Fatāwa Ibn Taymiyya*, v. 28, pg. 281.

[68] See Bonney, 113, and Laoust's article about Ibn Taymiyya in EI2, vol. 3, pg. 951.

Abū al-Suʿūd's Fatwa on Cash Endowments (Waqf al-Nuqūd): c. Tenth/Sixteenth Century

To analyze major fatwas from the latter period of the age of *madhhab* preponderance, a fatwa issued by Abū al-Suʿūd (d. 982/1574), an eminent jurist and judge in the history of Islam, has been chosen. Abū al-Suʿūd (Turkish transliteration: Ebu's- Su'ud) was the Ottoman Shaykh al-Islam from 1545 to 1574 CE),[69] at the height of Ottoman power during the reign of the Sultan Suleiman the Lawgiver (al-Qānūni) and as such was the top state-sanctioned religious jurist of his time. He was one of the greatest *muftī*s in the Ottoman Empire, and his major accomplishment was harmonizing Sharīʿa law with the laws/policies issued from the sultan that were known as *qānūn*.[70]

The issue that confronted Abū al-Suʿūd was the question concerning the legality of what was known as cash *waqf*s (*waqf al-nuqūd*). In the Islamic tradition, there had developed philanthropic foundations that were known as *awqāf* (sing. *waqf*), which consisted of stationary properties that were endowed for people's purposes such as schools, mosques, farms whose produce was donated, etc.[71] According to the Ḥanafī *madhhab*, the official Islamic legal doctrine of the Ottoman Empire, these *waqf*s had to be permanent and immovable properties, although there were several exceptions, such as weapons and farming tools that had been deemed as *waqf*-worthy properties by prophetic tradition (*ḥadīth*).[72]

69 Vikor, 213.

70 See Hodgson 110–111 and Vikor 213–214 for more on this. Burak (2015) argues that legal activities like harmonizing policies of the state with Islamic legal norms by the official Ottoman bureaucracy represented a kind of formation of an official Ottoman state *madhhab* (pg. 4) that was a sub-group of the larger Ḥanafī *madhhab*. This would mean that this official state *madhhab* would have its distinct doctrinal points and methodological approaches that were particular to it as a *madhhab*; this in my estimation would be the criteria of testability for the validity of such an argument. It will become evident in our analysis of Abū al-Suʿūd's fatwa that he displays no distinctness of legal approach in his fatwa other than observing the discursive rules of the Ḥanafī *madhhab* in his argument. The failure to display any distinctiveness in approach or doctrine of this supposed state *madhhab* implies that there was not a distinct official state Ottoman *madhhab*. So, this harmonization of government policies with Islamic law in which the likes of Abū al-Suʿūd were engaged represents more a normative scrutiny and legitimation of government policies (*qānūn*) than the forging of an official state legal institution.

71 For more on the description of a *waqf*, see Mandeville, 293.

72 MS (Abū al-Suʿūd), pg. 212. I am grateful to Dr. Murteza Bedir of Istanbul University, Turkey, for making this manuscript available to me. I would also like to thank Dr. Hamdi Ciligner of Sakarya University, Turkey, who patiently assisted me in navigating through the unclear script of the manuscript as well as some of the fatwas' legal intricacies.

In the ninth-/fifteenth-century Ottoman lands, the practice of taking cash money and designating it as a *waqf*[73] had developed where the endowed cash would be loaned or invested for a return that would eventually be utilized for philanthropic purposes.[74] By the first half of the sixteenth century, these cash *waqf*s grew in number to the point that they began to rival even traditional landed property *waqf*s.[75] What complicated matters further was that one of the most highly respected judges of the Ottoman Empire, Çivizade Muhittin Mehmet Efendi, issued a fatwa around the middle of the sixteenth century opposing the practice of cash *waqf*s.[76] This ruling threatened the legitimacy of this newly established and popular institution that was a source of finance around the western portions of the empire.

The issue had also been dealt with in a fatwa given by the predecessor of Abū al-Suʿūd, the previous Shaykh al-Islam of the Ottoman Empire Kamal Pasha, who legalized this practice in a fatwa he had issued earlier.[77] Yet the issue must have remained contentious as shown by Çivizade's fatwa prohibiting the practice, which in turn pressured Abū al-Suʿūd to issue a response fatwa[78] arguing for the legality of cash *waqf*s.

[73] Cizakca, 2000, 45. See also Mandeville, 290.

[74] Cizakca, 2000, 46.

[75] Mandeville, 292.

[76] Mandeville, 297.

[77] See Ibn Kamal Pasha's fatwa as edited and published by Tahsin Özcan "İbn Kemal' in Para Vakıflarına Dair Risâlesi" İslam Araştırmaları Dergisi, 2000, sayi: 4, s: 31–41. It is poignant to point out here that Burak (2015) claims that Ibn Kamal Pasha is one of the early Ottoman jurists who was pioneering an independent branch of the Ḥanafī *madhhab* consisting of the emerging official Ottoman learned hierarchy and that his work on the topology of the Ḥanafī *madhhab* (described earlier in footnote # 281) represents his attempt to do so (pgs. 66–67). This claim is misleading in that Ibn Kamal Pasha's topology in no way connects any Ḥanafī jurists in this work with reference to their relation to the Ottoman state but only discusses them with reference to their position in the Ḥanafī *madhhab* hierarchy. Even more relevant to this counterargument is that nowhere in his fatwa on cash *waqf*s that I am citing here does Ibn Kamal rely on his own political authority as Shaykh al-Islām (chief jurist) of the Ottoman Empire or the authority of its own learned hierarchy to legitimate his legal position on this matter. The entire fatwa is argued from the point of view of the wider Ḥanafī *madhhab* hierarchy (what I have called the *madhhab* predecessors and their later associates). So, if neither Ibn Kamal's theoretical works such as his topology of jurists nor his practical works such as this fatwa make reference to this Ottoman learned hierarchy in establishing legal authority and legitimation, this leaves Burak's claim about Ibn Kamal Pasha being an early pioneer for a distinct and independent branch of the Ḥanafī *madhhab* without much evidence.

[78] The fatwa of Abū al-Suʿūd is found in manuscript form in the Hacı Selim Ağa library in Istanbul, Turkey. I had obtained a copy of the manuscript during my research in Istanbul in the summer of 2011. It is based on this copy that I extract this data for my presentation of Abū al-Suʿūd's fatwa.

This generational debate between Ottoman jurists was an indication of their differences on what constituted proper Ḥanafī doctrine with relation to this new practice of cash *waqf*s. Despite the stronger political positions occupied by Kamal Pasha and Abū al-Suʿūd as the chief jurists of the empire, this did not diminish from Çivizade's *madhhab*ic legal authority to dispute with them. This assertion is further corroborated by the fact that the independent Ottoman jurist Mehmet Birgivi, who did not have a position in the Ottoman state's official religious hierarchy, issued several rejoinders to Abū al-Suʿūd's fatwa on cash *waqf* after it was issued.[79] This is a strong indication that the debate was primarily anchored in the *madhhab* (Ḥanafī) legal authority of the jurists rather than their official governmental status.[80]

Let us now turn to Abū al-Suʿūd's fatwa. There are many aspects of his fatwa and the historical circumstances that surround it that can be analyzed, but the focus of this analysis is on the forms of legal (*madhhab*ic) reasoning displayed by Abū al-Suʿūd. One of the early strategies that Abū al-Suʿūd adopted in this fatwa is to attempt to broaden the scope of the legal opinion of the second-/eighth-century jurist Muḥammad Ibn al-Ḥasan al-Shaybānī (750–804 CE), one of the foundational figures in the Ḥanafī school, on what properties can actually constitute a *waqf*.[81] One supposes from this strategy that Abū al-Suʿūd did not want to be seen as openly opposing the doctrines of his school and felt compelled, at least initially, to situate his argument within in the scope that had been outlined for *waqf*s by grand jurists such as al-Shaybānī. This shows the centripetal pull that *madhhab*s had on legal arguments of this period. Fatwas that were issued contrary to these doctrines had to at least address the established opinions and why they needed modification.

79 See al-Birgivi's fatwa against cash *waqf*s entitled *Risālat Buṭlān Waqf al-Nuqūd*. See also Mandeville, 304–306.

80 To bolster his main argument that the Ottoman learned hierarchy represented a formation of a distinct state *madhhab* within the larger Ḥanafī *madhhab* establishment, Burak claims – based on the statements made by several Shaykhs al-Islām (chief jurists) of the Ottoman Empire including Kamal Pasha himself – that opposing the rulings of this official religious hierarchy was reproachable and could even sanction punishment (pgs. 42–43). Yet, as is seen in al-Birgivi's several responses to Abū al-Suʿūd's fatwa, such reproach or supposed punishment was not realized in practice at least for those who had legal (*madhhab*) authority to pose such opposition regardless whether such authorities were a part of the official government bureaucracy or not.

81 MS. Ebussuud, *Risale fi vakfi'l-menkul*, Süleymaniye Ktp., Hacı Selim Ağa 299, vr. 10b, pg. 212.

It has already been mentioned that the understanding of a *waqf* in the Ḥanafī school was, with few exceptions, that it consisted of those properties that are immovable and permanent.

According to Abū al-Suʿūd, al-Shaybānī allowed for non-stationary or physically transferrable (*manqūlāt*) properties as *waqfs* based on the appeal to people's custom (*ʿurf*), on the legal grounds of *istiḥsān* (juristic preference).[82] Al-Shaybānī cites examples of non-stationary things that have been designated as *waqfs* based on *ʿurf*, or custom; those are things like saws, picks, and written Qurans (*maṣāḥif*). But al-Shaybānī excludes non-stationary things that custom (*ʿurf*) has not accepted such as clothes and animals. Abū al-Suʿūd tries to argue that just because al-Shaybānī lists certain moveable properties as being allowed to constitute *waqfs* and excludes others, this does not mean that he meant to limit the types of things that can be made into a *waqf* to these specified examples. Rather the allowance of moveable things to be made into *waqfs* depends on his general argument that it is the *ʿurf* (custom) of a particular place or time that determines what things are allowed for and what are not. That is the criterion for determining things that can be made into *waqf* and not the specific examples that were pointed out by al-Shaybānī.[83] The point here is that Abū al-Suʿūd wants to use this as a launching point to argue for the legality of cash *waqfs* that have been prohibited by previous jurists, including by some of the early master jurists of the Ḥanafī *madhhab*, namely, Abū Yūsuf and al-Shaybānī. He does this based on the principle of juristic preference (*istiḥsān*), thus legally sanctioning the custom (*ʿurf*) of instituting cash *waqfs* in his own era.

After having addressed the physically portable aspects of money and why that may not be a sufficient reason to exclude it from being a *waqf*, Abū al-Suʿūd deals with the second condition of why money or cash could not be made into a *waqf*, namely, the stipulation of the permanence (*baqāʾ*) of the property that is being made into a *waqf*. This second stipulation is a corollary of the first because immovability of the thing in question, like land or a building, is also an indication of its permanence. The issue that confronts Abū al-Suʿūd is that opponents of cash *waqfs* say that the actual items that make up a cash *waqf* [the cash in terms of *dirhams* and *dinars*] become spent in the process of transacting with them. That is, the

[82] MS. Ebussuud, *Risale fi vakfi'l-menkul*, Süleymaniye Ktp., Hacı Selim Ağa 299, vr. 10b, pg. 212.

[83] MS. Ebussuud, *Risale fi vakfi'l-menkul*, Süleymaniye Ktp., Hacı Selim Ağa 299, vr. 10b, pg. 212.

usual items made into *waqf*s like land or buildings when utilized do not lead to those very items being dispersed or effaced, hence satisfying the legal stipulation of the permanence of the item that is made into a *waqf*. On the other hand, with cash *waqf*s, the very items made into a *waqf* like cash get dispersed in the very process of utilizing this type of *waqf*, leading to the violation of the permanence clause for *waqf*s.

To clarify this matter, a word must be said about how cash *waqf*s were ideally to operate: The donor donates money as *waqf* whereby the cash is given to an entrepreneur to be invested in profitable ventures, whereby the entrepreneur keeps some of the profits of that venture and returns the original capital to the *wāqif* (the administrator of the *waqf*) who then lends it to another entrepreneur; therefore, repeating this process. The contention here is that the actual [*ʿayn*] cash [principal] that is made into a *waqf* is spent during the investment, leading to a loss of the item being made into a *waqf* and hence violating the stipulation of permanence for *waqf* items.[84] Abū al-Suʿūd replies to this argument by saying that although the actual [*ʿayn*] property of the *waqf* [in this case the cash] is dispersed in its utilization as a *waqf*, what remains of it, in this case, is its likeness [*mithl*], and that suffices to meet the stipulation of permanence.[85] In other words, the actual property made into a *waqf* does not have to be preserved so long as its essence is equally replaceable by another property that shares its exact qualities as in the case of money.

After overcoming the difficulty of cash *waqf*s not meeting the two conditions for *waqf*-worthy property, permanence and immovability, Abū al-Suʿūd must now deal with the tougher task of going up against the opinions of the grand jurists of the *madhhab*s on the legitimacy of this type of operation. He begins to deal with the fatwa of the Ḥanafī master jurists Abū Yūsuf and Muḥammad al-Shaybānī against the permissibility of cash *waqf*s. The explicit opinions of these master jurists present a real obstacle to Abū al-Suʿūd's objective to legitimize cash *waqf*s because he cannot, after all, go against the opinions of these master jurists of the *madhhab* and have his fatwa be taken seriously at the same time. This shows the centrality of the already established *madhhab* doctrine to the

[84] This is how the concept of cash *waqf*s was theoretically constructed, but as we will see later in this section, the bigger issue with cash *waqf*s as practiced in the Ottoman Empire had more to do with the transmutation of them into lending institutions based on usury. Nevertheless, Abū al-Suʿūd felt compelled in his fatwa to deal with the historical objections to cash *waqf*s as a construct.

[85] MS. Ebussuud, *Risale fi vakfi'l-menkul*, Süleymaniye Ktp., Hacı Selim Ağa 299, vr. 10b, pg. 213.

production of new legal rulings. Abū al-Suʿūd strategically handles this challenge by looking at the rationale of each of these two master jurists in order to present his argument later for the permissibility of cash *waqfs* that would not necessarily go against their legal principles although it may go against the letter of their fatwa against cash *waqf*s.

The rationale of Abū Yūsuf, one of the three original master jurists of the Ḥanafī school, sticks to the original rule on *waqf*s in that they must not be properties that are physically portable (*manqūlāt*) unless there is an explicit proof text (*naṣṣ*) [Quran or *ḥadīth*], such as in the case of weapons and beasts of burden, which then makes a legitimate exception to the rule. This proof text then becomes the grounds for *istiḥsān* (juristic preference) against the legal conclusions reached by *qiyās* (scriptural inference) about the legal norms defining *waqf*s.[86]

However, the rationale of al-Shaybānī, another one of the three original master jurists of the Ḥanafī school, makes an exception for *waqf*s that consist of physically portable properties in cases where *ʿurf* (custom) establishes a movable thing as a *waqf*. This *ʿurf* then becomes the basis for his *istiḥsān* against the *qiyās* that would otherwise make physically portable property not eligible to be a *waqf*. Both the proof text (*naṣṣ*) for Abū Yūsuf and the *ʿurf* (custom) for al-Shaybānī serve as the basis of the *dalīl* (legal argument) for *istiḥsān,* and that *istiḥsān* is what allows for the permanency clause for *waqf*s to be rendered dispensable claims Abū al-Suʿūd.[87]

Abū al-Suʿūd represents the argument of each of these master jurists, whether for or against cash *waqf*s, in a way that is consistent with the legal principles (*uṣūl*) that they claimed to have supported. Here, Abū al-Suʿūd was trying to use the very same rationale used by the master jurists (at least the Ḥanafī ones) to argue for the permissibility of cash *waqf*s. After having shown that *ʿurf* (custom) was used to establish the permissibility of certain illegitimate practices (from the point of view of regular Islamic norms) in certain eras and regions, Abū al-Suʿūd argues based on the *ʿurf* (custom) of his era that cash *waqf*s should be seen as legitimate even if they had not been permitted previously by the master jurists, because it was not the customary practice of their period.[88]

86 MS. Ebussuud, *Risale fi vakfi'l-menkul,* Süleymaniye Ktp., Hacı Selim Ağa 299, vr. 10b, pg. 215.

87 MS. Ebussuud, *Risale fi vakfi'l-menkul,* Süleymaniye Ktp., Hacı Selim Ağa 299, vr. 10b, pgs. 215–216.

88 MS. Ebussuud, *Risale fi vakfi'l-menkul,* Süleymaniye Ktp., Hacı Selim Ağa 299, vr. 10b, pg. 216.

Finally, Abū al-Suʿūd concludes his argument for the legitimacy of cash *waqf*s by dealing with the objection that the *ʿurf*, or social custom, of his era cannot be used as the basis to go against the *qiyās* because that type of *ʿurf* must be established by the *mujtahid* Imams (the master jurists of the legal schools). Abū al-Suʿūd responds to this objection by saying that the *ʿurf* itself does not have to be established by a *mujtahid* Imam because it is an empirical matter known by all. Abū al-Suʿūd says that what needs to be established by the *mujtahid* Imams (the master jurists) is whether *ʿurf* has legal ramifications for this case, and they have already done so as is apparent in al-Shaybānī's fatwa allowing for portable things to be considered *waqf*s so long as there is a socially recognized custom for that practice. Hence, as far as establishing the legal basis for *ʿurf* (custom) to act as a basis for a legal judgment to be rendered by *istiḥsān* (juristic preference), this is what must be established by a *mujtahid* (master jurist). But as far as applying these legal precepts to new situations, Abū al-Suʿūd claims that this is the prerogative of any *muftī* and need not be done by the *mujtahid* Imams[89] (see Figure 15 below).

Abū al-Suʿūd's fatwa[90] legitimated cash *waqf*s despite the fact that there continued to be resistance from some Ottoman Ḥanafī jurists, like al-Birgivi,[91] who opposed the legality of cash *waqf*s. Yet the form that cash *waqf*s took on in Ottoman Anatolia was different from their

89 MS. Ebussuud, *Risale fi vakfi'l-menkul*, Süleymaniye Ktp., Hacı Selim Ağa 299, vr. 10b, pgs. 216–217.

90 My presentation of the legal reasoning of this fatwa reveals that Abū al-Suʿūd relied completely on concepts from Islamic legal theory and structured positions within his *madhhab* to legitimate his legal position. Given the absence of any argument throughout the fatwa that relied on the status of the Ottoman learned hierarchy (like Ibn Kamal Pasha's previous fatwa on cash *waqf*) or his own officially sanctioned bureaucratic post, this calls into question the assertion made by Burak (2015) that the Ottoman learned hierarchy, as represented by figures like Abū al-Suʿūd, was forging a distinct state *madhhab*. Burak relies primarily on the use of circumstantial evidence from biographical dictionaries that focus on the Ottoman learned hierarchy to construct the argument for his case. Yet when examining the legal production of the jurists who make up this so-called emerging state *madhhab*, there is nothing in their legal reasoning to indicate that they saw themselves as legally distinct from any other contemporaneous Ḥanafī jurists, and they argue their positions from within the general framework of the Ḥanafī school and not from any special distinction of being a part of the official Ottoman state bureaucracy. This fact is evident from the fatwas on cash *waqf*s by Ibn Kamal Pasha and Abū al-Suʿūd, both of whom occupied the highest juristic position (in different time periods) in the Ottoman Empire as chief jurists. So, this begs the question, if there was indeed an official state *madhhab* that the Ottoman learned hierarchy represented, why did no distinct legal approach of this supposed *madhhab* come into play in their legal production?

91 See al-Birgivi's fatwa against cash *waqf*s entitled "Risalat Butlan Waqf al-Nuqūd."

conception in the historical legal debates. Some early Ḥanafī jurists (Zufar) used the business partnership model of cash *waqf*s that is known in Islamic law as *muḍāraba*. The way this model worked is that the cash *waqf* as the financier would take the endowed cash and transfer it to a would-be entrepreneur who would utilize the cash in a business venture and then would return the principle cash after a period of time to the cash *waqf* with additional amount of cash, presumably the shared profit of the business venture, that would be utilized by the *waqf* for pious social purposes.[92]

Historical evidence shows that many cash *waqf*s in the eleventh-/seventeenth-century Ottoman Empire worked on the constant profit return model of *istighlāl* rather than the profit and loss sharing partnership of *muḍāraba* that was worked out by those early Ḥanafī jurists who legitimated this practice, which was more likely what Abū al-Suʿūd had in mind when endorsing this practice.[93] Despite the different forms these institutions took on in practice, fatwas like the one issued by Abū al-Suʿūd alleviated the inhibitions that some sectors of Muslim society felt about cash *waqf*s as a result of the legal positions held by most legal schools against its practice. Fatwas like Abū al-Suʿūd's were very instrumental in changing traditionally held legal positions that were established in *madhhab* doctrines to open up new possibilities for change in the Muslim society.

Abū al-Sa'ûd's fatwa never quite settled the debate about the legality of cash *waqf*s among Ottoman Ḥanafī jurists as I pointed earlier. It did, however, win quite a bit of support from the Ottoman political authorities because the sultan's decree of 1548 ratified the practice of cash *waqf*s[94] partly due to the fact that it was legitimated by their Chief Jurist Abū al-Sa'ûd[95] and settled the matter from the perspective of the

92 Cizakca, 2000, 45–46.

93 See Cizakca, 2000, 46–47 for more on the business model of *istiqlāl*.

94 Imber, 144–145.

95 Burak (2015, 64) posits this relationship in reverse where the legal opinions of jurists of the Ottoman learned hierarchy were shaped by the sultanic edicts. Aside from a historical note about Abū al-Sa'ûd seeking the sultan's endorsement of his legal opinions (pg. 64), Burak furnishes no real evidence that sultanic edicts that endorsed certain fatwas actually altered the legal positions within the Ottoman branch of jurists from the Ḥanafī *madhhab*. The most one can say is that such edicts enforced the chief jurist's fatwas as was the case when Abū al-Sa'ûd's fatwa on cash *waqf*s, which was made into law for the Ottoman Empire. Burak's assertion that official Ottoman jurists were merely seeking minority opinions within in the Ḥanafī *madhhab* that were in concordance with sultanic *Kanun* (*qānūn*) law, thus making the real authority of those legal opinions rest on the *Kanun* rather than the institutions of Islamic law (pg. 64), is an overstatement in two respects. First, I have already discussed how the official Ottoman jurist Çivizade's

Ottoman Empire's regulations. His fatwa was instrumental in endorsing that social institution in the face of strong opposition by conservative-minded jurists who tried to undo this practice.

Al-Karakī's Fatwa on Kharāj *(Land Tax) c. Tenth/Sixteenth Century*

Another fatwa that I will examine here also dates from the tenth/sixteenth century, but this fatwa comes from a Shīʿī jurist instead of a Sunnī. The Safavid court at the beginning of its reign in the tenth/sixteenth century was recruiting Twelver Shīʿī scholars from outside Persia to help propagate Shi'ism among its newly conquered majority Sunnī Persian population. One of the first important Twelver Shīʿī scholars it was able to recruit from the Jabal ʿĀmil, a Shīʿī region of Syria, was ʿAlī b. ʿAbd al-ʿĀlī al-Karakī (d. 940/1532).[96] Being a forerunner of the Uṣūlī movement that would eventually gain ascendancy in Twelver Shi'ism,[97] he emphasized the role of the *ʿulamāʾ* as successors of the twelfth Imam of Twelver Shi'ism[98] in the latter's absence and advocated that competent scholars might practice *ijtihād* (legal effort and reasoning) to draw appropriate legal conclusions from the valid sources of the law. For Shīʿīs, those sources are Quran, *akhbār* (similar to the Sunnī notion of *ḥadīth* but including the authoritative reports of the twelve Shīʿī Imams), *ijmāʿ*, and *ʿaql* (reason).

fatwa on cash *waqf*s opposed the legal position of the Ottoman Chief Jurist before him, Ibn Kamal Pasha. Such vibrant debate and opposition between the Ottoman learned hierarchy themselves calls into question Burak's claim of their project to forge a state *madhhab* by endorsing the positions of Ottoman imperial law (*Kanun*). Second, all these jurists' argumentation relied solely on *madhhab*-centered legal reasoning, as we saw in detail with reference to Abū al-Sa'ûd's fatwa, without invoking in any way the authority of their official state status or imperial edicts to legitimate their opinions, which implies that their concern to a large degree was how to make the established legal norms of the *madhhab* address the political and social concerns of their age. Having said this, I do not intend to deny that political concerns did factor into their fatwas, but what I am calling into question is whether those considerations constituted a project of forging an independent state *madhhab* that was subservient to the exigencies of the state.

96 Arjomand, 1984, 107.

97 A legal movement that gained traction during the reign of the Safavid dynasty in Persia and legitimated the role of *ijtihād* (independent legal reasoning) in Twelver Shīʿī law. This position was opposed to the more conservative Akhbārī movement, which restricted the law to the literal implications of religious texts. For more on these movements, see Hallaq, 2009, 117, and Vikor, 128.

98 Twelver Shi'ism holds ʿAlī (the fourth Caliph) and eleven of his descendants as sacred persons, hence the name Twelver, whose teachings are as authoritative as the Prophet Muḥammad's teachings. For more on Twelver Shi'ism, see *Expectations of the Millennium: Shi'ism in History* by Dabashi, S. Nasr, and W. Nasr.

Al-Karakī promoted religious policies and interpretations that attempted to overcome Twelver Shīʿī reticence about the political establishment and tried to create harmony between the Twelver Shīʿī religious establishment and the Safavid court. Al-Karakī's innovations were opposed by many in the Twelver Shīʿī religious establishment throughout the tenth/sixteenth century, yet his initiatives eventually bore fruit in the subsequent century when more and more Shīʿī *ʿulamāʾ* became involved with the Safavid court, many of whose members were affiliated with al-Karakī as students or students of his students.[99] His initiatives eventually facilitated the recognition by the state of the Twelver Shīʿī *ʿulamāʾ* as the sole authorities in matters of religious affairs, thereby paving the way for the formation of a new Shīʿī hierocracy.[100]

There is one aspect of al-Karakī's work that interests us in this investigation and that is a treatise that he wrote on the issue of *kharāj* in 916/1510.[101] In Chapter 1 of my work, the issue of *kharāj* was dealt with from the perspective of its legitimation and its initial institutionalization by the second caliph of Islam, ʿUmar ibn al-Khaṭṭāb (d. 23/644). Al-Karakī revisits this issue in a different context with regard to its legitimacy in Twelver Shīʿī law, where ʿUmar's establishment of this political practice and the corollary institutions that stemmed from it were not seen as authoritative Twelver Shiʿism as he was neither recognized as a legitimate political nor a legitimate legal authority; hence, this practice needed legitimation on Twelver Shīʿī grounds.

Why was the issue of *kharāj* an important concern at this juncture in the life of the Twelver Shīʿī community? We recall that *kharāj* was a land tax that was implemented by the Muslim state on certain state-owned lands. Being a practice of political governance, Shīʿī jurisprudence for the most part neglected its discussion since the Twelver Shīʿī community was for most of Islamic history disenfranchised from the corridors of political power.[102] With the coming of the Safavid dynasty in Persia, the

[99] Newmans, EI2, v. 8, pgs. 778–779.

[100] Arjomand, 1984, 133. See also Arjomand, 184 in Dabashi, S. H. Nasr, and W. Nasr's *Expectations of the Millennium: Shi'ism in History*.

[101] Arjomand, 1984, 134. Although this work by al-Karakī was a treatise and not a fatwa per se, it functioned very much like a fatwa as it was trying to legally legitimate a much-debated issue in Twelver Shi'ism at the time, hence my treatment of it as a fatwa. For more on this debate, see Modarressi, *Kharāj in Islamic Law*. In addition, there were historical and political implications of this fatwa, which will not be the focus of this discussion. Instead, I pay greater attention to the legal reasoning and legal content employed in the fatwa.

[102] Modarressi, 47.

longest lasting political authority to officially proclaim Shīʿī teachings as the ideology of the state,[103] the situation changed and the disenfranchised Shīʿī community suddenly found itself with a privileged status within the circle of political power, and Twelver Shīʿī jurists now had to contend with legal issues that were of direct political concern.[104]

So what was al-Karakī's strategy in convincing his Shīʿī audience of the legality of *kharāj*? His strategy in seeking religious and legal legitimacy for *kharāj* was built on a two-pronged approach:

1. Appealing to the legal positions of the Shīʿī Imams with respect to *kharāj* that was administered by early Sunnī governments. This legal approach constituted the use of a unanimously agreed-upon source of jurisprudence among all Twelver Shīʿīs, which they called *akhbār*.[105] This was an appeal to the unique authoritative basis of Shīʿī law.
2. Appealing to previously established legal opinions of highly regarded Twelver Shīʿī jurists of the past, by which al-Karakī tried to assert that there was a consensus among these jurists on this issue.[106] This was an appeal to the authoritative opinions within Shīʿī law.

Now that I have given an overview of his approach to argumentation, what makes al-Karakī's treatise novel with respect to the established issue of the *kharāj* tax? Al-Karakī's treatment of *kharāj* is a general presentation of the subject and most generally speaking in line with the view that had already been established in Sunnī legal circles,[107] other than the fact that he utilizes Twelver Shīʿī sources of authority to vindicate this view instead of Sunnī ones.[108] Yet there are unique elements in his treatment

[103] Although the Buyid dynasty in tenth- and eleventh-century Baghdad was a Twelver Shīʿī dynasty that patronized Shīʿī scholars and the Shīʿī community, it nevertheless ruled in the name of the Abbasid Sunnī caliph, which meant that Sunnī political institutions remained intact throughout its rule.

[104] For more details on this point, see Modarressi, 48.

[105] See al-Karakī, pgs. 42, 49, 51, and 73, for examples of this.

[106] See al-Karakī, pgs. 45, 46, 47, and 71, for examples of this.

[107] See al-Mawardi, *Al-Aḥkām al-sulṭāniyya*, pgs. 262–270 for comparison with the position of Sunnī legal schools on kharāj.

[108] To place the legal implications of this debate on *kharāj* in its wider Islamic legal context, one may argue that al-Karakī was attempting to expand the range of consensus (*ijmāʿ*) around the issue of *kharāj*, which was already subject to consensus (*ijmāʿ*) within Sunnī *madhhab*s, to include the consensus of Twelver Shīʿī jurists by seeking its legitimation on terms conducive to Twelver Shīʿī legal tradition. While this argument in some respects resonates with Devin Stewart's (pg. 57) framing of the evolution

that bring nuance to the discussion of *kharāj*, especially in those parts where he tries to prove the legitimacy of *kharāj* from a religious point of view and the permissibility of the utilization of its resources by the general Muslim public even when the governing power is illegitimate from the Twelver Shīʿī perspective. This is where his treatise most resembles a fatwa, in that he was trying to establish a new legal position within the Twelver Shīʿī community, and this is where attention will be focused in this analysis.

The point of contention in Twelver Shīʿī law is not whether the *kharāj* tax was a legitimate practice in theory, but whether it can be collected and utilized in the absence of the legitimate ruler, a status the Twelver Shīʿīs limit to their twelve Imams and their deputies. Al-Karakī wants to argue that this practice is indeed legitimate even in the absence of legitimate rule. Al-Karakī argues that the absence of legitimate authority and even the presence of an illegitimate order does not obviate the obligation of *kharāj* for two reasons: (1) the abiding religio-legal obligation (*baqā' al-ḥaqq*) for the payment of the tax that is collected and paid for the sake of God and (2) the existence of those who have a right to its benefits (*wujūd al-mustaḥiqq*), that is, the Muslim public.[109] These two norms to which he refers represent the substantive reasons legitimating his legal position. He then forwards two formal types of legal proofs based on legal authority and authoritative precedence to vindicate his point of view, the first being reports (*akhbār*) from some of the Twelver Shīʿī Imams that concur with his view and the second being the alleged consensus of Twelver Shīʿī jurists on this point of view.

As for the first type of proof, he narrates various reports about Ḥasan, Ḥusayn, Jaʿfar al-Ṣādiq, Muḥammad al-Bāqir, and other Twelver Shīʿī Imams, showing where they endorsed the acceptance of benefits, employment, or purchasing of properties from their contemporary "illegitimate" authorities who derived their wealth from taxes like *kharāj*. The point in these reports (*akhbār*) from the Imams was to show that they accepted economic transactions with the wealth generated from the *kharāj* tax, thereby vindicating its legality even in situations where it was

of Twelver Shīʿī law as being under the centripetal influence of institutions of Sunnī jurisprudence, I would argue instead that al-Karakī's project represents Twelver Shīʿī law continuing to situate itself within the larger Islamic legal tradition and its discursive practices, which incorporated Sunnī and Shīʿī shared contributions (See Chapter 4 for elaboration) rather than viewing the development of Twelver Shīʿī law as being determined by the Sunni legal system as Stewart alleges (see Stewart pg. 21).

109 Al-Karakī, 76.

administered by a politically "illegitimate" regime.[110] Hence, by appealing to the Twelver Shīʿī Imams, there was undisputable authoritative precedence that was unique to Twelver Shīʿī legal theory for the legitimation of transacting with *kharāj* resources by ordinary subjects.

Yet these reports endorse the receiving of benefits from *kharāj* and do not necessarily endorse the collection and management of the *kharāj* by the illegitimate authorities.[111] Al-Karakī responds by stating that what is taken in *kharāj* from these lands is a right that has been established by the authority of Islamic law (Sharīʿa) (and not by political authority); hence, there is no objection to those taxes being collected. Since the collection of *kharāj* is dependent (*manūṭ*) on the command of the legitimate Imam and the fact that the legitimate Imam licensed Muslim transactions with *kharāj* properties collected by the illegitimate ruler, the question of the legality of its collection by the illegitimate authority becomes moot for al-Karakī.[112]

The second type of formal evidence that he brings to support his view for the legitimacy of the practice of *kharāj* under the reigns of an illegitimate authority is when al-Karakī argues for the consensus reached about this issue by post-Imamate-period Shīʿī jurists (presumably considered the equivalent of Sunnī *mujtahids*). Al-Karakī here cites the statements of such major jurists who preceded him as Muḥammad ibn Ḥasan al-Ṭūṣī (fifth/eleventh century),[113] al-Muḥaqqiq al-Ḥillī (seventh/thirteenth century),[114] al-ʿAllāma al-Ḥillī (eighth/fourteenth century),[115] al-Shahīd al-Awwal (ninth/fifteenth century),[116] and others.[117] The gist of their statements is that the wealth generated from the practice of *kharāj* is legitimate even when it is managed by an illegitimate authority. Moreover, al-Karakī claims that he did not find any dissenting claims in the statement of previous Shīʿī jurists on this issue, thereby constituting a consensus (*ijmāʿ*) of Shīʿī jurists[118] (see Figure 15).

110 Al-Karakī, 77.
111 Al-Karakī, 79–80.
112 Al-Karakī, 80. It is a moot point presumably because the Imams' authorization of transacting with *kharāj* properties is an implicit endorsement of their legitimacy given that the illegitimate authority is merely a conduit for the redistribution of Muslim wealth and not someone who usurps others' property.
113 Al-Karakī, 80–81.
114 Al-Karakī, 81.
115 Al-Karakī, 81.
116 Al-Karakī, 82.
117 Al-Karakī, 83.
118 Al-Karakī, 83.

Let us now explore the possible impact of this treatise/fatwa on subsequent Twelver Shīʿī thought and life. Modarressi points out in his work *Kharāj in Islamic law* that when Twelver Shīʿī legal works did address the issue of *kharāj*, they tended to do so from the perspective of duties of individuals toward the government with respect to *kharāj* and not the rights and responsibilities of the Muslim state with respect to *kharāj* in the same way Sunnī sources did. This is because even though Twelver Shīʿī law never recognized Sunnī Muslim governments as legitimate, it had to accommodate these governments in practice, and hence, on this basis, Shīʿī law works were obliged to address issues of *kharāj*, albeit in a fragmentary way,[119] so as to guide their Shīʿī subjects on how to deal with government policies on *kharāj*.

So, it is historically and politically significant that the timing of al-Karakī's treatise, which is the first extant work in Twelver Shīʿī law to deal with the issue of *kharāj* in its totality from the point of view of Twelver Shīʿī legal theory, coincides with the inception of an independent Twelver Shīʿī state (the Safavids). In his treatise/fatwa, he presents a legal argument to justify a governmental policy imposing *kharāj*, even in the face of strong opposition in the Twelver Shīʿī community to its legitimacy as demonstrated by the counterfatwas issued by contemporaneous Twelver Shīʿī scholars like al-Qāṭīʿfi and al-Ardbīlī.[120] This is because his probable aim was to change Twelver Shīʿī attitudes and discourse on government, especially in the wake of the inception of the Safavid state, which openly espoused Twelver Shīʿī ideology.

Aside from the possible sociopolitical impact of his ideas and actions, al-Karakī's fatwa expanded the scope and corpus of Twelver Shīʿī law to be more inclusive to issues of governance. Prior to his treatise on *kharāj*, there had been no independent treatment of the issue of *kharāj* in Twelver Shīʿī legal compendia. But after al-Karakī wrote his treatise, no fewer than eleven independent Twelver Shīʿī legal works were written about the subject of *kharāj* between the sixteenth and nineteenth centuries.[121] So his work, fitting with the historical circumstances in which the Twelver Shīʿī community found itself, generated lots of interest in an issue that had been practically neglected by the Twelver Shīʿī community prior to that.

119 See Modarressi 41–42 for list of chapters in Shīʿī legal works that contain discussions of *kharāj*.

120 See, for example, Muḥaqqiq al-Ardbīlī's *Risalatan fī al-kharāj* (two treatises on *kharāj*) as an example of counterfatwas to al-Karakī's treatment of *kharāj*. See also Modarressi 55–57 for more on these counterfatwas.

121 See Modarressi, 66, for a listing of such works.

On another note, how does al-Karakī's Shīʿī fatwa resemble that of the Sunnī fatwas and how does it differ? As far as similarities are concerned, al-Karakī's treatise/fatwa displays the usual legal formatting that Sunnī fatwas exhibit by seeking legitimacy of a particular legal position through appeal to the sacred text (discursive authority) and the legal precedence of those who interpreted those texts (hermeneutical authority). This is seen in his use of reports from the Twelver Shīʿī Imams, whose practice is as legally authoritative as the prophetic practice in Twelver Shīʿī legal theory, and the legal consensus of major Twelver Shīʿī jurist-consults from previous periods to support his own legal position. Even though with this position al-Karakī brings Twelver Shīʿī law closer to Sunnī law's position on the legitimacy of *kharāj*, he argues his view from the unique authoritative basis of Twelver Shīʿī law, namely, the authority of Twelver Shīʿī Imams and the consensus of Twelver Shīʿī jurists without appeal to the consensus of Sunnī jurists.[122]

As a jurist who is seen as a precursor to the Uṣūlī movement in Twelver Shīʿī legal theory, al-Karakī not only argues his position from the point of view of norms that are set by sacred texts but also corroborates his understanding within the framework of the consensus (*ijmāʿ*) of other Twelver Shīʿī jurists on the issue. Whether his claim of consensus of top Twelver Shīʿī scholars on this issue is accurate or not is not important here; what matters here is that his appeal to consensus makes his method of legal argumentation similar to that of his Sunnī counterparts and divergent from that of other Twelver Shīʿī jurists with Akhbārī proclivities, who eschew the notion that the law may be derived through a process of consensus (*ijmāʿ*) and/or intellect (*ʿaql*). Moreover, crucial to his project is to show that his understanding of the law on this issue not only is in line with the sacred norms as established by the Twelver Shīʿī Imams but also has precedents with other Twelver Shīʿī jurists, precedents that corroborate his application of those sacred norms

[122] Given that his approach was such attenuates Devin Stewart's main claim in his work *Islamic Legal Orthodoxy* that Twelver Shīʿī jurists sought to be included in the Sunnī-formed legal orthodoxy. Al-Karakī never appeals in his argument for support from Sunnī jurists or the legal arguments presented for *kharāj* from their *madhhabs*. In fact, on occasions throughout his fatwa he speaks rather disparagingly of Sunnīs and their legal positions, which makes it even more difficult to reconcile the fact that Twelver Shīʿī jurists were really seeking inclusion in the Sunnī-formed legal orthodoxy. What can be said more affirmatively by analyzing al-Karakī's fatwa is that its legal reasoning shows definite signs of being within the scope of the collectively negotiated Islamic discursive legal tradition (for more on formation and character of this legal tradition, see Chapter 4).

to the scenario that presents itself to him. This is very much in line with how Sunnī jurist situated their fatwas.

Where al-Karakī's fatwa differs from Sunnī fatwas of this period is that it is not confined by the legal hierarchy of *madhhab*s that came to dominate Sunnī law. Although he appeals to established precedents and the consensus of Twelver Shīʿī scholars, he does not appeal to them in such a way that these opinions necessarily confine the scope of his legal decision on the issue. Rather, his approach in these appeals is that of corroboration of his own independent decision as a jurist-consult of Twelver Shīʿī law. This is one of the ways in which the process of legal rationalization and utilization of legal authority differ in Twelver Shīʿī jurisprudence from its Sunnī counterpart. This independence in judgment becomes a permanent feature in Twelver Shīʿī legal practice even as the hierarchical structuration of the Twelver Shīʿī *madhhab* came into formation in the later period.[123]

To conclude, what al-Karakī's fatwa reveals is that it engages in many of the same discursive practices that characterize fatwas that originate in the Sunnī legal tradition. Despite the sectarian divide that existed between both camps, their legal discourses shared an uncanny similarity in both content and form. This similarity is a consequence of having a shared basis of legal authority in the form of a discursive legal tradition even when there are differences with regard to details of that basis. Therefore, there was a great deal of continuity in Islamic legal discourse even across various Islamic legal sub-traditions. This continuity can be explained by the fact that these sub-traditions were part of a greater Islamic discursive legal tradition that influenced their character.

Shah ʿAbd al-ʿAzīz Fatwa on Mughal Landholders' Ownership of Lands in Eighteenth–Nineteenth Century India

Shah ʿAbd al-ʿAzīz al-Dahlawī (1746–1824) was an Indian Ḥanafī jurist and scholar during the late Mughal Period and the son of the famous twelfth/eighteenth century Indian Muslim reformer Shah Walī Allāh al-Dahlawī (d. 1762). He acquired the mantle of leadership of his father's religious reform movement and spearheaded a political movement to combat the political and religious forces (Marathas, Sikhs, Shīʿa, and the British)

[123] For more on independent *mujtahid*s in Twelver Shi'ism, see Mangol Bayat, "The Uṣūlī-Akhbārī Controversy," 284, as well as Mahmud Ramyar and Leonard Binder, "Ijtihād and Marjaʿiyyat," 240, both of which are chapters in in Dabashi, S. H. Nasr, and W. Nasr's *Shi'ism: Doctrines, Thoughts and Spirituality*; see also Stewart, 229–230.

that had been tearing away at the Mughal Empire throughout the eighteenth century and into the nineteenth century, which was challenging the dominance and security of Indian Sunni Muslim community in the process.[124] Among his religious reform efforts was his issuance of fatwas on various religious, social, and political challenges that confronted Indian Muslim society and the rapidly disintegrating Mughal polity. From his collection of fatwas, I draw this fatwa for legal analysis, which addresses the proprietary claims of Mughal Indian landholders (*zamīndārs*).[125]

Although I was unable to determine the precise date of this fatwa, Shah ʿAbd al-ʿAzīz's fatwa was likely issued sometime after the British takeover of India and the British East India Company's subsequent declaration of the Permanent Settlement in 1889. This declaration converted Mughal state-owned properties managed by these landholders into their private property.[126] Those events probably spurred the questioner's inquiry regarding the status of these lands held by the landholders, even though neither the question nor the response provided information about the historical context of the fatwa.

While the fatwa was seemingly issued at the dawn of British colonialism in India, I still place this fatwa in the age of madhhab preponderance since Shah ʿAbd al-ʿAzīz addresses this concern from the perspective of the previously established doctrine of Islamic (Ḥanafī) law. Likewise, he enunciated his legal opinion in conversation with some of the opinions of prominent Indian Ḥanafī jurists of the Mughal era who were his predecessors and had addressed the same concern. Furthermore, his argument is based on the historical pedigree of these lands, their landholders, and the rights granted to them by the Mughal rulers of India before the arrival of the British.[127] As we will see in the next chapter, these considerations were increasingly marginalized from fatwas in the colonial and post-colonial age.

124 Rizvi, 78–80.

125 For a fuller exposition of this class, refer to Chapter 5, "The Zamīndārs," in Irfan Habib's work *The Agrarian System of Mughal India*. See also Shireen Moosvi's entry "Zamīndār" in EI2.

126 See Moosvi, EI2, 439, for more on the Permanent Settlement. I will say more about the British colonization of India in the next chapter. See also Luxemburg, pg. 353, and Rizvi, pgs. 57–58, for the British policy of privatization of land in India and its consequences on the peasant population.

127 I am indebted to Nadir Begum of Turath Foundation for translating this fatwa from Urdu into English, a translation that I used as the basis for my analysis. Ibrahim Khan of the University of Chicago assisted with the translation. In addition, I am thankful to Mufti Shujaath Ali, a resident scholar in Vancouver, Canada, for his assistance in locating similar fatwas from the period of Mughal India and confirming the accuracy

The questioner asked ʿAbd al-ʿAzīz, what are the laws for land and landlordism (*zamīndāri*) in India?[128] Furthermore, the questioner asks ʿAbd al-ʿAzīz to explain some technical legal terminology related to the legitimation of land grants made by Muslim (Mughal) political authorities. ʿAbd al-ʿAzīz initially responds to the second part of the question about a grantee's rights because it legally contextualizes the main concern about the status of landholdings in India. He says that there is disagreement (*ikhtilāf*) about this, and thus, there are two positions/narrations [within the Ḥanafī *madhhab*][129] The legal position that allows for the buying and selling of the [revenue rights of the][130] land grants (*iʿṭā'*) is conditioned on whether the political authorities have bestowed to the grantee perpetual benefit (*inʿām mu'abbad*) [of land

of the translation of this fatwa. Nevertheless, after reading over the translation of ʿAbd al-ʿAzīz's fatwa, it became clear that the original text of the fatwa used in the translation has some inconsistencies and seems incomplete. I corroborated this assessment by consulting the work of other scholars who concur with this view (See Rizvi, 215). These mistakes in the text seem to be a result of reproduction errors. I have remedied these inconsistencies by referring to other fatwas that Shah ʿAbd al-ʿAzīz relied upon in this fatwa to fill in the gaps in understanding.

128 To give historical context to this question, Muslim governments developed during the early medieval (post-classical) period a bureaucratic system of managing the land tax revenues (*kharāj*) from leasing public lands. They did so by administratively dividing public land areas into portions known as an *iqṭāʿ* and placing a landholder (*muqāṭiʿ*) as a manager of this portion who would collect the tax revenue from the peasants and keep a portion of this revenue as compensation for his services to the state (e.g., providing soldiers for the state) (see Hodgson, v. 2, pgs. 100–102). This administrative practice took on different names in different places within Muslim-governed lands in the latter half of the post-classical era. For example, in the case of Mughal-governed India, one of the several types of landholders was the "*zamīndārs.*" This type of landholder is the main subject of this fatwa.

129 Although ʿAbd al-ʿAzīz never explicitly mentions Ḥanafī madhhab with regard to this dispute, it is evident from his Ḥanafī-dominated Indian Mughal context that it is the positions of the Ḥanafī madhhab that are the objects of his analysis in this fatwa. See Rizvi, pg. 150, who affirms Shah ʿAbd al-ʿAzīz's commitment to the Ḥanafī madhhab in his rulings.

130 When discussing ownership rights of *zamīndārs*, often the language (e.g., *milk*) used in the fatwa gives the impression that by such designations, *zamīndārs* acquired inalienable proprietary rights to these land grants. However, Habib (pg. 159) shows that terms like *mālik* (owner) and *milkiyyat* (ownership) were used to describe the rights of some *zamīndārs* in Mughal documents that did not entail inalienable proprietary rights over the land as these terms may imply. Instead, such terms had much more restrictive implications in reality in that they merely meant that the *zamīndār* controlled some rights over the land revenue. This interpretation is further supported by the statement in the fatwa where ʿAbd al-ʿAzīz claims that if the king bestows ownership rights of land to a grantee, then the grantee will still have to pay the *kharāj* tax on it unless otherwise stated in the royal decree. *Kharāj* tax is only paid for leased public lands and not

revenue rights] by way of real perpetuity (*tabīd ḥaqīqatan*), which is explicitly stated in the royal decree (*farmān*), or if this perpetual right is presumed (*ta'b̄ id ḥukman*) when it is not stated explicitly by the royal decree.[131]

However, the other legal position/narration [within the Ḥanafī *madhhab*] is that buying and selling of the land grants is not permissible because such grants were bestowed as a pension (idrār) and/or were merited (*istiḥqāq*) [in place of some state service].[132] These terms imply temporary possession, thereby placing restrictions on the perpetuity of these grants.[133] 'Abd al-'Azīz reconciles these conflicting positions within the Ḥanafī madhhab by delineating the rights of the political authority to issue these grants. He says that if the head of the state (*imām*) grants publicly owned land (*bayt al-māl*) to someone by way of perpetual benefit, then the person acquired ownership [of its revenue].[134] However, if the head of state granted the land as a pension or based on some merit (*idrār* or *istiḥqāq*), then the land remains in the temporary possession of that person as a loan (*'āriyat*). By giving the head of state this right to dispense with public properties in this fashion, Abd al-'Azīz is tacitly invoking the Islamic legal principle of *al-siyāsa al-shar'iyya* (moral diplomacy or ethically legitimated political action). This principle grants the sovereign latitude to act independently within political affairs so long as his actions benefit the state and society and do not contradict any explicit rule of Islamic law.

private property, thus giving further credence to the interpretation of these various uses of terms for proprietorship as indicative of having ownership over the revenue rights and management of the land and not the land itself. Hence, my decision to qualify 'Abd al-'Azīz's use of the terms implying ownership (*milk*) and the like as having proprietary rights over its revenue and management. See also Moosvi, EI2, 438–439.

131 'Abd al-'Azīz, 575–577.

132 My rendering of the terms is based on Rizvi's translation of these terms in ft. 134 and ft. 135 on pg. 213.

133 'Abd al-'Azīz, 575–577.

134 The historical governance practices by previous Muslim regimes regarding public lands were that grants for landholding privileges were only temporary in place of services rendered to the state by the landholder. Such privileges could not be bought/sold or inherited since they were not inalienable proprietary rights (see Bromley, 205, and Inalcik, 114–115, for this policy in the Ottoman Empire, and see Katouzian pg. 20 and Lambton pg. 259 for how such landholdings were managed in Persia up till the nineteenth century). Despite this historical precedent, 'Abd al-'Azīz here seems to be affirming the Muslim head of state's privilege to grant permanent landholding revenue rights to grantees. This legal position does not seem to be 'Abd al-'Azīz's alone but is supported by earlier Mughal Ḥanafī jurists like Jalāl al-Dīn al-Thānīsirī, who is later cited by 'Abd al-'Azīz in this fatwa (see Rizvi, pg. 212, for more on al-Thānīsirī's position).

Furthermore, Abd al-ʿAzīz's conclusion reconciled the two seemingly conflicting legal positions within the Ḥanafī *madhhab* by asserting that each position merely addresses the differing intentions of the head of state behind bestowing such grants.[135] In this portion of his fatwa, it is evident thus far that ʿAbd al-ʿAzīz's strategy is to confine his analysis to the established legal doctrines of the Ḥanafī *madhhab*. But now that he set the legal context for such land grants, he proceeds to address the first part of the questioner's social inquiry that seeks to determine the status of the landholders' land (*zamīndārs*) in India. In this regard, he states that the customs [of landholding] in India are not in conformity with these rules, and the landholders now claim full ownership everywhere, thus leaving no remaining free land to the public domain (literally "owned by the state treasury") for which the aforementioned rules can apply.[136]

ʿAbd al-ʿAzīz addresses this overreach on public properties by referring to the legal opinions of a prominent tenth/sixteenth century Mughal Ḥanafī jurist by the name of Jalāl al-Dīn al-Thānīsirī (d. 991/1582), who addressed the issue of landholdings in India at his time in a fatwa treatise. Al-Thānīsirī argued like the Muslim-conquered lands of Iraq in the first/seventh century were declared by the Caliph ʿUmar as being in the public domain, claiming them for the state treasury.[137] Similarly, al-Thānīsirī argues that the lands in the initial Muslim conquest of India belonged to the public treasury and that the Indian landholders merely had the right of trusteeship (*tawliyat*) over them. ʿAbd al-ʿAzīz affirms this position by adding that the meaning of the term "*zamīndār*" is an indication of their limited role as landholders and not landowners.[138] Furthermore, the fact

135 ʿAbd al-ʿAzīz, 575–577. Later in his fatwa, after reconciling these two legal positions, ʿAbd al-ʿAzīz lists four logical scenarios that could explain the types of land grants in India. However, two of the scenarios listed in the published text were identical (scenario #2 and scenario # 4), thus reducing the total number of scenarios to three. Furthermore, scenarios #1 and #3 are almost identical in meaning, thus reducing the real scenarios to two. This reduction to two scenarios is despite the fact that ʿAbd al-ʿAzīz claims that scenario # 3 is a logical possibility but not a legally legitimate one, thereby alluding to some difference between scenarios #1 and #3 (see the text of the fatwa ʿAbd al-ʿAzīz, 575–577). Again, I believe this confusion is the result of reproduction errors, and after having several printed editions checked, they all seem to have reproduced the inaccurate text of the fatwa. Therefore, I had reduced my analysis to the only two seemingly different scenarios presented in the earlier portion of the fatwa when he was reconciling the different positions of the Ḥanafī madhhab on this issue.

136 ʿAbd al-ʿAzīz, 575–577.

137 Refer to Chapter 1 for this discussion.

138 See Habib, 138, who confirms this interpretation and gives the term's etymological (Persian) origin.

that Indian Muslim heads of state have often changed and dismissed such individuals from these positions is an indication that their original status was merely as landholders, and not landowners, in the true meaning of the term "*zamīndār*."[139]

Already we can observe in this portion of his argumentation that his strategy is to couch his legal position within the precedent set by his Ḥanafī (Indian) legal predecessors like al-Thānīsirī as well as the historical precedent set by Caliph ʿUmar before them. Similarly, he affirms al-Thānīsirī's use of *qiyās* (analogy) between the scenario of Iraq and the scenario of India, thereby triggering the transition of the legal ruling that was applied to the original case of Iraq to transfer over to the newer case of India. The *qiyās* that ʿAbd al-ʿAzīz affirms here is not the kind where the ruling on the original case was established through the scriptural authority of the Quran and *sunna* like most of the examples of *qiyās* showcased thus far. Instead, the original case (the scenario of Iraq and the Caliph ʿUmar's ruling on it) was established by *ijmāʿ* (consensus of Muslim jurists). This consensus regarding the legitimacy of the state to manage *kharāj* (public) lands was tacitly acknowledged even by Shīʿī scholars like al-Karakī.[140] This kind of *qiyās* based on a ruling reached by *ijmāʿ* is but another way that legal analogies are made in Islamic law.

ʿAbd al-ʿAzīz further bolsters his position by adding his own linguistic and historical observations that make landholders' widespread claims of land ownership spurious. Ultimately, he argues that all land in the landholders' possessions should be treated according to its original status as public land and not privately owned land unless proven otherwise.[141] By this assertion, he is implicitly employing an established legal principle known as *istiṣḥāb* (continuity),[142] which requires that any case's original rulings be maintained until some impinging factor necessitates a change in these rulings. By implicitly basing his argument on this principle, ʿAbd

[139] ʿAbd al-ʿAzīz, 575–577. For this last point, ʿAbd al-ʿAzīz seems to have reproduced the argument made earlier by an eighteenth century Indian Muslim jurist Muḥammad al-Tahānawī who also wrote a treatise on land law in India titled *Aḥkām al-Arāḍī*. See Zafarul Islam's article "Nature of landed Property in Mughal India: Views of an Eighteenth-Century Jurist" for a summary of this treatise. Nevertheless, Zafarul Islam affirms on pg. 302 of his article that al-Tahānawī's treatise liberally utilizes al-Thānīsirī's earlier treatise titled *Risala-Dar-Bai-Arazi*.

[140] See my analysis of his fatwa in the preceding section.

[141] ʿAbd al-ʿAzīz, 575–577.

[142] See Hallaq, 2009, 120, for his more nuanced translation of this term as "Assumption of Unaffected Continuity." Vikor defines *istiṣḥāb* as implying that "matters should continue as they are or in their natural state unless there is a reason to change them." (Vikor, 70)

al-ʿAzīz justified his ruling that these Indian lands that were subject of contention ought to be treated according to their original status as state owned until it can be determined how these land grants were distributed by the various Indian Muslim heads of state.

How is one to make such a determination? He states that this can be done by examining the past royal decrees (*farmāns*) to determine whether these heads of state bestowed these lands to the grantees for perpetuity (tabīd) or did they merely bestow them temporarily for the sake of granting pensions (*idrār*) or for rewarding merit (*istiḥqāq*) for various services rendered to the state. Nevertheless, he acknowledges the difficulty of undertaking this task, thus leading to a situation of continued ambiguity regarding such lands. ʿAbd al-ʿAzīz concludes his fatwa with a discussion of the possession/ownership of some lands in India by the nobility (*shurafā*), where the nature and origins of such possessions are less ambiguous than the previously mentioned category of land.[143] However, that brief discussion is of less concern for us here as the bulk of the fatwa concentrates on determining the legal status of the lands in possession of the landholders (*zamīndārs*). Moreover, there were some discussions on *kharāj* taxation (taxation on state lands) in the fatwa that is not germane to my analysis, and thus I have left those points out.

To sum up, ʿAbd al-ʿAzīz's fatwa highlights several important factors for the Islamic legal tradition. First, aside from demonstrating several already familiar Islamic legal concepts like *qiyās*, it also displayed the breadth of Islamic theory by utilizing new types of legal arguments, albeit implicitly, like *al-siyāsa al-sharʿiyya* and *istiṣḥāb* that we had not hitherto explored in this book. Secondly, it exhibited the historical character of fatwas, where the legal precedent of Thanisiri and Caliph ʿUmar played a determinate role in the legal outcome. In addition, as we saw in al-Karakī's fatwa earlier, it showed how Caliph ʿUmar's legal institutionalizations, like his establishment of public lands, continued to influence Islamic legislation more than a millennium after they were issued. Thirdly, the fatwa exemplifies the continued pull of established legal doctrine on jurists' legal practices and opinions in this period that I have designated as the era of *madhhab* preponderance. This pull is noticeable when ʿAbd al-ʿAzīz contextualized his discussion by first appealing to the legal positions within the established (Ḥanafī) doctrine on the issue of ownership of public lands (see Figure 17). This dynamic of situating one's legal opinions within the broader context of the legal opinions

[143] ʿAbd al-ʿAzīz, 575–577.

of one's school begins to be challenged in the subsequent period. I will investigate this matter further in the next chapter.

Furthermore, this fatwa indicates the role and limited rights Islamic law accords to the state regarding the relationship between law, state, and society. It shows that the Islamic legal tradition acknowledged that the state was a necessary institution for the law's full implementation, even though the law itself had developed with significant independence from the political sphere. This balance is another change in the Islamic legal tradition, further explored in the next chapter. Lastly, the ʿAbd al-ʿAzīz's fatwa showed how Muslims continued to rely on such legal and social devices as fatwas to navigate their drastically changing reality, like the disintegration of the Mughal Empire and the imposition of a new British colonial order in the world.

ʿUthmān Dan Fodio's Early Nineteenth-Century Fatwa Regarding Retrieving Property

ʿUthmān Dan Fodio (1754–1817) was a West African Mālikī Muslim jurist and scholar. He spearheaded a social and political reform movement in the late eighteenth and early nineteenth centuries in what is now known as northern Nigeria. Dan Fodio was a descendant of the Islamic scholarly class known as the Torodbe (Turudbe), which was ethnically mixed and carried out Islamization efforts across West Africa.[144] Growing up in this scholastic tradition, Dan Fodio took up teaching and preaching efforts early in his life to Islamize further the parts of sub-Saharan African societies that he viewed were fringe. Moreover, he advised the political authorities in Gobir (the Hausa dynasty) against unjust taxation and the freeing of political prisoners.[145] By the late eighteenth century, he gained a strong following for his religious message and social reform among the various people in the Hausalands in northern Nigeria.

As Dan Fodio's religious movement gained momentum, the Muslim Hausa rulers in Gobir felt threatened by the changes he introduced to the society. They, in turn, issued edicts banning Muslim proselytizing and conversion and the wearing of distinct Muslim clothing like turbans and veils, in addition to confiscating the properties of Dan Fodio's followers who were migrating to the town of Degal where Dan Fodio resided.[146]

[144] Lapidus, 420; Quick, 74; for more on the Turudbe, see Muhammad Shareef, "The Life of Shaykh Dana Tafa."

[145] Balogun, 276.

[146] El Masri, 10; Last, 12

Facing increasing religious persecution, Dan Fodio urged his followers in 1804 to emigrate (*hijrah*) from Gobir to the peripheral regions of the Hausalands to escape the grip of the political authorities. However, alarmed at the number of people who had joined Dan Fodio's emigration, the rulers forbade further emigrations and confiscated the emigres' properties.[147] Seeing no way out of the spiraling situation, Dan Fodio declared a jihad against the authorities in Gobir and eventually succeeded by 1808 in overthrowing the Hausa dynasty and establishing an Islamic state in that region known as the Sokoto Caliphate.[148]

These political events set the historical context of Dan Fodio's fatwa that I am investigating here. The fatwa is a chapter in a more extensive treatise written by Dan Fodio known as *Najm al-Ikhwān*. It is clear from the text of the fatwa that Dan Fodio issued it after his followers' victory over the Hausa rulers in Gobir, as its primary concern was how to deal with the properties that had been previously confiscated from the people by the Gobir authorities.

Some jurists in Dan Fodio's camp wanted to keep the status quo in maintaining such properties in the hands of those who possessed them or have them and other properties of the Gobir rulers appropriated by the state treasury of the new Sokoto Caliphate as war booty. Dan Fodio descents from this opinion and argues for the inviolability of the property rights of the original owners.[149]

Dan Fodio initiates his fatwa by putting the political scenario his newly founded state was facing into its historical and geographic context. He draws an analogy between the situation of Hausaland and that faced by the new emperor of the Songhai Empire of Mali in the late fifteenth and early sixteenth century, Askia al-Ḥājj Muḥammad, with the fall of his predecessor Sunnī ʿAlī. Askia asked the known Mālikī jurist from North Africa Muḥammad ʿAbd al-Karīm al-Maghīlī a series of questions regarding social challenges facing his rule that Sunnī ʿAlī created. Among these challenges was what to do with properties that Sunnī ʿAlī confiscated from people during his reign.[150] Following al-Maghīlī's precedent

147 Last, 23–24

148 Balogun, 279; El Masri, 12; Lapidus, 421.

149 I am grateful to Shaykh Adeyinka Muhammad Mendes, currently residing in Banjul, Gambia, for providing me with the text of this fatwa and the references to many of the secondary sources used in this presentation of Dan Fodio's life and works.

150 For more on this exchange/fatwa, see John O. Hunwick's translation and commentary titled: *Sharia in the Songhai: The Replies of Al-Maghīlī to the Questions of Askia Al-Hajj Muhammad* (1985).

and the ruling found in a text authored by his brother ʿAbd Allāh, Dan Fodio asserts that if anyone were to see his property (in possession of someone else) and can prove that it is his/hers, then they may take it back without compensation. This repossession can occur under any circumstance the original owner finds it, even if s/he takes it from someone who might have acquired it by sale, gift, or inheritance. This position says Dan Fodio is because its buyer, heir, or receiver is equivalent to the usurper (*ghāṣib*) if that person knew of the usurpation.[151]

Dan Fodio continues in his fatwa to restate his brother's position saying that statements of previous jurists about leaving alone properties that the unjust rulers had granted to others needed contextualization. He claims that those statements only applied to the disposed-of properties from the state treasury (*bayt al-māl*) that circulated among many, leading to the inability to trace its original owners. Therefore, tracing these properties would only bring more harm (*mafāsid*) than good. But what one can prove ownership of certainly allows them to repossess it. Likewise, the same ruling should apply to the Fulani tribes,[152] who claim Islam and who usurped the wealth of each other. As for their political authorities (*al-salāṭīn*) and their assistants, whose wealth is entirely illegitimate (*al-mustaghriq al-dhimma*)[153] [because they usurped it], those in charge should not return those properties to them because they do not belong to them. Thus, they belong to the state treasury.[154]

As for those whose properties that are not unlawful (*lam yakun minhum mustaghriq al-dhimma*) and they can prove that this was their wealth, they may simply take it wherever they find it. The only exception to this rule is if taking back one's property would lead to a situation of greater vice (*munkar*). In this case, one should abandon one's claim to repulse the harm (*mafsada*) that is likely to accrue. Yet, this does entail that repossessing one's own property is illegal. Dan Fodio says that this is the implication of al-Mughili's position, and it is apparent to anyone who knows what is found in the legal manuals.[155]

Dan Fodio then says that it is incumbent upon the rulers and all of the muftis to explain to the people that such wealth (that leads to greater vice

151 Dan Fodio, 240.

152 One of the three major ethnic groups, along with the Hausa and the Tuareg, occupying Hausaland.

153 I am thankful to Dr. Waleed Mosaad, a resident scholar in Allentown, Pennsylvania, for clarifying the meaning of this phrase within the context of Mālikī law.

154 Dan Fodio, 240.

155 Dan Fodio, 240.

if repossessed) is still illegal/illegitimate [for exchange]. This fact should be made known so that those ignorant of the matter do not become misguided regarding the legality/legitimacy of that property because that legitimization of that ill-gotten wealth is an even greater moral transgression than the offense of merely utilizing or exchanging it. This clarification is necessary because some will assume what was acquired of this ill-gotten property (*al-amwāl al-ma'kūla*) before his jihad against those who claim to be Muslim [i.e., the Hausa monarchs] is permissible for them to utilize. This assumption will prevail if people don't hear the rulers and jurists objecting to this matter but only if such objections do not lead to a situation of more significant harm (*mafsada*). This course of action is necessary because it is wrong to leave matters undifferentiated/ambiguous (*ijmāl*) when differentiation/clarity (*tafṣīl*) is required.[156]

Thus far, Dan Fodio asserts the right of repossession of those whose property had been confiscated irrespective of when that dispossession took place. He is going against those jurists who seem to believe that what had been illegitimately taken by these political authorities and had been widely circulated is no longer subject to the right of repossession. Therefore, these properties may continue to be exchanged and utilized by the public.

Dan Fodio then takes further exception to those jurists and judges who distinguish between the implementation of Islamic law before and after Dan Fodio's caliphate-conquered Alkalawa (the capital of Gobir). He claims that such judges assume that the situation before the takeover is not subject to Islamic law. Thus, however, the properties were transacted; they were to receive a post-facto legitimacy without differentiating between such properties. But if these properties were transacted after the establishment of Dan Fodio's (Islamic) political authority in Hausaland, they are more cautious in investigating the origin of properties. Dan Fodio says that this is an apparent mistake because the rulings of Islamic law applied to the same degree before and after the conquest of areas [and the establishment of Islamic governance]. He says this position is well established in the books of Islamic law, and whoever claims otherwise needs to provide the proof.[157]

Dan Fodio asserts that even stranger than the previous position of such jurists is their position on those who have a peace treaty with Muslims. They claim that what has been usurped from Muslims by the

[156] Dan Fodio, 240–241.
[157] Dan Fodio, 241.

unbelievers who had a peace treaty with them or those who claim to be Muslim before the conquest of Alkalawa, those properties are not to be investigated. Moreover, if the rightful owner were to find their (usurped) property, then s/he has the choice to repurchase it from them or leave it in their possession. Dan Fodio claims that these jurists and judges legitimize the transaction of unbelievers with the usurped properties of Muslims, and he found this legal opinion objectionable.[158]

After broadly stating his legal opinion on these issues, Dan Fodio begins a detailed restatement of his position but now contextualizes it within the established rulings of the Mālikī *madhhab*:

1. The Muslim properties that were usurped by the Hausaland rulers before this time and have been bought by others should not be investigated to determine their original owners because this would produce greater harm, as is stated in the Mālikī law book al-*Miʿyār* by al-Wansharīsī.
2. But these properties are only permissible for exchange as long as their owners are not identified because they are properties whose actual owners are unknown. To support this position, he cites a passage from another Mālikī law manual *Shurb al-Zallāl*: "As for the property whose rightful owners are unknown, it is permissible for utilization."
3. But if these properties are now found by their rightful owners and s/he has proof of ownership, then s/he may immediately take them without [legal] recourse. Moreover, even if this property is found with the usurper's heirs, those the usurper had gifted the property to, or with the one who had bought it from the usurper, the rightful owner could repossess the property. Dan Fodio says this position is well established in yet another Mālikī law text, *al-Mukhtaṣar*, and its commentaries. This opinion, he says, is the popular (*al-mashhūr*) opinion in the Mālikī *madhhab* despite the minority who claim that what has been taken by force should be reclaimed through purchase.[159]
4. As for the properties of the Fulanis whom Dan Fodio was fighting against and others who claim to be Muslim and those who align with them, they should not return their properties to them because all their properties were attained illegally (*mustaghriq al dhimma*). The exception to this ruling were those whose properties

[158] Dan Fodio, 241.
[159] Dan Fodio, 241–242.

were legitimate and could be distinguished from the majority. Nevertheless, most of these ill-gotten properties ought to be transferred to the state treasury (*bayt al-māl*). He supports this position by quoting the famous Mālikī jurist al-Burzulī, who affirms the legality of these appropriations for the state treasury.[160]

5. Here, Dan Fodio repeats his earlier criticism of those jurists who apply different rulings depending on the timing of his conquest of the Hausaland. But this time, he points to the source of this mistaken understanding as that they were universalizing what was particular. Here, he refers to the specific peace agreement between his group and the Tuareg peoples who resided in Gobir before its defeat by Dan Fodio. This agreement entitled the Tuareg to a return of their property in Gobir when Dan Fodio's armies took it over. After presenting an elaborate discussion about the different positions of previous Mālikī jurists regarding the inalienability of the Muslim-owned properties living in the abodes of war (*dar al-ḥarb*), he says that despite their agreement, they were unable to fulfill this pledge of returning Tuareg property in its entirety.[161] He then justified his position by stipulating that what was usurped from Tuareg [by the previous rulers of Gobir] before Dan Fodio's victory in al-Alkalawa would not be returned to them since they resided in the abode of war (*balad al-ḥarb*). This opinion, he says, is supported by a strong position within Mālikī *madhhab* that says that all properties existing in the abode of war were subject to confiscation by an Islamic state even if Muslims previously owned them.

On the other hand, what they had taken from the Tuareg after the conquest of Hausaland would be returned to them since the entire region had come under the rule of Islam, making their property rights inalienable. He says that under this exceptional circumstance, the victory in Hausaland became a historical marker for the restriction of some Islamic rulings.[162]

[160] Dan Fodio, 242. To underline the influence of al-Maghīlī on Dan Fodio, it is important to note that Dan Fodio's citation of al-Burzulī is exactly reproduced from al-Maghīlī's earlier cited replies to Askia (see pg. 89–90 in Hunwick's *Sharia in the Songhai*). In addition to Dan Fodio citing al-Maghīlī at the beginning of his fatwa, his reproduction of what is found in al-Maghīlī's fatwa is yet another indication that this fatwa had influenced Dan Fodio's opinions on this issue.

[161] It is unclear from the text of the fatwa as to why Dan Fodio's government was unable to fulfil the pledge in the agreement to return the property of the Tuareg.

[162] Perhaps he means here his suspension of the ability to execute his agreement with Tuareg, which would have been required in Islamic law.

Yet the mistake these jurists make is that they generalize the limits from this exceptional case to all Islamic rulings.[163]

6. Related to the previous point, Dan Fodio objects to the strange position taken by those jurists who say that no one should interrogate the properties usurped from Muslims by non-Muslims with which they had a peace agreement before the conquest of Hausaland. This non-interference is because the agreement renders what is in possession of these non-Muslims inviolable. Dan Fodio justifies his objection by saying that such actions are not permissible in accordance with the consensus (*ijmāʿ*) of Muslim/ Mālikī jurists.

   Instead, the rulings of Islamic law should apply to these non-Muslims who have usurped these properties as they would apply to the Muslims. The exception to the position is that if applying the letter of the law leads to more significant harm, they should be abandoned to stave off this ḥarm. Dan Fodio concludes this point (and the fatwa) by summarizing the Mālikī jurists' legal debates regarding the property rights of non-Muslims who convert to Islam.[164] This discussion is tangential to the main issue he was trying to settle and not pertinent for our purposes.

Ultimately, Dan Fodio's ruling supports peoples' rights to reclaim their usurped properties under any conditions except those situations that would lead to greater upheaval/corruption (*mafsada*). This latter position echoes the fundamental principle behind Islamic law: "to promote the common good and deter corruption (*jalb al-maṣlaḥa wa dar' al-mafsada*)." This principle seems to be the driving force behind Dan Fodio's fatwa and the only consideration that tempers his position of the inviolability of peoples' property rights. Alternatively, one may interpret Dan Fodio's concern about avoiding harm as a manifestation of the unique Mālikī legal precept of *sadd al-dharī'ah* (blocking the pathways to harm). This concept implies that some act may be legal in its own right, but if it leads to something unlawful, then it too is considered unlawful. By pointing out the possibility that repossession of one's confiscated properties (something that is legal) can lead to a greater harm (something that is illegal), Dan Fodio was taking into consideration this legal idea (see Figure 17).

[163] Dan Fodio, 242–243.
[164] Dan Fodio, 243–245.

Case	Ruling/fatwa	Legal reasoning	Jurist	Madhhab
Do minor children have the right to reach maturity to pardon their father's murderer?	Yes. **Note:** Ibn Rushd's fatwa was arguing against the established position of the Mālikī madhhab	1. Quranic and *ḥadīth* evidence indicates the right of the family to pardon or punish 2. *Qiyās* to stated scripture implies that children cannot be stripped of this right on account of their minority status 3. *Istiḥsān*, which is used by the jurists of the school to establish the right of the agnates over the children, is not a stronger legal principle than *qiyās* in the Mālikī school 4. The primacy of pardoning over punishment in scripture	Ibn Rushd (al-Jadd) Eleventh–twelfth-century Islamic Spain (Andalusia)	Mālikī
Is it permissible to wage jihad (war) against other Muslims (i.e., Tatars)?	Yes	1. Quran and *ḥadīth* give license for Muslims to fight other Muslims who transgress 2. Early Muslim caliphs and the early predecessors all sanctioned fighting against renegade Muslims (e.g., Khawārij) 3. Ijmāʿ: All master jurists of the *madhhab*s (Mālik, Abū Ḥanīfa, al-Shāfiʿī, and Ibn Ḥanbal) sanctioned fighting against earlier Muslim rebel groups	Ibn Taymiyya Thirteenth–fourteenth-century Mamluk Syria and Egypt	Ḥanbalī **Note:** Ibn Taymiyya does not restrict himself to arguing within his own school (Ḥanbalī) because of the less structured nature of the Ḥanbalī school and his own proclivities toward independent *ijtihād* (legal reasoning)

FIGURE 17 Fatwa in the age of preponderance of legal schools

Are cash endowments (*waqf al-* <u>nuqūd</u>) legitimate enterprises when they lack the two conditions for a *waqf* in Islam, immovability and permanence?	Yes. **Note:** Master jurists of the Ḥanafī school (Abū Yūsuf and al-Shaybānī) argued against the legitimacy of these types of foundations	1. Al-Shaybānī does allow for some movable items to be made into *waqf*s based on the prevailing custom (*ʿurf*), which can be extended to cash *waqf*s 2. As for the dispersal of the cash and its impermanence, the likeness (*mithl*) of the cash does remain as an endowment even though the actual cash (*ʿayn*) endowed gets dispersed. Hence, the permanence clause is satisfied 3. *ʿUrf* (customary practice) has already been established as a legal source for the legitimization of practices by the master jurists. When cash *waqf*s were banned by early master jurists, it is because they were not a part of the *ʿurf* of that period, but they have become so now since *ʿurf* always changes. Hence, cash *waqf*s can be seen as legitimate	Abu al-Suʿūd. Sixteenth-century Ottoman Turkey	Ḥanafī

FIGURE 17 (cont.)

Is the collection and utilization of *kharāj* (land tax) a legal practice in Twelver Shīʿī law in the absence of a legitimate government?	Yes. **Note:** Twelver Shīʿī scholars viewed Islamic regimes of the time as illegitimate because they did not adhere to Twelver Shīʿī political theory of the legitimate ruler	1. Twelver Shīʿī Imams endorsed the acceptance of benefits, employment, or purchasing of properties from the contemporary "illegitimate" authorities, who derived their wealth from taxes like *kharāj* 2. Post-Imamite-period Shīʿī *mujtahid*s (independent jurists) were in virtual consensus (*ijmāʿ*) that the wealth generated from the *kharāj* tax is legitimate for utilization even if the government was illegitimate	Al-Karkī. Sixteenth-century Safavid Iran	Twelver Shīʿī
Are Indian lands that are in the possession of the landholders (*zamīndārs*) their private property?	No	1. *Qiyās:* Indian land is public property because it is conquered land analogues to seventh-century Iraq 2. *Istiṣḥāb* (continuity): Public land remains under the joint ownership of the community under the management of the state unless a reason is given necessitating a modification of this status	Shah ʿAbd al-ʿAzīz Eighteenth–nineteenth-century late Mughal India	Ḥanafī

FIGURE 17 (cont.)

		3. *Al-siyāsa al-sharʿiyya* (moral diplomacy): The head of the Muslim state may bestow the revenue and management of public lands to grantees on a temporary or permanent basis if some state benefit is accrued from such an action. But the land always remains in the public domain		
Can owners repossess their confiscated properties without recourse to the law?	Yes, so long that they have proof of ownership	1. Precedent: Fatwa of al-Maghīlī affirming the right to repossess one's property 2. *Jalb al-maṣlaḥa wa dar' al-mafsada* (to promote the common good and deter corruption): Avoiding harm/corruption is an overarching concern when applying rules 3. *Sadd al-dharī'ah* (blocking the pathways to harm): If retrieving one's confiscated property would lead to greater societal harm, then this course should be abandoned 4. Established Mālikī doctrine: Majority opinions within this school affirm the right of unqualified repossession	ʿUthmān Dan Fodio Eighteenth–nineteenth-century West Africa	Mālikī

FIGURE 17 (cont.)

Nevertheless, Dan Fodio positioned his universal guiding precepts and his opinion on property rights within the context of the Mālikī legal debates surrounding these issues. This fact is evident in his strategy of citing the works of previous Mālikī jurists like al-Maghīlī, al-Wansharīsī, al-Burzulī, and others who pervade the fatwa. All this points to the overarching character of fatwas in this period of *madhhab* preponderance that they had to be situated within the web of opinions comprising the Islamic legal schools.

However, Dan Fodio's fatwa displays some distinguishing features. First, by citing the fatwa of his earlier Mālikī predecessor al-Maghīlī regarding a similar scenario confronting earlier Muslim states in West Africa, he created a legal analog (qiyās) between the scenarios he faced with that of what occurred earlier in the same geographic context. This strategy is similar to what Shah ʿAbd al-ʿAzīz employed in his fatwa. Yet there are differences between the two in that Dan Fodio references the precedent that emerged from his geographic context rather than the precedent set elsewhere. Using this maneuver, he acknowledges the precedent set by earlier jurists from across the Muslim world. Still, he also highlighted the indigenization of the Islamic legal tradition in the African context, which is exemplified by referencing the legal exchange between the jurist al-Maghīlī and Emperor Askia. This indigenization was both a growing reality in sub-Saharan Africa and a part of Dan Fodio's agenda of social and political reform.

CONCLUSION

In the previous chapters, the evolution of the Islamic legal tradition through the practice of fatwas was outlined. Fatwas played a constitutive role in forming that legal tradition both substantively in terms of providing the matter of legal doctrine and formally in terms of the legal rationale that was embedded in them that became the prototype of the Islamic legal discourse. Hence, fatwas were a fundamental element in the emergence of the Islamic legal tradition.

As this tradition emerged, it exerted its influence on the jurisprudential activity of fatwas. Like all traditions, the Islamic legal tradition viewed historical legal discourses, institutions, and experiences as foundational and normative. In this respect, Islamic legal discourse and tradition represent what Harold Berman calls historical jurisprudence where the past "is the source of 'standards' for the interpretation and promulgation of laws, and for the normative goals of the legal system."[165]

This was clearly illustrated in the consistent appeal of Muslim jurists through the ages to the judgments that had been established through historical precedent and the institutionalized practice of previous generations of Muslim jurists (i.e., in the form of *madhhab*s) as guides and standards for how contemporary Islamic jurisprudence would be determined. That had been the guiding ethos of Islamic jurisprudence from the very early stages, but with the imposition of colonialism on Muslim lands in the nineteenth century, for the first time in over a millennium of Islamic history, this ethos came into question from a new Muslim elite who sought to break from this tradition. It will be the subject of the remaining part of this study to assess the effects of this modern discourse on Islamic law in particular and the Islamic legal tradition in general.

[165] Chase, 3. For more on Berman's concept of historical jurisprudence, see Edward Chase's article entitled "Law and Theology" in *A Companion to the Philosophy of Law and Legal Theory*, Blackwell Reference Online.

6

Colonialism, Islamic Law, and the Post-Colonial Fatwa

INTRODUCTION

Until now, we have talked about the evolution of the Islamic legal tradition in the first twelve hundred years of Islam and how the fatwa played an integral role in that development and how, reciprocally, it was affected by that development. The development of that tradition was something that was gradual and organic. This began to change toward the beginning of the nineteenth century with the rise of European power in the world that brought about a new set of attitudes and ways of thinking about the world. But most importantly, the rise of European power brought about a new world order that would change the entire global social, economic, and political dynamic. Those sweeping changes would equally affect the Muslim world and in particular the developmental trajectory of Islamic law. In the next few sections, I outline illustrations of colonization and semi-colonization of the Muslim world in the nineteenth and twentieth centuries in order to provide a political context for the changes in Islamic law. After which the investigation will turn to an analysis of some colonial and post-colonial fatwas to see the sort of new trajectories Islamic law is undergoing.

EUROPEAN COLONIZATION OF THE MUSLIM GEOGRAPHIC PERIPHERY IN THE NINETEENTH CENTURY

British Colonization of Muslim-Ruled India

In 1757, the British, in collaboration with the British East India Company, defeated the local Muslim rulers of Bengal in the Battle of Plassey and gained control of the Indian regions of Bengal.[1] This was India's richest province, and through the resources afforded to the British by the acquisition of Bengal, they managed to gain control over all of India over the next sixty years, both the Muslim-ruled and the smaller Hindu-ruled portions of it.[2] The introduction of English machine-produced textiles brought ruin to the Bengali cotton weaving industry as Indian textiles could not compete with British-manufactured goods on the world market and eventually turned Bengal into an agricultural economy for the production of jute and indigo as raw materials for the core industrialized regions of the world economy and not for local food production for its own subsistence.[3]

Yet British colonialism did not simply remain within the confines of political and economic exploitation of India. As Hallaq points out, British commercial interests "were intimately connected with the particular vision of a legal system structured and geared in such a manner as to accommodate an 'open' economic market. The legal system was, and continued to be, the template that determined and set the tone of economic domination."[4] Nevertheless, the British did not directly impose British law on Indians but instead preferred a multi-tiered legal system whereby the British legal structure would be superimposed on native Indian laws, whether those laws were Hindu or Muslim, where British judges would adjudicate civil matters in accordance with Muslim and Hindu law.[5] This necessitated the eventual translation of Islamic legal compendia into English so as to give British judges direct access to Islamic legal statutes so as not to rely on Muslim *qāḍī*s (judges), whom they did not trust, to adjudicate legal issues that arose among the Muslim population. This led to the translation of the Ḥanafī Islamic legal compendium *al-Hidāya* into

[1] Metcalf and Metcalf, 53.

[2] Metcalf and Metcalf, 55; see also Hodgson, v. 3, 213.

[3] Metcalf and Metcalf, 76–77; Hodgson, v. 3, 211.

[4] Hallaq, 2009, 371–372. Elaborating on the economic and political purposes of the British colonial judicial system in India and British Malaya, Hussin says: "Jurisdiction in the early days of the colonial state was not delegated – it had to be built The definition of jurisdiction as territory links space and power, and in the colonial project control over territory was at the forefront of the colonial agenda. Treaties like Allahabad and Pangkor were part of the effort to secure control over a discrete space (Bengal and Perak), for economic reasons first and foremost: the rich resources of these states and the opportunities they presented for British trading interests." (Hussin, 89–90)

[5] Hallaq, 2009, 372. But even where Islamic law was theoretically given jurisdiction in the colonial state, this jurisdiction remained a place to intervention by the colonial juridical system, rendering this supposed jurisdiction of Islamic law superfluous. See, for example, the case of Naderah Begum in Iza Hussin's *The Politics of Islamic Law* (pg. 105).

English as the Ḥanafī school of law was the legal doctrine to which most Indian Muslims adhered.[6]

As Hallaq asserts, the translation of *al-Hidāya* amounted to its codification, which made this legal compendium cease to function in the way it previously had, because it restricted the juridical discretion of the *jud*ges and replaced "the native's system of interpretive mechanisms by those of English law."[7] Furthermore, the translation/codification of *al-Hidāya* severed its organic relatedness to the Islamic juristic and hermeneutical tradition by excluding considerations of customary norms, which were essential to the functioning of Islamic law, especially at the level of application.[8]

Yet the initial exclusion of customary consideration from the interpretation and implementation of the now reified Islamic legal texts in British India proved to be inadequate, and customary law was then given reconsideration as a source of law in late nineteenth-century India. Michael Anderson states: "Frustrated by the inadequacy of religious texts and native law officers, British administrators in the latter half of the nineteenth century began to focus upon custom as a source of law."[9] Yet

[6] Hallaq, 2009, 374. Hallaq says: "The immediate purpose of these translations was to make Islamic law directly accessible to British judges who deeply mistrusted the native maulvis advising them on points of law." (Hallaq, 2009, 374). Elaborating on this point, Hussin says: "By replacing the multiple and messy opinions of jurists with a brief and translated code of Ḥanafī law on personal status, the British attempted to limit the discretion of Muslim legal professionals, allow British judges to pronounce on Islamic law using an authoritative code, and subject the content of Islamic law to the forms and logics of British judicature" (Hussin, 85).

[7] Hallaq, 2009, 375–376. Speaking of the methods of subversion of native laws by the British colonial government in its Muslim territories even when it was declared that such laws were operational in their limited domains, Hussin says: "Another principle of law which allowed the gradual increase of English legal content in the legal systems of India, Egypt, and Malaya was the sense that Islamic law simply did not cover all eventualities, and where the Quran and classical texts were silent, English law or British judgment could fill in the blanks. The reliance on textual forms of law and the rise in codification of Islamic law, as well as the concomitant reduction in Islamic legal interlocutors working in the courts who could interpret new cases in light of Islamic legal principles, or using shari'a jurisprudential techniques, contributed further to the sense that Islamic law was a finite and fixed resource" (Hussin, 139).

[8] Hallaq, 2009, 376. In this regard, Hussin notes: "The Hastings Plan set aside the local practices of Hindus and Muslims in Bengal, which were mixtures of religious, customary, group, caste, class, and regional norms and institutions, in favor of the laws of the Quran and the Shasters [A treatise of authoritative instruction for Hindus]. In doing so, British officials and courts significantly reduced the realm and status of custom and customary law, privileging the classical texts of gradually homogenizing religions" (Hussin, 141; additions in brackets are from the author).

[9] As quoted in Hussin, 141. Speaking of British effort at the collection and codification of Indian customary law, Hussin says: "In the Punjab in 1872, for example, revenue officers

the impulse to implement customary laws was more than a result of the perceived inadequacies of Islamic legal texts; it was also as a stratagem to undermine the growing empowerment of native officers using Islamic law to intervene in the workings of British colonial policies. Hussin states:

That they [customary laws] were put in place is a sign firstly that the [Hastings] Plan had not managed to achieve its aims solely through the unification and definition of Islamic law, but also that native law officers were becoming an obstacle to the administration of colonial policies, perhaps in part because of the fact that a strictly defined Islamic law gave them a measure by which British actions could be judged and potentially found wanting. The choice of custom, then, was a new political strategy, but it encountered some of the same problems as that of the Hastings Plan, reifying otherwise varied and contingent practices into fixed and flattened codes. Whereas customary practices "necessarily entailed a reinterpretation of community standards and the interpreter's position within them... very real struggle over what the standards were in the first place... what the British called 'customary law' was inherently incompatible with the epistemological dictates of codification" (Hussin, 141–142; additions in brackets are from the author).

The superimposition of British legal structure on Islamic law in India was a form of symbolic violence on the Islamic legal system in India. As Hallaq states: "*Ijtihādic* hermeneutics was the very feature that distinguished Islamic law from modern codified legal systems, a feature that permitted this law to reign supreme in, and accommodate, as varied and diverse cultures, sub-cultures, local moralities and customary practices as those which flourished in Java, Malabar, Khurasan, Madagascar, Syria, and Morocco. But insofar as judicial practice was concerned, the bindingness of a ruling according to the specifically British doctrine of precedent deprived the *qāḍī* of the formerly wider array of opinions to choose from in light of facts presented in the case. Once the determination of law in a specific case was made binding, as would happen in a British court, the otherwise unceasing hermeneutical activities of the Muslim muftī-cum-author jurist would have no place in judicial life."[10]

Yet even this hybrid form of Islamic law in India that was known as Anglo-Muḥammadan law did not survive past the first century of British

were sent to record customary land-holding practices in order to better the system for collection of revenue. These attempts at collecting, standardizing, and then codifying custom functioned along the same principles as the Hastings Plan of a century earlier. That they were put in place is a sign firstly that the Plan had not managed to achieve its aims solely through the unification and definition of Islamic law, but also that native law officers were becoming an obstacle to the administration of colonial policies, perhaps in part because of the fact that a strictly defined Islamic law gave them a measure by which British actions could be judged and potentially found wanting."

[10] Hallaq, 2009, 381.

colonialism in India. Shortly after the Sepoy Mutiny in 1857, the British began to abolish aspects of Islamic law, such as Islamic legal procedures and criminal law and evidence. By the end of the nineteenth century, all indigenous forms of law were supplanted by British law with the exception of family law and certain aspects of property transactions.[11]

French Colonization of Algeria

French colonization of Algeria began in 1830 when the French invaded Algiers and continued with the subsequent takeover of the rest of Algeria over the next forty years. French colonization of Algeria had a different character than British colonization in India in that it took the form of settler colonialism whose main feature was an appropriation of Algerian land by French settlers who came from France seeking to exploit the new economic opportunities that were afforded to them by this colonization.[12]

French colonialism in Algeria functioned by dispossessing the natives of their land, making those lands available to French colonists. During the period of 1830 to 1940, the colonized Algerians lost 3,445,000 hectares of land to the French.[13] These land confiscations impoverished the

[11] Hallaq, 2009, 383. Elaborating on these events, Hussin states: "The Government of India Act of 1858 was a victory for the reformers who wanted authoritarian control over British India, and represented a consolidation of colonial power. The East India Company was removed from its governmental role in India, and this role was passed to the queen, whose representative would be the secretary of state for India, who had wide powers with few checks. This new system of government included the passing of laws (Acts, as opposed to Company Regulations) which were to unify India under a single legal system, beginning with the replacement of Islamic criminal law and procedure (with the Code of Civil Procedure 1859, Code of Criminal Procedure of 1861, and the Evidence Act of 1872). High courts were instituted in all the provincial capitals, and the local administration of justice was taken into the ambit of the increasingly centralized state" (Hussin, 120).

[12] Abū-Nasr, 252.

[13] Naylor, 6. Speaking of the confiscation of communal properties in Algeria by the French, Luxemburg states: "Communal property had to be disrupted in order to gain the economic assets of the conquered country; the Arabs, that is to say, had to be deprived of the land they had owned for a thousand years, so that French capitalists could get it. Once again the fiction we know so well, that under Moslem law all land belongs to the ruler, was brought into play. Just as the English had done in British India, so Louis Philippe's governors in Algeria declared the existence of communal property owned by the clan to be 'impossible'. This fiction served as an excuse to claim for the state most of the uncultivated areas, and especially the commons, woods and meadows, and to use them for purposes of colonisation. A complete system of settlement developed, the so-called *cantonnements* which settled French colonists on the clan land and herded the tribes into a small area. Under the decrees of 1830, 1831, 1840, 1844, 1845 and 1846 these thefts of Arab family land were legalised" (Luxemburg, 360–361).

Algerians, as a reduction in the land also meant that they could raise less livestock and produce less wheat. While the population of Algerian Muslims increased, their holdings of livestock decreased by one-quarter between 1865 and 1900.[14] After 1871, with an increased appropriation of their lands, Algerians either became laborers for European-owned farms or turned to sharecropping of those lands for a fifth of the produce.[15] So, by 1900, according to official estimates, the Algerian Muslim population owned 37% of the country's wealth, even while there were eight times as many Algerians as there were Europeans.[16]

On the political front, the repression of the Algerian population grew ever more intense with each passing day of colonization. For example, the *Code de l'indignat* that was promulgated by the French colonial authorities in 1881 stated that colonial administrators could enact severe penalties on the Muslim population of Algeria for any one of forty-one specified offenses without any legal procedure. Outlining some of these measures, Abu-Nasr says: "Civil administrators could detain Muslims without trial, place them under surveillance, and order collective penalties and the sequestration of property. Muslims, furthermore, could no longer leave the districts without obtaining a special permission from the authorities. This code was periodically administered until 1927."[17]

Yet if this was the political and economic devastation that was wrought on Algerian society from French colonization, this colonization also brought about the alienation of Algerians from their cultural and religious heritage. Like the British, the French increasingly reduced the role of Islamic law in Algerian Muslim society by reducing the types of cases that could be settled through that law and then reducing the number of Sharīʿa courts. The *qāḍī*s (judges) lost the right to deal with cases concerning landed property in 1886, and criminal cases could

[14] Abu-Nasr, 270. Showing the effects of land confiscations on the Algerian natives' capacity to earn income through animal husbandry, Luxemburg notes: "French methods of oppressive taxation had the same tendency, in particular the law of June 16, 1851, proclaiming all forests to be state property, which robbed the natives of 6,000,000 acres of pasture and brushwood, and took away the prime essential for animal husbandry" (Luxemburg, 361).

[15] Citing an example of how land dispossession reduced many Algerians into sharecroppers, Luxemburg says: "In 1873, 1,000,000 acres were French property. But the capitalist companies, the Algerian and Setif Company which owned 300,000 acres, did not cultivate the land at all but leased it to the natives who tilled it in the traditional manner, nor were 25 per cent of the other French owners engaged in agriculture" (Luxemburg, 363–364).

[16] Abu-Nasr, 270.

[17] Abu-Nasr, 269.

only be dealt with by French jury courts, where French settlers were the jurors.[18] There were originally 300 Sharīʿa courts in Algeria, but with the introduction of new policies that would further subdue Algerians under French domination, the number of these courts decreased from 180 to 60 in the period between 1870 and 1890. In the areas where non-Arab Berber tribes (Kabyle) resided, these courts were abolished altogether in 1874, under the guise that the Berbers were not sufficiently Muslim and ought to be governed by their own customary laws.[19]

In conclusion, in the areas where Muslim societies experienced direct colonial occupation in the nineteenth century such as Algeria and India, the reform efforts were much more sudden and direct where colonial governments directly imposed colonial political and economic institutions to uproot the native institutions that had previously maintained the newly colonized societies. Law was one of the primary institutions that the colonial establishment used to re-configure traditional Muslim society into a modern secular one.

EUROPEAN HEGEMONY OVER MUSLIM GEOGRAPHIC HEARTLANDS IN THE NINETEENTH CENTURY

European pressure on the Muslim geographic heartlands in the Near East in the late eighteenth and early nineteenth century did not come in the form of direct colonialism as in the case of the Muslim geographic periphery, although by the end of the nineteenth century and early twentieth century, the same fate befell the Muslim heartlands as well. Owing to this lag, European colonialism in the Middle East began in the form of political pressure that Muslim ruling elites internalized by witnessing European technical superiority and their own military and economic weakness vis-à-vis European powers. This impotence became manifest in various wars Muslims had with these powers from the late eighteenth century, such as the Ottoman–Russian wars of 1768–1774, 1787–1792, and 1806–1812; the Russian annexation of the Crimea in 1783; Napoleon's temporary conquest of Egypt in 1798–1801; and the Russian wars with Persia/Iran of 1722–1735. These factors inspired Muslim rulers in these regions to reform their militaries, government bureaucracies, and economic institutions in order to catch up with Europe, as in the case of the Tanzimat reforms in the Ottoman Empire (1839–1876). Let us take a

[18] Vikor, 245.
[19] Vikor, 245.

closer look at those changes that took place in the core Muslim regions such as the Ottoman lands and Egypt.

The Ottoman Empire (Centered in Modern-Day Turkey)

The purpose of the Tanzimat reforms was to remedy the weaknesses within the political bureaucracy, economy, and military from which the empire suffered in the face of growing European assertiveness and aggression in world affairs. The reforms first began in the political and economic administration of the empire. The government was now organized based on European models of governance with ministries and ministers, which set responsibilities and areas of governance that they managed.[20] These political reforms also had their economic effects. For instance, the abolition of the traditional army corps of the Janissaries, who were also guildsman participating in manufacturing and were strong advocates of economic protectionism, opened avenues to the economic liberalism that was demanded by European powers. This protectionism had meant that raw materials were sold to the guilds by local or foreign suppliers at controlled prices. Yet the Treaty of Balta Limani in 1838 concluded between the British and the Ottoman sultan removed these measures that protected Ottoman manufacturers from European competition.[21] This elimination of protectionism and the rise of the price of raw materials left most Ottoman manufacturing guilds bankrupt.

[20] Showing how Tanzimat reforms led to the creation of Western-style institutions of governance, Noah Feldman says: "These rescripts gave rise, however, to new institutions, whose status was harder to pin down in constitutional terms. The 1839 document was followed by the creation of a 'supreme council for judicial regulations', a body that both acted as a court of appeal and drafted new legislation. Its members were unelected, but they made their decisions by majority vote. The sultan agreed in advance to abide by those decisions, thereby creating a body with real (if constrained) decision-making authority. Eventually, after several experiments with different distributions of power, the successor institution was split in 1867 into two bodies, one legislative and one judicial-appellate" (Feldman, 70).

[21] Donald Quataert, 764. Charles Issawi speaks to the political motivations of the Ottomans for concluding this economically unfavorable treaty with the British: "The sultan's conflict with Muhammad Ali of Egypt made the Porte willing to accommodate Britain and, in return for that country's help, to grant its main demands, which were aimed even more at Egypt than at Turkey. The result was the Anglo-Turkish Commercial Convention of 1838 [Treaty of Balta Limani]. This prohibited all monopolies, allowed British merchants to purchase goods anywhere in the empire without payment of any taxes other than import or export duty (or its equivalent in interior duty), and imposed duties of 3 percent on imports, 12 percent on exports, and 3 percent on transit" (Issawi, 19; what is found in brackets are additions of the author).

The eventual extinction of Ottoman guilds made the Ottoman economy into a supplier of raw materials whose market value was determined by European manufacturers.[22]

The Tanzimat reforms achieved little in terms of modernizing Ottoman society and keeping it independent from foreign control, which was its main goal. Yet, there were unintended religious and political consequences of these reforms. On the political front, the new generation of Ottoman citizens, who were educated in new secular bureaucratic schools, were exposed to European political ideas and became increasingly secularized in their outlook given their European-style education. Moreover, they came to expect that some European political ideals would have to be implemented in the empire if it was to truly modernize.[23]

On the religious and cultural front, education that had been mainly carried out by the traditional *ʿulamāʾ* class was now being increasingly centralized and administered by the state. For example, in 1869, the Ottoman state enacted the Regulation of Public Education Acts, prepared under the direction of the French Minister of Education, which "brought the different schools of the empire under a single comprehensive system."[24] But the continued decline of the status of Muslim scholars in the empire did not stop there; there was the establishment of independent legal educational institutions like Nāʾibs College (founded in 1854–1855) for the training of judges. Their focus was on the legal practice sanctioned in the new courts more than on the traditional study of legal compendia that had served as the backbone of traditional juristic training. This institution "issued diplomas in the name of the College as a corporate entity, and teachers- instead of issuing the *ijāza* as independent pedagogical authorities- were now relegated

[22] Hallaq, 2009, 398–400. Wallerstein cites the observations of historians on the economic effects of the adoption of these policies on the Ottoman economy in the nineteenth century: "Despite a whole series of political and economic countermeasures attempted by the Sublime Porte beginning with the measures of Selim III in 1793–1794, by 1856 one English author talks of the fact that the manufacturing industry has 'greatly declined' in Turkey and that Turkey now exported raw materials which later returned there in a manufactured form. By 1862, another British author's comment has an even more decisive tone: 'Turkey is no longer a manufacturing country'" (Wallerstein, v. 3, 151).

[23] McCarthy, 302. As an indication of the new Ottoman intelligentsia's Europeanized liberal outlook, here is a statement made by one of the prominent leaders of the Young Ottomans by the name of Namik Kemal: "One would think it (i.e., the Tanzimat) to have been made as a surety for the *life, property, and honor of every individual*. But the truth of the matter is that it was proclaimed for the purpose of securing the life of the state" (Voll, 92 emphasis added).

[24] Hallaq, 2009, 413.

to the rank of institutional functionaries, thus becoming contained by, and absorbed into, this corporate personality on behalf of an increasingly centralizing state."[25] The full consequences of these changes become manifest in the twentieth century when both Islamic law and the *ʿulamāʾ*, who were its vanguard, would lose their preeminent status in Muslim society.

Modernization and Colonization of Egypt

Although Egypt was technically a part of the Ottoman Empire, after Napoleon's invasion in 1798 and subsequent three-year French occupation, Egypt became an autonomous Ottoman regency that independently ran its own affairs once it was freed from this brief period of French colonization. Yet independence from the Ottomans did not mean that Egypt in the nineteenth century was free from other outside influence. The dominance of European powers in world affairs also became apparent to Egyptians from its conquest by France. Hence, the newly instated non-Egyptian rulers of Egypt in the nineteenth century, Muḥammad ʿAlī and his successors, set it on a course of "modernization" that would solidify their own hold over the country as well as fend off further European encroachment. This push toward modernization would cause a dramatic disruption in Egyptian economic, social, and religious life.

For example, under the counsel of French advisors, Muḥammad ʿAlī sought to gain control over various aspects of Egyptian civil society like the *ʿulamāʾ*. He achieved this by taking control of the *waqf*s (religious endowments) from which they derived their subsistence and making them dependent on state salaries.[26] The state's confiscation of *waqf*s weakened the independence of the *ʿulamāʾ* and their educational institutions in the nineteenth century because it brought to an end many colleges that were rivals to the al-Azhar University, the premier Islamic university in Cairo, and later made many other colleges subordinate to the head of al-Azhar (Shaykh al-Azhar).[27] The purpose of such educational centralization measures was to further state control over civil society institutions. All of these measures made many of the *ʿulamāʾ* increasingly withdraw from

[25] Hallaq, 2009, 418.
[26] Lapidus, 514; Hallaq, 2009, 420; Skovgaard-Petersen, 43.
[27] Skovgaard-Petersen, 46. Despite this, the supremacy of the reconfigured al-Azhar was tempered by the fact that "1872 was the year of the opening of the teacher training College Dar al-Ulum. This institution was the first challenge to the Azhar monopoly over teacher training" (Skovgaard-Petersen, 45).

public life in the nineteenth century to protect their narrow spheres of education and the judiciary.[28]

Furthermore, to advance his modernization efforts of Egypt, Muḥammad ʿAlī began to send Egyptian students to France early in his reign. Along with technical subjects that they studied, they also learned French law and upon their return to Egypt began to translate French codes[29] that would eventually be put into effect in Egypt in the second half of the nineteenth century under the rule of Muḥammad ʿAlī's successor and grandson Khedive Ismāʿīl (r. 1863–1879). "Modernizing" (read Europeanizing and centralizing) reforms in the first half of the nineteenth century continued with vigor in new social spheres in the second half under Khadive Ismāʿīl. Under the reign of Ismāʿīl, for example, the government opened up many "modern" schools that encouraged European culture among the new Egyptian elite.[30]

Despite such reforms, by the third quarter of the nineteenth century, Egypt would lose its sovereignty to European states. Because of the high costs of the modernization projects that it undertook, it incurred heavy debts from European financial institutions. This made it eventually declare bankruptcy. A European managed debt administration was then imposed on Egypt in 1875.[31] Egyptians resented these impositions,

[28] Lapidus, 514.

[29] Hallaq, 2009, 422.

[30] Hodgson, v. 3, 240; Mitchell, 75. Mitchell gives the following example of the establishment of new European-style schools: "The new schooling introduced earlier in the century under Muhammad Ali had been intended to produce an army and the particular technicians associated with it; schooling was now to produce the individual citizen. To understand what was envisaged in a system of civilian schooling, two important innovations from the 1840s can be picked out as an indication, the 'model school' (al-maktab al-unmudhaji) in Cairo and the Egyptian school in Paris. I will begin with the model school, which had been set up by Ibrahim Adham in 1843 in a large room attached to the military primary school. Its purpose had been to introduce into Egypt the so-called Lancaster method of schooling ... The Lancaster or 'mutual improvement' schools had been developed for the instruction of the industrial classes in England The Lancaster school, like the factory, consisted of a single large room, which contained rows of benches with individually numbered places for up to a thousand pupils. Each bench constituted a 'class' of eight or ten pupils, and was under the supervision of a senior pupil who monitored the behaviour and work of the other students. At the command of a whistle or bell each class moved from its bench to one of the boards that were placed on the walls around the room, and stood on a semi-circular line marked on the floor around it. The boards were numbered in a sequence of ascending difficulty..." (Mitchell, 69).

[31] Hodgson, v. 3, 241; Lapidus, 515. Speaking about the general economic effects of this European debt administration of Egypt, Owen says: "Between 1876 and 1880 a number of projects were devised by Egypt's foreign creditors to regulate its financial affairs. They all had two main characteristics. First, they combined an unwillingness to reduce

which eventually sparked the 'Urabi Revolt in 1882 that sought to eliminate European control in Egyptian affairs.[32] To suppress the widespread revolt, the British directly occupied Egypt, initiating the phase of direct colonialism in Egypt[33] that would last in various forms till the 1950s.

SECULAR NATIONALISM AND ISLAMIC REFORM IN THE TWENTIETH-CENTURY MUSLIM WORLD

In the twentieth century, European colonialism went unabated. In fact, during this century, there was an increase of the span of regions that succumbed to European imperial control. As far as the Muslim world was concerned, after World War I, only several Muslim countries remained free from direct colonial control even though they also incurred some form of colonial occupation: modern Turkey, Saudi Arabia, Iran, and possibly Oman even though it was under British suzerainty. This near total domination by European powers over Muslims and the ill-fated response of Muslims to that domination changed the material and political conditions on the ground, and this led to the growth of modern sociopolitical movements that sought to bring an end to colonialism in the Muslim world as well as remedy its weaknesses that were factors leading to the colonization of Muslim lands.

the size of the funded (public) or of the floating debts with a considerable over-estimate of the annual sums which the country could afford to pay in interest and amortization. The result was the impositions of burdens greater than Egypt could bear, particularly in the depressed agricultural conditions of the late 1870s. Second, each scheme involved an increasing degree of European financial control, whether viewed in terms of the numbers of foreign officials appointed to supervise the various arrangements or in terms of their power" (Owen, 130).

[32] Hussin says: "Colvin, the chief European financial advisor to the khedive, while sympathizing with the 'liberal' elements in Egypt argued that the problem was 'Urabi's insistence on reclaiming financial control by Egyptians: 'The European interests engaged in Egypt were far too various and important to permit of the engagements contracted by the Khedive being placed at the mercy of Egyptian soldiery or of an inexperienced native administration'" (Hussin, 129).

[33] Hodgson, v. 3, 241. Speaking of the consequences to Islamic law in Egypt suffered by British occupation, Hussin says: "The aftermath of the revolt and the British occupation for the shape and content of Islamic law was to persuade Egyptian governing elites of the administrative and political wisdom of adopting codes based on French models. The promulgation of a civil code on the French model in 1882 was aimed at halting the incursion of British officials into Egyptian administration at the same time that it made the formal incorporation of Egypt into the British Empire seem less likely. It also was a step toward the equalization of Egyptians and Europeans before the law, since this code meant that both populations (in the Mixed and Native Courts) would be governed by the same bodies of law" (Hussin, 131).

Among the newly formed secular and Western-educated elite, who were products of European-style schools at home or abroad, the path to freedom and progress was through intensifying the modernization efforts that had begun in some Muslim regions in the previous century. Modernization for this group in some ways meant Westernization because aping values and customs was the easiest and fastest path to modernization.[34] Those values included nationalism because every Western society was based on an "intense sense of the nation."[35] For secular Muslim colonial elites, to be modern was to imagine their communities as nations. This gave rise to ethnic nationalism. By the late nineteenth century, for example, for the first time in the multi-ethnic and multi-religious Ottoman Empire, the Arab Western-educated elite began to speak of an Arab fatherland, while their Turkic counterparts began to emphasize the Turkish nature of the ruling elite within the empire.[36]

In Egypt, for example, the nineteenth-century Egyptian Westernizer Rifāʿa Rāfiʿ al-Ṭahṭāwī spoke of past Egyptian glories, and within the larger Muslim community "there were special national communities (i.e., Egyptian) that were deserving of loyalty."[37] The same analysis applies to movements in other Muslim nations such as the Young Tunisians in Tunis or the Pan-Turkish Jadidi movement in Central Asia.[38] Eventually, nationalism became the political vehicle by which to eliminate Western domination in Muslim lands in the twentieth century and the basis for

[34] Speaking of the Western proclivities of some of the elite in British Malaya in the late nineteenth century, Hussin makes the following observations about the British coronated future Sultan of Johor: "In this endeavor, Abu Bakar's Westernization was viewed as an asset by his colonial observers, ... Sir Harry Ord, Governor General of Singapore, who characterized him in 1868 as 'in his tastes and habits ... an English gentleman, as a ruler is anxious to promote in every way the advancement and civilization of his people, and he is the only Rajah in the whole Peninsula, or the adjoining States, who rules in accordance with the practice of civilized nations. He is deeply attached to the British Government and nation, and feeling with their support and encouragement he is most likely to benefit his country he takes no steps of importance in administration without the advice of the local government, whilst he is ready at all times to place the whole resources of his country at our disposal'" (Hussin, 158).

[35] Hodgson, vol. 3, 246. Some even conflated nationalism with Westernization. For example, the late nineteenth-/early twentieth-century Egyptian nationalist leader Mustafa Kamil stated in 1906: "We have realized for over a century now that nations cannot lead an honorable life unless they follow the path of Western civilization. We were the first oriental people to shake hands with Europe, and we shall certainly continue along the path we have taken" (cited in Voll, 98).

[36] Voll, 94.

[37] Voll, 96.

[38] See Voll pgs. 100 and 124.

the reorientation of Muslim societies into nation states,[39] which were an extension of the artificial partitions already established by colonialism.[40] Moreover, the Muslim secular elite were often committed to a liberal constitutionalism in the first half of the twentieth century.[41] But in the second half of the twentieth century, after achieving independence from their colonial masters, their commitments took on a more socialist hue.[42]

Yet the rise of Muslim modernism among some Muslim groups, that is, the adoption of Western liberal ideas by some Muslims through contact with the West or its institutions, did not always engender secular outlooks among other groups of educated Muslim elites in the nineteenth and twentieth centuries. Another group that came into being was Islamic reformers who advocated new Islamic solutions to the current crisis faced by Muslims, but were different in their approach to Islam from the tradition-oriented conservative *ʿulamāʾ*, although many of these reformers were from the *ʿulamāʾ*. Islamic reformers often approached the authoritative textual sources of Islam (the Quran and *Ḥadīth*) from the point of view of Western rationalism.[43]

Their agenda had two interrelated goals: First, they sought a progressive Islamic program that would remedy Muslim material decadence and spiritual malaise by showing that Islam was compatible with modern values; second, they wanted to combat the Western perception that Islam was an irrelevant force in the modern world.[44] They sought to revive Islam by reassessing the authority of tradition and hence rejected traditional notions such as *taqlīd* (following the authority of medieval Islamic schools of law and theology) and advocated a new *ijtihād* (independent rethinking) based on the authoritative textual sources of Islam so as to keep Islam relevant to its modern context.[45] Two representative nineteenth-century figures of Islamic reform were Sayyid Aḥmad Khān in India and Muḥammad ʿAbduh in Egypt, whose ideas gave birth to Islamic reform movements of the twentieth century.

With regard to Islamic law, the twentieth-century disciples of these reformers advocated legal positions that broke with the established Islamic legal discourse that had held sway over Muslim societies for

[39] See Lapidus 518–519 for how this process took shape in the case of Egypt.
[40] Schulze, 28.
[41] Lapidus, 519; Voll. 94.
[42] Hodgson, v. 3, 369.
[43] Waines, 196.
[44] Waines, 196.
[45] Waines, 196.

over a millennium. For example, Rashīd Riḍā (d. 1935), Muḥammad ʿAbduh's Syrian disciple, advocated the setting aside of legal doctrines that were based on *madhhabs* so as to reformulate Islamic law based on its legal sources (Quran and *Ḥadīth*). So, his was a call for a new *ijtihād* to be applied to issues about which there had already been a consensus among the legal schools; this proposal was essentially calling for the legal doctrines of the *madhhabs* to be abandoned.[46]

In conclusion, the colonial experience spawned new ideological movements in the Muslim world that were seeking the best path forward to cope with a European imposed world order and an increasingly attractive Western worldview. The ideological responses to that challenge were varied, but they all underlined how Islamic tradition and society had to change to meet the demands of the new world that European colonial powers had been forging. The views of these reformers varied from those who sought to exclude religion from public life altogether and those who felt that the religion of Islam should continue to play a role in the public square, although they advocated an Islam whose concepts and tradition were sufficiently revamped to deal with the modern European notion of progress.

MODERNITY AND THE CHANGE IN THE STATUS OF ISLAMIC LAW IN MUSLIM SOCIETIES

The following synopsis delineates some of the areas where the workings of Islamic law (i.e., Sharīʿa) have been disrupted in the colonial and post-colonial period. This will help the reader assess the extent to which political, economic, and social changes that have occurred in the nineteenth and twentieth centuries have impacted Islamic legal tradition over the past two centuries so as better to appreciate the sociohistorical impetuses that are possibly leading to a transformation of that legal tradition. Two primary areas are identified where Islamic law had been reconfigured in the colonial and post-colonial period: institutional and discursive. Both of these areas can be broken down into two different yet overlapping periods: the colonial period (c. 1800–1950) and the post-/neo-colonial or nation state period (c. 1920 till the present). There is some overlap between the two periods depending on the various timelines over which Muslim nations were able to shed their colonial overrulers. This

[46] Hallaq, 1997, 215. Later in this study, I will carefully examine one of Rashīd Riḍā's fatwas where he illustrates how legal opinions could be issued outside *madhhab* strictures.

exposition will begin by assessing the institutional changes that Islamic law has undergone in the colonial and post-colonial periods and then move on to the discursive ones.

Institutional Changes in Sharīʿa

Colonial Period

In the nineteenth century, under colonial rule or foreign pressure, Sharīʿa law in many Muslim regions was restricted to adjudicate matters of family law and pious endowments and was stripped of jurisdiction over criminal and commercial law.[47] An example of this is the Ottoman adoption of European penal and commercial codes.[48] In addition, European pressure to set up separate courts in Muslim regions that would handle cases involving Europeans (e.g., Egyptian mixed courts) led to the growth of secular courts and restrictions on religious courts.[49] Post-colonial states eventually abolished this bifurcation of roles where religious courts were simply subsumed under the new secular courts, now called national courts in Egypt, and this further limited the jurisdiction of the Sharīʿa to issues such as family law.[50]

Moreover, these legal reforms in the jurisdiction of Islamic law ultimately reduced the role of the *ʿulamāʾ*, who were the traditional representatives

[47] Asad, 2003, 211.

[48] Hallaq, 2009, 407. See also Asad, 2003, 210. Commenting on how such adoptions transformed the very character of criminal law in the Ottoman state, Ruth Miller (2005) shows how the orientation of Ottoman criminal law had shifted from "crimes against victims," for which this law was embedded in its social context and defined by Islamic moral principles, to the "victimless crime category" that accompanied the increasing bureaucratization of Ottoman state and society for which such an abstraction of the law concomitantly redefined the relations between religion, society, and state (Miller, 6–7).

[49] See Hallaq, 2009, 422–425. Speaking about the continuous limitations put on Islamic courts during the period of their reformation in late nineteenth-century Egypt, Skovgaard-Petersen notes: "From being the courts in the country, albeit hampered by the wide khedival interference in criminal and other matters, the Sharia Courts ... were by 1883 reduced in scope and importance to third place after the Mixed and National Courts. They were by then only dealing with matters of personal status law and *waqf* and *hiba* (gift)..." (Skovgaard-Petersen, 60).

[50] See Asad, 2003, 211 and 215. Elaborating on the effects on Islamic law that such measures had, Asad says: "When the shari'a is structured essentially as defining personal status in the law, it is radically transformed ... what happens to the sharia (sic) is not curtailment but transmutation. It is rendered into a subdivision of law that is authorised by the centralizing state ... it is secularised in distinctive ways." Commenting on Asad's statement, Hussin says: "This process of secularization does not revolve around the separation of church and state or the removal of religion to the private sphere but around the right and ability of the state to assign religion its role and to define that role as a subsidiary of the state" (as cited in Hussin, 198).

of Sharīʿa in society. These modernizing reforms were really intended to strengthen the hand of the secular state at the expense of civil society, and this was done through increasing the centralization of the state and widening its intrusion into the realm of public affairs.[51] For example, during the nineteenth-century Ottoman Empire, the period of Tanzimat reforms that led to the increasing bureaucratization of the state, Sultan Mahmud II (in 1826) and his advisors created the Ministry of Imperial Pious Endowments, "which brought the administration of the major *awqāf* (or '*waqf*s', charitable endowments) under the central administration where *waqf*s were previously under the independent control of families and religious scholars and organization."[52] The pious endowments, which traditionally were the material base of the *ʿulamāʾ*, passed out of their hands into state control, further weakening the independence of this group.[53]

Nation-State Period

With the formation of Muslim nation states in the early twentieth century, the removal of legislative authority from the hands of Muslim jurists was almost complete. Whereas the jurists controlled the legislative and judicial functions in the pre-colonial state, these functions were transferred to the "modern" nation-state in the form of a secular legislature and judiciary. Pre-colonial sovereigns in the Muslim world were subject to the law and were not its makers, while the modern nation-state "arrogated to itself the status of legislature and at the same time a position above the law."[54] Centralization in the modern nation-state was the

[51] Feldman asks a question as to how the traditional *ʿulamāʾ* in the Ottoman Empire were undermined by modern reforms. He partially explains that historical process as follows: "When their [the *ʿulamāʾ*s] authority is juxtaposed with the issuance of the various Ottoman codes, it can be seen that these new institutions went very far toward displacing the scholars' traditional function of declaring the content of the law. The constitution of 1876 went much further. It created two elective bodies, a chamber of deputies and a senate, with responsibility for lawmaking. Courts were authorized separately, to be staffed by judges whose qualifications would be specified by law. A single provision declared, in an almost circular fashion, that affairs touching upon the shariʿa would be tried by shariʿa tribunals – the only mention of traditional Islamic courts anywhere in the document. The same provision restricted civil affairs to the civil courts" (Feldman, 69–71; what is in brackets are the additions of the author).

[52] Hallaq, 2003–2004, 255–256.

[53] Voll 91.

[54] Hallaq, 2003–2004, 254–255. Feldman illustrates this in the case of Iraq: "Postwar written constitutions in British and French protectorates typically treated the shariʿa as just another set of legal rules to be applied by judges appointed by the state. The Iraqi constitution of 1925, for example, established a constitutional monarchy in which the legislative power was vested in an elected parliament" (Feldman, 82).

main process that was employed to take control of the law.[55] Modern Muslim nation-states wrested Islamic law from the control of Muslim jurists. For example, in Syria and Iraq, polygamy was prohibited unless it was permitted by the religious judge (*qāḍī*), "who must be satisfied that the husband is financially capable of maintaining more than one wife."[56]

Even in areas where Islamic law was allowed to have jurisdiction, there was a move away from legal doctrines that were determined by the classical Islamic legal schools (*madhhab*) toward a formulation of law based on pan-*madhhab* considerations by the use of the legal mechanism of *talfīq* (amalgamating rulings from different schools). In the pre-colonial period, Islamic law was only operationalized through the particular *madhhab* adopted by the state, but with the formation of the nation-state, that was no longer a consideration. Examples of how modern Muslim nation-states used this dubious legal mechanism to legislate were the Sudanese and Egyptian laws that legalized the right of the deceased to dispose of his or her inheritance in accordance with his or her own judgment and preference, a legal position that actually was in agreement with Twelver Shīʿī law but not with the major Sunnī schools. This was despite the fact that both Sudan and Egypt were Sunnī majority countries and Sunnī schools of law only allow for the disposal of the inheritance in accordance to prefixed shares. This type of amalgamation of law (*talfīq*) had not been practiced in previous eras.[57]

Discursive Changes in Sharīʿa

Colonial Period

During the nineteenth century, the Ottoman *Tanzimat* reforms brought about changes in Islamic law and its respective institutions. Prior to these modernization efforts, Islamic law had been embodied in the form of fluid interpretive legal texts that were the reference point for how legal matters were decided. This practice changed in the Ottoman Empire in the latter part of the nineteenth century, when Islamic law took the form of a rigidly codified law, as was the case in the legal work known as the *Majalla*, so as to emulate European models of law.[58]

55 Hallaq, 2003–2004, 255.

56 See Layish, 95.

57 For more on this notion of *talfīq* or amalgamation of law and its usage by Muslim nation-states, see Hallaq, 2009, pg. 448.

58 For more details see Hallaq, 2009, 411–412. Also, Asad, 2003, 210–211. Speaking about the far-reaching and unintended political consequences of the promulgation of the *Majalla*, Feldman says: "Under the classical Islamic constitution, the condition for the

The Nation-State

Discursive changes in Islamic law during this period were of two types: state-based reforms and non-state-based reforms. As for state-based reforms, the injunctions of Islamic law were codified into statutory provisions. Codifying the religious law brought about its nationalization because Sharīʿa-based injunctions that were incorporated into legal statutes were seen strictly as national-territorial statutes; hence, they were interpreted within the framework of the nation-state as opposed to the framework of the Islamic legal tradition where trans-regional legal commentary informed the public about how to understand the law.[59] Codifying Islamic law in a statutory form made it no longer bound by the rules of Islamic legal theory and methodology that had been developed by generations of Muslim jurists; indeed, it was now determined by national legislatures who were ignorant of the origins and implications of these laws.[60]

administrative regulations was that the shari'a authorized the ruler to issue these regulations. Ultimate authority rested with the shari'a. The regulations had legal force, theoretically speaking, because the shari'a allowed them to exist. But by issuing the Mecelle [i.e. *Majalla*], which purported to state the content of the shari'a, the executive implied that the shari'a itself had authority only insofar as it was incorporated into a legal document issued by the ruler and his state. This was a historic reversal, even if its effects were not immediately apparent. Ultimate authority now rested not with the law, but with the ruler" (Feldman, 64; what is found in brackets is the addition of the author).

59 Hussin comments on how the codification of Islamic law changed not only its form but also its function: "Can legal codes which function within a context starkly different than that where they originated coexist within a single national system without distortion of their intent, function, and meaning? When principles of the shari'a are taken to govern women and children, families, and property, and placed alongside commercial codes taken from Western legal systems and administrative law created to serve a new nation, plurality may not be the most accurate representation of the relationship between these legal codes. Pluralism implies that Islamic law functions within the personal status law of the postcolonial nation as an autonomous domain within the national legal system. But the function and meaning of Islamic law as contained within a personal status or family law is contingent upon the workings of the entire system of which it is a part. The circumstances within which this 'plurality' was arrived at were rife with power inequalities, and the particular type of plurality which was achieved looks less like the coexistence of separate but equal elements of different legal systems within one structure than it resembles a peculiar legal Frankenstein creature – different functional elements pieced together to achieve a singular and unique purpose, the other parts of each system discarded by design" (Hussin, 224–225).

60 Layish, 96. Skovgaard-Petersen asks a critical question about how the codification of Islamic law changed its practice: "What is the difference between applying a methodology and a code? First, it can be observed that the code is to be universally applied in the same way, leading to a unification of results. It is promulgated by the government who can thereby exert control over the legal system. It is a standardization that leaves

As for non-state reforms, there were growing calls for reform within circles of Muslim intelligentsia who wanted to reformulate the classical Islamic legal doctrines of the Islamic legal schools *(madhāhib)* into new legal doctrines that were reformulated strictly based on scriptural sources (Quran and *Ḥadīth*) to suit contemporary conditions.[61] This is best illustrated in efforts by reformists, who sought to innovate legal rulings that did not adhere to the traditional legal schools. An example of this is Sayyid Sābiq's legal work *Fiqh al-Sunna*. Also, there were calls for a shift away from legal methodologies that were traditionally agreed upon, methods ranging from widely held principles such as *qiyās* (analogical reasoning) to methodologies that were not as overtly applied in legal reasoning such as *maṣlaḥa* (utility) and *ʿurf* (customary practice). This is evident in Rashīd Riḍā's rejection of *qiyās* and its displacement with *maṣlaḥa*[62] as well as ʿAbd al-Wahhāb Khallāf's elevation of the prominence of *ʿurf* in legislation.[63]

European impositions on Muslim society, such as the European calls for modernization, impacted the manner in which Islamic law was reconfigured both institutionally and discursively. This challenge solicited responses from various Muslim circles, yet the intricacies and transformations of modern life happened so quickly, so drastically, and even violently that Muslim circles had difficulty adapting and keeping pace as they struggled to address the totality and extent of that challenge with the socio-legal tools that Muslim tradition had developed for agrarian-based societies. This situation led to the call for radical change within segments of the Muslim intelligentsia. The key point here is to see whether these

little room for individual variations. The judge is supposed to concentrate his efforts in establishing the exact nature of the case, whereupon it should be relatively simple to consult the code. This procedure forms a contrast to the skills needed to derive judgements according to the *uṣūl al-fiqh* [Islamic legal theory and methodology]" ((Skovgaard-Petersen, 64; what is in brackets is a clarification by the author).

61 Commenting on how some modern reformist Muslim thinkers rejected adherence to a *madhhab* (*taqlīd*), Zaman says the following about reformers like Rashīd Riḍā: "Taqlid, to Rida, was the diametrical opposite of ijtihād – a view he shared with Muslim modernists. In his multifaceted diatribes against taqlid, Rida argued that rigid adherence to the schools of law had divided the community into warring factions, that the eponymous founders of the schools as well as other early masters had been turned into veritable icons all but worshipped by the people, that taqlid had deadened people's mental faculties, and that, in alliance with sellouts among the ʿulama, the rulers had used taqlid in support of their despotism. Above all, taqlid had set up barriers between the people and what God had intended to be their unmediated access to the Quran" (Zaman, 2012, 77).

62 Hallaq, 2009, 506. This point will be illustrated in my detailed analysis of one Rashīd Riḍā's fatwas below.

63 Hallaq, 2009, 509.

calls for change, both then and now, promise to have a lasting impact on the Islamic legal tradition by filtering into its core discourses.

FATWAS IN THE AGE OF COLONIALISM

One of the ways to assess the practical impact of the colonial experience on Islamic law is to examine fatwas from this period, especially those pronounced by Muslim scholars who called for reform. Hence, we will examine the fatwas of Rashīd Riḍā (1865–1935). Riḍā was a Muslim reformist scholar in the colonial period who was originally from Syria but later settled in Egypt. He was a protégé of the nineteenth-/twentieth-century reformist Egyptian scholar Muḥammad ʿAbduh (d. 1909). Riḍā's reformist agenda consisted of advocating for a reexamination of the foundational textual sources of Islam (the Quran and *ḥadīth*) independent of traditional approaches to interpreting these texts, as was the case when their legal content was being interpreted strictly through the lens of the *madhhab*s. Riḍā's and ʿAbduh's reformist ideas had currency in places as far off as India and Indonesia[64] and were disseminated through the journal *Al-Manār*, which Riḍā published from 1898 until the time of his death in 1935.[65] One of Riḍā's fatwas that is the subject of this analysis is found in *Al-Manār*.

Two fatwas related to *ribā* (usury) that Riḍā issued at two different stages of his career will be investigated in this section. One fatwa was issued in 1907 in response to a request for a fatwa from Calcutta, India, which I designate as the Calcutta fatwa. The other fatwa was issued in 1928 in response to a request for a fatwa from Hyderabad, India, which will be designated here as the Hyderabad fatwa. The purpose of looking at these fatwas, both of which focus on the issue of usury, is to examine the progression of Riḍā's reformist agenda throughout his career. From this, we can assess in very practical terms how the Islamic legal discourse was undergoing a transformation during the height of the colonial period of Muslim history.

The first fatwa, the Calcutta fatwa, was published in Al-Manār journal.[66] A summary of the question that was posed to Riḍā is as

[64] The influence of Riḍā's ideas on India will be demonstrated in the subsequent fatwas that will be analyzed in this section. See also Zaman, 2012, 121. For ʿAbduh's and Riḍā's influence on Indonesia, see Kaptein, 116.

[65] For more on the life and works of Rashīd Riḍā, see Zaman, 2012, 6–11. See also Hallaq, 2009, 504–509.

[66] *Al-Manār* (Jumādā al-Ūlā 1325 AH), vol. 10, pg. 359 as reproduced in the Shamela Library (version 3.61).]

follows: Muslim businessmen in Calcutta receive money transfers through European banks, and after maintaining a balance in these banks for a period, they receive a fixed annual percentage increase (2 rupees on a 100 rupees) in their account even though these merchants did not stipulate this as a precondition for these services. The questioner wants to know: Is it allowed for the merchants to take this increase to their savings? Moreover, he asks Riḍā to respond from the point of view of the four (Sunnī) *madhhab*s and only after this to present his personal view.[67]

Riḍā first responds by recognizing that the questioner is essentially asking whether the transaction that was described constitutes *ribā* (usury). Complying with the wishes of the questioner, Riḍā then defines *ribā* according to the established Sunnī schools of law and then evaluates whether this transaction constitutes *ribā* according to those definitions. Riḍā claims that in the Ḥanafī school, any preconditioned stipulation of increase (*faḍl*), whether tangible or intangible, on material exchanges constitutes *ribā*. But Riḍā says that since there was no stipulated precondition by the merchants to the stated increase, this transaction does not constitute *ribā* according to the Ḥanafī definition. He then presents the point of view of the Shāfiʿī school on *ribā*, which is defined as any contract that exchanges specific items that are not known to have equal value or where there is a delay in delivery of one or both items exchanged. He then says that since the transaction described by the questioner contains no contract, this transaction does not constitute *ribā* for the Shāfiʿī school either.[68]

Riḍā then pursues a different strategy in his fatwa to categorize this new type of commercial transaction that hitherto had not been directly dealt with in previous Islamic rulings. Riḍā says that this case of money transfers that were turned into savings resembles the category of entrusted items (*wadīʿa*) that is commonly addressed in Islamic law. But the entrusted items in this case, the money left in the bank by the businessman, are more like loans than entrusted items because the banks transact with that money and return other than the actual money that was entrusted. Many jurists, especially the Ḥanafīs, says Riḍā, have clearly stipulated that any loan that accrues benefits is considered *ribā* (usury), a position they supported with *ḥadīth*s. Riḍā says if anyone

[67] *Al-Manār* (Jumādā al-Ūlā 1325 AH), vol. 10, pg. 359 as reproduced in the Shamela Library (version 3.61).

[68] *Al-Manār* (Jumādā al-Ūlā 1325 AH), vol. 10, pg. 359 as reproduced in the Shamela Library (version 3.61).

holds this belief, then he needs to act according to it[69] and hence declare this transaction illegitimate.

Yet, Riḍā asserts that examination of the proof texts (*dalīl*) that support this position that any loan that accrues benefits is considered *ribā* (usury), such as the *ḥadīth* "Every loan that has accrued benefit is *ribā* (usurious)," shows that the proof text is weak in terms of its authenticity, and some scholars have claimed that it is even fabricated. In addition, he states that there are *ḥadīth*s to the contrary whereby Riḍā cites a few *ḥadīths* in his fatwa showing the Prophet Muḥammad repaid debts by giving back more than what was actually owed like a *ḥadīth* narrated by Jaber ibn ʻAbd Allah that the Prophet repaid him a debt by giving him more than what was loaned.[70]

Riḍā claims that this series of proof texts (*ḥadīth*s) is a strong indication that giving back extra on a loan is legitimate so long as there is no indication that increase was a precondition of the debt. But if the added payback to the amount of the loan is preconditioned, then there is a consensus among scholars that this transaction is prohibited.[71]

Riḍā then concludes his fatwa by clarifying that the Quranic prohibition on *ribā* (usury) is applicable to the exploitative type of usury (what he calls *ribā al-nasīʾa*) where the lending party exploits the inability of the debtor to pay back by compounding the interest. To bolster his interpretation of the relevant Quranic verses, he cites the opinions of the master jurists Mālik and Ibn Ḥanbal that concur with his interpretation of these verses.[72] He then says that the scenario spelled out by the questioner does not contain this exploitative element within the commercial transaction. Here, he claims that the bank merely invests the loan given to it by the lender and in return willfully gives him/her a portion of the profit at the end of a stipulated period without any precondition or contract. He ultimately concludes that this modern interest-based transaction is legitimate from the point of view of Islamic law because it resembles what the Prophet had done with his debts by willingly giving back more than what was owed[73] (see Figure 18).

69 *Al-Manar* (Jumadi al-Awwal 1325 AH), vol. 10, pg. 359 as reproduced in the Shamela Library (version 3.61).
70 *Al-Manar* (Jumadi al-Awwal 1325 AH), vol. 10, pg. 359 as reproduced in the Shamela Library (version 3.61).
71 *Al-Manar* (Jumadi al-Awwal 1325 AH), vol. 10, pg. 359 as reproduced in the Shamela Library (version 3.61).
72 *Al-Manar* (Jumadi al-Awwal 1325 AH), vol. 10, pg. 359 as reproduced in the Shamela Library (version 3.61).
73 *Al-Manar* (Jumadi al-Awwal 1325 AH), vol. 10, pg. 359 as reproduced in the Shamela Library (version 3.61).

More than twenty years after issuing the Calcutta fatwa, Riḍā issued another fatwa, in 1928, that directly deals with the issue of *ribā* (usury) in reference to the interest that accrued from savings or charged on loans from Western banks. This fatwa is known to some as the Hyderabad fatwa.[74] The fatwa that Riḍā issues consists of four parts in accordance with the four questions asked to him by the Muftī of Hyderabad. The muftī prefaced his question with his own lengthy fatwa on the issue, where he argued for the permissibility of interests on loans. Yet after presenting his judgment on the issue, the Muftī of Hyderabad solicited the views of other scholars on the matter where he also requests Riḍā to give his opinion. The Muftī of Hyderabad's fatwa on interest accrued on bank loans, and his questions are reproduced in the beginning part of the Riḍā's book *al-Ribā wa al-Muʿāmalāt fī al-Islām*,[75] which is followed by Riḍā's fatwa on the issue. It is this text that is the source of the current analysis.

The entirety of Riḍā's responses to the Muftī of Hyderabad's questions will not be dealt with here, but particular aspects of his responses pertaining to legal reasoning will be assessed. Like the earlier Calcutta fatwa, Riḍā, in this fatwa, argues for the permissibility of interest on loans, even reproducing some of the same arguments of his earlier fatwa. Yet there are some nuances in his argument in the Hyderabad fatwa that were not articulated in the earlier fatwa and that will be the focus of this analysis. Here are the salient points of the Hyderabad fatwa, especially as it contrasts with his earlier discussion on the subject of *ribā*:

First, in the earlier Calcutta fatwa, Riḍā was much more conciliatory toward the opinions of the *madhhabs*, or schools of law, where in accordance with the questioner's wishes, he provides some of the positions of the Sunnī legal schools on *ribā* even as he diverges to give his own opinion on the issue that is contrary to theirs. In contrast, in the very introduction to the Hyderabad fatwa, Riḍā clearly establishes his difference with the opinions of jurists that adhere to the *madhhabs* because he criticizes the Muftī of Hyderabad for interpreting the proof texts (Quran and *ḥadīth*) on this issue through the interpretive lens of (traditional) jurists (i.e., how the *madhhab* jurists have interpreted these proof texts). Moreover, Riḍā says that his fatwa will be strictly based on the Quran and *sunna* and not

74 For an English translation of this fatwa, see http://elgamal.blogspot.com/search?q=Rashīd+Riḍā+on+Ribā+--+II:+The+Hayderabad+fatwa. For further background on this fatwa, see Zaman's discussion of the fatwa on pgs. 128–129 of his book *Modern Islamic Thought in a Radical Age*. Cambridge University Press. Cambridge: 2012.

75 See Riḍā, pgs. 2–46.

based on one of the opinions found in the *madhhabs*.[76] This is in contrast to the Calcutta fatwa, where he cites traditional *madhhab* jurists who agree with his opinion on *ribā*.

Second, in the earlier Calcutta fatwa, he asserts that what was meant by *ribā* (usury) in the Quran is the exploitative type of usury (*ribā al-nasīʾa*) and not ordinary interest, and he supported this interpretation by citing the verse in *Sūrat Āl ʿImrān* (3:13) that says that the believers should not engage in the "doubling" of interest when the creditor is unable to pay the loan. This very same verse was quoted in the Hyderabad fatwa, but what is different between the two fatwas is that in the Calcutta fatwa, Riḍā cites the two master jurists Mālik and Ibn Ḥanbal who give this interpretation of the verse saying that it was a response to the customary practice of usury in pre-Islamic Arabia.[77] On the other hand, in the Hyderabad fatwa, he does not appeal to these authorities, but instead relies on a report from ʿUmar b. al-Khaṭṭāb that claims that the Prophet passed away before clarifying the meaning of the other verse concerning *ribā* in *Sūrat al-Baqara*, which is one of the last verses revealed in the Quran (i.e., the verse cited by Muftī of Hyderabad in his questions).[78]

So, Riḍā concludes that the meaning of *ribā* in the verse found in *Sūrat al-Baqara* must also be taken as a designation of the customary practice of *ribā* of the pre-Islamic age, which was of the exploitative kind where there was a doubling or compounding of the interest paid. In addition, it is this definition of *ribā* that should be the agreed-upon interpretation of the previously revealed verse on *ribā* in *Sūrat Āl ʿImrān* (3:13).[79] Moreover, he dismisses the idea that was traditionally asserted that the *ḥadīth* of the Prophet that stipulated the equivalent exchange of barley, wheat, salt, dates, gold, and silver played any role in interpreting the Quranically abstract term *ribā* in the cited verse (i.e., the *ribā* verse in *Sūrat al-Baqara*) because he claims the historical report of ʿUmar negates that possibility (see Figure 18).[80]

The striking point to be made about this discussion is that in both the Calcutta and the Hyderabad fatwas, Riḍā asserts the same conclusion that the term *ribā* as utilized/prohibited in the foundational texts of Quran and *ḥadīth* does not imply the contemporary practice of interest on loans, but instead is aimed at the historically established exploitative practice

[76] Riḍā, 47.
[77] See reference mentioned earlier.
[78] Riḍā 49–50.
[79] Riḍā, 49–50.
[80] Riḍā, 49–50.

of doubling and redoubling of interest. Yet the modes of legal reasoning employed in both fatwas were remarkably different. In the Calcutta fatwa, Riḍā did not hesitate to cite the opinions of the master jurists that supported his view, but in the Hyderabad fatwa, he eschews any reliance on the opinions of the schools of law or their masters, which is consistent with the statements he made in the introduction of that fatwa.

The third and final point to be made here is that Riḍā corroborates the Muftī of Hyderabad's assertion that benefit or increase (interest) accrued by a loan does not constitute *ribā* (usury) because there is no direct textual evidence from the foundational sources of the religion (Quran and *ḥadīth*) that stipulate that. Moreover, Riḍā concurs with the muftī that the evidence used by the traditional jurists to prohibit benefit (interest) accrued by a loan as *ribā* (usury) is one of the two: a weakly corroborated *ḥadīth* or an analogical argument (*qiyās*) to other decrees on *ribā* found in the foundational texts (Quran and *ḥadīth*). He then proceeds to refute both of these reasons. As for the *ḥadīth* "Every loan that has accrued benefit is *ribā* (usurious)," he had already argued the earlier Calcutta fatwa for its inauthenticity,[81] and he affirms that here. As for the arguments based on *qiyās* (analogy), Riḍā agrees with the *muftī* that the analogical arguments employed by the traditional jurists to prove their point were in a sense false analogies (*qiyās maʿa fāriq*), but Riḍā says that even if the analogies were sound, the necessities or needs of the time allow us to negate the legal implications of that analogy.[82]

Now that I have summarized some of the salient points of the Hyderabad fatwa, I make the following observation about the maturation of Riḍā's approach to law and fatwa as well as how his ideas reflected the impetus for reform that was increasingly being called for in certain circles within the Muslim world during that period:

1. By comparing Riḍā's Calcutta fatwa with his Hyderabad fatwa, one can discern Riḍā's growing disregard for and questioning of traditional authority. This is seen in several facets of his two fatwas. First, in both fatwas, Riḍā goes counter to the prevailing legal opinion about *ribā* (usury) that had been agreed upon by most jurists of the *madhhab*s by claiming that an increased return (*faḍl*) on a loan did not constitute usury. Second, in the Hyderabad fatwa, there is a complete disregard for *madhhab*-based legal

81 See argument summarized earlier.
82 Riḍā, 51–52.

Case	Ruling/fatwa	Legal reasoning	Jurist	Madhhab
Is it allowed for merchants to take an increase on their bank deposits that are a result of international transfers? Give answer according to Sunnī *madhhabs*. Calcutta Fatwa 1907	Yes, because that is not *ribā* (usury)	1. Because the increase is not a precondition, it is not *ribā* in the Ḥanafī school 2. Because the money transfer contains no contract stipulating an increase, the increase is not *ribā* in the Shāfiʿī school 3. The *ḥadīth* that states that "every loan that accrues a benefit is *ribā*'" is a weakly corroborated *ḥadīth* 4. Modern bank interest resembles the increase that the Prophet would give beyond the price in some of his transactions; hence, bank interest is not *ribā* (~*qiyās*)	Rashīd Riḍā Egypt/Syria	None
Is the interest that is applied to loans and savings in Western banks considered *ribā* (usury)? Hyderabad Fatwa 1928	No, interest is not *ribā*	1. The usury that is prohibited in the Quran and in the *ḥadīth* was an exploitative type of usury where there is a doubling of the debt, not modern day interest 2. No sound legal evidence that an increase on a money transaction constitutes *ribā*, because the scriptural evidence that is cited for it is weak or misinterpreted, or the legal arguments employed by the *madhhabs* to justify this position are unsound	Rashīd Riḍā	None

FIGURE 18 Fatwa in the age of colonialism: Rashīd Riḍā's fatwas on usury (*ribā*)

reasoning, which is reflected both in his own argument and stated intentions in the introduction of the fatwa. Although he never restricted himself to *madhhab* opinions in his earlier Calcutta fatwa, he did display greater regard to the traditional authority of the *madhhab*s by citing their views as was requested by the questioner, especially where those views agreed with his. This regard is wholly absent in his later Hyderabad fatwa as we mentioned. Yet Riḍā was not alone in calling into question these types of traditionally established Muslim institutions. This was a hallmark of many reformists of this period who wanted to do away with those types of institutions, which they believed were responsible for the stagnation of Muslim civilization.[83]

2. Riḍā, like most reformists, wanted to independently reinterpret the sacred scriptures free from the traditionally established interpretation, so as to fit the exigencies of the times. This is more clearly demonstrated in his Hyderabad fatwa, where he departs from the traditional established interpretation of *ribā* (usury) defined as any increased return on a debt and questions the evidence used to demonstrate the validity of this definition. He then proceeds to offer his own scriptural and historical arguments for why that is not the case. This is demonstrated in his reinterpretation of the verse on *ribā* in Sūrat al-Baqara as meaning exploitive types of usury that were already established by an earlier verse in the Quran in Sūrat Āl ʿImrān and not ordinary interest, as previous scholars had asserted. In this respect, he re-evaluates the historical sources to forward evidence (ʿUmar's report and linguistic analysis of the quranic verses) that demonstrates his position contrary to established tradition. The purpose of this reinterpretation is ultimately to show that Islam is not a hindrance to progress and can accommodate contemporary realities.[84]
3. In his discussion of Riḍā's methodology of law, Hallaq says that Riḍā never denies the status of *qiyās* (analogical reasoning) in Islamic law but that he did view it as problematic because of its restrictiveness.[85] Although Riḍā does not directly address the issue of *qiyās* in the Calcutta fatwa, he certainly displays this critical attitude toward

[83] Refer to the section mentioned earlier that discusses the agenda of Muslim reformists of this period. See also Zaman, 2012, 6.
[84] For more on this point, see Zaman, 2012, 8.
[85] Hallaq, 2009, 506.

it in the Hyderabad fatwa, where he claims that the needs of the time necessitate that we negate the legal implications of *qiyās* made by traditional jurists that corroborate their understanding of *ribā*.[86] Riḍā's argument here in some sense resembles the Ḥanafīs' usage of the legal principle of *istiḥsān*, or juristic preference, where they counter the ruling produced by *qiyās* in favor of another ruling that produces more favorable results. Yet Riḍā does not refer to this principle in his argument, especially given the fact that he chided his Ḥanafī muftī interlocutor who sought the fatwa for restricting his argument to consideration within the Ḥanafī *madhhab*. Instead, Riḍā claims it is the exigencies of his age that authorize the negation of the *qiyās*,[87] which is an argument that essentially appeals to another principle of jurisprudence, *maṣlaḥa* (public interest), and one that Riḍā believes lies at the core of determining the Islamic law of human transactions, or *mu'āmalāt*.[88] The appeal to *maṣlaḥa* for reshaping Islamic law in the colonial period was not only a beckoning call of Riḍā and other reform-minded thinkers of his age but is also heralded even by reformers today.[89]

In conclusion, what the analysis of Riḍā's fatwas shows us is that the colonial experience had a profound impact on how Islamic law came to be negotiated both in theoretical and in practical terms. Some of the most fundamental institutions, especially those concerning Islamic law, were now being interrogated by certain circles of Muslims because it was alleged that it was those institutions that had stifled the progress of Muslim civilization and hence opened the doors for colonial domination. In the next section, an assessment will be made of whether some of the legal ideas that Muslim reformers advocated in the colonial age had an impact on the production of Islamic law, particularly fatwa in the post-colonial period.

FATWA IN THE POST-COLONIAL AGE

This final section of the chapter presents an analysis of fatwas issued in the post-colonial period as a barometer for assessing the impact of "modernity" on Islamic law in light of the sweeping changes that have taken place

86 Riḍā, 52.
87 Riḍā, 52.
88 For more on Riḍā's advocacy of *maṣlaḥa*, see Hallaq, 2009, 508.
89 There is an increasing number of books that are published even in English that call for a more *maṣlaḥa*-oriented legal thinking. See, for example, the ideas and works of Yusuf al-Qaradawi, Gamal Eldin Attia, Jasser Auda, and Aḥmad Al-Raysuni.

in the Muslim world over the past two hundred years. This study has noted the influence of European ideas and colonialism on the theoretical aspects of the legal discourse of the reformists in the twentieth-century Muslim world, but did the discourse of the reformists have an effect on the subsequent practical discourse of Islamic law as represented by fatwas? Moreover, how have the changes that were initiated in the colonial period affected Islamic legal institutions in the post-colonial period?

The remaining portion of this study will examine the fatwas of post-colonial Muslim legal institutions and *muftis*. These fatwas will be divided into two sections. The first section will contain fatwas from the era of post-colonial Muslim nation-states as the formation of this new type of state in the twentieth century has changed the political and institutional context in which fatwas are issued. For this task, I will analyze a fatwa from the Grand *Muftī* of the Sultanate of Oman Aḥmad Khalīlī (1975–present) and a fatwa from the former Supreme Jurist/Leader of the Islamic Republic of Iran, Ayatollah Khomeini (r.1979–1989). The second section will examine the fatwas from a post-colonial global Muslim institution: the IIFA of the Organisation of Islamic Cooperation (OIC). The creation of these types of institutions are a reaction to the increasing fragmentation of the global Muslim body in the age of nation-states. Then, I will close this chapter with some preliminary conclusions about the character of fatwas in the post-colonial age.

FATWAS IN THE ERA OF POST-COLONIAL MUSLIM NATION-STATES

Ahmad Khalīlī's Fatwa on Blood Transfusion, Grand Muftī of Sultanate of Oman

Institutional Context of the Fatwa and the Muftī

Aḥmad Khalīlī is the Grand Muftī of the Sultanate of Oman, the only modern state where Ibāḍīsm predominates, and he has occupied this position since 1975. He also sits at the height of the hierarchy of the Ministry of Awqaf and Religious Affairs (MARA), whose function is to regulate Islamic institutions and activities of the country, which includes mosques, endowments (*awqāf*), Friday sermons, the issuance of fatwas, etc.[90] MARA started taking shape shortly after the inauguration

[90] Al-Kharusi, Muscat; August 13, 2015. Ministries of religious affairs are a common bureau in modern Muslim states where such organizations came into being with the twentieth-century formation of Muslim nation-states so that these new founded states could harness religion for the purposes of state formation and national cohesion.

of Sultan Qaboos in 1970 as a part of his efforts to develop the country along the lines of bureaucratic formalism. It was known as the Ministry of Endowment and Judicial and Islamic Affairs in 1981. The judiciary was separated from that ministry in 1997 where the department then became the Ministry of Awqaf and Religious Affairs.[91]

The Committee on Ifta (Hay'at al-Iftā') is a department within MARA, which the Grand Mufti is also the head of, where he issues fatwas that are of national concern (i.e., contemporary issues that affect the wider Omani public). Khalīlī does not always issue fatwas exclusively from the perspective of the established Ibāḍī *madhhab* when it comes to contemporary issues. Rather he evaluates contemporary issues based on the broadest forms of Islamic legal reasoning (*dalā'il shar'iyya*) and public interest (*maṣlaḥa*),[92] a fact that is corroborated by the fatwa I will analyze here. Khalīlī at times has issued fatwas that went against the established position of Ibāḍī *madhhab*. An example of such a fatwa is his legitimation that Friday prayers can be held outside of big cities.[93] Khalīlī is also a mufti within the IIFA of the Organization of Islamic Cooperation (OIC)[94] where he represents the Sultanate of Oman.

Khalīlī's fatwa that is being examined here is about the legitimacy of medical blood transfusion for patience. Blood in Islamic law was seen as ritually impure excrement, thus making the intake/ingestion of blood into the human body a dubious activity. The fatwa is taken from one of Khalīlī's publications on the contemporary revival of Islamic law. The date of the fatwa is not indicated in the source, but I presume that it was issued sometime after 1975 when he assumed his position as Grand Muftī of the Sultanate of Oman; since it was then, it would have been incumbent upon him to deal with the issues of wide public concern.

Al-Khalīlī's Fatwa on Medical Blood Transfusion

Aḥmad Khalīlī seeks to legally legitimate the act of blood transfusion for those who medically need it. Al-Khalīlī begins his fatwa by giving some legal context mentioning the earlier opinions of most modern Omani jurists when the possibility of blood transfusion first came to their attention, claiming that at that stage Oman was an isolated state that did not have a good grasp of modern advances. As a result, many of its jurists declared blood transfusion illegitimate because blood in the traditional

[91] Al-Salimi, 151.
[92] Al-Kharusi, Muscat; August 13, 2015.
[93] Al-Kharusi, Muscat; August 13, 2015.
[94] The OIC and fatwas from its fatwa academy will be analyzed later in this chapter.

schools of Islamic law was seen as ritually impure, thus making it unlawful to medicate with impurities. Al-Khalīlī retorts that he opposes those fatwas building his case on the legal principle that "necessity licenses prohibitions," a principle, he says, that is supported by the Quran, Prophetic practice (*sunna*), and consensus (*ijmā*ʿ) of Muslim jurists.[95]

Al-Khalīlī begins by demonstrating how this principle is validated in the Quran when it allows for the consumption of four prohibited things when necessity requires so: pork, alcohol, blood, and what has been ritually slaughtered to other than God.[96] He then sights authoritative precedence by stating that jurists from all four Sunni schools of law including jurists within the Ibāḍī school agreed on this understanding of the Quranic injunctions. Moreover, in cases of necessity, these jurists state that it is not just an option to consume these prohibited things but a legal requirement that would be deemed morally reprehensible if one were to forgo this option at the expense of their survival. These jurists cite Qur'anic junctions in their arguments that support their judgment: "Don't expose yourself to destruction" (2:195) and "Don't kill yourselves..." (4:29).[97]

Once al-Khalīlī establishes the legitimacy of consuming prohibited products in situations of necessity, he then proceeds to conclude by analogy that treatment through blood transfusion should be viewed as even more legitimate. Al-Khalīlī says that necessity would not even be required if it is merely deemed probable that with the blood transfusion the patient could avoid some harm. To support this position, he cites the prophetic allowance for the traditional practice of wet cupping where blood is extracted from the body for medical treatment. He says that if such an ancient medical practice was allowed for treatment in a previous era, then our more advanced medical knowledge and technologies place us even in a better position to determine the proper course of treatment through blood transfusion without harm to the patient or the donor.[98]

Al-Khalīlī then responds along rational lines to an unnamed objector to blood transfusion who likened the act to separated organs. His response starts by listing the differences between organ transplant and blood transfusion. Yet the objector raises another objection, claiming that no one can know with certainty whether the patient's life depends on the blood transfusion. Al-Khalīlī retorts that this claim does not consider

[95] Al-Khalīlī, 102.
[96] Al-Khalīlī, 103.
[97] Al-Khalīlī, 103–104.
[98] Al-Khalīlī, 104–105.

the precision involved in modern medicine. But even if the claim about the uncertainty of the results of the medical procedure were true, the implementation of the aforementioned legal principle "necessity licenses prohibitions" only requires the preponderance of necessity to be established, and not its certainty, for the relaxation of prohibitions.[99] In this counterargument, al-Khalīlī was implicitly referencing a principle within classical Islamic legal theory that norms are established for the likeliness of the occurrence of events/actions and not based on the certainty of their occurrence.

Furthermore, one of the main pieces of evidence that the objector forwards for his position is a *ḥadīth* that says: "Allah did not make your healing from things that are forbidden to you." Despite the questionable pedigree of the *ḥadīth* in that its attribution to the prophet is disputed (see footnote #1 in al-Khalīlī, 103), al-Khalīlī nevertheless takes the *ḥadīth* seriously and engages in scriptural hermeneutics to reconcile this statement with his overall position. He says that the implication of this *ḥadīth* should be restricted to situations where one would not need to resort to prohibited things to be treated, but when there is a necessity to resort to such things, they can no longer be considered prohibited because of the Quranic statement: "He [God] has distinguished/designated what is forbidden for you except in situations of necessity." (6:119). It is particularly in these situations that al-Khalīlī says the *ḥadīth* does not apply (Khalīlī, 107).

This hermeneutical maneuver that he undertakes here is using a norm arising from one scriptural statement to modify the scope of cases to which the norm of another scriptural statement is applied to. This is known in Islamic legal theory as "particularizing the universal" (*ḥaml al-ʿāmm ʿalā al-khāṣṣ*).

Al-Khalīlī concludes his fatwa by supporting the position of legitimating blood transfusion for medical purposes with a broadly recognized *ḥadīth* of his own that shows that things that are prohibited to consume in normal circumstances are allowed in exceptional cases. The *ḥadīth* refers to a group of people who visited the Prophet in Medina and became ill. Among the prescriptions that the Prophet prescribed to cure their particular illness was drinking the urine of camels. Al-Khalīlī reasons from this prophetic prescription that although a majority of jurists from the schools of law including the Ibāḍī *madhhab* concluded that camel urine is impure and thus prohibited for consumption, the Prophet

[99] Al-Khalīlī, 106.

permitted them to drink it for the sake of treatment. This he says is a legal indication that those necessities that license a prohibition include the necessities of medical treatment [even if the life of the patient may not be in immediate danger]. Al-Khalīlī then cites a few more prophetic statements where the Prophet allowed for items forbidden for use under normal circumstances (wearing of gold and silk) were allowed by him to be used for medical treatment of even minor issues.[100] Through such analogical reasoning to established norms and practices, al-Khalīlī legitimizes the new practice of blood transfusion (see Figure 19).

Al-Khalīlī utilizes numerous approaches of legal reasoning to legitimate his fatwa. It is to be expected that he would use scriptural texts like Quran and *ḥadīth* as the fundamental sources for deriving the legal norms that would support his views. Furthermore, the methods of the derivation of such scriptural norms are arrived at by traditionally sanctioned hermeneutical and legal strategies like analogy (*qiyās*), particularizing the universal, etc. But what is most unusual about al-Khalīlī's approach is using a universally accepted legal principle across the different *madhhabs*, "necessities license prohibitions," as the starting point of his argument rather than appealing to the rules of his Ibāḍī *madhhab* as was so usual with the fatwas from the post-classical period. Moreover, he also appeals to the consensual positions of Muslim jurists from across the madhhabs for interpreting these sacred texts that concur with his legal position.

Types of legal rationale manifested in al-Khalīlī fatwas

Case	**Fatwa**	**Legal reasoning**
Is medical blood transfusion legal given the ritual impurity of blood?	- Medical blood transfusion is allowed	1. Legal principle: Necessity licenses prohibitions 2. Analogy (*qiyās*) to consumption of prohibited products to save one's life or heal someone as found in Quran and *sunna* 3. Historical consensus (*ijmāʿ*) of Muslim jurists from all *madhāhib* that intake of prohibited things is allowed/mandated to save one's life or heal them

FIGURE 19 Fatwa in the era of the post-colonial Muslim nation-states I: blood transfusion.

[100] Al-Khalīlī, 107–108.

Al-Khalīlī's strategies in legal reasoning suggest a tilt toward greater inclusivity in post-colonial fatwas and a step away from *madhhab* exclusive legitimation even though muftis like al-Khalīlī situate themselves within an established *madhhab*. Greater communication between the global Muslim communities has heightened jurists' sensitivity to employing a more universal language to communicate their juristic opinions. Perhaps there is a recognition by post-colonial jurists that there is a greater need to employ inter-madhhab and trans-madhhab reasoning in modern fatwas to resolve the intricate issues that are presented to them in modern life.

The Fatwas of the Supreme Jurist/Leader of Islamic Republic of Iran: Ayatollah Khomeini's

Fatwa on Gender Interaction in the Public Sphere

POLITICAL AND INSTITUTIONAL CONTEXT OF THE FATWA. As a reaction to the secularizing reforms and the despotic character of the Pahlavi dynasty in Iran during the twentieth century, a people's revolution led by Ayatollah Khomeini took place against the regime in 1979 where an Islamic system of governance headed by clerics was eventually established. The new government consisted of a combination of selected clergy and elected officials. At the very head of the government is the Supreme Leader/Jurist (*al-Faqīh*), a position first assumed by Ayatollah Khomeini (r.1979–1989), who had the final say on political matters related to the state. Then comes the Guardian Council that is made up of high-ranking clergy who monitor policies and laws to ensure that they are consistent with Islamic norms. There are also executive (president) and legislative (parliament) branches of government who are elected officials whose task is to legislate and execute laws for the Islamic Republic.[101]

The scope of this discussion will center on a fatwa by Ayatollah Khomeini, as a recognized religious authority and political head of state, that played a crucial role in influencing issues of governance in the first decade of the Islamic Republic. Hence, my analysis will focus on the impact of his fatwas on public policy rather than their modes of legal reasoning to display the social and political dimensions of fatwas in modern times. The particular fatwas analyzed here are his fatwas addressing the

[101] For an in-depth study of the revolution and its aftermath, see Said Arjomand's *The Turban for the Crown: The Islamic Revolution in Iran*. New York, NY: Oxford University Press, 1988.

content of Iranian television after the revolution. My information on this issue has been obtained through my interview with Muhammad Rafsanjani, who was the Minister of Radio and Television (1981–1994) when these fatwas was issued in the late 1980s.

AYATOLLAH KHOMEINI'S FATWA ON IRANIAN TELEVISION FILMS. As the Iranian Revolution was a modern political experiment on how to run a government based on Islamic norms, there were challenges to managing media in the newly formed Islamic Republic. Radio and TV were frowned upon by the traditional Iranian clerics because they saw them as corrupting forces in society. My informant told me that Ayatollah Khomeini was not principally against radio or TV as a communication medium but was against their content having a socially corrupting influence. The challenge was how to define criteria that would act as guidelines for deciding what content of radio and TV is corrupting (*ḥarām* or Islamically prohibited to use my informant's language).

So, when certain programs were aired on radio and TV in the post-revolutionary period in the 1980s, they came under severe criticism by conservative clerics as being un-Islamic (*ḥarām*) because they featured women and men interacting and talking with each other. The accusation by conservatives was that these programs are no different from the period of the previous Iranian regime, and so in their eyes, very little had changed in terms of entertainment in the Islamic Republic. Since Muhammad Rafsanjani was in charge of these communication mediums during this period, the criticism of conservatives became focused on him.[102]

In 1987, criticism of radio and television programs came to a head when a prominent conservative Iranian scholar named Ayatollah Haram Mohammadi Gilani, who was also a member of the Guardian Council, criticized Muhammad Rafsanjani in a Friday sermon for allowing such programs to be broadcast. To bolster his argument, Ayatollah Gilani also referred to a prior legal ruling indicating the illegality of such types of programing by the Supreme Leader of the Islamic Republic Ayatollah Khomeini stated in his earlier legal dissertation before becoming head of Iran known as *Taḥrīr al-Wasīla*. Muhammad Rafsanjani felt unable to respond to Ayatollah Gilani because of his powerful position and sought a fatwa from Ayatollah Khomeini that would clarify the legality of the TV programs and music that was being broadcast on Iranian media.[103]

[102] M. Rafsanjani, Tehran; January 1, 2017.
[103] M. Rafsanjani, Tehran; January 1, 2017.

In response to this request, Ayatollah Khomeini issued a fatwa claiming that the programs currently being broadcast on Iranian media did not pose a problem from the point of view of Sharīʿa (Islamic law); even indicating that many of the programs had something to teach people.[104] Furthermore, the fatwa addressed the issue of observing sporting events, saying that it too was not a problem to observe even when men were not observing proper Islamically mandated dress, which was also a bone of contention of the conservatives.[105]

Nevertheless, Khomeini's fatwa was not a blanket endorsement of the existing television programs because he stipulated two things that must be observed when making and observing these TV films. First, the makeup artist ought to be a *maḥram*.[106] This meant that a non-relative male makeup artist should not come into physical contact with female actors and vice versa during the process of preparing these actors for filming. Muhammad Rafsanjani said this point in the fatwa came from Ayatollah Khomeini's study of film credits that showed that they often contained a single makeup artist despite there being both male and female actors on the film set. Secondly, he cautioned the observing audience of these films not to come to such programs having lustful intentions in mind. That is, they should be observing these programs for their entertainment value and artistic expression (see Figure 20).[107]

Ayatollah Ali Akbar Rafsanjani, at the time speaker of the parliament, announced Ayatollah Khomeini's fatwa in his Friday sermon and said that the fatwa made it clear that observing existing programs on Iranian TV and radio posed no social or moral risk. Muhammad Rafsanjani added that Ayatollah Khomeini's fatwa silenced the conservative criticism of television and radio programs and allowed for a more open atmosphere for the production and distribution of such programming.[108]

[104] The Persian text of Khomeini's fatwa was printed on the cover of the Iranian Persian language magazine *Saroush* (published: 29 Aban, 1372, of the solar Hijri calendar). In addition, the text of the fatwa was also printed on pg. 20 of the same publication along with the accompanying article discussing the fatwa and the story surrounding it.

[105] M. Rafsanjani, Tehran; January 1, 2017.

[106] *Maḥrams* are those who are in position to observe and come into physical contact with members of the opposite sex. Usually such individuals would have a close familial relationship and thus are ineligible to marry from whom they have such familial relationships.

[107] M. Rafsanjani, Tehran; January 1, 2017.

[108] M. Rafsanjani, Tehran; January 1, 2017.

Ayatollah Khomeini's Silent/Implicit Fatwa on Women in Television

On another occasion during the1980s, the Supreme Leader of the Islamic Republic, Ayatollah Khomeini, influenced public policy through religious action. In this case, the religious action was implicit rather than an explicit fatwa. A news-anchor woman on Iranian television named Maryam Riyazī presented the news in the 1980s, which some conservatives objected to because they did not feel that women should appear on TV. Once again, this posed a problem for Muhammad Rafsanjani, the Minister of Radio and Television. Muhammad Rafsanjani said that she was an excellent news anchor, and he responded to her critics by saying that most males ought to be occupied with defending the country in its war in Iraq and not with playing these roles (M. Rafsanjani, Tehran; January 1, 2017).

As the criticisms of this case went unabated from conservative camps, Muhammad Rafsanjani then went to Ayatollah Khomeini to ask for his judgment (fatwa) on the issue. After some days of deliberation, Ayatollah Khomeini handed Muhammad Rafsanjani the text of his weekly televized address to the Iranian people, usually presented by his son Aḥmad Khomeini, and asked him to have Ms. Riyazī deliver his televized address for that week (M. Rafsanjani, Tehran; January 1, 2017). This substitution showed Ayatollah Khomeini's tacit approval of the right of women to play such public roles and silenced the critics. They understood that commissioning the anchorwoman to read his weekly address, he approved of her position. In conclusion, although Ayatollah Khomeini never explicitly pronounced a judgment in this case, that could be considered a fatwa. This is because fatwas are, by their very nature, explicit pronouncements. Nevertheless, observers may consider his actions an implicit fatwa since it served the function of judging the legitimacy or illegitimacy of an action or position (see Figure 20).

The Role of Fatwa in Iranian Governance

The use of fatwas to determine public policy not only represents a process of embedding religious norms that counter secularizing trends that were advanced in the twentieth-century Middle Eastern societies but also represents the continuity of traditional forms of ethico-legal legitimation of public practice despite the new techniques of government employed by the Iranian revolutionary regime. The usage of traditional forms of legal legitimation such as the issuance of fatwas within a system of republican governance implies a confluence in the forms of governance practiced by the early regime. This regime sought to preserve the authoritativeness of discursively based Islamic institutions even as it legitimizes bureaucratic forms of administration of public affairs as represented by institutions like the Ministry of Radio and Television.

Yet treating the fatwas of Khomeini in this instant as binding has a larger significance to both the institutions of Islamic legal tradition as well as modern understandings of governance. This is because the newly formed political office that Khomeini occupied under the political doctrine of *vilāyat-i faqīh* (Rule of the Jurist) now gave his pronouncements a politically binding character. It resulted in the political routinization of the voluntary socio-religious association of *marja'-i taqlid*,[109] the highest epistemic religious authority in Shī'i Islam. This transformation of a voluntary and strictly ethico-legal institution into a political one gave its new formulation a political sanction and a politically binding character that it did not previously possess even though it had a morally binding character to the members who subscribed to it.

This newly formed politico-juridical institution of *vilāyat-i faqīh* gave this form of governance a theocratic character. At the same time, the system's validation of political participation of the public in governance represented by the electoral process and forms of procedural legitimation of political norms represented by the legislature gives this system of governance a democratic character. This hybrid form of governance is far more constrained by religiously established norms and the clergy, thus making it theocentric. Yet there existed incongruencies between these two component practices of legitimation. This led to an ad hoc manner of settling disputes in the first decade of the revolution through the fatwas of Khomeini.

Furthermore, Khomeini's fatwa on Islamic legality of male-female interactions in public life perhaps set a new legal precedence in traditional Twelver Shī'i law by loosening the restrictions on roles and interactions of women in the public square. Yet, this precedence was not set through some sort of secular democratic procedure, but through the religious-legal practice of fatwa issuances that gave this new precedence a

[109] A voluntary association is a consensual grouping of individuals that is governed by a set of rules (Weber 1978, VI, 52). *Marja'-i taqlid* is a Twelver Shī'i juridical institution that developed in the nineteenth century as a way of organizing the religious practice of the Shī'i laity around the religio-legal pronouncements of recognized Twelver Shī'i jurists designated as *marja* ' (Moussavi, 104). The Shī'i religious practitioners choose the recognized *marja'* they wish to follow. Moussavi (1986) argues that the political

religiously sanctioned ethical dimension based on religiously sanctioned principles. Hence, these fatwas led to the re-embedding of religious ethics in the public sphere and the subsequent de-secularization of social and political action.

It is important to highlight that the legitimation of women's participation in the public sphere and the modes of that legitimation were religious. An Islamic legal practice like fatwa issuances was the primary vehicle that normalized these positions, thereby increasing the political space for religious action. Khomeini's fatwas legitimating male-female interaction in the public sphere were laden with ethical considerations of the proper propriety that must be observed in such interactions (restricting male-female physical contact and moral admonitions to the viewer of such programs). Hence, fatwas were a means of embedding religio-ethical precepts to govern domains in what is normally viewed as the sphere of the secular (television programming) and subject primarily to "secular"

Political and social significance of Ayatollah Khomeini's fatwas

Case	Fatwa	Political and social significance
Can men and women come into close contact during film making and is observing such interactions legal?	- Gender interactions in this context are legitimate if males and females do not come into physical contact with one another	1. Established the boundaries of legitimate gender interactions in contemporary Muslim society. 2. Created a space for traditional Islamic legal practices like *iftā'* to legitimate modern Muslim governance practices
	- The public observance of such interactions is legal	3. De-secularizes the Muslim public sphere
		4. Expanded Islamic media content
Can women have public roles like serving as news anchors?	Yes	Legitimated women's participation in the Muslim public sphere

FIGURE 20 Fatwa in the era of the post-colonial Muslim nation-states II: gender interaction and women's participation in the Muslim public sphere.

institution of *vilāyat-i faqīh* that was theorized and established by Ayatollah Khomeini himself, in fact, has its historical and epistemological antecedents in the legal institution of *marja'-i taqlid*.

considerations (means of program production, the esthetic quality of the programming, etc.).

FATWAS IN THE ERA OF POST-COLONIAL GLOBAL MUSLIM INSTITUTIONS: THE OIC AND THE IIFA

Historical Background of the OIC and the Institutional Context of the IIFA's Fatwas

The Organization of Islamic Cooperation (OIC), formerly known as the Organisation of the Islamic Conference, is an intergovernmental organization that arose out of the need to increase cooperation between Muslim states in an era of the post-colonial nation-state system.

Fostering "Islamic solidarity" between Muslim nation-states was the key objective in the organization's formation[110] in the post-colonial era. The initial impetus for the call of cooperation came about in light of an Israeli arson attack on the Al-Aqsa Mosque, a Muslim holy shrine, in Jerusalem in August 1969. Muslim governments were called upon to hold a summit to condemn the Israeli occupation of Palestine.[111] An initial organizing meeting, the First Islamic Summit, took place in September 1969 in Rabat, Morocco,[112] in the aftermath of newly formed Muslim nation-states freeing themselves from the European colonial yoke during the 1950s and 1960s. Thirty-six Muslim nation-states were invited to the summit, but only twenty-five attended.[113]

The OIC membership of Muslim nation-states has grown since its inception in 1969. It now has fifty-seven member states,[114] although some of those states are not majority Muslim states but have significant populations of Muslims (e.g., Gabon). The organization has also established many subsidiary organizations that promote its goal of Islamic solidarity. One such organization is the International Islamic Fiqh Academy (IIFA), created at the OIC's Third Islamic Summit Conference in Mecca in 1981.[115] The OIC's stated purpose for this body was to gather "religious scholars and intellectuals in various cultural, scientific, social and economic disciplines from various parts of the Muslim world

110 İhsanoğlu, 2.
111 See al-Ahsan, 1992, 108.
112 Al-Ahsan, 1988, 18; İhsanoğlu, 26.
113 İhsanoğlu, 26.
114 See İhsanoğlu, 219–220.
115 Al-Ahsan, 1988, 36.

to study problems of contemporary life and to engage in original effective *ijtihād* (legal reasoning) with the view to providing solutions, derived from Islamic tradition and taking into account developments in Islamic thought, for these problems."[116]

The membership of the IIFA consists of "expert jurists and scholars of Islamic jurisprudence and various other sciences."[117] The purpose of the academy is to foster Islamic unity by promoting adherence to an Islamic jurisprudence that engages contemporary issues in order to provide Islamic solutions that are both effective and authentic.[118] The idea is to bring about a renewal of Islamic jurisprudence that reconciles the differences between Islamic legal schools by emphasizing their common ground through a process of collective *ijtihād* (legal reasoning) on modern problems.[119] In other words, the academy recognizes that problems in the post-colonial world are too complex to be dealt with strictly by the traditional approaches and methodologies of Islamic law and require a more collective effort that brings together authoritative legal scholars ("muftīs") from the various legal schools to collaborate toward a trans-*madhhab* approach to resolving these problems. This approach is partly substantiated by the fact that the muftīs that are chosen for the fatwa committees come from all across the Muslim world and have various *madhhab* affiliations.[120]

To corroborate these assertions, the current administrative director of fatwas at the IIFA, ʿAbd al-Qāhir Muḥammad Qamar, states in a paper that he delivered at a conference in Kuwait in 2007[121] that among the objectives of the IIFA is to work toward the renewal of Islamic law by means of its internal development and advancement utilizing Islamic legal theory (*uṣūl al-fiqh*) and the aims and principles of Islamic law (*maqāṣid* and *qawāʿid al-Sharīʿa*).[122] So it may be observed from this statement that the IIFA vision for renewing Islamic law is in some respects a conservative one given that the means of renewal take into consideration traditional Islamic legal principles, methods, and goals as the means by which this renewal should take place and is not the sweeping overhaul of

116 As quoted in İhsanoğlu, 33.
117 İhsanoğlu, 42.
118 İhsanoğlu, 42, 91–92; See also al-Ahsan, 1988, 36.
119 İhsanoğlu, 92–93.
120 See www.fiqhacademy.org.sa/ members (*al-aʿḍāʾ*) page for the current list of scholars that are members of IIFA.
121 This paper was obtained via email through personal communication with Dr. Qamar.
122 Qamar, 12.

Islamic legal practices and institutions that many Muslim reformists had called for.[123]

Nevertheless, there are points of divergence between the IIFA's vision of renewal and the ways in which Islamic law was practiced in the pre-colonial period; one example is the fact that the IIFA does not see the necessity of restricting rulings within the confines of the traditional doctrines of the Islamic legal schools. In this respect, Qamar states that one of the goals of the IIFA is to bring together jurists from the various Islamic legal schools so they can converge on those points where they share common ground yet remain respectful of their divergences.[124] As alluded to earlier, Islamic rulings of the past were produced in light of existing doctrines (precedents) and legal methodologies within a particular legal school. In attempting to bring about a convergence of the various approaches to the production of Islamic law, the IIFA is engaging in novel legal practices that hitherto had not been practiced by previous generations of legal scholarship.

An Examination of the IIFA's Fatwas

For the purpose of illustrating the theoretical points stated in the section mentioned earlier, this section will commence with an examination of the fatwa literature issued by the IIFA in the field of commercial and financial transactions, as this is one of the areas of Islamic law that has undergone the most dramatic change with the imposition of the global capitalist system. The point here is that modern financial practices that developed in the West and are the standard mode of operation in global financial institutions pose a challenge to Muslim economic ethics and law, a challenge that Muslims are trying to negotiate through the use of traditional legal practices such as the fatwa. Therefore, we always need to keep in mind how Islamic legal discourse and institutions are being slowly reconstituted to adapt to the challenges of colonialism and its aftermath.

With this in mind, five fatwas (or *qarārāt* – resolutions – as the IIFA calls them)[125] have been selected to serve as a sample for this case study of contemporary post-colonial fatwas. These fatwas are about the following five topics: abstract rights, Islamic stocks (*sukūk*), endowing shares and

[123] See the previous two sections of this chapter for examples of how reformists like Rashid Riḍā attempted to introduce sweeping changes to Islamic law.

[124] Qamar, 12.

[125] See Qamar (15, n. 1), who claims that these fatwas were called resolutions (*qarārāt*) according to the terminology of the contemporary convention when agreements are reached at conferences.

stocks, health insurance, and international trade. But before any discussion ensues about the actual fatwas, a few brief remarks are called for here on the deliberation procedures for such fatwas. While the muftīs on the fatwa committees of the IIFA make their deliberations on the particular issues at the conferences that are convened for these deliberations, they are presented with detailed research studies on the subject of consideration from various specialists prior to their deliberations. Hence, the discussions of the Muslim experts are informed by detailed studies from those who are experts in finance and economics.[126] It is not until they have read/heard the expert analysis that they come to some legal resolution on the matter being considered.[127] They recognize that issues arising in the post-colonial age are too complicated simply to be addressed by a muftī without the mediation of an expert in that field who can help the muftī better understand the nature of the process or phenomenon that he seeks to engage.

Instead of analyzing each fatwa individually, these fatwas will be examined in light of some common themes that emerge from them. This approach to the analysis is justified by the fact that all the fatwas are issued from the same fatwa-making body – the fatwa committees of IIFA – and display a similarity of certain substantive and procedural legal characteristics that facilitate this approach to the analysis. With that said, two basic common themes emerge from this analysis, both of which revolve around the broad unifying theme of continuity and change in Islamic law. Those two themes are, first, the conscious connection of the new IIFA rulings to the historically established doctrines of Islamic law and thereby a tacit admission of the continued influence of the Islamic discursive legal tradition on legal production today and, second, the types of legal rationale that are employed in the justifications of their positions. In the following paragraphs, each of these points will be discussed in more detail.

Relationship of IIFA Fatwas to Established Islamic Law

The resolutions (fatwas) of the IIFA are not made in a vacuum but assume a body of legal knowledge of which their resolutions are an extension. In other words, the legal decisions that are reached and presented give the impression that these decisions are reached in light of already established and agreed-upon legal principles and doctrine and that these new legal

[126] See a sample of these research studies that were presented to the muftīs of the IIFA nineteenth Session on *Tawarruq* at the following site: www.isra.mymedia-centredownloads accessed July 4, 2013.

[127] Qamar, 19.

decisions are merely trying to elaborate and apply these classical principles to the contemporary context. For instance, in Resolution 178, the IIFA tries to delineate the specific characteristics of a legitimate Islamic stock (*sakk*);[128] the decision reached by the IIFA says: "The Islamic stock (*sakk*) should be issued in accordance with a Sharīʿa (legal and legitimate) contract, and it takes on all of its legal rulings."[129]

The resolution goes on to spell out some of those conditions of a legitimate Islamic financial contract, but what is of greater concern here is that this statement indicates that the IIFA already assumes that there are established Sharīʿa rules for contracts that are to be taken into consideration when formulating guidelines for Islamic stocks. Hence, there is an implicit analogy between traditionally established financial contracts and between the newly established financial contracts of *sukūk*. So, it seems that the IIFA is not necessarily arguing for the legitimacy or illegitimacy of a certain issue by appealing to the discursive sources of Islamic law like the Quran and *ḥadīth*, nor is it appealing to new legal principles by which it is arriving at its decision. Rather, there is an assumption of an established body of legal doctrine (symbolized by the term Sharīʿa) that needs to be adhered to, albeit modified for these new cases under consideration. There is no appeal to any specific legal doctrine of any of the classical schools (*madhāhib*), but there is an impression from the language used in these legal decisions that the legal doctrine to which it is appealing is a simple matter of consensus among the different schools of Islamic law (see Figure 21).

Similarly, in another fatwa concerning the matter of endowing (stock) shares (*waqf al-ashum*), Resolution 181, the IIFA states that both permanent and temporary endowments are legitimate endowments. This rule is established because *sukūk* (Islamically legitimated stocks) are obviously temporary properties that would need this justification in order to be

[128] *Sukūk* (sing. *sakk*) has been sometimes translated as Islamic bonds instead of stocks. Yet many within Islamic finance circles have recognized that translating it as bonds is misleading because bonds are usually denoted as debts to the issuer, while stocks are shares in an investment. Since bonds are debts and pose no risk of loss to the investor, they are considered interest-bearing loans and hence prohibited in Islamic law, while stocks by design are profit-and-loss-sharing equities, which are permissible in Islamic law. Since *sukūk* are essentially equity shares that are made compliant with the norms of Islamic law, the more accurate denotation for them is stocks rather than bonds. See the AAIOFI *Shari'ah Standards* manual under the entry "Sukūk" for the elaboration of this point.

[129] Resolution number 178 (19/4) regarding "Sukūk, its contemporary applications and its circulation." www.fiqhacademy.org.sa/ accessed February 3, 2014. Translation from Arabic is mine.

utilized as an Islamically legitimate endowment. They also assert that an endowment may be movable, money, or even a benefit.[130] It is interesting here that their definition of endowments seems to build on Abū al-Suʿūd's sixteenth-century fatwa on cash *waqf*s[131] and at the same time diverges from it in other respects. Abū al-Suʿūd argued for the legitimacy of endowments, or *waqf*s, made from transportable properties as a way of legitimating the idea that cash could be made a *waqf*. This is in light of the fact that the major jurists of the *madhhab*s did not approve of this.[132]

The fact that the IIFA's fatwa committee has now taken this point for granted indicates that Abū al-Suʿūd's legal position has had a lasting impact on Islamic law. They have stated that cash *waqf*s can be endowable properties and hence no longer a point of controversy or debate, as was the case in the sixteenth century. Also, like Abū al-Suʿūd, the IIFA claims that cash (as a particular example of a transportable property) can be made into a *waqf*. Yet the IIFA seems to depart from Abū al-Suʿūd's position in terms of the temporariness of the endowment. It should be stated here that the second condition for endowments – according to the doctrines of Islamic legal schools – is that the endowment must be permanent. Abū al-Suʿūd does not question this premise other than to establish that cash (*nuqūd*) can be considered permanent from the point of view of its exchangeability. Yet the IIFA's resolution goes further than all of these by declaring that temporary property can be made into a *waqf*. The rationale for this contrarian position vis-à-vis previously established legal doctrine is not provided in the text of the fatwa/resolution, but the ruling is, nevertheless, taken as is, and it is a prerequisite for the establishment of their positions for the legitimacy of endowing shares and *sukūk*.

After stating their general position on endowments, members of the IIFA are now in position to state their ruling on the legitimacy-endowing shares and *sukūk*. They claim that endowing shares and/or *sukūk* are legitimate in view of the Sharīʿa.[133] As these fatwas/resolutions barely provide any rationale for these legal positions in the text of the fatwas themselves, one can only presume that the disregard for the previous preconditions of permanence and immovability of endowment properties

[130] Resolution 181 (19/7) www.fiqhacademy.org.sa accessed February 18, 2014. See also the translation of Resolution 181 at www.ifikr.isra.my accessed January 27, 2014. Translation by Ibrahim Ali and Mohammad Ashadi Mohd. Zaini.

[131] For more on this fatwa, please refer to the analysis of it in the previous chapter.

[132] See the detailed analysis of this fatwa in Chapter 5 of this work.

[133] Resolution 181 (19/7) www.fiqhacademy.org.sa accessed February 18, 2014. See also the translation of Resolution 181 at www.ifikr.isra.my accessed January 27, 2014. Translation by Ibrāhīm ʿAlī and Mohammad Ashadi Mohd. Zaini.

is the key factor as to why shares and Islamic stock, despite the volatile nature of these properties, can be seen as endowment properties. The issue of legal rationalization will be discussed in the next section.

Yet even after establishing that previously unqualified properties (transportable and temporary) can be turned into endowments, the same resolution of the IIFA places stipulations on these non-traditional forms of *waqf*s. In this regard, they first stipulate that the preeminent (*aṣl*) position on endowed shares is that they remain intact (*baqāʾuhā*) while the profits (returns) from these shares are to be used for the purposes of the endowment and not for trade on the market. This statement is an interesting parallel to Abū al-Suʿūd's position concerning cash *waqf*s where he states that the cash endowed in a cash *waqf* remains essentially intact (although not actually intact) in the form of a loan/investment, because its likeness remains while the profits that are accrued from the cash are spent on perpetuating the aim of the cash *waqf* (i.e., for further loans and investments).[134] So, it seems that the IIFA is building on the sort of legal positions and rationale that Abū al-Suʿūd established earlier or is taking that legal rationale for granted.

In addition, the IIFA states that if the company from which the shares were endowed is liquidated or the value of the stocks (*sukūk*) has been paid, then the original endowment may be exchanged for other properties – such as estates or shares in other companies or *sukūk* – based on the conditions of the endower or on the condition that the new property will serve the preponderant interests of the endowment.[135] This stipulation mirrors the traditional position on *waqf*s according to which *waqf*s may be sold and exchanged for other properties if the new property is in a position to accrue greater benefits for the original endowment[136] (see Figure 21).

It may be concluded from what has been presented thus far about the relationship of IIFA resolutions to previously established doctrines of Islamic law that the IIFA seems to build on the already established rulings within the classical legal compendiums. However, these rulings show some important forward movements, for example, in the

[134] MS. Ebussuud, Risale fi vakfi'l-menkul, Süleymaniye Ktp., Hacı Selima Ağa 299, vr. 10b. pg. 214.

[135] Resolution 181 (19/7) "Endowing shares, sukūk, material rights and benefits," www.fiqhacademy.org.sa, nineteenth session, accessed February 18, 2014. Translation rendered was done in conjunction with referencing to the translation of this resolution by www.ifikr.isra.my accessed January 27, 2014. Translation by Ibrahim Ali and Mohammad Ashadi Mohd. Zaini.

[136] See this ruling stated in Abū al-Suʿūd's fatwa on cash *waqf*s MS. Ebussuud, Risale fi vakfi'l-menkul, Süleymaniye Ktp., Hacı Selima Ağa 299, vr. 10b. pg. 214.

Connections between IIFA fatwas and past legal doctrines		
Case	**Fatwa**	**Relation to past legal doctrines**
What is a legitimate Islamic stock (*sakk*)?	**Resolution 178:** One that is issued in accordance with Sharīʿa rules for a contract	- Assumes previously established body of legal norms/rules that govern even this modern financial instrument (*sakk*)
Can stock shares be endowed (*waqf al-ashum*)?	**Resolution 181:** Even though shares are temporary and transportable properties, they can be endowed	- Implicitly builds on the legal arguments of Abu al-Suʿūd that endowments can be temporary and transportable

FIGURE 21 Fatwa in the era of the post-colonial Muslim global institutions I: connections between IIFA fatwas and past legal doctrines

understanding of what properties or benefits can be considered endowable, such as shares and stocks, which were not financial instruments in the pre-colonial era. Here the circle is expanded to include new types of endowables that are the consequence of the invention of contemporary business practices. Yet the acceptance of these new business products as legitimate endowables is built on previous advancements in the legal discourse to which later generations of post-classical jurists, such as Abū al-Suʿūd, contributed. Hence, the leap between the classical and the contemporary rulings, as evidenced by the IIFA fatwas, is not as wide as it might have been without the changes that had already taken place in the classical legal positions during the post-classical period.

Types of Legal Rationale Manifested

Earlier statements alluded to the fact that the IIFA's resolutions do not state the legal rationalizations for its positions in the text of its fatwas. That said, the rationales for these fatwas are subject to robust debate between the muftīs at the fatwa sessions that were held for the sake of settling these issues as evidenced by the publications of the full proceedings of these sessions, which are made available by the IIFA in electronic and hard copy formats. Even though the complete rationale underlying individual fatwas is never fully and explicitly stated in the text of the fatwa (resolution), some rationale for the IIFA positions is occasionally expressed in the texts of the resolutions/fatwas. From these brief statements, we can make some interesting observations about the types of legal rationalizations employed by the members of the IIFA in reaching its conclusions.

The first interesting observation to note about the IIFA's approach to legal reasoning is that it issued two resolutions endorsing increased consideration for the legal methodologies of *maṣlaḥa*, or public interest (Resolution 141 in 2004),[137] and *ʿurf*, or customary practice (Resolution 47 in 1988)[138] in contemporary fatwas. The fact that the IIFA decided to take resolutions explicitly endorsing the increased consideration of these two legal concepts, without endorsing other forms of legal reasoning, is significant because it seems to vindicate the reformist agenda of twentieth-century Muslim reformists, such as Riḍā and Makhlouf, who advocated greater implementation of these two legal concepts in contemporary Islamic legal reasoning.[139]

Even though the IIFA's resolutions on *maṣlaḥa* and *ʿurf* do not introduce many nuances to the classical formulation of these legal concepts, the resolutions' significance lies in the fact that they signify a new attitude or orientation among scholars/muftīs of the IIFA councils (and possibly other contemporary muftīs): an orientation that gives priority to less pronounced Islamic legal concepts. More specifically, the muftīs who comprise the IIFA's fatwa committees are trying to loosen the hold of textual (scriptural) hermeneutics on Islamic law, a hold that has been perpetuated through previously prominent legal concepts such as *qiyās* (analogical reasoning). In addition, these resolutions signal that they would like to loosen the hold of the authority of legal precedence on contemporary rulings especially as represented in the legal doctrines of the Islamic legal schools, or *madhāhib*.

For example, with respect to loosening the hold on established precedence of past legal doctrines, their resolution on *ʿurf* states the following: "The Muslim jurist, whether a muftī or a judge, should not be confined (*jumūd*) to what is reported (*manqūl*) in the books of (previous) jurists without giving due consideration to the changing of custom (*ʿurf*)."[140] This is an explicit statement that the IIFA is trying to open the doors

[137] See full resolution at www.fiqhacademy.org.sa/qrarat/15-7.htm accessed March 21, 2014.

[138] See full resolution at www.fiqhacademy.org.sa/qrarat/5-8.htm accessed March 21, 2014.

[139] See the previous two sections of this chapter for a more detailed discussion of these points.

[140] See Resolution 47 on *ʿurf* at www.fiqhacademy.org.sa/qrarat/5-8.htm accessed January 27, 2014. Translation mine.

for fresh legal reasoning and loosen the hold of the authoritativeness of *madhhab* legal doctrines, which make up the content of those legal compendiums to which the resolution alluded.

This is an indication that there is a greater receptivity among some post-colonial muftīs to giving greater attention or pronouncement to legal reasoning based on public interest (*maṣlaḥa*) and custom (*ʿurf*) when formulating new legal rulings. By giving these context-based legal methodologies greater consideration in contemporary legal reasoning, they lessen the role that other (text-based) legal precepts like *qiyās* (analogical reasoning) and/or legal precedence might play in the current legal discourse (see Figure 22). There is some suggestion that this new attitude toward legal rulings and reasoning is not only theoretically endorsed but actualized in the resolutions/fatwas of the IIFA. This is because there are occasional references to *maṣlaḥa* and *ʿurf* in the rationale of the textual pronouncements of their resolutions/fatwas.

For example, in Resolution 43 (al-Ḥuqūq al-Maʿnawiyya), the IIFA took on the issue of the legality of abstract rights with respect to company trademarks, copyrights, and inventions. It is interesting that the committee of scholars who deliberated on these issues took the position that those abstract rights are "the specific rights of the owner" and that s/he has the right to gain monetary benefit from them. The justification that they give for such a position is that these abstract rights have acquired a monetary value in the contemporary *ʿurf* (customary practice).[141] The interesting point here is that the IIFA explicitly referred to *ʿurf* as the legal basis for this decision and did not refer to scriptural authority or previous legal doctrine on this matter. This gives some indication that contemporary Islamic law may be taking on a more contextual hue in contrast to the textual and precedent-oriented legal tradition. Moreover, this ruling is in some sense innovative from the point of view that traditional doctrines of Islamic law did not consider abstract rights as something that can be monetized in the way they are today, something to which this fatwa alludes to, as it was not the customary practice of previous eras (see Figure 22).

In another example, in Resolution 149, the IIFA tackled the issue of the legality of health insurance (*al-taʾmīn al-ṣiḥḥī*). Previous to the colonial period, health insurance and similar types of contracts would have been

[141] Resolution 43 (1988), regarding "Abstract Rights" at www.fiqhacademy.org.sa/qrarat/5-4.htm accessed February 4, 2014. Translation by author with assistance from translation found at Fatwa and Translation Unit of www.ifikr.isra.my accessed January 27, 2014.

viewed as illegal from the perspective of classical Islamic law. The rationale for such a prohibition was that these types of contracts contain too much uncertainty (*gharar*) to be valid business contracts.[142] The uncertainty (*gharar*) in the health insurance contract lies in the fact that there is an exchange of something that is determined (the cost of the insurance premium) for something that is undetermined (the coverage if and when the insured gets sick). Yet given the pervasiveness and overreliance on health insurance in the post-colonial globalized health system, the IIFA took on the subject trying to bring a new perspective on the issue. The IIFA could not ignore entirely the established ban on such contracts, but it had to take into consideration the pressing social circumstances surrounding contemporary health systems. Hence, its strategy for legitimating health insurance was to find a way to minimize the issue of uncertainty (*gharar*) while at the same time declare the necessity of insurance in the current context.

Based on these pressing circumstances, the IIFA decided to legitimate insurance policies that are issued directly from health centers that provide health services. Their justification is that the degree of uncertainty (*gharar*) in this kind of contract is too small or negligible and therefore not a violation of the norms of Islamic financial transactions. It is not quite clear how the IIFA's legitimated type of insurance policy would have a lesser degree of ambiguity than conventional health insurance, as the IIFA does not provide the rationale for its decision. But one presumes that it may have to do with the not-for-profit status of these health centers issuing such insurance contracts. The reason for this assumption is that the IIFA stipulates conditions for the validity of such insurance policies, and in one of these conditions, it says that the health center may only charge the recipient for services that were actually rendered and not for presumed services as is the case with private (conventional) insurance companies.[143] Although it does not explain the exact workings of their legitimated insurance policy, it may be surmised from the stated condition that the insurance contract would use the premium toward setting up some sort of declining balance for the insured that the insured party would use as needed, with the unused balance eventually being returned to the insured. Hence, the level of uncertainty (*gharar*) of the exchange in this contract is negligible.

[142] See Ibn Rushd's *The Distinguished Jurist's Primer*, trans. Nyazee, v. 2, 179 for discussion of the criteria for sale contracts that contain *gharar* (uncertainty) and the illegitimacy of such contracts.

[143] See Resolution 149 (16/7) on Health Insurance: www.fiqhacademy.org.sa/qrarat/16-7.htm accessed February 20, 2014.

Yet there are more pronounced reasons, which are relevant to the issue of *maṣlaḥa* (public interest), for why such insurance contracts would be legitimate for the IIFA. According to the resolution, the need for health insurance has become necessary for the preservation of life, mind, and progeny, which are fundamental aims that Islamic law seeks to sustain.[144] This rationalization for the legitimacy of health insurance is interesting because it is directly linked to the foundational legal principles (*maqāṣid*) of the Sharīʿa: the preservation of life, religion, mind, progeny, and wealth. It is based on these fundamental principles that *maṣlaḥa*, or public interest, is determined.[145] Hence, the IIFA, in invoking these principles in their rationale, essentially appealed to an argument of public interest (*maṣlaḥa*) when legitimating this restricted form of health insurance (see Figure 22).

Furthermore, Resolution 181 on endowing shares, which was discussed in the previous section, also refers to the aims (*maqāṣid*) of Sharīʿa when arguing for the legality of these types of endowments. In the same resolution, it also refers to the criteria of *maṣlaḥa* when stipulating the conditions for when the supervisor of these endowed shares may engage in a transaction with these shares so as to preserve a preponderant public interest (*maṣlaḥa rajiha*) for the endowment[146] (see Figure 22).

All of these cases give an indication that when classical (discursive and hermeneutical authority) legal considerations are not a factor in establishing the rule or when then classical rulings do not meet contemporary circumstances, the IIFA resorts to more open-ended rational considerations of *maṣlaḥa* (public interest or common good) or *ʿurf* (customary practice) in its fatwas. So, its mode of legal rationalization seems to give quite a bit of prominence to these concepts in ways that were not so explicit in the rationalizations of past rulings of Islamic law. Even though concepts like *maṣlaḥa* and *ʿurf* were classically formulated authoritative legal methodologies and even as they constituted the implicit basis for much of classical Islamic legal rulings, explicit appeal to them in the past legal rationale was far more limited in scope than the way they have been appealed to in the fatwas of the IIFA. This may be a new development in the manner of post-colonial Islamic legal reasoning.

144 See Resolution 149 (16/7) on Health Insurance: www.fiqhacademy.org.sa/qrarat/16-7.htm accessed February 20, 2014.

145 See IIFA Resolution 141 on Maṣlaḥa for the connection between *maṣlaḥa* and the aims (*maqāṣid*) of the Sharīʿa: www.fiqhacademy.org.saqrarat15-7.htm.pdf accessed January 28, 2014.

146 Resolution 181 (19/7) "Endowing shares, sukūk, material rights and benefits," www.fiqhacademy.org.sa, nineteenth session, accessed Febuary18, 2014.

Types of legal rationale manifested in IIFA fatwas		
Case	**Fatwa**	**Legal significance/reasoning**
Should *maṣlaḥa* and *ʿurf* be given greater consideration in formulating fatwas?	**Resolution 47** and **Resolution 141:** *Maṣlaḥa* and *ʿurf* should be given greater consideration in contemporary fatwas	- Loosens the hold of classical legal doctrines on the formulations of fatwa - Allows for alternative forms of legal reasoning in the formulation of fatwa
Are abstract rights (*al-ḥuqūq al-maʿnawiyya*) like copyrights and trademarks legitimate properties that deserve legal protection?	**Resolution 43:** Abstract rights are the specific rights of the owner	- Abstract rights were not considered properties that were explicitly protected in classical Islamic law - Yet, contemporary *ʿurf* (customary practice) has given such properties a monetary value that should be protected by the law
Is health insurance (*al-taʾmīn al-ṣiḥḥī*) an Islamically legitimate business transaction?	**Resolution 149:** Health insurance policies issued by health centers are legitimate	- The uncertainty (*gharar*) in these policies is too small to be considered a violation of the norms of Islamic business contracts - *Maṣlaḥa* (public interest) dictates that health insurance these days is a necessity to preserve the fundamental aims of life (*maqāṣid al-Sharīʿa*) in Islamic law

FIGURE 22 Fatwa in the era of the post-colonial Muslim global institutions II: types of legal rationale manifested in IIFA fatwas

PRELIMINARY CONCLUSIONS ABOUT POST-COLONIAL FATWAS

In his study on the development of the Ḥanafī *madhhab*, Brannon Wheeler asserts that in the post-classical period, future scholarship in the Ḥanafī school was only authoritative if it could demonstrate that its "conclusions were consistent with the conclusions of the previous generation of scholarship."[147] This statement can be taken more broadly to mean that its conclusions are consistent in principle with the previous conclusions and not necessarily exact in content as in applying the same legal and

[147] Wheeler, 228.

interpretive principles of previous generations of jurists. This statement perhaps can be generalized to all the classical legal schools of Islam.

But if this is how Islamic jurisprudence was conducted in the pre-colonial period, how could we describe this jurisprudence in the post-colonial era as represented in fatwas issued by the OIC's IIFA and the fatwas of officials of post-colonial Muslim nation-states? With regard to this, two observations are made as to the character of post-colonial fatwas: First, it is a kind of historical jurisprudence in that it takes established legal norms and rulings as a reference point for its own rulings; second, it is a sort of hybrid jurisprudence in that it is not merely an extension of those historically established legal norms and rulings, but it is a product of a new legal rationale that is addressing novel sociohistorical conditions.

As for the historical nature of the post-colonial fatwa, IIFA fatwas seem to assume a body of Islamic legal doctrine and principles that are the launching point for its own contemporary fatwas. For example, in the fatwas (Resolution 147)[148] concerning the trade of international commodities and conditions that govern that trade (al-Asʾila al-Dawliyya wa-Ḍawābiṭ al-Taʿāmul Fīhā), it draws several scenarios on how this trade can take place, and then they pronounce their judgment with respect to each case. In each case, the IIFA makes reference in its rulings to already established legal rulings that legitimate its own position. For instance, when it describes the first two types of transactions where both the commodity and its payment are exchanged on the spot (or what is effectively on the spot as guaranteed by the marketplace), it declares that these transactions are legal in accordance with "the known conditions for sales."[149] The language "known conditions" indicates that there are previously established rules to which it is referring and an indication that its judgments are taking place with clear reference to these established legal norms.

As for the hybrid character of the post-colonial fatwa, it has been shown how the IIFA's fatwas often employ more context-driven legal rationales such as *maṣlaḥa* and *ʿurf* in the legitimation of its fatwas and rely less on previously established authoritative doctrines of particular Islamic legal schools. Yet its fatwas do not strictly rely on legal concepts and methodologies like *maṣlaḥa* (public interest) or new deductions from scriptural (Quran and *ḥadīth*) proof texts, but are anchored in a set of formerly

148 See www.fiqhacademy.org.sa/qrarat/16-5.htm accessed March 25, 2014.

149 Resolution 147 (16/5) "International Commodities and the Conditions of their Transactions." www.fiqhacademy.org.sa/qrarat/16-5.htm accessed February 20, 2014.

agreed-upon legal norms and principles that must be reapplied and reinterpreted to meet the demands of new realities facing Islamic law. In this reapplication, fresh legal methodologies and approaches such as *maṣlaḥa* and *ʿurf* are being employed more overtly and frequently than may have been the case in the past. Hence, the legal products (fatwas) are not entirely new, nor are they a rehash of legal doctrines of the past. Thus, what we end up with is a product that is marked by hybridity in various ways.

But what does this characterization of the post-colonial fatwa tell us about the impact of the call for a new *ijtihād* (legal reform through new legal reasoning) made by modern Muslim reformers? The IIFA's fatwas, as prototypical post-colonial fatwas, neither meet the overhaul of Islamic law that was demanded by some reformers like Rashid Riḍā nor are they a continuation of the Islamic jurisprudence of old. This is because IIFA fatwas are not attempting to derive new legal norms from the scriptural sources of the law through the use of novel hermeneutical techniques as demanded by those reformers, nor does it stick to the pre-established legal positions as demanded by traditionalist *muftīs*. Instead, the IIFA's fatwas and those of the *muftīs* of post-colonial Muslim nation-states display sufficient innovation in legal rulings and application of legal rationale that render its judgments as constituting a new *ijtihad*. But at the same time, they display enough conservatism and consistency with pre-established legal norms that lend a sense of continuity of character to their jurisprudence; herein lies the hybrid nature of the post-colonial fatwa.

Judging from this, one may assert that the Muslim encounter with the colonial and neocolonial Western global order seems to have made an impact on Muslim legal discourse that, while not totally effacing the legal tradition, has created a discursive shift in both the substance and the form of Islamic legal discourse. What this says is that Islamic law continues to evolve in response to constantly changing historical conditions even as the pace of change in the contemporary period requires novel applications of established rules to deal with that change. Despite the disruptive nature of historical change that has swept the Muslim world over the last two centuries, the evolution of Islamic law remains anchored in a set of legal principles that are both historically established and remarkably adaptive to the realities that confront it. Such shifts in Islam's legal discourse do not cause it to lose its authentic Islamic character.

Conclusion

This study has retold the history of Islamic law from the perspective of one of its practices, *iftāʾ*, or the art of issuing fatwas. This was possible because fatwas can be seen as the fundamental building blocks from which the law was constructed, and having this unique position, they are capable of telling us a lot about the development of Islamic law. This is because, even though the whole is more than the sum of its parts, the constituent elements that make up the whole still have bearing on its character. It is with this in mind that I have adopted this approach to the study of Islamic law.

This study has shown how fatwas contributed to the formation and transformation of an Islamic legal discourse and tradition. This is because this discourse and tradition in some respects arose organically out of resolutions to Muslim problems, and these resolutions often took the form of fatwas. This was not the only constituent that made up the discourse and tradition, yet it played a very instrumental role. Out of the materials of fatwas, particular forms of legal rationale emerged that would go on to constitute the legal discourse of Islamic legal theory. In addition to this, Islamic legal doctrines were informed by fatwas, which went on to become the basis of these doctrines. Some of the legal authorities who uttered these fatwas came to occupy a special place in Islamic history, so much so that legal institutions, *madhhab*s, became identified with them. All of these components, which have their discursive origins in the fatwa, went into making a peculiar Islamic legal tradition that shaped subsequent legal practice.

Yet fatwas were not simply instrumental in shaping Muslim law, but they also played a pivotal role in representing and shaping Muslim society. This was so because of the very nature of fatwas. Fatwas are both discursive and dialogical engagements between the Muslim public and its religious specialists, and these characteristics are important for social change. They are discursive engagements in the sense that fatwas are statements that instruct their audience on proper religious and social practice and dialogical engagements because they are social exchanges between the public and the religious elite. In this way, fatwas functioned as indicators of prevailing social attitudes because they often reflected what was being debated at any given time. But more importantly, fatwas facilitated social transformation by legitimating new practices that brought about change.

These features of a fatwa were displayed repeatedly in various periods of Muslim history covered in this study. Time and time again, the Muslim public reached out to religious specialists to seek guidance for various new challenges that confronted it, and the way that these religious specialists often addressed these concerns was through the agency of fatwas. Fatwas were used either to condone or condemn certain actions or positions, and in doing so, they facilitated change in some directions and hindered change in other directions. So, in this way, fatwas were the instrument that allowed Islamic law to keep its flexibility in the face of changing circumstances.

Yet throughout all the various periods of transformations within Islamic law, it always maintained an essential identity of being a discursive legal tradition because it was grounded in the fundamental and normative discourses of the Quran and the early traditions. No matter what form Islamic law took in the various stages of its evolution, it was always positioned with respect to these discourses. This is exemplified by the fact that even the quintessential Islamic legal practice of fatwa had its discursive origins in the Quran. In fact, fatwas were attempts at extending the reach of those Quranic norms in history. This is still very much the case today, when modern Islamic legal discourse still draws its authenticity from newer interpretations of Quranic norms.

Yet despite this stability in the Islamic legal tradition, the Islamic legal discourse seems to be undergoing a discursive shift. Changes in the legal methodologies employed in contemporary jurisprudence, such as the greater frequency of evoking *maṣlaḥa*, constitute a shift in Islamic legal discourse toward a contextually based methodology of jurisprudence that moves away from the textually dominated discourse and precedent-oriented justifications in pre-colonial times. That is because the employment of legal tools such as *maṣlaḥa* as legal rationale represents a mode of legal production that gives greater consideration to social utility and context; while previously jurists had greater reliance on tools like *qiyās* that sought to bind the law more tightly to the sacred text.

My brief analysis of contemporary fatwas shows that *maṣlaḥa* and *ʿurf* have come into greater prominence as tools in evaluating contemporary legal concerns and in the issuance of fatwas. This approach has its advantages in that it allows a lot of room for social context to play a larger role when considering legal issues. This larger role for a context-driven methodology has legal implications in that it takes place at the expense of the more text-based legal hermeneutics of the authoritative discourses. In this case, fatwas become less a function of direct deductions from legal textual sources, such as the Quran and *ḥadīth*, and more a function of social circumstances.

Yet what remains to be seen is whether this contemporary trend among some Muslim thinkers and jurists toward these contextually oriented legal devices represents a lasting shift away from the traditionally textually oriented legal methodology that will change the orientation of the Islamic legal tradition or whether it is a passing phenomenon that will not have a lasting impact. This question can only be answered with further research and reflection.

However, this apparent shift in the legal discourse, in my assessment, has not as of yet changed the fundamental character of the Islamic legal tradition. It remains very much tied to its discursive roots of the Quran and *ḥadīth* as the fundamental source of values and starting point for this tradition. This quality of the Islamic legal tradition remains stable even amid the calls for change in more recent times. For example, Muslim reformists like Riḍā never question the authority of these sacred scriptures even when they called into question the traditional interpretations of them. Moreover, the contemporary fatwas of the IIFA and the fatwas of other *muftī*s showcased here show that they are enunciated very much in conversation with the traditionally established hermeneutical authority of that discursive tradition even when they do not always come to the same legal conclusions as the previously recognized legal doctrines.

This constancy is an indication of the durability of this discursive legal tradition despite the tremendous challenges that Muslim societies and institutions have faced in the past two hundred years as a result of the drastic restructuring of the global order. Whether this tradition continues to survive remains to be seen, yet its survival depends on its ability to adopt and adapt newer modes of reasoning and discursive practices that are in consonance with its character and help maintain its vibrancy under ever-changing circumstances. This is what the debates in Muslim societies over the past century and a half have been about: when and how does one adopt new ideas and practices in ways that do not alter a tradition's core identity. As far as the Islamic legal tradition is concerned, if its fatwas are any indication, the tradition's core identity remains intact despite the shifts in focus within it. This underlines the adaptability of this tradition to changing circumstances and how fatwas play a fundamental role in this process.

Glossary

***adab al-fatwā*:** the protocols by which a proper fatwa should be issued.

***ahl al-ḥadīth*:** "Advocates of *ḥadīth*." A scholarly movement in the second century of Islam that advocated sole reliance on *ḥadīth* for the derivation of Islamic legal rulings with little recourse to legal opinion or reason.

***ahl al-raʾy*:** "Advocates of *raʾy*." A scholarly movement in the second century of Islam that advocated reliance on rational and pragmatic considerations (i.e., *raʾy*) for the derivation of Islamic legal rulings along with recourse to *ḥadīth*.

Akhbārīs: "Advocates of *akhbār* (authoritative traditions)." A Twelver Shīʿī movement whose prominence was during the sixteenth–eighteenth century that sought to make reports from the Shīʿī Imams the sole source of Shīʿī law. They opposed the Uṣūlīs. Comparable to the earlier Sunnī *ahl al-ḥadīth* movement.

***al-faqīh al-mustaqill bi madhhab imāmihi*:** an independent jurist who can make legal deductions utilizing his own legal school's principles and doctrines.

***al-Hidāya*:** an authoritative Ḥanafī legal compendium.

***al-ḥuqūq al-maʿnawiyya*:** abstract rights such as copyrights, patents, and trademarks.

al-Sawād: the fertile area in Iraq that was designated as the first *kharāj* land by the conquering Muslim state in the seventh century CE.

***al-siyāsa al-sharʿiyya*:** moral diplomacy or ethically legitimated political action.

***al-taʾmīn al-ṣiḥḥī*:** health insurance.

asbāb al-nuzūl: the occasions of revelation. Reports that shed light on the historical circumstances that accompanied the revelation of certain Quranic verses.

aṣl: in the context of law, a principle that is seen as the source or foundation for law.

athar (pl. ***āthār***): a report about the religious opinions and practices of the early generation of Muslims that was deemed authoritative for determining Muslim doctrine or religious practice.

awlā: having more priority.

āyatullāh ("Ayatollah"): the highest title given to a scholar within Twelver Shiite Islam. A high-level jurist (*mujtahid*) within Twelver Shiism.

dalālāt al-lafẓ: legal significations of a scriptural term.

dihqans: landlords in the late Sassanian Empire.

dīwān: a record of government public expenditures.

faqīh: a person learned in Islamic law.

fatwā: any statement, oral or written, that establishes the legitimacy or lack thereof of an action or position and is pronounced by someone who is vested with legal authority whether the origins of that authority lay in political institutions or the religious and social sphere.

fayʾ: a type of spoils that are acquired without armed conflict that is withheld by the Muslim state to be utilized for the public's interest.

fī maʿnā al-manṣūṣ: a legal position that is not directly found in the legal doctrine yet is directly implied by it.

fiqh: authoritative Islamic legal rulings that make up the content of Islamic law. A product of a distillation process of previous fatwas.

ghanīma: a type of spoil taken after an armed conflict that is distributed to the participants in the battle.

gharar: a level of uncertainty in social or economic contracts/transactions that can lead to disputes.

ghayr manṣūṣ: a legal position that is not found in the legal doctrine or legal source texts (Quran and *ḥadīth*).

ḥadīth: reports that convey the Prophet Muḥammad's sayings or actions.

ḥalāl: Islamically lawful or allowed.

ḥamalet al-ʿilm: Bearers of Knowledge. An Ibāḍī designation to those scholars who were deemed authoritative to define their distinct school of law and theology.

ḥarām: Islamically unlawful or prohibited.

ḥukm (pl. ***aḥkām***): a legal ruling.

ʿibādāt: a legal category denoting matters of ritualistic worship (e.g., prayer, reading the Quran, fasting, etc.).

Ibāḍīism: A little known third sect of Islam that arose from the events of first Muslim civil war in the first/seventh century. Developed its distinct school of law whose legal doctrine was centered around the legal opinions of a select group of first-/seventh- and second-/eighth-century Baṣran jurists.

***iftāʾ*:** the practice of issuing a fatwa. Sometimes designated as *futyā*.

***iḥtiyāt*:** taking precaution or exercising scrupulousness in legal rulings usually by adopting the more demanding position.

***ijmāʿ*:** a binding consensus of Muslim scholars (jurists) on an issue. The third source of Islamic law in Sunnī Islam after the Quran and *sunna*.

***ijtihād*:** An act of independent legal reasoning used to arrive at a legal resolution for a case.

***ʿilla*:** ratio legis. The legal cause that substantiates a legal ruling.

***istiftāʾ*:** the process of requesting a fatwa.

***istiḥsān*:** juristic preference for a legal ruling even though it may run counter to a scripturally or analogically derived ruling. It is operationalized to counter a ruling derived by *qiyās* because of the jurist's perception that ruling leads to unfavorable consequences. A legal device used primarily in the Ḥanafī school's legal methodology.

***istiṣḥāb*:** continuity of a legal ruling where the original ruling is maintained until some factor requires for that ruling to change.

***istiṣlāḥ*:** the process of choosing a legal position based on public interest or considerations of the common good.

***jalb al-maṣlaḥa wa darʾ al-mafsada*:** "to promote the common good and deter corruption." Muslim jurists affirm this foundational principle as underlying all Islamic rulings.

***junub*:** being in a state of greater ritual impurity caused by the emission of semen.

***khabar aḥad*:** a historical report that is narrated with a chain of transmission that is not recurrent (see *mutawātir*).

***kharāj*:** a land tax levied on the occupants of state-owned farmland (*see also* al-Sawād).

***madhhab* (pl. *madhāhib*):** a legal school consisting of a voluntary association of Muslim jurists who adhere to and cultivate the legal doctrine and ideas of an early jurist whose opinions were viewed as authoritative.

***maʿnā*:** a term used by al-Shāfiʿī to denote the legal attribute that linked two legal cases together analogically making the ruling for the original case the ruling for the other. A precursor to *ʿilla*.

maqāṣid al-Sharīʿa: the religious and social aims that Islamic law purports to achieve.

marjiʿal-taqlīd: a Twelver (Imāmī) Shīʿi juridical institution that developed in the nineteenth century as a way organizing the religious practice of the Shiite laity around the religio-legal pronouncements of recognized Twelver Shīʿi jurists designated as a *marjiʿ*. This level of jurist would be akin to the *mujtahid fī al-madhhab* (independent jurist within the school) category within the Sunnī juristic hierarchy.

marjūḥ: a subordinate or inferior legal ruling in a legal school/doctrine.

masālik al-aqyisa: approaches to legal reasoning.

maṣlaḥa: considerations of public interest that go into formulating a legal ruling. One of the precepts of Islamic legal theory.

muʿāmalāt: a legal category denoting matters of human transactions (e.g., buying, selling, marriage, divorce, etc.)

muḍāraba: investment partnership in which one party acts as a venture capitalist and the other party acts as a manager of the investment capital.

muftī: a jurist-consult who has the authority to issue fatwas.

mujtahid muṭlaq: a master jurist who has the authority to establish his own legal doctrine.

mujtahid: a jurist who has the capacity for independent legal reasoning to derive Islamic law from its sources.

mujtahidūn fī al-masāʾil: dependent jurists who can make legal deductions about particular issues within the rules of a legal school.

muqallid: someone who follows the jurisprudence of a jurist (*mujtahid*).

murajjiḥ: a legal scholar who determines a preponderant legal ruling within a legal school/doctrine.

mustaftī: one who seeks a fatwa.

mutamayyizūn: those who excel in extracting the preponderant legal rulings of a legal doctrine

mutawātir: a report that is transmitted recurrently.

naṣṣ: authoritative legal text (Quran and *ḥadīth*) used to derive legal rulings.

nawādir: rare legal rulings.

qaḍāʾ: juridical decision made by a judge (*qāḍī*)

qarār: resolution

qāṭiʿ: definitive or certain (in reference to knowledge) (opposite to *ẓannī*).

qawāʿid: principles (of law)

qiyās: legal analogy. Analogical reasoning in which the ruling of one case that is established by scriptural writ or consensus applies to another case based on a common attribute (*ʿilla*). A foundational legal concept in Islamic legal theory.

raʾy: deriving Islamic law based on rational and pragmatic rather than scriptural considerations.

rājiḥ: preponderant legal position in a legal school or doctrine.

ribā al-faḍl: a type of usury in which there is an increase in one of the commodities exchanged.

ribā al-nasīʾa: a type of usury in which there is a delay in one of the commodities exchanged.

ribā: usury.

sadd al-dharīʾah: "blocking the pathways to harm." This legal principle implies that some act may be legal in its own right, but if it leads to something unlawful, then it too is considered unlawful. This legal device is distinctly applied by the Mālikī school.

***sakk* (pl. *sukūk*)**: an Islamic stock.

salaf: ancestors. A designation for the first few generations of Muslims who are seen to have represented an ideal Islam.

Sharīʿa: the articulation of divine law as an expression of God's will for humanity.

***shaykh al-islām* (*şeyhülislam*)**: the grand muftī in the Ottoman Empire and highest religious authority.

***sunna* (pl. *sunan*)**: the established practice of authoritative persons, which initially designated the practices of the early generations of Muslims. Later, utilized to signify the established practices of the Prophet Muḥammad.

taʿdiyat al-ḥukm: transmission of an established ruling to a new case.

taḥrīr: editing a fatwa for the purpose of including its content in legal doctrine.

tajrīd: the process of stripping a fatwa of its superfluous elements so that its core ruling may be included in legal doctrine.

takhrīj: extracting the preponderant legal ruling of a legal doctrine that is consistent with the established legal principles that govern that particular legal school.

takhṣīṣ al-ʿilla: particularizing the ratio legis. Narrowing the scope of the legal cause that substantiates the legal ruling.

talfīq: indiscriminately constructing a legal doctrine from the existing rulings of the various schools.

talkhīṣ: summarizing the content of a fatwa in order to extract its most essential elements that should be included in formulating Islamic laws.

***taqlīd*:** the process of following the legal rulings of a legal school or *mujtahid*.

***taqrīr*:** affirming the validity of the ruling of a fatwa so that the ruling can be included in legal doctrine.

***tayammum*:** alternative ritual purification.

***ʿulamāʾ* (sing. *ʿālim*):** scholars, especially in relation to the religious sciences.

***ʿurf*:** customary practice.

***uṣūl al-fiqh*:** Islamic legal theory and methodology of jurisprudence.

Uṣūlīs: a Twelver Shīʿī movement rising to prominence in the sixteenth century that sought to base Shīʿī law on rational as well as traditional considerations. They opposed the Akhbārīs.

***waqf* (pl. *awqāf*):** an endowment of property that is used for the benefit of the public.

Vilāyat-i-Faqīh: The novel Shīʿī political doctrine developed by Ayatollah Khomeini in the 1970s that asserted that the right to politically rule over society belonged to Muslim jurists. It is the current system of governance in the Islamic Republic of Iran since the Iranian Revolution in 1979.

***yasʾalūnaka*:** "they ask you about…" One of two Quranic phrases used as a literary device to foreshadow several Quranic fatwa proclamations that encouraged the activity of fatwa seeking.

***yastaftūnaka*:** "they seek your advice…" The other Quranic phrase used as a literary device to foreshadow several Quranic fatwa proclamations that encouraged the activity of fatwa seeking.

***ẓāhir al-riwāya*:** the preponderant ruling within the Ḥanafī school.

***zakāh*:** alms tax that is levied on every capable Muslim and is the third pillar of Islam.

***ẓannī*:** speculative, non-definitive, or probable knowledge (opp. of *qāṭiʿ*).

Bibliography

ʿAbd al-ʿAzīz, Shah. *Fatawa ʿAzīzī*. Karachi: H.M. Saeed Company, 1987.

Abū Ghānim, Bishr Ibn Ghānim al-Khursāni. *Al-Mudawanna al-Kubrā*. Vol. 3, edited by Bājū, Muṣṭafā ibn Ṣalāḥ. Musqaṭ: Wizārat al-Turāth wa al-Thaqāfa, 2007.

Abu Nasr, Jamil M. *A History of the Maghrib in the Islamic Period*. New York: Cambridge University Press, 1987.

Abū Yūsuf, Ya'coub Ibn Ibrāhīm. *Kitāb al-Kharāj*. Beirut, Lebanon: Dar al-Ma'rifah, 1979.

Abū Zahra, Muḥammad. *Tarikh Al-Madhahib Al-Islamiah Fi l-Siyasah Wa Al-Aqa'Id Wa Tarikh Al-Madhahib Al-Fiqhhiyyah*. Cairo, Egypt: Dar al-Fikr al-Arabi, ND.

Ahsan, Abdullah. *Ummah or Nation? Identity Crisis in Contemporary Muslim Society*. Leicester, UK: The Islamic Foundation, 1992.

Ahsan, Abdullah. *The Organization of the Islamic Conference: An Introduction to Islamic Political Institution*. Herndon, VA: The International Institute of Islamic Thought, 1988.

Al-Aghbarī, Ismā'īl ibn Ṣāliḥ. *Al-Ibāḍiyya Bayānu Ḥirāsat al-Dīn wa-Siyāsat al-Dunyā*. Musqaṭ: Wizārat al-Thaqāfa wa al-shu'ūn al-dīniyya, 2013.

al-Amali, Zayn al-Dīn Ibn Ali (Al-Shahīd al-Thānī). *Munyat Al-Murid Fi Adab Al-Mufid Wa Al-Mustafid*, edited by Al-Mukhtāri, Riḍā. Shia Online Library, 1409 AH. Maktab al-'Alam al-Islami. Accessed at: Shia Library Online in June 2012 at the following link www.shiaonlinelibrary.com.

al-Ḥimsī, Līna. *Tārīkh al-Fatwa fi al-Islām: wa Aḥkāmuha al-Sharʿiyya*. Damascus, Syria: Dar ar-Rashīd, 1996.

al-Juwaynī, Abū al-Maʿālī. *Qiyath Al-Umam Fi Al-Tiyath Al-Dhulam*, edited by Abdul-Mun'im, Fu'ad and Mustafa Hilmi. Alexandria, Egypt: Dar Al-Da'wah, ND.

al-Karakī, Al-Muhaqiq. Al-Kharjiyyat. 1992CE–1413 AH. Mu'assassat Al-Nashr Al-Islami, 1413 AH. Downloaded from Shia Online Library (www .shiaonlinelibrary.com/) November, 2013.

al-Khalīlī, Aḥmad. Bayān Āthār al-Ijtihād wa al-Tajdīd fī Tanmiyyat al-Mujtama'āt al- Islāmiyya. Ministry of Endowments and Religious Affairs. Muscat, Oman, 2010.

al-Kharusi, Kahlan al-. Āthār Al-Rabī' b. Habīb: Edition and Study. First Edition. Harrassowitz Verlag, 2016. https://doi.org/10.2307/j.ctvckq4k5. Downloaded from JSTORE: April 12, 2022.
al-Kharusi, Kahlan. Interview. Muscat: Ministry of Endowments and Religious Affairs, August 13, 2015.
al-Khidhri, Muḥammad. *Tarikh Al-Tashri' Al-Islami*. Second Edition. Beriut Lebnon, 1997. Dar Al-Qalam
Al-Kindī, Ibrāhīm. *Al-Ḥukm al-Shar'i fī al-Mīzān al-Uṣūlī*. Damascus: Dār Qutaybah, 2000.
Al-Kūfī, Muḥammad ibn Sulaymān. *Kitāb al-Muntakhab*. Sana: Dar Al-Hikmah al-Yemaniyyah, 1993.
al-Nawawī, Abū Zakariya Yaḥya ibn Sharaf. *Adab al-Fatwa Wa Al-Muftī Wa Al-Mustaftī*. Damascus, Syria: Dar Al-Fikr, 1988.
al-Salimi, Abdulrahman. The Transformation of Religious Learning in Oman: Tradition and Modernity. *Journal of the Royal Asiatic Society* 21 2 (April 2011): 147–157.
al-Sāyis, Muḥammad 'Alī. *Tafsīr āyāt al-Aḥkām*, edited by Al-Subki, Abdul Latief, Muḥammad Ibrāhīm Karsun. Beirut, Lebanon: Dar Ibn Katheer, 1996.
al-Sāyis, Muḥammad 'Alī. *Tarikh al-Fiqh Al-Islami*. Beirut, Dar al-Fikr. ND:
al-Shāfi'ī, Muḥammad Ibn Idris. *Kitāb al-Umm V.4*. Cairo, Egypt: Dar Al-Wafa', 2004.
al-Shāfi'ī, Muḥammad Ibn Idris. *Al-Risāla fī Usul al-Fiqh: Treatise on the Foundation of Islamic Jurisprudence*. Translated by Khadduri, Majid. Second Edition. Cambridge, UK: Islamic Text Society, 1987.
al-Shamela Library Software (Version 3.61). Downloaded from: www.shamela.ws.
al-Shaybānī, Muḥammad Ibn Al-Ḥasan. *Kitāb al-Āthār*, edited by Al-Mansouri, Aḥmed 'Isa. First Edition. Vol. 1–2. Cairo, Egypt: Dar Al-Salaam, 2006.
al-Shaybānī, Muḥammad Ibn Al-Ḥasan. *Kitāb al-Ḥujjah 'Ala Ahl Al-Madinah*, edited by al-Kaylani, Mahdi Ḥasan. Third Edition. Beirut, Lebanon: 'Alam Al-Kitāb, 1983.
Al-Shaybānī, Ṭāriq Sāsī. *Al-Ibāḍiyya Uṣūluhā wa A'lāmuhā wa Atharuhā fī al Taqrīb Bayn al-Madhāhib al-Islāmiyya*. Ribāṭ: Al Munaẓẓama al-Islamiyya li'l-Taribiyya wa al-'Ulūm wa al-Thaqāfa, 2013.
al-Tilimsānī, 'Ali Ibn Muḥammad. *Takhreej al-Dalalat Al-Sam'iyyah*. Cairo, Egypt: Al-Majlis Al-'A'ala Lil-Shou'oun Al-Islamiyyah, 1995.
al-Tirmidhi, Muḥammad Ibn Isa. *Jami' Tirmidhi [Al-Jami' Al-Sahih Sunan Al-Tirmidhi]*. Translated by Maulana Fazal Aḥmed and Rafique Abdul Rahman. Vol. 1. Karachi, Pakistan: Darul Ishaat, 2007.
Anjum, Ovamir. "Islam as a Discursive Tradition: Talal Asad and His Interlocutors." *Comparative Studies of South Asia, Africa and Middle East* 27 3 (2007).
Ansari, Zafar Isḥāq. "Islamic Juristic Terminology before S(h)afi'i: A Semantic Analysis with Special Reference to Kufa." *Arabica* 19 3 (1972): 255–300.
Ansari, Zafar Isḥāq. "The Early Development of Islamic Fiqh in Kufah with Special Reference to the Works of Abū Yūsuf and Shaybani." PhD, McGill University, 1966.
Aristotle. *Nicomachean Ethics*. Translated by Robert Bartlett and Susan Collins. Chicago: University of Chicago Press, 2011.

Arjomand, Said Aamir. "The Law, Agency, and Policy in Medieval Islamic Society: Development of the Institutions of Learning from the Tenth to the Fifteenth Century." *Comparative Studies in Society and History* 41 2 (1999): 263–293.

Arjomand, Said Aamir. *The Turban for the Crown: The Islamic Revolution in Iran*. New York: Oxford University Press, 1988.

Arjomand, Said Aamir. *The Shadow of God and the Hidden Imam: Religion, Political Order, and Societal Change in Shiite Iran from the Beginning to 1890*. Chicago, IL: The University of Chicago Press, 1984.

Asad, Talal. *Formations of the Secular: Christianity, Islam, and Modernity*. Stanford, CA: Stanford University Press, 2003.

Asad, Talal. *The Idea of an Anthropology of Islam*. Washington, DC: Center for Contemporary Arab Studies, 1986.

Auda, Jasser. *Maqāṣid Al-Sharīʿa: A Beginner's Guide*. London, UK: The International Institute of Islamic Thought, 2008.

Awass, Omer. "Fatwa, Discursivity, and the Art of Ethical Embedding." *Journal of the American Academy of Religion* 87 3 (September 2019): 765–790.

Balogun, Isma'il A. B. "The Life and Work of the Mujaddid of West Africa, 'Uthmān B. Fūdī Popularly Known as Usumanu Ḍan Fodio." *Islamic Studies* 12 4 (1973): 271–292.

Berkey, Jonathan. *The Formation of Islam: Religion and Society in the Near East 600–1800*. Cambridge, UK: Cambridge University Press, 2003.

Berman, Harold J. "Toward an Integrative Jurisprudence: Politics, Morality, History." *California Law Review* 76 4 (1988): 779–801.

Bernand, M. "Kiyas." In *The Encyclopedia of Islam: Volume V*, edited by Bosworth, C. E., E. Van Donzel, B. Lewis and C. H. Pellat, 238–242. Leiden: Brill, 1986.

Bonney, Richard. *Jihad: From Quran to Bin Laden*. New York: Palgrave-McMillan, 2004.

Bove, Paul. "Discourse." In *Critical Terms for Literary Study*, edited by Lentricchia, Frank and Thomas McLaughlin, 50. Chicago, IL: University of Chicago Press, 1990.

Bromley, Simon. "'The State System in the Middle East: Origins, Development, and Prospects'." *Blackwell Reference Online*, edited by Youssef M Choueiri. Blackwell Publishing, 2005. Accessed April 28, 2009. www.blackwellreference.com/subscriber/tocnode?id=g9781405106818_chunk_g9781405106818 31.

Burak, Guy. *The Second Formation of Islamic Law: The Hanafi School in the Early Modern Ottoman Empire*. New York: Cambridge University Press, 2015.

Chase, Edward. "Law and Theology." In *A Companion to Philosophy of Law and Legal Theory*, edited by Patterson, Dennis. Blackwell Publishing, 1999. Blackwell Reference Online. March 24, 2008.

Cizakca, Murat. *A History of Philanthropic Foundations: The Islamic World from the Seventh Century to the Present*. Istanbul, Turkey: Bogazici University Press, 2000.

Cizakca, Murat. *A Comparative Evolution of Business Partnership*. New York: Brill, 1996.

Cohen, Hayyim J. "The Economic Background and the Secular Occupations of Muslim Jurisprudents and Traditionist in the Classical Period of Islam." *Journal of the Economic and Social History of the Orient* 13 1 (1970).
Cook, Michael. *Commanding Right and Forbidding Wrong in Islam*. New York: Cambridge Univesity Press, 2000.
Dan Fodio, 'Uthmān. *Mukhtārāt min Mu'allafāt 'Uthmān Dan Fodio*. Samaru: Iqra'ah Publishing House, ND.
Dennet, Daniel. *Conversion and Poll Tax in Early Islam*. Delhi: Idarah-I Adabyat-I Delli, 1950.
Djait, Hichem. "Al-Kufa." In *The Encyclopedia of Islam: Volume V*, edited by Bosworth, C. E., E. Van Donzel, B. Lewis and C. H. Pellat, 345–351. Leiden: Brill, 1986.
Dutton, Yasin. *The Origins of Islamic Law: The Quran, the Muwaṭṭa, and Madinan Amal*. Surrey, UK: Curzon Press, 1999.
El Masri, Fathi Hasan. *A Critical Edition of Dan Fodio's Bavan wuiub al-hiijra 'ala l-'ibad*. Oxford: Oxford University Press, 1978.
El Shamsy, Aḥmed. *The Canonization of Islamic Law: A Social and Intellectual History*. New York: Cambridge University Press, 2013.
Ennāmī, 'Amr Khalīfah. *Studies in Ibāḍīsm*. Musqat: Ministry of Endowments and Religious Affairs, ND.
Euben, Roxanne. *Enemy in the Mirror: Islamic Fundamentalism and the Limits of Modern Rationalism*. Princeton, NJ: Princeton University Press, 1999.
Feldman, Noah. *The Fall and Rise of the Islamic State*. Princeton, NJ: Princeton University Press, 2008.
Franscesca, Ersilia. "Ibāḍī Law and Jurisprudence." *The Muslim World* 105 2 (April 2013): 209–223.
Gilbert, Joan E. "Institutionalization of Muslim Scholarship and Professionalization of the Ulama' in Medieval Damascus." *Studia Islamica* 52 (1980): 105–134.
Gran, Peter. *Islamic Roots of Capitalism: Egypt, 1760–1840*. Austin: University of Texas Press, 1979.
Habib, Irfan. *The Agrarian System of Mughal India: 1556–1707*. New York: Asia Publishing House, 1963.
Haidar, Najam. *The Origins of the Shi'a: Identity, Ritual, and Sacred Space in Eighth-Century Kufah*. Cambridge: Cambridge University Press, 2011.
Hallaq, Wael. "Groundwork of the Moral Law: A New Look at the Quran and the Genesis of Sharī'a." *Islamic Law and Society* 16 3–4 (2009): 239–279.
Hallaq, Wael. *Sharī'a: Theory, Practice, Transformations*. New York: Cambridge University Press, 2009.
Hallaq, Wael. *The Origins and Evolution of Islamic Law*. New York: Cambridge University Press, 2005.
Hallaq, Wael. "Juristic Authority Vs. State Power: The Legal Crisis of Modern Islam." *Journal of Law and Religion* 19 2 (2003–2004): 243–258.
Hallaq, Wael. *Authority, Continuity, and Change in Islamic Law*. New York: Cambridge University Press, 2004.
Hallaq, Wael. "From Regional to Personal Schools of Law? A Reevaluation." *Islamic Law and Society* 8 1 (2001): 1–26.

Hallaq, Wael. "The Authenticity of Prophetic Ḥadīth: A Pseudo-Problem." *Studia Islamica* 89 (1999): 75–90.

Hallaq, Wael. "From Fatwa to Furu: Growth and Change in Islamic Substantive Law." *Islamic Law and Society* 1 1 (1994): 29–65.

Hallaq, Wael. "Was al-Shāfiʿī the Master Architect of Islamic Jurisprudence?" *International Journal of Middle East* 25 4 (1993): 587–605.

Hallaq, Wael. "Logic, Formal Arguments and Formalization of Arguments in Sunnī Jurisprudence." *Arabica* 37 3 (1990): 315–358.

Hallaq, Wael. "The Use and Abuse of Evidence: The Question of Provincial and Roman Influences on Early Islamic Law." *Journal of the American Oriental Society* 110 1 (1990): 79–91.

Hallaq, Wael. "Non-Analogical Arguments in Sunnī Juridical Qiyās." *Arabica* 36 3 (1989): 286–306.

Hallaq, Wael. "The Development of Logical Structure in Sunnī Legal Theory." *Islam* 64 (1987): 42–67.

Hallaq, Wael. *A History of Islamic Legal Theories: An Introduction to Sunnī Usul al-fiqh*. New York: Cambridge University Press, 1997.

Hasan, Aḥmed. *Principles of Islamic Jurisprudence: The Command of the Sharīʿa and Juridical Norms*. Islamabad, Pakistan: Islamic Research Institute, 1993.

Hasan, Aḥmed. *The Early Development of Islamic Jurisprudence*. Islamabad, Pakistan: Islamic Research Institute, Islamic University, 1970.

Haykel, Bernard. *Revival and Reform of Islam*. New York, NY: Cambridge University Press, 2003.

Hilli, al-Hasan Ibn Yusuf (Al-Allāma). *Mabadi' Al-Wusul Fi 'Ilm Al-Usul*, edited by Al-Baqaal, 'Abdul Al-Hussein Muḥammad Ibn Ali 1404 AH. Tehran: Maktab al-'Alam al-Islami, 1984 (1404).

Hodgson, Marshall. *Rethinking World History: Essays on Europe, Islam and World History*. New York, NY: Cambridge University Press, 1993.

Hodgson, Marshall. *The Venture of Islam: Conscience and History in a World Civilization*. Vol. I–III. Chicago, IL: University of Chicago Press, 1974.

Hoyland, Robert. *Seeing Islam as Others Saw It: A Survey and Evaluation of Christian, Jewish, Zoroastrian Writings on Early Islam*. Princeton, NJ: The Darwin Press Inc, 1997.

Humphreys, Stephen. *Islamic History: A Framework for Inquiry*. Minneapolis, MN: Bibliotheca Islamica, 1988.

Hunwick, John. *Sharia in the Songhai: The Replies of Al-Maghīlī to the Questions of Askia Al- Hajj Muhammad*. Oxford, UK: Oxford University Press, 1985.

Hussin, Iza. *The Politics of Islamic Law Local Elites, Colonial Authority, and the Making of the Muslim State*. Chicago, IL: University of Chicago Press, 2016.

Ibn ʿābidīn, Muḥammad Ameen. *'Uqud Rusum Al-Muftī*. Lahore, Pakistan: Suhail Academy, 1976.

Ibn Anas, Mālik. *Kitāb Al- Muwaṭṭa'*, edited by Muḥammad Fouad 'Abdul-Baqi. Vol. 1–2. Beirut, Lebanon: Al-Maktabah Al-Thaqafiah, 1988.

Ibn Anas, Mālik. *Al-Muwaṭṭa' [Kitāb Al- Muwaṭṭa']*. Translated by 'Aisha Abdul Rahman at Tarjumana Bewley and Ya'cub Johnson. Norwich, UK: Diwān Press, 1982.

Ibn 'Ashur, Muḥammad Al-Tahir. *Treatise on Maqāṣid Al-Sharī'a*. Translated by Mohamed el-Tahir el-Mesawi. Herndon, VA: International Institute of Islamic Thought, 2006.

Ibn Rushd, Abū Waleed Muḥammad Ibn Aḥmad (Al-Jadd). *Fatāwa Ibn Rushd, V.2*, edited by Al-Talili, Mukhtar Ibn Tahir. Beirut, Lebanon: Dar Al-Qarb Al-Islami, 1987.

Ibn Rushd, Muḥammad Ibn Aḥmed. *The Distinguished Jurist's Primer V.2*. Translated by Nyazee, Imran Ahsan Khān. Reading, UK: Garnet Publishing Limited, 1996.

Ibn Rushd, Muḥammad Ibn Aḥmed. *The Distinguished Jurist's Primer V.1* [Bidayat Al- Mujtahid]. Translated by Nyazee, Imran Ahsan Khān. Reading, UK: Garnett Publishing Limited, 1994.

Ibn Taymiyya, Ṭaqī ad-Dīn Aḥmad. *Muslims under Non-Muslim Rule*. Translated by Michot. Beaverton, OR: Yaḥya Interface Publications, 2010.

Ibn Taymiyya, Ṭaqī ad-Dīn Aḥmad. *Majmu' Fatāwa Ibn Taymiyya, V.28.*, edited by Al-Jazar, 'Amer and Anwar Al-Baz. Saudi Arabia: Majma' al-Mālik Fahd lildiba'ah wa al-Nashr, 2004. www.waqfeya.com/book.php?bid=1747.

Ibn Taymiyya, Ṭaqī ad-Dīn Aḥmad. *Al-Masa'Il Al-Mardiniyyah*, edited by Al-Masri, Khalid ibn Muḥammad Ibn 'Uthman. Amman, Jordan: Dar Al-Flah, ND.

Ibn Taymiyya, Ṭaqī ad-Dīn Aḥmad. *Al-Fatāwa Al-Kubra*, V.3., edited by 'Ata, Muḥammad and Mustafa 'Ata. Beirut, Lebanon: Dar Al-Kutub Al-'Ilmiyyah, 1987. www.waqfeya.com/book.php?bid=775.

Ihsanoglu, Ekmeleddin. *The Islamic World in the New Century: The Organization of the Islamic Conference*. New York, NY: Columbia University Press, 2010.

Imber, Colin. *Ebu's-su'ud*. Stanford, CA: Stanford University Press, 2009.

Inalcik, Halil and Donald Quataert, eds. *An Economic and Social History of the Ottoman Empire, 1300–1914*. New York, NY: Cambridge University Press, 1994.

Islam, Zafarul. "Nature of Landed Property in Mughal India Views of an Eighteenth Century Jurist." *Proceedings of the Indian History Congress*. Indian History Congress. 36 (1975): 301–309.

Issawi, Charles. *An Economic History of the Middle East and North Africa*. New York, NY: Columbia University Press, 1982

Kaptein, Nico. "The Voices of the Ulema: Fatwas and Religious Authority in Indonesia." *Archives de sciences sociales des religions* 125 (janvier–mars 2004): 115–130. file:///Users/omerawass/Downloads/assr-1038.pdf

Katouzian, Homa. *The Political Economy of Modern Iran: Despotism and Pseudo-Modernism 1926–1979*. London, UK: McMillan Press LTD, 1981.

Kearney, Richard. *Twentieth-Century Philosophy. Routledge History of Philosophy*, edited by Richard Kearney. Vol. VIII. London, UK: Routledge, 1994.

Keddie, Nikki R. *Roots of Evolution: An Interpretive History of Modern Iran*. Binghamton, NY: Yale University Press, 1981.

Khān, Qāḍī. *Al-Fatāwa Al-Hindiyya, V.1. (Printed on margins of Al-Fatāwa Al-Hindiyyah by Shaikh Nizam)*. Second Edition. Al-Bulaq, Egypt: Dar Al-Sader, 1310 AH.

Khin, Mustafa Sa'īd. *Āthār Al-'Ikhtilaf Fi Al-Qawa'Id Al-Usuliah fi 'Ikhtilaf Al-Fuqhha'*. Beirut, Lebanon: Mu'asasat al-Risālah, 1998.

Krygier, Martin. "Law as Tradition." *Law and Philosophy* 5 2 (1986): 237–262.

Lambton, Ann. *Landlord and Peasant in Persia: A Study of Land Tenure and Land Revenue in Persia*. London, UK: Oxford University Press, 1953.

Lane, Edward William and Stanley Lane-Poole *The Arabic–English Lexicon*. Beirut, Lebanon: Librairie du Liban, 1968.

Laoust, Henri. "Ibn Taymiyya." In *The Encyclopedia of Islam: Volume III*, edited by Lewis, B., V. L. Menage, C. H. Pellat and J. Schacht, 951–955. Leiden: Brill, 1986.

Lapidus, Ira. *A History of Islamic Societies*. Second Edition. New York, UK: Cambridge University Press, 2002.

Lapidus, Ira. "State and Religion in Islamic Society." *Past and Present* 151 (1996): 3–27.

Lapidus, Ira. "The Evolution of Muslim Urban Society." *Comparative Studies in Society and History* 15 1 (1973): 21–50.

Last, Murray. *The Sokoto Caliphate*. London, UK: Longmans, Green, and CO LTD, 1967.

Layish, Aharon. "The Transformation of the Sharīʿa from Jurists' Law to Statutory Law in the Contemporary Muslim World." *Die Welt Des Islams, New Series* 44 1 (2004): 85–113.

Lowry, Joseph. "Does Shāfiʿī Have a Theory of 'Four Sources' of Law?" In *Studies in Islamic Legal Theory*, edited by Weiss, Bernard, 23–50. Leiden: Brill, 2002.

Luxemburg, Rosa. *The Accumulation of Capital. Tr. Agnes Schwarzschild*. London, UK: Routledge, 2003.

Mackintosh-Smith, Tim. *Arabs: A 3000 Year History of Peoples, Tribes, and Empires*. New Haven, CT: Yale University Press, 2019.

Madelung, Wilfred. "Zaydiyya." In *The Encyclopedia of Islam: New Edition (Ei2)*, edited by Bianquis, Th., C. E. Bosworth, E. Vandonzel, W. P. Heinrichs and P. J. Bearman, Vol. XI, 477–481. Leiden: Brill, 2002.

Madison, Gary B. "Hermeneutics." In *Routledge History of Philosophy: The Twentieth Century – Continental Philosophy*, edited by Kearney, Richard, 240–288. New York, NY: Routledge, 1994.

Mahmood, Saba. *Politics of Piety: The Islamic Revival and the Feminist Subject*. Princeton, NJ: Princeton University Press, 2005.

Mailloux, Steven. "Interpretation." In *Critical Terms for Literary Study*, edited by Lentricchia and McLaughlin, 121–134. Chicago, IL: University of Chicago, 1990.

Mandaville, Jon E. "Usurious Piety: The Cash Waqf Controversy in the Ottoman Empire." *International Journal of Middle East Studies* 10 3 (1979): 289–308.

McCarthy, Justin. *The Ottoman Turks: An Introductory History to 1923*. New York, NY: Addison Wesley Longman Limited, 1997.

Melchert, Christopher. *The Formation of Sunnī Schools of Law, 9th–10th Centuries CE*. Leiden, NL: Brill, 1997.

Metcalf, Barbara D. and Thomas R. Metcalf. *A Concise History of Modern India*. New York, NY: Cambridge University Press, 2006.

Miller, Ruth. *Legislating Authority: Sin and Crime in the Ottoman Empire and Turkey*. New York, NY: Routledge, 2005.

Mitchell, Timothy. *Colonizing Egypt*. New York, NY: Cambridge University Press, 1988.

Moosvi, Shireen. "Zamindar." In *The Encyclopedia of Islam: New Edition (EI2)*, edited by Bianquis, Th., C. E. Bosworth, E. Vandonzel, W. P. Heinrich and P. J. Bearman, 438–439. Leiden, NL: Brill, 2002.

Motzki, Harald. *Analyzing Muslim Traditions: Studies in Legal, Exegetical and Maghazi Ḥadīth*. Leiden, NT: Brill, 2010.

Motzki, Harald. *The Origins of Islamic Jurisprudence: Meccan Fiqh before the Classical Schools*. Leiden, NL: Brill, 2002.

Moussavi, Ahmad. "The Theory of Vilayat-i Faqih: Its Origins and Its Appearance in Shiite Juristic Literature." In *State Politics and Islamby Mumtaz Ahmad.* Indianapolis, IN: American Trust Publications, 1986.

Mu'ammar, 'Ali Yaḥyā. *Al-Ibāḍiyya fī Mawkib al-Tārīkh*. Al-Seeb, Oman: Maktabat al-Ḍāmirī li'l-Nashr wa al-Tawzī', 2008.

Nasr, Seyyed Hossein, Hamid Dabashi, and Seyyed Vali Reza Nasr, eds. *Expectations of the Millenium: Shi'ism in History*. Albany, NY: State University of New York, 1989.

Nasr, Seyyed Hossein, Hamid Dabashi, and Seyyed Vali Reza Nasr, eds. *Shi'ism: Doctrines, Thought and Spirituality*. Albany, NY: State University of New York Press, 1989.

Newman, A. J. "Safawids: Religious Trends." In *The Encyclopedia of Islam: Volume 8*, edited by Bosworth, C. E., E. Van Donzel, W. P. Heinrichs and G. Lecomte, 777–781. Leiden, NL: Brill, 1995.

Nyazee, Imran Ahsan Khan. *Theories of Islamic Law: The Methodology of Ijtihād*. Islamabad, Pakistan: Islamic Research Institute, 1994.

Ozcan, Tahsin. "Ibn Kemal'in Para Vakiflarina Dair Risalesi." *Islam Arastirmalan Dergisi* 1 4 (2000): 31–41.

Quateart, Donald. *The Age of Reforms, 1812–1914. Pt. 4 of an Economic and Social History of the Ottoman Empire, 1300–1914*, edited by Inalcik, Halil and Donald Quataert. New York, NY: Cambridge University Press, 1994.

Quick, 'Abdullah Hakim. "Aspects of Islamic Social Intellectual History in Hausaland: Uthman Ibn Fudi, 1774–1804 C.E." University of Toronto: Dissertation, 1995.

Ra'ana, Irfan Mahmud. *Economic System Under 'Umar the Great: A Treatise on Muslim Economy in the Early Seventh Century*. Lahore, Pakistan: Sh. Muḥammad Ashraf, 1991.

Radin, Max. "Tradition." In *Encyclopedia of the Social Sciences*, edited by Seligman, Edwin R. A. and Alvin Johnson, Vol. 15, 62–67. New York, NY: The Macmillan Company, 1963.

Rafsanjani, Mohammad. Interview. Tehran: Cancer Research, Treatment, and Training Institute, January 1, 2017.

Riḍā, Rashīd. *Al-Ribā wa al-Mu'āmalāt fī al-Islām*. Cairo, Egypt: Maktabat Al-Qahirah, 1960.

Riyāḍ, Muḥammad. *Usul Al-Fatwa Wa Al-Qadha' Fi Al-Madhab Al-Mālikī*. Casablanca, Morocco: Dar al Bayda, 1996.

Rizvi, Sayid Athar Abbas. *Shah Abdul Aziz: Puristanism, Secterian, Polemics, and Jihad*. Canberra, AU: Marifat Publishing House, 1982.

Sadeghi, Behnam. *The Logic of Law Making in Islam: Women and Prayer in the Legal Tradition*. Cambridge, UK: Cambridge University Press, 2013.

Salaymeh, Lena. *The Beginnings of Islamic Law: Late Antiquity Islamicate Tradition*. Cambridge, UK: Cambridge University Press, 2016.

Salaymeh, Lena. *The Oral and Written in Early Islam*. Translated by Vagelpohl, Uwe, edited by Montgomery, James. New York, NY: Routledge, 2006.

Schulze, Reinhard. *A Modern History of the Islamic World*. Translated by Azodi, Azizeh. New York, NY: New York University Press, 2000.

Shareef, Muhammad. "The Life of Shaykh Dan Tafa." Sankore Institute of Islamic African Studies. ND.

Shatzmiller, Maya. "Economic Performance and Economic Growth in the Early Islamic World." *Journal of the Economic and Social History of Orient* 54 (2011): 132–184.

SidAḥmed, Abdel Salam and Anoushirvan Ehteshami, eds. *Islamic Fundamentalism*. Boulder, CO: Westview Press, 1996.

Skovgaard-Petersen, Jakob. *Defining Islam for the Egyptian State: Muftīs and Fatwas of the Dār al-Iftā*. Leiden, NL: Brill, 1997.

Sonn, Tamara. *Islam: A Brief History*. Second Edition. West Sussex, UK: Wiley-Blackwell, 2010.

Stewart, Devin J. *Islamic Legal Orthodoxy: Twelver Shīʿī Responses to the Sunnī Legal System. Salt Lake City* Utah: The University of Utah Press, 1998.

Stodolsky, V. Y. A New Historical Model and Periodization for the Perception of the Sunnah of the Prophet and his Companions. Doctoral Thesis. Chicago, IL: Department of Near Eastern Studies, University of Chicago, 2012.

Tucker, Judith. *In the House of the Law Gender and Islamic Law in Ottoman Syria and Palestine*. Berkeley, CA: University of California Press, 1998.

Vaglieri, Veccia. "Ibn ʿAbbās." In *The Encyclopedia of Islam: Volume V*, edited by Gibb, H. A. R., J. H. Kramers, E. Levi-Provencal and J. Schacht, 40–41. Leiden, NL: Brill, 1986.

Vikor, Knut S. *Between God and Sultan: A History of Islamic Law*. New York, NY: Oxford University Press, 2005.

Voll, John Obert. *Islam: Continuity and Change in the Modern World*. Boulder, CO: Westview Press, 1982.

Waines, David. "Islam." In *Linda Woodhead's Religion in the Modern World*. First Edition, edited by Linda, Woodhead, 182–202. New York, NY: Routledge, 2002.

Wallerstein, Immanuel. *The Modern World System III: The Second Era of Great Expansion of the Capitalist World-Economy 1730–1840*. Berkeley, CA: University of California Press, 2011.

Weber, Max. *Economy and Society: An Outline of Interpretive Sociology*, edited by Guenther Roth and Claus Wittich. Vol. 1–2. Berkeley, CA: University of California Press, 1978.

Wheeler, Brannon. *Applying the Canon of Islam: The Authorization and Maintenance of Interpretive Reasoning in Ḥanafī Scholarship*. Albany, NY: State University of New York Press, 1996.

Wilkinson, John. *Ibadism: Origins and Early Development in Oman*. Oxford, UK: Oxford University Press, 2010.

Wink, Andre. *Al-Hind: The Making of the Indo-Islamic World. Vol. II: The Slaving Kings and the Islamic Conquests:11th–13th Centuries*. Leiden, NL: Brill, 1991.

Zaman, Muḥammad Qasim. *Modern Islamic Thought in a Radical Age: Religious Authority and Internal Criticism*. Cambridge, UK: Cambridge University Press, 2012.

Zaman, Muḥammad Qasim. "The Caliphs, the Ulama, and the Law: Defining the Role and Function of the Caliph in the Early 'Abbāsid Period." *Islamic Law and Society* 4 1 (1997): 1–36.

Zysow, Aron. The Economy of Certainty: An Introduction to the Typology of Islamic Legal Theory. Doctoral Thesis. Boston, MA: Department of Near Eastern Studies, Harvard University, 1984.

Index

AAIOFI *Shari'ah Standards* manual, 242
abandoned property, 52, 54, 57
Abbasid caliphate, 77, 142
'Abd Allah ibn 'Abd al-Azīz, 54, 55, 141
'Abd Allah ibn Baraka, 143
'Abd al-'Azīz, 178–185, 196, 263, *See also* Shah 'Abd al-'Azīz
'Abd al- Razzāq al-Ṣan'ānī, 4
'Abd al-Qāhir Muḥammad Qamar President of IIFA, 239
'Abd al-Wahhāb Khallāf, 217
abiding religio-legal obligation, 174
abode of war, 190
abrogation, 81, 127
abstract rights, 240, 247, 250, 257
Abū 'Ubaydah Muslim ibn Abī Karīmah, 52–56, 139–142
Abū al-Ma'ālī al-Juwaynī, 122, *See also* al-Juwaynī
Abū al-Su'ūd, 163–170, 243–245
Abū Ḥanīfa, 40, 43, 48, 50, 51, 57–71, 73, 79, 84, 95, 96, 98–100, 109, 126, 128, 131, 132, 160, 161, 193
  ish'ār, legal practice of, 60, 64
  istiḥsān, legal principle of, 61–2
Abū Sa'īd al- Kudamī, 142
Abū Ya'coub al-Warajalanī, 143
Abū Yūsuf, 30–32, 43, 51, 52, 59, 60, 96, 98, 99, 126, 128, 131, 166–168, 193, 263, 265
  legal response of, 51
adab al-fatwa. *See* the etiquette of fatwa
adab al-fatwā, 7, 138, 144, 257
'adilla
  legal evidence, 126, *See also* legal evidence
administrator of the *waqf*, 167
advocates of *athar*, 107
advocates of *ḥadīth*, 50, 54, 78, 92, 97, 98, 109, 142
advocates of opinion, 63
advocates of *ra'y*, 58, 78, 80, 107–110, 142
advocates of reason, 49, *See also* ahl al-ra'y
advocates of the *ḥadīth*, 110
agnates, 155, 156, 158, 192
āḥād
  singular chain of transmission, 51, 52, 97, 100, 107
Aḥkām al-Quran, 98
Aḥkām al-Arāḍī
  land law in India, 183, *See also* land law in India
ahl al-ḥadīth, 44, 49, 50, 58, 63, 65, 79, 81, 97, 108
ahl al ra'y, 44, 47, 49, 50, 63, 79, 81
Ahmad Hasan, 60
Aḥmad Ibn Ḥanbal, 158, 160, 161, 162
Aḥmad Ibn Kamāl Pashazadeh, 131, *See also* Ibn Kamāl
Aḥmad ibn.'Isa ibn Zayd, 136
Aḥmad Khalīlī, 227, 228, *See also* Grand Muftī of the Sultanate of Oman
Aḥmed Khān, 211
aims of Islamic law. *See* spirit of the law
aims of the law, 50, 92

Akbar, 152, 234, *See also* Mughal Empire
akhbār, 171, 173, 174, 257, *See also* authoritative reports
Akhbārī movement, 171
al- Awazajandī, 104
al- Muhadhdhab, 103
al- Muwaṭṭa', 102
al- Shaybānī, 98, 126, 128, 166, 168, 193
al- Wansharīsī, 196
Al-'Awātibī, 143
al-'Allāma al-Ḥillī, 138, 175
al-amwāl al-ma'kūla, 188, *See also* ill-gotten property
Al-Aqsa Mosque, 238
al-Ardbīlī, 176
al-As'ila al-Dawliyya wa-Ḍawābiṭ al-Ta'āmul Fīhā
  trade of international commodities and conditions that govern that trade. *See* trade of international commodities and conditions that govern that trade
al-Awzā'ī, 43, 50, 51, 57, 110
al-Azhar, 207
al-Azhar University, 207
al-Bazdawī, 132
al-Birgevi. *See* Birgevi
al-Burzulī, 103, 190, 196, *See also* Mālikī jurist
alcohol, 17, 18, 19, 229
al-Dabūsī, 98, 99
al-Faqīh
  Supreme Leader/Jurist, 232, *See also* Supreme Leader/Jurist
al-Fasīḥ, 134
Al-Fatāwa Al-Hindīyya, 153
Algeria, 54, 142, 202–204
Algerian Muslims, 203
Algerian society, 203
al-Hādī, 71, 72–74, 136, *See also* al-Hādī ilā al-Ḥaqq, Yaḥyā ibn al-Ḥusayn
  crop farming, 72–73
  decision on the prophetic report, 74
  marriage contract, 59
al-Ḥaṭṭāb, 103
al-Hidāya, 199, 200, 257
al-Ḥujja 'alā ahl al-Madīna, 66
al-Ḥuqūq al-Ma'nawiyya. *See* abstract rights
  abstract rights, 247
'Alī, 40, 43, 95, 171, 207, 208, 243, 264
'Alī b. 'Abd al-'Ālī al-Karakī, 171, *See also* al-Karakī
al-Jarrāḥ, 132
al-Jaṣṣāṣ, 98, 133
al-Juwaynī, 122–124, 126, 128, 264
  legal opinions, 122
al-Kanz, 134
al-Karakī ('Alī b. 'Abd al-'Ālī al-Karakī), 152, 171–178, 183, 184, 264
Alkawala
  capital of Gobir, 188, *See also* Gobir
al-khaṣm
  litigant, 53
al-Khaṭīb al-Baghdādī', 79
al-Kudamī, 143, 144, *See also* Abū Sa'īd al- Kudamī
al-Kūfī, 72
al-Mabsūṭ, 127
al-Maghīlī, 186, 190, 196, *See also* Muḥammad 'Abd al-Karīm al-Maghīlī
al-maktab al-unmudhaji
  model school, 208, *See also* modern schools
al-Manār, 218, *See also* Rashīd Riḍā
al-Mi'yār, 189, *See also* al-Wansharīsī
al-Mudawanna al-Kubrā, 53
al-Mughili, 187
al-Muḥaqqiq al-Ḥillī, 175
al-mujtahidīn fī al-shar', 131, *See also* master jurists
al-Mukhtār, 134
al-Mukhtaṣar, 103, 189
  Mālikī law manuel, 189
al-Mūṣilī, 134
al-mustaghriq al-dhimma, 187
al-mustaqill bi-madhhab imāmihi, 124
al-Muwaṭṭa', 45, 48
al-Nasafī, 103
al-Nawawī, 103, 264
al-Qāsim ibn Ibrāhīm al- Rassī, 71, 136
al-Qātī'fi, 176
al-Qudūrī, 134
al-Rabī' ibn al-Ḥabīb, 53, 56, 58, 140, 141
al-Rāzī al-Jaṣṣāṣ, 133
al-Ribā wa al-Mu'āmalāt fī al-Islām, 221, *See also* Rashīd Riḍā
al-Riḥla fī ṭalab al-ḥadīth, 79
al-Risāla, 21, 25, 35, 62, 80, 85, 86
al-Sarakhsī, 61, 98, 132
al-Shāfi'ī, 25, 43, 59, 62, 63–65, 68–71, 73, 79–82, 85–89, 92, 95–100, 102, 109, 112, 156, 160, 161, 193, 259, 267
  financial liability of children, 62–63
al-Shahīd al-Awwal, 175

al-Shahīd al-Thānī, 138
al-Shaybānī, 48, 51, 60, 84, 96, 99, 102, 126, 127, 131, 143, 165–169, 264
al-Shaykh al-Mufīd, 137
al-siyāsa al-shar'iyya
  ethical diplomacy, 151, 181, 184, 257, *See also* ethical diplomacy
al-Ṭaḥāwī, 98, 99, 132
al-ta'mīn al-ṣiḥḥī
  health insurance, 247, 257, *See also* health insurance
alternative ritual purification. *See* tayammum
al-Thaljī, 98, *See also* Muḥammad ibn Shujā' al-Tha
Al-Thānīsirī, 182, *See also* Jalāl al-Dīn al-Thānīsirī
al-Wansharīsī, 189
'amal ahl al-Madînah, 97, *See also* 'the practice of the people of Medina
amalgamation of rulings, 215, *See also* talfīq
A'mash, 40
ambiguity, 19, 54, 55, 184, 248
'āmm
  universal implication, 51
'Ammār ibn Yāsir, 27
'Amr ibn al-'Āṣ, 22
analogical deduction, 63
analogical reasoning, 24, 25, 60, 62, 63, 86, 89, 93, 109, 217, 225, 231, 246, 247
analogy, 21, 22, 46, 48, 49, 55, 62, 69, 73, 79, 80, 84, 86–88, 90, 99, 119, 137, 139, 156, 162, 168, 183, 186, 223, 229, 231, 242, 260
Anatolia, 150, 169
al-Marghīnānī, 134
Anglo-Muḥammadan law, 201
animals
  predatory animals, 62, 90, 166
'aql, 137, 171, 177, *See also* reason and
  legal compensation, 45, 57
  reason, 73
aqyisa wa-ṭuruq, 124
  methodology, 124
Arabia, 26, 32, 39, 44, 142, 209, 222, 268
Arabs, 26, 44, 202, 269
arbitrary judgment, 89
Aristotel, 10, 38, 76
āriyat
  loan, 181, *See also* loan
asbāb al-nuzūl, 17, 18, 258
Askia, 186, 190, 196, 268, *See also* Askia al-Ḥājj Muḥammad
Askia al-Ḥājj Muḥammad, 186, *See also* Songhai Empire
'aṣr, 23
'Aṭā' ibn Rabāḥ, 41
athar, 54, 85, 96, 107, 108, 110, 142, 144, 258, *See also* authoritative precedence; tradition
āthār, 44–46, 49, 50, 56, 58, 71, 76, 258, *See also* traditions
Athar al-Rabī', 141
āthārists, 49, 108, *See also* traditionists
Aurangzeb, 152, *See also* Mughal Empire
authentic report, 50
Authenticity of Early Islamic Legal Material, 3–5
authoritative discourses, 19, 38, 76, 119, 255
authoritative doctrine, 149, 251, *See also* ẓāhir al-riwāya
  ẓāhir al-riwāya, 126, 127, 128
authoritative hierarchy, 162
authoritative norm, 65
authoritative precedence, 229
authoritative reports, 171
authoritativeness of *ḥadīth*, 50
authority, 8, 16, 18, 20, 21, 25, 26, 28, 34, 35, 39–42, 46, 50, 52, 56, 58, 71–74, 79, 95, 96, 99, 100, 105–107, 112, 115, 117–119, 121, 135–139, 141, 143, 145, 149, 150, 153, 155, 158, 159–162, 164, 165, 170, 172–175, 177, 178, 181, 183, 188, 205, 211, 214, 215, 223, 232, 236, 246, 247, 249, 255, 258, 260, 261
authority construction, 96
autonomy, 150
awqāf. *See waqf*
ayatollah, 138
Ayatollah Ali Akbar Rafsanjani, 234
  Islamic Republic of Iran, 234
Ayatollah Haram Mohammadi Gilani, 233
Ayatollah Khomeini, 227, 232–235, 237, 262, *See also* Supreme Jurist/Leader of the Islamic Republic of Iran
āyatullāh, 138, 258, *See also* ayatollah
'ayn, 167, 193, *See also* specified property
Ayyubid, 147, 148

baqā', 166, 174, *See also* permanence
baqā' al-ḥaqq
  abiding religio-legal obligation, 174, *See also* abiding religio-legal obligation

barley, 65, 222
Baṣra, 27, 39, 52, 57, 142
Baṣran authorities, 55–57, 139
Baṣran jurist, 56
Baṣran legal authorities, 58
Baṣran lineage of jurists, 55
Battle of al-Ṣiffīn, 161
Battle of Plassey, 198
Battle of al-Jamal, 161
bayt al-māl, 181, 187, 190, *See also* state treasury
Behnam Sadeghi, 35
Bengal, 198–200
Bengali cotton weaving industry, 199
Berber tribes, 204
Berbers, 204
Birgevi, 165, 169, *See also* Mehmet Birgevi
blocking the pathways to harm, 191, 195, 261
blood, 156, 228–230, 231
blood money, 156
blood transfusion, 228–231
bread, 66, 70
British colonialism, 179, 202
British colonization in India, 202
British commercial interests, 199
British East India Company, 179, 198
British Government, 210
British judges, 199
British legal structure, 201
British occuppation of Egypt, 209
bughāh
  renegades, 161, *See also* renegades
bureaucratic forms of administration, 236
bureaucratic schools, 206
bureaucratization of the state
  modern reforms, 214
business contracts, 248, 250
business partnership, 170
business practices, 245
business products, 245
Buyid Dynasty, 173

Cairo, 23, 147, 207, 208, 263, 264, 271
Calcutta, 218, 221–225
Calcutta fatwa, 218, 221
Caliph ʿUmar. *See* ʿUmar ibn al-Khaṭṭāb
caliphate, 29, 32, 35, 40, 77, 78, 147, 148, 152, 161, 188
caliphs, 40, 108, 192
camel urine, 230
cantonnements, 202
capital, 167, 188, 260
carcass, 90
carrion meat, 61
case law, 102
cash *waqf*s, 163–170, 193, 243–245
Caspian Sea, 71, 136
Central Asia, 26, 39, 147, 148, 210
centralization, 207, 214
centralizing state, 202, 213
chain of narration, 50, 51
chain of transmission, 51, 52, 97, 99, 110, 111, 259, *See also* genealogy of a report
charitable endowments, 207, *See also* waqf
Charles Hirschkind, 118
Chief Jurist, 170, *See also* Shaykh al-Islām
Christians, 105
civil society, 3, 149, 207, 214
civil war
  first civil war, 40, 259
civil wars, 40, 41, 105, 161, 162
civilization, 8, 11, 113, 210, 225, 226
Çivizade Muhittin Mehmet Efendi, 164
clemency, 157
Code de l'indignat, 203
Code of Civil Procedure [of] 1859, 202
Code of Criminal Procedure of 1861, 202
codified Mongol traditions, 160
Codifying Islamic law
  modern Muslim states, 216
coloniality, 2, 5, 7, 179, 185, 198–204, 209–215, 218, 226, 227, 238, 240, 245, 252, 254
colonial juridical system, 199
colonial policies, 200, 201
colonial state, 199
colonialism, 2, 7, 12, 179, 197, 199, 202, 204, 209, 211, 227, 240
commercial law, 213
commercial transaction, 219, 220
commodity, 30, 31, 47, 48, 251
commodity exchange, 48
communal property, 202
communicative, 19, 110, 112, 119, 121
communicative activity, 121
communicative practice, 119
community, 17, 18, 26, 29, 82, 99, 105, 106, 112, 117, 121, 135–138, 141, 172–174, 176, 194, 201, 217
Companions of the Prophet, 108
company trademarks. *See* abstract rights

compendiums
legal compendiums, 103
compilations of prophetic traditions, 96
compound interest, 220
conceptual framework, 106
conceptual transformations, 80, 112
conquered lands, 29, 30, 32, 182
consensus, 35, 54, 62, 73, 82, 83, 87, 88, 93, 97, 109, 112, 122, 126, 127, 131, 137, 139, 143, 145, 159, 173–175, 177, 178, 183, 191, 194, 212, 220, 229, 231, 242, 259, 260 , *See also ijmā'*
constant profit return model, 170
constitutionalism, 211
consuming prohibited products, 229
consumption, 18, 20, 90, 91, 229, 230, 231
context-driven methodology, 255
contextually oriented legal devices, 255
continuity of law, 35
contract, 59, 219, 220, 224, 242, 245, 248, 249
converting to Islam, 27
copper, 66, 67, 70
copyrights. *See* abstract rights
Cordoba, 154
corpus of *ḥadīth*, 118
court decisions. *See* qaḍā'
courts, 102, 149, 200, 202, 203, 206, 213, 214
crime, 156, 213
"crimes against victims, 213
criminal law, 154, 202, 203, 213
crops farming, 61, 62, 73–74
shared ownership of field, 74
Crusaders, 147
custom, 41, 61, 75, 116, 151, 166, 168, 169, 193, 200, 201, 246, 247. *See also* 'urf
customary laws, 201, 204
customary practice, 222

dalā'il
indications/proofs, 86, 228, *See also* proofs
dalā'il shar'iyya, 228
dalīl, 168
proof text, 220, *See also* proof texts
Damascus, 27, 39, 57, 148, 159, 263, 264, 266
Dan Fodio, 185–191, 196, 266
dar al-ḥarb
abode of war, 190, *See also* abode of war
Dar al-Ulum College
Egypt, 207
dates, 65, 70, 171, 222
Dāwūd al- Ẓāhirī, 95
ḍayā', 73, *See also* farm fields
debts, 208, 220, 242
Degal, 185
dependent jurist, 201
deposition of the sultan, 151
de-secularization, 237
dhihqāns, 33
dialectic development, 80
dialectic process, 119, 144
dialogical activity, 3, 6, 14
dialogical character, 3, 10, 112
dialogical engagements, 254, *See also* dialogical interactions
dialogical interaction, 10, 119, 121
dialogical manner, 6, 14, 112, 117
dialogical mode of interaction, 16
dialogical process, 3, 6, 10, 14–16, 19, 112, 117, 119–121, 254
dialogically negotiated discursive tradition, 10
dialogically negotiated engagement, 112
dialogically negotiated tradition, 121
differentiation of political and religious authorities, 43
diffusion of *ḥadīth*, 50, *See also* mashhūr
discourse
Islamic legal discourse, 1, 2, 6–8, 14–16, 19, 20, 39, 41, 42, 58, 76, 79, 80, 87, 96, 97, 108–111, 114, 117, 138, 142, 143, 162, 176, 227, 245, 247, 252–255
discursive changes in Islamic law, 216
discursive engagements, 254
discursive learning, 105
discursive legal tradition, 117, 118, 155, 178, 254, 255
discursive methods, 119
a discursive barometer. *See* fatwas and social change
discursive practice, 10, 14, 16, 25, 36, 101, 105, 120, 121, 173, 178, 25
discursive process, 144
discursive rules, 7, 115, 128, 130, 145, 146, 153, 163
discursive shift, 252, 254
discursive statements, 10, 106, 111
discursive tradition, 9
Islamic legal discursive tradition, 114
legal discurive tradition, 10, 114, 117, 118, 120, 121, 255

discursive transformations, 80
discursively-based Islamic institutions, 236
dīwān, 33, 258, *See also* registry
drinking the urine of camels, 230

Ebu's- Su'ud. *See* Abū al-Su'ūd
ecclesiastic bodies, 144
economic market, 199
economic protectionism, 205
economy, 102, 199, 205, 206
edible food, 61
education, 206, 208
Egypt, 26, 32, 33, 39, 64, 79, 147, 148, 192, 200, 204, 205, 207–211, 213, 215, 218, 224, 263, 264, 266, 269, 270
Egyptian laws, 215
Egyptian mixed courts, 213
embedding religio-ethical precepts
  fatwas, 237
Emperor Askia, 196
endowable properties, 243
endowing shares, 240, 242, 243, 249
endowing shares and stocks, 241
Ennami, 55, 141, 142, 143
entrepreneur, 167, 170
entrusted items, 219
epistemic authority, 100, 145
epistemological certainty, 51
Epistemological Foundations of *Iftā'*, 15
established legal ruling, 155
estates, 34, 244
ethical diplomacy, 151
ethical legitimacy, 42, 43
ethical norms, 39
ethico-legal norms, 78
  traditional norms, 235
European banks, 219
European colonialism, 204, 209
European encroachment, 207
European managed debt administration, 208
European notion of progress, 212
European powers, 198, 204, 205, 207, 209
European-style education, 206
European-style schools, 208
Evidence Act of 1872, 202
exchange, 3, 47, 48, 65–70, 186, 188, 189, 196, 222, 248
  unequal exchange, 68
exchange by volume or weight, 66
exchange of goods, 65
exchange of silver, 48
exchanged on the spot, 65, 66, 251, *See also* Usurious Transactions
exchanging gold and silver, 48, *See also* 'like for like' rule
excrement, 228
execution, 155
exploitative practice
  ribā, 222
exploitative type of usury, 220, 222, 225
extracting, 30, 98, 103, 260, 261, *See also* tajrīd

faḍl
  increase, 219, 223, 261
false analogies, 223
family law, 202, 213, 216
faqīh, 124, 257, 258
farm fields, 73
farmān, 184, *See also* royal decrees
  royal decree, 181, *See also* royal decree
farming, 73, 163
farms, 72, 163, 203
fasting, 21, 23, 82, 83, 258
Fatāwa Qāḍī Khān, 126
father obligation to support children, 63
Fatimids, 147
fatwa(s), 1–16, 18–25, 27, 28, 29, 31–36, 38–40, 46, 47–49, 52–69, 71, 72, 77–79, 84, 94, 95, 101–104, 112, 114, 115, 117, 119–124, 126, 128–132, 134, 135, 137–141, 144–146, 148, 149, 151–160, 162–172, 174, 176–180, 182–187, 190–192, 196, 198, 212, 217–223, 225–237, 239–247, 249–254, 257, 259–262, *See also* fatwa
  discursive activity of fatwa, 94
  political practices, 34
  social transactive character, 121
  non-binding nature, 8
  primordial legal matter, 102
  social change, 3, 12, 212
Fatwa-i 'Alamgiri, 153, *See also* Al-Fatāwa Al-Hindīyya
fatwas and legal doctrine, 102
fay', 30, *See also* spoils of war
feudal estates system, 34
fī ma'nā al- manṣūṣ. *See also* implicit in the stated doctrine
  implicit in the stated doctrine, 124

financial instruments, 245
financial liability of children, 62
fiqh, 9, 80, 93, 101–104, 119, 143, 258, 267, *See also* legal doctrine
Fiqh al-Sunna, 217
foreign invaders, 160
formal rationality, 24
formalist theory hermeneutics, 108
foundations of the Islamic legal schools, 100
France, 202, 207, 208
French colonialism, 202
French colonists, 202
French colonization, 202, 203, 207
French colonization of Algeria, 202
a fortiori, 72, 128
  bi-l-awlā, 80
French law, 208
French occupation of Egypt, 207
French settlers, 202, 204
Friday sermon, 233, 234
fruits, 61, 67
Fulani tribes, 187
Fulanis, 189
Fustat, 26, 39, *See also* Egypt

Gabon, 238
gambling, 17–19, *See also* games of chance
games of chance, 17, 19
ghanīma, 31, 258, *See also* spoils of war
gharar
  uncertainty, 248, 250, 258, *See also* transactional uncertainty
ghāṣib
  usurper, 187, *See also* usurper
ghayr manṣūṣ, 124, 258
Ghazan, 159
Ghaznavids, 147
Ghiyāth al-umam, 122
gift, 213
global capitalist system, 240
Gobir, 185, 186, 188, 190, *See also* Hausa Dynasty
gold, 48, 65, 67–70, 222, 231
governance, 30, 142, 172, 176, 181, 188, 205, 232, 235–237, 262
governance practices, 181
government, 56, 102, 105, 150, 163–165, 176, 190, 194, 200, 202, 204, 205, 208, 210, 216, 232, 233, 235, 258
government institutions, 150
Grand *Muftī* of the Sultanate of Oman, 227
"Great Synthesis," 119
greater good, 30, 32, 35
Guardian Council, 232, 233, *See also* Islamic Republic of Iran

ḥadīth, 4, 20–23, 44, 47, 49–52, 54–56, 58, 61–64, 66, 67, 69, 71, 73, 76, 78–83, 85, 87, 88, 92, 96–100, 106, 108–111, 116–120, 122, 123, 130, 142, 143, 155, 157, 160, 161, 163, 168, 171, 192, 211, 212, 217, 218, 220–224, 230, 231, 242, 251, 255, 257, 258, 260
ḥamalat al-ʿilm
  True Bearers of Knowledge, 141–143, *See also* True Bearers of Knowledge
ḥaml al- ʿāmm ʿalā al-khāṣṣ
  particularizing the universal, 230, *See also* particularizing the universal
Ḥammād, 40
Ḥanafī, 26, 43, 51, 52, 59, 61, 79, 88–93, 96, 97, 98, 99, 103, 107, 126–134, 149, 151, 153, 158, 163–170, 178–184, 193, 194, 199, 200, 219, 224, 226, 250, 257, 259, 262, 272
  predatory animals and birds, cases of, 90
Ḥanafī *madhhab*, 127, 128, 131, 163–165, 170, 180, 181
Ḥanafī school, 26, 59, 96–99, 126, 127, 128, 130–131, 134, 165, 166, 168, 169, 193, 200, 219, 224, 250, 259, 262
Ḥanbalī, 158, 162, 192, 193
Ḥanbalī school, 158, 159, 193
Ḥanbalī tradition, 159
ḥarām, 233, 258
  Islamically prohibited. *See* Islamically prohibited
harm, 187, 188
Harold Berman, 196
Harold Motzki, 4
Harran, 148
Hārūn al-Rashīd, 32
Ḥasan ibn ʿAlī, 41, 165, 174, 175, 264
Ḥasan al-Baṣrī, 41
Hastings Plan, 201
Hausa Dynasty, 185, 186
Hausa monarchs, 188
Hausa rulers, 186
Hausaland, 185, 186–191, 271
Hay'at al-Iftā'
  The Committee on Ifta, 228, *See also* Ministry of Awqaf and Religious Affairs (MARA)

ḥazā, 53, 54
acquire, 52
head of state, 181, 182, 184, 232
health insurance, 241, 247, 248, 249, 250, 257
health system, 248
hermeneutical authority, 107, 121, 160, 177, 255
hermeneutical discourses, 119
hermeneutical function, 119
hermeneutical methods, 76
hermeneutical reasoning, 20
hermeneutical techniques, 36
hermeneutics, 22, 32, 94, 107, 108, 156, 157, 201, 246, 255
hiba, 213
gift. *See* gift
Hijaz, 43–46, 49–51
hijrah
emigrate, 186
Hindu, 199, 200
Hindu law
Britsh India, 199
historical jurisprudence, 251
ḥujja, 72
legal proof, 72, 126, *See also* legal proof
ḥujjat al-Islām, 138
ḥukm, 90, 91, 139, 258, 261, *See also* ruling
human transactions, 226
Ḥusayn ibn ʿAlī, 75, 174
hybrid form of governance, 236
hybrid jurisprudence, 251
hybridity
modern fatwa, 13
Hyderabad, 218, 221–226
Hyderabad fatwa, 218

Ibāḍī, 52, 54–56, 58, 139–144, 228–231, 258, 266
Ibāḍī *athar*, 144
Ibāḍī hermeneutical authority
ḥamalat al-ʿilm, 143
Ibāḍī jurists, 142
Ibāḍī law, 142–144
Ibāḍī legal discourse, 142, 143
Ibāḍī legal school, 140
Ibāḍī legal tradition, 140
Ibāḍī *madhhab*, 141–144, 228, 230, 231, *See also* Ibāḍī school
Ibāḍī practice, 143
Ibāḍī school, 229
Ibāḍīsm, 140, 142–144, 227, 266
Ibn Kamal Pasha, 164
Ibn ʿAbd al-Azīz, 56
Ibn ʿAbbās, 18, 40, 41, 56, 271
Ibn ʿĀbidīn, 130–134, 268
Ibn Ḥanbal, 21, 131, 193, 220, 222
Ibn Jarīr al-Ṭabarī, 95
Ibn Masʿūd, 28, 48
Ibn Rushd, 103, 154–158, 192, 248, 268
Ibn Rushd al-Jadd, 103, 154
Ibn Taymiyya, 23, 148, 158–162, 192, 268, 269
Ibrāhīm al-Nakhaʿī, 47, 49, 140
legal authorities, 48
silver ring, cost of, 47
idrār
pension, 181, 184, *See also* pension
iftāʾ, 2, 3, 5–8, 14–17, 20–25, 28, 32, 34, 35, 36, 38–40, 77, 81, 94, 101, 103, 115, 117, 128, 130, 144, 146, 154, 157, 237, 253, 259, *See also* issuance of fatwas
iḥāza
possession of abandoned property, 54
iḥtiyāṭ
precaution, 54, 57, 140
IIFA
International Islamic Fiqh Academy, 227, 228, 238–252, 255, *See also* International Islamic Fiqh Academy
context-driven legal rationales, 251–252
trade of international commodities, 251
ijāza, 206
ijmāʿ, 109
consensus, 62, 73, 80, 82, 83, 87, 88, 93, 98, 100, 109–122, 131, 137, 139, 143, 171, 173, 175, 177, 183, 191, 194, 229, 231, 259
ijmāʿ of innovation, 82, 83
ijmāʿ of interpretation, 82, 83
ijmāl
undifferentiated, 188, *See also* undifferentiated
ijtihād, 22–25, 55, 73, 81, 84–86, 109, 121, 122, 126–128, 132, 138, 144, 171, 193, 211, 212, 217, 239, 252, 259, *See also* legal competence
ikhtilāf
disagreement, 180, *See also* disagreement
Ikhtilāf al-Fuqahāʾ, 98

Ilkhanid, 148, 159
ʿilla, 90
legal cause, 87–91, 259, 261, *See also* legal cause
ill-gotten property, 188
Imam, 135, 137, 171, 173–175, 177, 194, 257, *See also* head of the state
leader, 55, 137, 171, 175, 265
Imāmī, 135–139, 151, 260
Imāmī legal school, 138, *See also* Imāmī madhhab
Imāmī legal theory, 138
Imāmī *madhhab*, 137
Imāmī Shīʿism, 137
immovability, 166, 167, 193, 243
impediment, 91
imperial court, 151, 152
implicit in the stated doctrine, 124
impurity, 22, 90, 100, 229, 231
inalienable proprietary rights, 180, 181
inʿām muʾabbad, 180, *See also* perpetual benefit
indefinitive, 99
indemnity, 46
independent jurist, 121, 124–128, 132, 133, 137, 157, 158, 257, 260, *See also* jurists
independent legal judgment, 123, *See also* mujtahid
independent reasoning, 55, 56, 62, 86
India, 150, 152, 178–180, 182–184, 194, 198–202, 204, 211, 218, 266, 268, 270
Indian Muslim heads of state, 183, 184
injunction, 23, 29, 31, 61, 62, 69, 87, 92, 99, 139
institution of the caliphate, 29
institutions, 2, 5–7, 11–13, 77, 78, 95, 101, 102, 104, 113–115, 118, 120, 121, 130, 131, 135, 136, 139, 146, 147, 149, 150, 152, 167, 170, 172, 173, 196, 200, 204–208, 211, 214, 215, 225–227, 236, 240, 253, 255
instruments of universal valuation, 67
insurance companies, 248
insurance policy, 248
insurance premium, 248
integrative jurisprudence, 162
intentionalist theory hermeneutics, 107
interest, 223, *See also* benefit accrued by a loan
interest-based transaction, 220
inter-madhab reasoning, 232
International Islamic Fiqh Academy, 227, 228, 238, 251
international trade, 241
interpretive scheme of the *sunna*, 98
intoxicants, 17
intoxicated person, 154
inviolability of the property rights, 186
iqṭā, 180
Iran, 137, 148, 159, 194, 204, 209, 227, 232, 233, 262, 265, 269
Iranian clerics, 233
Iranian Revolution, 233, 262
Iranian television, 233, 235
Iraq, 26, 29, 31–33, 39, 43–46, 49, 54, 57, 71, 79, 107, 136, 142, 148, 152, 182, 183, 194, 214, 215, 235, 257
Iraqi legal school, 48
Iraqi legal tradition, 59
Iraqi school
regional schools, 46, 50, 59, 60, 73, 84, 89
iron, 66, 67, 70
irrigation systems, 33, 34
ishʿār
flesh incision, 60, 61
Islamic civilization, 3, 8, 103
Islamic expansion, 39, 44, *See also* Muslim expansion
Islamic financial contract, 242
of Islamic criminal law, 202
of Islamic legal theory, 216
Islamic financial transactions, 248
Islamic jurisprudence
fiqh, 9, 83, 95, 110, 197, 239, 251, 252
Islamic law, 1–3, 5, 7–9, 11, 12, 16, 21, 22, 24–26, 28, 31, 35, 36, 38, 42, 43, 48, 52, 58, 59, 61, 69, 71, 78, 80, 81, 87, 92, 93, 94, 100, 101–105, 110, 111, 113–116, 121, 122, 130, 131, 135, 140, 145, 146, 148, 149, 153,160, 163, 170, 175, 176, 181, 183, 185, 188, 190, 191, 197–201, 203, 207, 209, 211–213, 215–220, 225, 226, 228, 229, 234, 239–244, 246–250, 252–254, 258–261
development of, 12, 149
formation of, 115–116
judges and courts activity, 102
stagnation thesis of, 12

Islamic legal discourse, 1, 3, 6, 7, 25, 36, 39, 76, 78, 84, 108, 116, 120, 162, 178, 196, 211, 218, 240, 252, 253, 254
Islamic legal discursive tradition, 118
Islamic legal institutions, 7, 12, 28, 227
Islamic legal norms, 5, 6, 39, 45, 163
Islamic legal rulings, 7, 43, 249, 257, 258
Islamic legal system, 77, 113, 149, 201
Islamic legal theory, 22, 78, 81, 93, 94
  development of, 80
  formation of, 94
Islamic legal tradition, 2, 3, 5, 6, 10, 11, 15, 22, 24, 29, 31, 39, 65, 74, 78, 112, 114, 115, 117–121, 142–144, 173, 184, 185, 196–198, 212, 216, 218, 236, 253–256
Islamic legal tradition in the African context, 196
Islamic norms
  Quranic norms, 8, 43, 168, 232, 233
Islamic polity, 32
Islamic reform movements, 211
Islamic Republic of Iran, 232
Islamic society
  formation of Islamic society, 8, 41, 104, 112
Islamic solidarity, 238
Islamic state, 186
Islamic stocks, 240, 242
Islamic system of governance, 232
Islamic vision, 105
Ismāʿīlīs, 83
isnād, 111, *See also* chain of transmission
Israel, 238
Israeli occupation, 238
istighlāl, 170, *See also* constant profit return
istiḥqāq, 181, 184, *See also* merited right
istiḥsān
  juridical preference, 60, 61–63, 65, 80, 85, 86–93, 100, 109–111, 121, 156, 166, 168, 259, *See also* juridical preference
  juristic preference, 156, 157, 166, 168, 169, 226
  legal principle, 61–62
istiṣḥāb, 184
  continuity, 183, *See also* continuity
Istiṣlāḥ
  arguments of public interest, 92
  seeking the public interest, 61, 62, 65, 86, 88, 92, 93, 100, 119, 259
iʿṭāʾ
  land grants, 180, *See also* land grants
Ithnā ʿAshariyya, 87, *See also* Shīʿī

Jabal ʿĀmil, 171
Jaber ibn ʿAbd Allah, 220
Jabir ibn Zayd, 52, 53, 55, 56, 139
  legal right to reclaim property, 52
Jadidi movement, 210
Jaʿfar al-Ṣādiq, 43, 174, 95
Jaʿfarī, 135, 151
Jalāl al-Dīn al-Thānīsirī, 181, 182
jalb al-maṣlaḥa wa darʾ al-mafsada
  to promote the common good and deter corruption, 191, *See also* to promote the common good and deter corruption
Janissaries, 205
Jerusalem, 238
jewelry, 48
Jews, 105
jihad, 162, 186, 188, 192
judges, 102, 149, 150, 164, 188, 189, 199, 200, 203, 206, 214
judiciary, 208, 214, 228
junub, 22
juridical decisions. *See* qaḍāʾ
juridical rulings. *See* qaḍāʾ
juridical verdicts. *See* qaḍāʾ
jurisdiction, 86, 199, 213, 215
jurisprudence, 32, 44, 55, 62, 63, 76, 78, 79, 83, 84, 95, 101, 136, 137, 162, 172, 173, 178, 196, 197, 226, 251, 252, 254, 260, 262
jurist consult, 103, *See also* muftī
juristic approach, 55
juristic competence, 121
juristic inference, 156
juristic preference, 61–64, 80, 86, 88, 90, 109, 156, 166, 168, 169, 226, 259
jurists, 1, 2, 6–8, 25, 32, 35, 36, 39, 42–44, 49, 50, 54–56, 58–60, 61, 62, 65, 66, 71, 76–79, 81–84, 88, 90–104, 107, 109, 112, 115, 116, 120–122, 126, 127, 130, 132, 134–135, 137–145, 148, 151, 156–158, 160–162, 164–170, 173–175, 177, 179, 183, 184, 186–194, 196, 197, 200, 214, 216, 219, 220–223, 226, 228–232, 239, 240, 243, 245, 246, 251, 255, 259, 260, 262

independent jurists, 150
legal specialists, 9, 37, 43, 96, 120
master-jurists, 95

Kabyle
Berber tribes, 204, *See also* Berber tribes
kalāla, 15
Kanun. *See* qānūn
Kanz al- Daqā'iq, 103
khabar aḥad, 99, 259
single chain of transmission, 99, *See also* single chain of transmission
Khalīl ibn Isḥāq, 103
Khalīlī, 227–232, 264, *See also* Aḥmad Khalīlī
kharāj, 33, 172–177, 180, 183, 184, 194, 257, 259, *See also* taxation
Kharāj in Islamic Law, 176
khāṣṣ
particular implication, 51, 230
Khawārij, 161, 162, 192
Khaybar, 30
Khedive Ismā'īl, 208
Khomeini's fatwa, 234
kissing, 21, 23, 24
Kitāb al-Muntakhab, 136, 264
Yaḥyā ibn Hussein, 72, *See also* Yaḥyā ibn Hussein
Kitāb al-Aḥkām, 72, 136
Yaḥyā ibn Hussein, 72, *See also* Yaḥyā ibn Hussein
Kitāb al-Athār, 47–49, 65, 102, 264
Kitāb al-Kharāj, 30, 32, 263
Kitāb *al-Umm*, 65, 102, 264
knowledge, 39, 41, 42, 51, 52, 55, 74, 78, 79, 82, 99, 105, 106, 108, 120, 122, 229, 241, 260, 262
Kufa, 26, 28, 39, 44, 45, 54, 57, 64, 82, 96, 265, 266
Kufan authorities, 50, 57
Kufan scholars, 40
Kufan school, 48
kutub al-furū', 135

lā ḍarara wa lā ḍirār
Do no harm, and neither harm should be done on to you, 74, *See also* Do no harm, and neither harm should be done on to you
Lancaster schools
modern schools, 208
land grants, 180–182, 184
land law in India, 183
land tax, 29, 172, 180, 259
landholders, 178–180, 182–184, 194
landholding privileges, 181
laughter invalidate ritual purification, 85
laughter invalidates ritual prayer, 84
law. *See* Islamic law
legal (*madhhab*ic) reasoning, 165
legal activity, 76, 77, 94, 95, 104, 139, 144
legal approach, 44, 46, 47, 49, 54, 56, 77, 100, 101, 140, 163, 169, 173
legal attribute, 67, 88, 259
legal authorities, 9, 28, 39, 46, 48, 49, 56, 59, 97, 116, 117, 121, 165, 253
legal cases, 46, 47, 60, 80, 84, 124, 132, 259
legal cause, 87, 89, 90, 91, 259, 261
legal charter
Chater of Medina, 105
legal compendia, 104, 134, 158, 176, 199, 206
legal compendiums, 102–104, 244, 247
legal competence, 121, 126
legal concepts, 2, 80, 82, 88, 94, 100, 111, 112, 119, 184, 246, 251
legal debate, 47, 81, 95, 106, 170, 191, 196
legal decisions, 15, 24, 27–29, 36, 76, 78, 124, 241, 242
legal deductions, 20, 49, 257, 260
legal discourses, 77, 78, 116, 118, 119, 121, 139, 178, 196
legal doctrine, 1, 9, 48, 71, 72, 79, 95, 97, 102, 103, 123, 124, 127, 128, 132, 135, 136, 137, 140, 141, 145, 158, 159, 163, 184, 196, 200, 242, 243, 247, 251, 258–262
Islamic legal doctrines, 2, 6, 7, 12, 15, 36, 43–45, 49, 59, 76, 78, 101–104, 114–116, 119, 120, 122, 123, 130, 134, 136, 139, 144, 148, 149, 157, 158, 182, 212, 215, 217, 246, 247, 250, 252, 253, 255
legal evidence, 126
legal formations, 6, 114
legal injunctions, 63, 93, 98, 107, 122
legal institution, 20, 138, 102, 164, 236, 237
legal issues, 16, 21, 41, 58, 80, 86, 107, 130, 173, 199, 255

legal judgments, 36, 84, 88, 102, 122, *See also* legal decisions
legal maxim, 18
legal method, 47, 109
legal methodological tools, 25
legal methodologies, 2, 6, 14, 21, 28, 37, 51, 74, 80, 81, 93, 95, 130, 131, 217, 240, 246, 247, 249, 252, 254, 255, 259
legal norms, 8, 24, 25, 36, 52, 53, 58, 61, 66, 69, 71, 78, 105, 117, 120, 130, 168, 170, 231, 245, 251, 252
legal opinions, 1, 4, 10, 14, 24–26, 28, 42, 53, 54, 56, 59, 60, 62–65, 68, 71–73, 76, 95–98, 100, 108, 120, 121, 124, 126–127, 131, 134–136, 138–142, 144, 155, 157, 158, 170, 173, 182, 184, 212, 259
legal practice. *See* Islamic legal practice
legal precedent, 15, 29, 32, 48–50, 62, 74, 96, 153, 184
legal principles, 2, 35, 47, 61, 63, 68, 69, 73, 74, 92–94, 101, 120, 127, 131–132, 156–158, 168, 181, 183, 192, 200, 226, 229, 230, 239, 241, 242, 249, 252, 261
legal pronouncements, 7, 65, 102, 236, 260
legal proof, 126
legal questions, 1, 16, 72, 103
legal reasoning
  Islamic legal reasoning, 2, 6, 8, 14, 20–25, 34–36, 39, 55, 60–63, 65, 71, 73, 74, 77, 78, 81, 84, 86, 92–95, 98, 109, 122–124, 126–128, 130, 132, 133, 169–172, 177, 193, 217, 221, 223, 225, 228, 231, 232, 239, 246–247, 249, 250, 252, 259, 260
legal reforms, 213
legal responses. *See* fatwas
legal schools
  Islamic legal schools, 2, 7, 12, 27, 52, 59, 78, 94–96, 100–102, 104, 113, 115, 116, 120–122, 124, 126, 131, 135, 138, 139, 144, 146, 153, 157, 158, 160, 169, 170, 173, 196, 212, 215, 217, 221, 239, 240, 243, 246, 251, 252
legal synthesis, 110, 142
legal system, 113, 173, 197, 199, 202, 216
legal technique, 34, 76
legal theorist, 25, 35, 60, 84, 87, 92, 93, 98–101, 115, 121, 122, 130, 142
legal theory, 6, 7, 21, 24, 25, 28, 34, 48, 49, 78, 80, 81, 85, 87, 93, 94, 100–102, 113, 114, 116–119, 121, 127, 135, 136, 138, 139, 143, 146, 153, 156, 157, 169, 175–177, 216, 230, 239, 253, 260–262
legal tradition, 5, 10, 11, 29, 35, 71, 78, 112, 114, 115, 117–121, 177, 178, 196, 255, *See also* Islamic legal tradition
legally preponderant position, 131
legislative authority, 214
legislature, 214, 236
legitimacy, 8, 16, 25, 34, 42, 52, 59, 78, 92, 98, 105, 109, 111, 123, 143, 148, 152, 156, 161, 164, 167, 169, 172–177, 183, 188, 193, 228, 229, 235, 242–243, 249, 258
legitimate authority, 174
legitimate rule, 174
legitimation, 20, 41–43, 92, 99, 101, 109, 110, 118, 141, 164, 172, 173, 175, 180, 228, 232, 235–237, 251
Lena Salaymah, 4, 113
liberal ideas, 211
lines of legal authority, 52
loan, 181
'like for like' rule, 73

Mabādi' al-Wuṣūl, 138
madhāhib, 31, 59, 94, 102, 115, 120, 121, 123, 217, 231, 242, 246, 259, *See also* madhhab
madhhab, 2, 7, 58, 59, 65, 71, 78, 84, 94–96, 99, 101, 115, 122–124, 126–128, 130–132, 134–150, 153, 155–159, 161–167, 169, 170, 173, 177–182, 184, 189, 190, 192, 193, 196, 197, 212, 215, 217, 218, 221, 223, 224, 226, 228, 230–232, 239, 243, 247, 250, 253, 257, 259, 260, *See also* Islamic legal schools
madhhab predecessor, 72, 145
madhhab preponderance, 130, 147, 150, 153, 163, 179, 184, 196
Madinan authorities, 50, 57
mafāsid
  harms, 187, *See also* harm

mafsada
harm, 187, 188, 191, 195, 259, *See also* harm
maḥram.
male guardian, 234
Majalla
Ottoman codification of Islamic law, 215
majoritarian schools, 145, *See also* Sunnī schools
Makhlouf, 246
male-female interaction, 236, 237
Mālik, 35, 42, 43, 45, 48, 59, 61–62, 64, 65, 67–71, 95, 97–100, 102, 108, 110, 131, 160, 161, 193, 220, 222, 268
legal reasoning, use of, 61
principle of public interest, 61
Mālik ibn Anas, 35, 43, 45, 48, 59, 61, 64, 67, 70
Mālikī doctrine, 155, 158, 195
Mālikī jurist, 190
Mālikī law manual, 189
Mālikī *madhhab*, 155, 157, 189, 190
Mālikī school, 59, 156, 158, 192, 261
Mālikī tradition, 156
Mamluks, 147–149, 159, 162, 192
Mamluk state, 148
maʿnā, 63, 86, 87, 124, 258, 259
mānīʿ, 91, *See also* impediment
manqūlāt
physically transferrable properties, 166, 168, *See also* physically transferrable properties
manṣūṣ, 124, 258
maqāṣid al-sharīʿa, 35, 92
maqāṣid of the Sharīʿa
aims of Islamic law, 249
MARA, 227, 228, *See also* Ministry of Awqaf and Religious Affairs (MARA)
marjaʿ, 139, 236, *See also* Twelver Shīʿi jurists
Twelver Shīʿi independent jurist, 139
marjaʿ-i taqlid, 236
Twelver Shīʿi juridical institution, 236, 237, *See also* Twelver Shīʿi juridical institution
marjūḥ
weak legal opinions, 131, 260
marketplace, 251
marriage, 59, 60, 143, 159, 260
Marw, 26, 39
Maryam Riyazī
Islamic Republic Iran, 235
masālik al-aqyisa, 124, 260
mashhūr
widely circulating ḥadīth, 51, 52, 107
maṣlaḥa, 30, 31, 34, 35, 61, 92, 195, 217, 226, 228, 246–252, 254, 255, 259, 260, *See also* greater good, public interest
ontological and epistemological status, 35
maṣlaḥa mursala, 34, 92
Masrūq, 40
master jurists, 95–97, 126, 131, 132, 162, 166–169, 193, *See also* jurists
Max Weber, 135
maximizing benefit and minimizing harm
legal maxim, 18
Maymūna, 20
means of legal reasoning
means of legal reasoning. *See* means of legal reasoning
Mecca, 17, 39, 40, 79, 238
Mecelle. *See* Majalla
medical knowledge, 229
medical practice, 229
medical treatment, 231
Medina, 17, 26, 39, 44–46, 48, 54, 57, 64, 71, 74, 75, 79, 82, 96, 97, 105, 111, 230
Medinan legal tradition, 61
Medinan line of transmitters, 54
Mehmet Birgevi, 165
merchants, 205, 219, 224
merited right, 181
metals, 48, 67, 69, 70
methodological foundations of fatwa
Quranic discourse, 16, 100
Middle East, 118, 150, 204, 265, 267, 268, 270
milk. *See* inalienable proprietary rights
inalienable proprietary rights, 180
milkiyyat
ownership, 180, *See also* ownership
Ministry of Awqaf and Religious Affairs
Oman, 227
Ministry of Endowment and Judicial and Islamic Affairs
Oman, 228

Ministry of Imperial Pious Endowments
  Ottoman Empire, 214
minor children, 155–157, 192
mithl, 167
Mixed courts, 213
mobility of Muslim scholars, 78
model school, 208, *See also* modern school
modern discourse, 197
modern life, 217, 232
modern medicine, 230
modern socio-political movements, 209
modern values, 211
modern world, 211
modern schools, 208
modernity, 7, 226
modernization, 207, 208, 210, 215, 217
modes of rationality, 77
money, 17, 156, 164, 166, 167, 219, 224, 243
Mongol, 147, 158, 160
Mongol invasion, 147, 148
moral diplomacy. *See* ethical diplomacy
morally reprehensible, 229
Morocco, 238
mosques, 147, 152, 163, 227
Motzki. *See* Harold Motzki
mu'āmalāt, 226, *See also* human transactions
Mu'ādh ibn Jabal, 17, 30
mu'āmalāt
  human transactions, 127, 260, *See also* human transactions
muḍāraba, 167, 170, 260, *See also* business partnership
  profit and loss sharing partnership, 170
muftī, 3, 14, 36, 102, 103, 115, 122–124, 126–132, 134, 137, 138, 144–146, 149–151, 153–155, 163, 169, 187, 201, 223, 226–228, 232, 241, 245–247, 252, 255, 260, 261
  categories of, 122
Muftī of Hyderabad, 221–223
Mughal, 150, 152, 178–183, 185, 194, 266, 268
Mughal Empire, 178, 185
Mughal India, 152, 183
Mughal political authorities, 180
Mughal state-owned properties, 179
Muḥammad 'Abd al-Karīm al-Maghīlī, 186
Muḥammad 'Abduh, 211, 212, 218
Muḥammad al-Bāqir, 43, 174
Muḥammad 'Alī, 207, 208
Muḥammad al-Shujā' al-Thaljī, 79
Muḥammad al-Tahānawī, 183
Muḥammad Ibn al-Ḥasan al-Shaybānī, 165
Muḥammad ibn Ḥasan al-Ṭūṣī, 175
Muḥammad ibn Idrīs al-Shāfi'ī, 59
Muḥammad ibn Shujā' al-Thaljī, 96
Muḥammad ibn Sulaymān al-Kūfī, 72, *See also* al-Kūfī
Muhammad Rafsanjani
  Minister of Radio and Television, 233–235
mujtahid, 121–124, 126–130, 137, 138, 144, 158, 159, 169, 258, 260, 262
  independent legal reasoning, 122
mujtahid mustaqill, 138
mujtahid muṭlaq. *See also* independent jurist
  independent jurist. 193
  master jurist, 128, 144, 260, *See also* master jurist
mujtahidūn fī al-madhhab, 131, *See also* independent jurists
mujtahidūn fī al-masā'il, 132, 260
  independent jurists in particular legal cases, 132, *See also* independent jurists in particular legal cases
mukharrijūn, 132, *See also* takhrīj
mullā, 138
munkar, 187, *See also* vice
Munyat al-Murīd, 138
muqallid
  dependent jurist, 128
muqāṭi', 180, *See also* landholder
murajjiḥs, 158
murajjiḥun, 133
  give preponderance to one opinion over another, 133
Murder, 154
Muṣannaf, 4, 56, 140
Muslim civilization, 225
Muslim community, 6, 14, 17–19, 26, 28–30, 39–42, 82, 104–106, 108, 110, 113, 117, 120, 161, 178, 210, 232
Muslim empires, 150
Muslim expansions, 41
Muslim geographic heartland, 147, 204
Muslim geographic periphery, 204
Muslim legal institutions, 227

Muslim legal subjects, 117
Muslim nation-states, 214, 215, 227, 238, 251, 252
Muslim public, 3, 42, 43, 174, 237, 254
Muslim public sphere, 42, 237
Muslim society, 1, 3, 7, 9, 11, 12, 32, 42, 77, 78, 107, 108, 112, 130, 146, 147, 170, 178, 203, 204, 207, 211, 217, 235, 237, 254, 255
Muslim world, 2, 5, 44, 49, 79, 82, 97, 111, 136, 147, 150, 152, 154, 196, 198, 209, 212, 214, 223, 227, 238, 239, 252
Muslims, 1, 6, 8, 19, 26, 27, 35, 38, 41, 42, 77, 78, 82, 105, 113, 136, 149, 153, 159–162, 184, 185, 188, 190–192, 200, 203, 204, 209, 211, 226, 238, 240, 258, 261, 268
Muslims states, 153
Musnad al-Rabīʿ, 53, 141
Mustafa Kamil, 210
mustaftī, 14, 260
mustaghriq al dhimma, 189
mutamayyizūn
  distinguish strong from weak opinions, 134, 260
mutawātir
  transmitted recurrently, 99, 259, 260, *See also* recurrent transmission

Nāʾibs College, 206
Najm al-Ikhwān, 186
Napoleon, 204, 207
naskh
  abrogation, 81, 127, *See also* abrogation
naṣṣ, 168, 260, *See also* proof text
nation, 210–212, 214–216, 227, 238, 251, 252
nation states, 211, 214
national courts, 213
nationalism, 210
nationalization, 216
nation-state, 214–216, 227
nawādir, 134, 260
Near East, 28, 39, 41, 147, 204, 265
necessity licenses prohibitions, 229, 231
  legal principle, 229
Nigeria, 185
Nizamiyya colleges, 148
non-textually based methods, 121
non-Muslims, 191
non-perishable food
  perishable food, 68
non-scriptural based reasoning, 35
normative practices, 34
North Africa, 26, 41, 142, 150, 186, 268
nuqūd
  cash, 243
Nur al-Dīn al-Salīmī, 144

OIC. *See* Organisation of Islamic Cooperation(OIC)
Oman, 54, 142, 209, 227, 228, 264, 270, 272
Omani jurists, 228
opinion, 15, 23, 29, 31, 40, 44, 46, 47, 49, 54, 56, 60, 63, 66, 68, 73, 74, 76, 82–84, 86, 88, 96, 99, 108–111, 126–128, 134, 141, 143, 156–158, 165, 179, 186, 189, 190, 196, 221, 223, 257
  legal opinion, 56
oral document, 106
Organisation of Islamic Cooperation, 227, 238
origins and development of Islamic law. *See* Islamic law
orphan, 17–19, 30, 31, 48, 49, 57
Ottoman adoption of European penal and commercial codes, 213
Ottoman bureaucracy, 163
Ottoman citizens, 206
Ottoman dynasty, 148
Ottoman economy, 206
Ottoman Empire, 150, 163–165, 167, 169–171, 181, 204, 205, 207, 210, 214, 215, 261, 266, 268, 270
Ottoman jurist, 165, 170
Ottoman lands, 164, 205
Ottoman manufacturing guilds, 205
Ottoman state, 150, 163, 165, 169, 206, 213
Ottoman state *madhhab*, 163
Ottoman sultan, 205
Ottoman-Russian wars, 204
Ottomans, 150, 205–207
owner, 180
ownership, 180

Pahlavi Dynasty, 232
Palestine, 79, 148, 238, 271
pan-*madhhab*, 215

pardon, 155–157, 192
particularizing the universa
legal principle, 230
patents. *See* abstract rights
peace treaty, 188
peasant, 34, 179
pedagogic purposes, 20
pension, 181, 184
People of the Book
community, 105, 106
permanence, 166, 167, 193, 243
Permanent Settlement in 1889, 179
perpetual benefit, 180, 181
perpetuity, 181, 184
Persia, 26, 150–152, 171, 172, 181, 204, 269
personal status law, 213, 216
phronesis, 10, 38, 76, *See also* Aristotle
phronetic character. *See* phronesis
physically transferrable properties, 166
pietistic groups, 106, 108, 110
piety-minded, 42
pious endowments, 213, 214
religious endowments. *See* waqf
plot shares, 74
plots, 29, 74
Pluralism, 216
political and economic exploitation of India, 199
political authorities, 32, 40–43, 141, 158, 161, 170, 175, 180, 181, 185–188
political doctrine of Rule of the Jurist, 236
political economy, 29
political elite, 42, 148
political establishment, 43, 106, 151, 172
political fragmentation, 77, 78, 147, 150
political fragmentation of the caliphate, 78
political institutions, 8, 29, 173, 237, 258
political integration, 150
political leadership, 29, 40, 41
political prisoners, 185
political reforms, 205
political sovereign, 151
portable properties, 168
post-caliphate period, 147
postclassical period, 2, 7, 250
postcoloniality, 2, 7, 12, 179, 212, 216, 226, 227, 232, 238–240, 247, 249, 251–252
postcolonial fatwas, 240, 251, 252
postcolonial jurists, 232
postcolonial muftīs, 247
postcolonial nation, 216
postcolonial nation-state system, 238
post-Imamate-period Shīʿī jurists, 175
post-prophetic fatwas, 26
post-prophetic period, 6, 14, 26–28, 40
post-Shāfiʿī era, 78, 81
post-Shāfiʿī period, 87, 112, *See also* post-Shāfiʿī era
practical reason
phronesis, 10
practical reasoning. *See* phronesis
legal practice, 1–11, 14–17, 19–33, 38–40, 42, 43, 45–46, 48–51, 54–56, 58, 60–62, 71, 73, 74, 77, 79, 82, 83, 85, 92–94, 96, 97, 99, 102, 104, 106–112, 114–119, 121, 122, 136, 137, 141–143, 146, 149, 153, 154, 157, 161, 164, 165, 168–172, 174, 175, 177, 178, 180, 193, 194, 196, 197, 201, 206, 215–217, 222, 229, 231, 236, 237, 246–247, 249, 250, 253, 254, 258–262
practice of the people of Medina, 111
prayers, 22, 23, 49, 83, 228
precaution. *See* iḥtiyāṭ
precedence, 24, 29, 32, 36, 40, 46, 49, 54, 56–58, 96, 97, 140, 144, 158, 174, 175, 177, 229, 236, 246, 247
precedent, 35, 40, 46, 48, 50, 55, 56, 58, 73, 75, 85, 97, 108, 110, 141, 142, 144, 153, 156, 158, 181, 183, 186, 196, 197, 201, 247, 254
predatory birds, 90, 91
predecessor, 72, 87, 101, 140, 145, 164, 186, 196
preemption, 156
pre-Islamic Arabia, 222
preservation of life, religion, mind, progeny, and wealth
aims of Islamic law, 249, *See also* aims of Islamic law
pre-Shāfiʿī era, 82
pre-Shāfiʿī period, 84, 91, *See also* pre-Shāfiʿī eraprey
profession of faith, 160
profit, 167, 170, 220, 242, 244, 248
profit and loss sharing partnership, 170
prohibit benefit accrued by a loan
interest, 223
prohibition, 18, 20, 23, 61, 66, 67, 91, 220, 231, 248
proliferation of *ḥadīth*, 79, 142

proof texts, 96, 155, 168, 221, 222, 251
property, 48, 52–54, 56, 140, 162, 164, 166–168, 175, 179, 180, 186–191, 194–196, 202, 203, 206, 216, 243, 244, 262
Prophet Muḥammad, 14–17, 20–22, 25, 26, 28–30, 35, 39, 40, 48, 50, 65, 67, 111, 117, 135–137, 161, 171, 220, 258, 261
prophetic authority, 20, 22
prophetic fatwas, 24, 26, 28
prophetic injunction, 69
prophetic norm, 55, 56
prophetic report, 54, 55, 65, 74, 99, *See also* ḥadīth
prophetic sayings, 44
prophetic statement, 68, 74, *See also* prophetic report
prophetic traditions, 25, 49, 55, 67, 69, 76, 79, 96, 117
protectionism, 205
proto-jurist
  Kufan, 45, 47, 49, 52
prudence. *See* phronesis
public domain, 182, 194
public interest, 30–32, 34, 60–62, 86, 88, 92, 119, 226, 228, 246–247, 249–251, 258–260, *See also* greater good
public lands, 180, 181, 183, 184, 194
public order, 151
public ownership, 30
public policy, 232, 235, 236, *See also* fatwa and public policy
public practice, 235
public properties, 181, 182
public sphere, 237
public square, 212, 236
public treasury. *See* state treasury
punishment, 155–157, 165, 192

qaḍāʾ, 8, 36, 40, 260
Qāḍī Khān, 126–129, 134
qāḍīs, 149, 150, 199, 201, 203
Qamar. *See also* ʿAbd al-Qāhir Muḥammad Qamar
qanīma, 29
qānūn
  Ottoman law, 151, 163, 164, 170
qāṭiʿ, 82
  certain knowledge. *See* certain knowledge
  definitive, 99, 262, *See also* definitive
qawāʿid
  legal principles, 132, 260, *See also* legal principles
qiyās, 21, 22, 25, 48, 49, 55, 57, 59, 60, 62–64, 73, 79–81, 84–93, 98–100, 109, 119–121, 123, 137, 139, 156, 157, 168, 169, 183, 184, 192, 196, 217, 223–225, 231, 246, 247, 255, 259, 260, *See also* analogy
qiyās maʿa fāriq. *See* false analogies
Quran, 6, 14–22, 24, 25, 29–31, 41, 42, 44, 51, 61, 62, 73, 76, 80–82, 87, 88, 93, 96–100, 105–107, 116–120, 122, 123, 130, 137, 143, 155, 157, 159, 160, 168, 171, 183, 192, 200, 211, 212, 217, 218, 221–225, 229, 231, 242, 251, 254, 255, 258–260, 265–267
Quranic discourse, 39, 41, 42
  social transformation, 41
Quranic ethical ideals. *See* piety-minded
Quranic ethico-legal norms, 6, 39
Quranic ethos, 42
Quranic injunctions, 32, 61, 229
Quranic legal norms, 117
Quranic legislation, 19
Quranic norms, 18, 43, 117, 118, 254
Quranic norms in history
  fatwas, 254
Quranic prohibition, 220
Quranic statements, 15, 16

Rabat, 238
Rabīʿat al-Raʾy, 45–46, 57, *See also* Rabīʿa ibn Farrūkh
  compensation, 45
radio and TV, 233
rājiḥ
  legally preponderant position, 131, 261, *See also* legally preponderant position
Rashīd Riḍā, 35, 212, 217, 218, 224, 252
Rāshidūn Caliphate, 40, *See also* caliphate
rasm al-muftī, 126
rationale
  legal rationale, 2, 21, 24, 28, 29, 31, 36, 37, 39, 48, 54, 59, 66, 69, 87, 91, 118, 124, 153, 155–157, 168, 196, 241, 243, 244, 247–249, 251–254
rationality, 8, 24, 47, 77, 81, 87, 88, 106, 107, 113, 118
  scriptural rationality, 106

rationalization, 2, 178, 244, 249
ra'y, 24, 44–46, 47, 49, 50, 52, 54–56, 58, 60, 63, 71, 76, 78–81, 84–86, 88, 96, 107–110, 143, 257, 261
ra'y-ḥadīth legal paradigm, 96
reason, 18, 20, 38, 42, 46, 49, 53, 54, 73, 76, 85–88, 90, 106, 107, 137, 151, 156, 166, 171, 183, 194, 248, 257
reasoning faculties, 17
Reconquista, 147
reform
  Islamic reform, 2, 130, 178, 185, 196, 204, 211, 217, 218, 223, 226, 252
reformists, 217, 225, 227, 240, 246, 255
regional centers of Islamic law, 43
regional school, 26, 49, 63
regionally established legal practice, 97
Regulation of Public Education Acts, 206
religious action, 237
religious authorities, 39–43, 48, 106, 107, 137
religious courts, 213
religious establishment, 40, 148, 151–153, 172
religious ethos, 42
religious institutions, 150
religious learning, 41
religious practices, 10, 39, 82, 120, 121
religious specialists, 10, 40, 41, 43, 76, 107, 112, 254, *See also* religious specialists
reports, 4, 5, 27, 30, 31, 48, 50, 52, 54, 55, 107, 109, 110, 171, 174, 175, 177, 257, 258
republican governance, 236
a recurrent transmission, 149, *See also* mutawātir
revelation, 15–17, 73, 88, 258
revenue for the state, 33
ribā al-nasī'a, 220, 222, 261, *See also* exploitative type of usury
ribāwī, 65, *See also* usurious
Riḍā, 246, 255
Rifāʿat al- Ṭahṭāwī, 210
right of possession, 53, 54
right of repossession, 188
right of trusteeship, 182
rightful benefactors, 174
Risala-Dar-Bai-Arazi, 183
ritually impure, 90, 228, 229
royal decree, 180, 181
Russian annexation of the Crimea, 204
Rustumī Dynasty, 142
Ruth Miller, 213

Saba Mahmood, 118, 120
sacred places, 160
sacred texts, 112, 118, 119, 121, 156, 161, 177, 231
sadd al-dharī'ah. *See also* blocking the pathways to harm
  Mālikī legal precept, 191, 195, 261
ṣadr
  religious state official, 152
Safavid court, 171, 172
Safavid dynasty, 151, 152, 171, 172
Safavid state, 152, 176
Safavids, 150–152, 176
ṣāḥib al-zāriʿ
  crop farmer, 73
Saʿīd b. Jubayr, 40
Saʿīd ibn al-Musayyib, 45, 47, 49
sakk. *See* sukūk
ṣalāh, 48, 50, 57, 84, 160, *See also* prayer
saliva, 90
  bird saliva, 91
salt, 65, 70, 222
Sanaʿa, 39
Sassanid, 33, 35
savings, 219, 221, 224
Sawād, 29, 32–34, 257, 259
sayl, 73, *See also* stream
Sayyid Sābiq, 217
Schacht, 4, 40, 269, 271
scholars, 22, 30, 31, 40, 78, 79, 82, 83, 85, 87, 130, 135, 137, 138, 147, 151, 152, 171, 173, 176–179, 183, 194, 206, 214, 218, 220, 221, 225, 238, 239, 246, 247, 258, 259, 262, *See also* ulamā'
schools of law, 6, 7, 27, 28, 35, 44, 49, 58, 59, 84, 87, 93, 95, 96, 101, 114, 115, 137, 138, 145, 146, 152, 156, 158, 159, 162, 163, 206, 208, 210, 211, 215, 217, 219, 221, 223, 229, 230, 261
scriptural evidence, 26, 34, 62, 71, 86, 90, 224
scriptural hermeneutics, 6, 14, 230
scriptural injunctions, 34, 61–63, 65, 83
scriptural rationality, 106, *See also* rationality

scripturally based reasoning, 65, *See also* qiyās
scripturally derived norms, 65
secular courts, 213
secular legislature, 214
secular state, 214
secularization, 213, 237
secularizing reforms, 232
seek your advice. *See* yastaftūnaka
Seljuk dynasty, 148
Seljuks, 147
semen, 99, 259
Sepoy Mutiny in 1857, 202
sexual excitement. *See* kissing
Sha'bī, 40, 46
shādhdh. *See* āḥād
  anomalous, 51
Shāfiʿī, 59, 60, 63, 68, 69, 71, 78–82, 84–87, 89, 97, 98, 103, 109, 112, 122, 131, 158, 219, 224, 269
Shāfiʿī school, 59
Shah ʿAbd al-ʿAzīz, 178, 179
Shah Walī Allāh al-Dahlawī, 178
shahada, 160
sharecropping, 203
shareholders, 74, 75
Sharḥ Maʿānī al-Āthār, 98
Sharīʿa, 78, 150, 151, 153, 160, 161, 163, 175, 203, 212–216, 234, 239, 242–243, 245, 249, 250, 259, 261, 265, 267–269 *See also* sharia
Sharīʿa courts, 150, 203, 204
Sharīʿa law, 78, 151, 153, 163, 213
Shaykh al-Azhar
  head of al-Azhar, 207
shaykh al-Islam, 151, 164
sheep, 20, 23, 61
Shi'ism, 171
Shīʿī, 71, 87, 93, 135–137, 139, 143–145, 151, 152, 171–178, 183, 194, 215, 257, 262, 271
  Zaydī, 71
Shīʿī hierocracy, 172
Shīʿī Imams, 174, 175, 177
Shīʿī institutions, 135, 152
Shīʿī Islam, 135, 137, 139, 151, 236
Shīʿī jurisprudence, 172
Shīʿī jurists, 175
Shīʿī law, 171–174, 176–178, 194, 215, 257, 262
Shīʿī legal schools, 139
Shīʿī legal theory, 135
Shīʿī *madhhabs*, 139
Shīʿī scholars, 183
Shurb al-Zallāl
  Mālikī law manual, 189
silk, 231
silver, 47–48, 57, 65, 67–70, 222
social attitudes and fatwas, 254
social change, 3, 7, 146, 254
social context, 213, 255
social convention, 106
social mechanism, 106
social problem, 14
social sphere, 8, 60, 258
social transformation, 41, 254
social world, 106
socio-legal mechanism. *See* fatwa
Sokoto Caliphate, 186, 269
soldiers, 29–33, 180
Songhai Empire of Mali, 186
Southern Arabia
  Oman/Yemen, 142
sovereign. *See* head of state
sovereignty, 208
Spain, 147, 192
specified property, 167
speculative transaction, 82, 99, 262
spirit of the law, 35, 156, *See also* aims of the law
spoils of war, 17, 31, 32
  ghanīma and fay', 31
state, 2, 8, 22, 26, 30, 32, 33, 40, 43, 84, 102, 105, 108, 112, 123, 136, 137, 147–153, 163–165, 169, 170, 172, 176, 179–187, 190, 194, 199, 202, 203, 206, 207, 212–217, 227–229, 232, 238, 243, 245, 257–259
state *madhhab*, 163, 169, 170
State of greater ritual impurity, 22
state property, 203
state treasury, 33, 182, 186, 187, 190
state-owned lands, 172
stationary properties, 163
stratification of *muftīs*, 134
stream, 73–75
Stream of Mahrūr, 74
strong drink. *See* intoxicants
sub-Saharan Africa, 196
Sub-Saharan African societies, 185
substantive rationality, 24
Sudanese laws, 215

Sufyān al-Thawrī, 43
sukūk
Islamic stocks, 240, 242–244, 249, 261, *See also* Islamic stocks
Sulayman the Lawgiver, 163
sultan, 150, 151, 163, 170, 205
a single chain of transmission, 148, 149
Sultan Mahmud II
Ottoman Empire, 214
Sultan Qaboos, 54
Oman, 228
Sultanate of Oman, 228
sunan, 97, 110, 111, 261
sunna, 40, 45–46, 55, 57, 73, 74, 93, 96–100, 110, 111, 117, 122, 137, 143, 183, 221, 229, 231, 259, 261
Sunnī, 28, 30, 40, 43, 59, 87, 93, 95, 100, 122, 124, 131, 135–140, 142–145, 147, 151, 152, 158, 160, 171, 173, 175–178, 215, 219, 221, 224, 257, 260, 267, 270, 271
Sunnī ʿAlī, 186, *See also* Songhai Empire
Sunnī law, 135, 139, 144, 177, 178
Sunni Muslim, 178
Sunnī Muslim orthodoxy, 147
Sunnī schools, 215
Sunnīzation of Ibāḍīsm, 143
Supreme Jurist/Leader of the Islamic Republic of Iran, 227
Supreme Leader/Jurist, 232
Sūrat Āl ʿImrān
ribā, 222, 225
Sūrat al-Baqara
ribā, 222, 225
Syria, 32, 33, 39, 43, 50, 147, 148, 158, 159, 162, 171, 192, 201, 215, 218, 224, 263, 264, 271
systemization of Islamic law, 130

taʼb̄ id ḥukman
presumed perpetual right, 181
ṭabaqāt
levels, 131
tabīd
perpetuity, 181, 184, *See also* perpetuity
taʿdiyat al-ḥukm
transitiveness of the rule, 139, *See also* transitiveness of the rule
tafṣīl
differentiated, 188
Taḥrīr al-Wasīla.
Ayatollah Khomeini, 233
taḥrīr wa-taqrīr, 124
tajrīd, 103, 261
extracting, 103
takhrīj
extrapolation, 132, 261, *See also* extrapolation
takhṣīṣ
particularization, 89, 91, 261
Talal Asad, 9, 114, 116, 118, 120, 265
discursive tradition, 116–117
talfīq
amalgamation of rulings, 215, 261
talkhīṣ, 103, 261
abridgment, 104, *See also* abridgment
Tanzimat, 204–206, 214, 215, *See also* Tanzimat reforms
Tanzimat reforms, 204–206, 214, 215
Taqī al-Dīn Aḥmad Ibn Taymiyya, 159, *See also* Ibn Taymiyya
taqlīd, 72, 132, 159, 211, 217, 260, 262
Tatar invasions, 162, *See also* Mongol invasions
Tatars, 159, 160–162, 192, *See also* Mongols
tawliyat
right of trusteeship, 182, *See also* right of trusteeship
tax, 29, 30, 33, 48, 57, 82, 161, 173, 174, 180, 194, 205, 262
taxation, 33–35, 184, 185, 203
tayammum, 22, 23, 262
techniques of government, 235
text-based legal hermeneutics, 255
textual authority, 106, 118, 119, 160
textual evidence, 56, 223
textual hermeneutics, 22, 24, 25
textuality, 86, 106
textually oriented legal methodology, 255
The Committee on Ifta, 228
The Dialogical Style of the Quranic Discourse
Quran, 15
the etiquette of fatwa, 115
the practice of the people of Medina, 97
the Prophet, 6, 14–18, 20–31, 35, 39–41, 46–48, 50, 52, 53, 55, 58, 65–69, 74, 99, 108, 110, 111, 135–137, 157, 161, 171, 220, 222, 224, 230, 258, 261
the West, 211, 240
things exchanged by counting, 68
Timurid, 148

to promote the common good and deter corruption, 191
Torodbe
West African Islamic scholarly class, 185, *See also* West African Islamic scholarly class
trade of international commodities and conditions that govern that trade, 251
tradition, 3–6, 8–10, 14, 16, 18, 20, 21, 24, 28, 32, 35–38, 41, 43, 45, 46, 49, 59, 61, 66, 67, 69, 71, 72, 76, 78, 83, 88, 95, 98, 99, 101, 105, 107, 108, 110–121, 140, 142–144, 155, 159, 160, 163, 173, 177, 178, 185, 196–198, 200, 211, 212, 217, 225, 239, 241, 247, 252–255
traditional authority, 223
traditionalism, 44, 45, 58, 71, 107, 108, 110
traditionist, 46, 50, 51, 79, 85
transaction, 65, 66, 68, 70, 189, 219–220, 224, 249, 250
transactional uncertainty, 248
transitiveness of the rule, 139
trans-madhab reasoning, 232
transmitters of reports, 50
traveling, 23
treasury, 33, 34, 182, 187, 190
Treaty of Balta Limani, 205
True Bearers of Knowledge," 141
Tuareg, 187, 190
Tunis, 210
Turkey, 148, 163, 164, 193, 205, 206, 209, 266, 270
Twelver Shīʿī, 151, 171, *See also* Imāmī Shīʿī
Twelver Shīʿī doctrine, 152
Twelver Shīʿī Imams, 177
Twelver Shīʿi juridical institution, 236
Twelver Shīʿī jurists, 177, 236
Twelver Shīʿī law, 215, 236
Twelver Shīʿī legal theory, 176, 177
Twelver Shīʿī religious establishment, 151, 152, 172
Twelver Shīʿī state, 176
Twelver Shīʿīs, 152, 173, 174
Twelver Shīʿism, 152

ʿulamāʾ, 78, 147, 148, 150–152, 171, 172, 206, 207, 211, 213, 214, 262
scholars. *See* scholars
ʿUmar. *See also* ʿUmar ibn al-Khaṭṭāb
ʿUmar ibn al-Khaṭṭāb, 17, 21, 30–35, 40, 48, 172, 182–184, 222, 225, 271
ʿUmar ibn ʿAbd al-ʿAzīz, 42
ʿUmar ibn al-Khaṭṭāb, 17, 172
Umayyad, 41–43, 136, 141
Umayyad Dynasty, 136
Ummayad caliphate, 40
unclaimed property, 53
undifferentiated, 188
universal ethical norms, 39
universal rule, 69
universalization and diffusion of this prophetic *sunna*, 111
universalization of *istiḥsān*, 111
ijmāʿ, 110
ʿUqūd rasm al- muftī, 131
ʿurf, 75, 151, 166, 168, 169, 193, 217, 246–247, 249–252, 262, *See also* custom
urine, 100, 230
usufruct, 30, 33
uṣūl al-fiqh, 7, 22, 25, 78, 80, 81, 93, 97, 100–102, 118–121, 127, 146, 153, 216, 262, 239, *See also*. Islamic legal theory
uṣūl al-madhab, 100, 100, *See also* foundations of the Islamic legal schools
foundations of the Islamic legal schools, 100
Uṣūlī movement, 171
usurious exchanges, 66, 67, 69, *See also* usurious transactions
usurious transactions, 66, 69, 71
usurpation, 105, 187
usurped property, 189
usurper, 187, 189
usury, 47, 57, 65–71, 161, 218–225, 261, *See also* interest
Urabi Revolt, 209
ʿUthmān Dan Fodio
West African Mālikī Muslim jurist, 185, 195, 266
utilization of skin of dead sheep, 20

"victimless crime," 213
value system, 35
values, 8, 18, 24, 35, 41, 69, 106, 157, 210, 211, 255

verse (quranic), 15, 17–20, 30, 31, 98, 156, 222, 225
vice, 34, 187
victim, 155, 156
vilāyat-i faqīh, 236, 237
  Rule of the Jurist, 236, *See also* political doctrine of Rule of the Jurist
voluntary association, 135, 236, 259

wadīʿa
  entrusted items, 219, *See also* entrusted items
Wael Hallaq, 15, 34–36, 42–44, 61, 78–80, 82, 84–88, 90–93, 95–97, 102–104, 110, 120, 131, 133, 149, 151, 154–158, 171, 183, 199–202, 206–208, 212–215, 217, 218, 225, 226, 267
  religious and legal practices, 78–79
walī
  male guardian, 59, 64
waqf, 163–170, 193, 213, 242–245, 262
  cash waqf, 163
waqf al- ashum
  endowing shares, 242, *See also* endowing shares
waqf al-nuqūd
  cash waqfs, 163, *See also* cash waqfs
*waqf*s
  religious endowments, 163–170, 193, 207, 214, 243–244
wāqif
  the administrator of the waqf, 167, *See also* administrator of the waqf
war booty, 32, 162, 186
war spoils. *See fay'*
wars of apostasy, 161
water, 21, 22, 72–75, 100
water management, 72
weak legal opinions, 131
wealth, 17–19, 29, 31, 48, 49, 57, 59–60, 64, 174, 175, 187, 194, 203, 249
weapons, 163, 168
wearing of gold, 231
weight, 66–70, 157
West Africa, 185, 195, 196, 265
Western banks, 221, 224
Western civilization, 210
Western domination, 210
Western historical criticism, 4, 5
Western legal system, 216
Western rationalism, 211
Western worldview, 212
Westernization, 210
Western-style institutions, 205
wet cupping, 229
wheat, 65, 70, 203, 222
women's participation in the public sphere, 237
wujūd al- mustaḥiqq, 174, *See also* rightful benefactors

Yaḥyā ibn al-Ḥusayn, 71, 136, *See also* al-Hādī ilā al-Ḥaqq, al-Hādī
Yasa, 160, *See also* codified Mongol traditions
yasʾalūnaka, 15–18, 262
yastaftūnaka, 15, 16, 262
Yemen, 39, 71, 72, 75, 79, 136, 142
Young Tunisians, 210

ẓāhir al-riwāya, 126–128, 134, 262
Ẓāhirīs, 87
zakāh, 48, 57, 160, 161, 262, *See also* alms giving
zamīndāri, 180
zamīndārs
  landholders, 178, 180, 182, 184, 194, *See also* landholders
ẓannī
  speculative/indefinitive, 82, 99, 260, 262, *See also* indefinitive; speculative
  speculative knowledge, 82, 99, 260, *See also* speculative knowledge
Zayd, 43, 46, 53–55, 57, 58, 71, 95, 136, 140–142, *See also* Zayd ibn Ali
Zayd ibn ʿAlī, 95, 136
Zaydī, 71–73, 75, 93, 100, 135, 136, 144
  legal school, 73
Zaydī Islam, 71, 72, 136
Zaydī legal doctrine, 71, 136
Zaydī *madhhab*, 136, 137
Zaydī political theology, 136
Zaydī School, 137
Zaydī state
  Yemen, 136
Zaydīsm, 72
Zayn al-Dīn ibn Muḥammad ibn ʿAlī, 138, *See also* al-Shahīd al-Thānī
Zengid, 147
Zengid-Ayyubid state, 147
Zufar, 170

For EU product safety concerns, contact us at Calle de José Abascal, 56–1°,
28003 Madrid, Spain or eugpsr@cambridge.org.

www.ingramcontent.com/pod-product-compliance
Lightning Source LLC
LaVergne TN
LVHW041621060526
838200LV00040B/1383

* 9 7 8 1 0 0 9 2 6 0 8 7 9 *